DATE DUE			

ADVANCES IN MOTIVATION AND ACHIEVEMENT

Volume 3 • 1984

THE DEVELOPMENT OF
ACHIEVEMENT MOTIVATION

ADVANCES IN MOTIVATION AND ACHIEVEMENT

A Research Annual

THE DEVELOPMENT OF ACHIEVEMENT MOTIVATION

Volume Editor: JOHN G. NICHOLLS
Purdue University

Series Editor: MARTIN L. MAEHR
Institute for Child Behavior
and Development
University of Illinois, Urbana-Champaign

VOLUME 3 • 1984

 JAI PRESS INC.

Greenwich, Connecticut   *London, England*

CONTENTS

LIST OF CONTRIBUTORS

Terry Adler

Department of Psychology
University of Michigan

James P. Connell

Department of Psychology
University of Rochester

Jacquelynne Eccles (Parsons)

Department of Psychology
University of Michigan

Susan Harter

Department of Psychology
University of Denver

Heinz Heckhausen

Max-Planck-Institut für
Psychologishe Forschung
West Germany

Saul M. Kassin

Department of Psychology
Williams College

Mark R. Lepper

Department of Psychology
Stanford University

Carol Midgley

Department of Psychology
University of Michigan

Arden T. Miller

Department of Leadership and
Foundations
Morehead State University

John G. Nicholls

Department of Education
Purdue University

Glyn C. Roberts   Motor Performance Laboratory
                                 University of Illinois,
                                 Champaign

Klaus Schneider   Fachbereich Psychologie, der
                                Phillips-Universtät Marburg
                                West Germany

Deborah J. Stipek   Graduate School of Education,
                                University of California at
                                Los Angeles

Colleen F. Surber   Department of Psychology
                                University of Wisconsin at Madison

John R. Weisz   Department of Psychology
                                University of North Carolina at
                                Chapel Hill

INTRODUCTION

Who can doubt the importance placed on achievement and achievement motivation in our society? Concern about success in school, on the playing field, and in careers is ubiquitous and the right motivation is widely assumed to enhance our chances of success. But success and achievement should not be construed too narrowly. Achievement behavior is best construed as behavior wherein one's competence is at issue. We might gain a sense of accomplishment or competence by making a useful contribution to the lives of others instead of gaining higher grades or incomes than them (Kaltenbach & McClelland, 1958).

A sense of competence can be seen as a critical half of what David Bakan (1966) calls the duality of human existence. In Erich Fromm's (1941) terms, individual development "succeeds" only when individuals succeed in uniting with the world in love and productive work: work that "affirms the individuality of the self and at the same time . . . unites the self with man and nature" (p.287). Many other theorists have assigned great importance in personality to a sense of competence (e.g., de Charms, 1968; Deci, 1980; M. B. Smith, 1969; White,

1959, 1973). In view of the importance of the topic, it is surprising that this is the first volume devoted specifically to the study of age-related changes in the nature of achievement motivation or the basis of feelings of competence.

Until recently, many psychologists would probably have taken "The development of achievement motivation" to refer to the developmental stability, antecedents, and behavioral consequences of individual differences in the achievement motive. The work of McClelland, Atkinson, Clark, and Lowell (1953) on the need to achieve fostered interest in such questions and contributed to the link, in the minds of many, between achievement motivation and "the achievement motive." For workers in the tradition of McClelland and Atkinson (Atkinson & Feather, 1966) there is more to research on achievement motivation than the study of the achievement motive. The term motivation refers to "the interaction dynamics of many factors in a given person-environment relationship involving goal-directed experience and behavior." (Heckhausen, 1967, p. 2). The achievement motive (McClelland et al., 1953) or the motives to approach success and avoid failure (Atkinson & Feather, 1966) are not seen as independent causal entities. They are seen as part of the person-environment interaction. Their antecedents have been sought and their role in achievement behavior is presumed to depend on situational factors. Nevertheless, these approaches have stimulated relatively little interest in age-related change in the cognitive, affective, and situational factors that mediate or direct achievement behavior. In short, developmental change in the nature of achievement motivation is not of central importance in these perspectives.

At the Fels Research Institute, Vaughn and Virginia Crandall and their associates developed a social learning approach based on the work of Rotter (1954) that did not employ a general achievement motive construct (Crandall, 1967, 1972). Variations in task preferences, intensity of effort, and persistence on different types of task (e.g., physical, academic, and intellectual) led to doubts about the explanatory value of a single trait-like achievement motive. In this approach, achievement behavior on any given type of task is seen as a function of the value placed on attaining competence, expectancies of success, standards of success, and locus of control (Crandall, Katkovsky, & Preston, 1960). The antecedents of individual differences have been of interest to the Fels researchers and the Fels longitudinal sample has provided unique and fascinating data (e.g., Crandall & Battle, 1970). Age-related changes in achievement behavior and its determinants have been of interest at Fels (e.g., Crandall & Rabson, 1960). Nevertheless most of their studies and many others reviewed by V. J. Crandall (1963) focused on individual differences and their developmental and situational determinants.

The relative lack of interest in developmental change in the nature of perceived competence and achievement motivation is also illustrated by the contents of the only previous volume of papers on achievement motivation in children (C. P. Smith, 1969). Most of the chapters of that volume deal with the nature, determinants, and consequences of group and individual differences in achievement-related constructs. A notable exception is Veroff's (1969) chapter. Veroff proposed three stages of development of achievement motivation: autonomous competence, social comparison about achievement, and autonomous achievement motivation integrated with social comparison strivings. His proposal that, at about the age of six, children become more likely to evaluate their competence with reference to the performance of others (social comparison) has generally been borne out. The proposal also helped stimulate a considerable amount of developmental research in achievement settings (Ruble, in press; Suls & Sanders, in press).

Attribution theory approaches to achievement motivation (Weiner, 1972) have fostered increased interest in developmental change. In attributional, approaches, cognitive constructs such as perceived ability and causal attributions play the mediating role that, in McClelland and Atkinson's approaches, had been assigned to achievement-related motives. Because cognitive processes play an enlarged role in these newer approaches, they have opened the way for use of the relatively sophisticated theories and methods of the psychology of cognitive development. There had been some earlier interest in age-related changes in the cognitive basis of achievement behavior (Bialer, 1961; Cromwell, 1963; Heckhausen, 1967). Much of this reflected the impact of Rotter's (1954) social learning theory and, in particular, his concept of locus of control. Harter's (1974, 1978) work on effectance motivation is also significant.

Nevertheless, a number of reviews bear testimony to the growing influence of attribution theory on developmental research in this domain (Dweck & Elliot, 1983; Frieze, 1981; Heckhausen, 1982; Kassin, 1981, Ruble, 1980; Weiner & Kun, 1976; Weisz & Stipek, 1982). The number of these recent reviews also reflects the steadily growing body of research on age-related changes in achievement cognition, affect, and behavior. This body of recent research and theory made production of this volume appear timely.

Though all the chapters of this book deal with age-related changes, individual differences have not been ignored. In fact, our increased understanding of age changes in achievement motivation has begun to open the way for consideration of individual differences within different levels of developmental maturity. Nevertheless the emphasis is on developmental change.

I have resolved the problem of ordering the chapters by placing them roughly in sequence of the ages of the children considered in each and by placing those wherein a wider range of factors are considered toward the end. I am reluctant to do much more in the way of categorizing the different contributions. The authors can and should speak for themselves about their purposes and positions. It may, however, be of some value to readers if I note common and unique concerns of the different chapters. All except that by Kassin and Lepper deal, to a greater or lesser degree, with changes in perception of factors that can cause success or failure or with expectancies of success and failure. This includes children's understanding of concepts such as luck, ability, difficulty, and effort, the ways they make judgments of ability, effort, or chances of success, and perceptions of own competence and control over outcomes. Kassin and Lepper focus on perceived control over action: on perceived reasons or responsibility for achievement behavior rather than success or failure. This is also one of the concerns of Eccles, Midgley, and Adler and Harter and Connell. Harter and Connell also focus on the causal interdependence of different achievement-related constructs at different ages. The impact of the environment on motivation is a central concern of Roberts and Eccles et al.. Roberts focusses on the relatively neglected field of children's sport whereas Eccles et al. consider age-related changes in the academic environment.

It is noteworthy that, until recently, there has been less interest in developmental change in cognition, affect, and behavior in the domain of achievement than in other social domains such as morality. I believe that the contributors to this volume show that there have been considerable recent gains in knowledge in the domain of achievement motivation. Readers will also discern plenty of new problems of theoretical and practical interest. We are unlikely to have to wait long for the next volume on this topic.

John G. Nicholls
Volume Editor

ACKNOWLEDGMENTS

Preparation of this chapter was supported in part by NSF Grant BNS 7914252, University of Illinois and Harvard University subcontracts. Suggestions by Martin Maehr are gratefully acknowledged.

REFERENCES

Atkinson, J. W., & Feather, N. T. (Eds.), *A theory of achievement motivation*. New York: Wiley, 1966.

Bakan, D. *The duality of human existence: An essay on psychology and religion*. Chicago: Rand McNally, 1966.

Bialer, I. Conceptualization of success and failure in mentally retarded and normal children. *Journal of Personality*, 1961, *29*, 303–320.

Crandall, V. C. Achievement behavior in young children. In W. W. Hartup (Ed.), *The young child: Reviews of research*. Washington, D.C.: National Association for the Education of Young Children, 1967.

Crandall, V. C. The Fels study: Some contributions to personality development and achievement in childhood and adulthood. *Seminars in Psychiatry*, 1972, *4*, 383–397.

Crandall, V. C., & Battle, E. S. The antecedents and adult correlates of academic and intellectual achievement effort. In J. P. Hill (Ed.), *Minnesota Symposium on Child Psychology* (Vol. IV). Minneapolis: University of Minnesota Press, 1970.

Crandall, V. J. Achievement. In H. W. Stevenson (Ed.), *Child psychology: Sixty-second yearbook of the National Society for the Study of Education*. Chicago: University of Chicago Press, 1963.

Crandall, V. J., Katkovsky, W., & Preston, A. A conceptual formulation for some research on children's achievement development. *Child Development*, 1960, *31*, 787–797.

Crandall, V. J., & Rabson, A. Children's repetition choices in an intellectual achievement situation following success and failure. *Journal of Genetic Psychology*, 1960, *97*, 161–168.

Cromwell, R. L. A social learning approach to mental retardation. In N. R. Ellis (Ed.), *Handbook of mental deficiency*. New York: McGraw- Hill, 1963.

de Charms, R. *Personal causalition: The internal affective determinants of behavior*. New York: Academic Press, 1968.

Deci, E. L. *The psychology of self-determination*. Lexington, Mass.: D. G. Heath, 1980.

Dweck, C. S., & Elliot, E. S. Achievement motivation. In E. M. Hetherington (Ed.), *Carmichael's manual of child psychology*, 1983.

Frieze, I. H. Children's attributions for success and failure. In S. S. Brehm, S. M. Kassin, & F. X. Gibbons (Eds.), *Developmental social psychology*. New York: Oxford University Press, 1981.

Fromm, E. *Escape from freedom*. New York: Holt, Rinehart, Winston, 1941.

Harter, S. Pleasure derived by children from cognitive challenge and mastery. *Child Development*, 1974, *45*, 661–669.

Harter, S. Effectance motivation reconsidered: Toward a developmental model. *Human Development*, 1978, *21*, 34–64.(a)

Heckhausen, H. *The anatomy of achievement motivation*. New York: Academic Press, 1967.

Heckhausen, H. The development of achievement motivation. In W. W. Hartup (Ed.), *Review of child development research* (Vol. 6). Chicago: University of Chicago Press, 1982.

Kaltenbach, J. E., & McClelland, D. C. Achievement and social status in three small communities. In D. C. McClelland, A. L. Baldwin, U. Bronfenbrenner, & F. L. Strodtbeck (Eds.), *Talent and society: New perspectives in the identification of talent*. Princeton, NJ: Van Nostrand, 1958.

Kassin, S. M. From laychild to "layman": Developmental causal attribution. In S. S. Brehm, S. M. Kassin & F. X. Gibbons (Eds.), *Developmental and social psychology: Theory and Research*. New York: Oxford University Press, 1981.

McClelland, D. C., Atkinson, J. W., Clark, R. W., & Lowell, E. L. *The achievement motive*. New York: Appleton-Century-Crofts, 1953.

Rotter, J. B. *Social learning and clinical psychology*. Englewood Cliffs, NJ: Prentice-Hall, 1954.

Ruble, D. N. A developmental perspective on theories of achievement motivation. In L. J. Fyans (Ed.), *Achievement motivation: Recent trends in theory and research*. New York: Plenum, 1980.

Ruble, D. N. The development of social comparison processes and their role in achievement-related self-socialization. In E. T. Higgins, D. N. Ruble & W. W. Hartup (Eds.), *Developmental social cognition: A socio-cultural perspective*. New York: Cambridge University Press, in press.

Smith, C. P. (Ed.). *Achievement-related motives in children*. New York: Russell Sage, 1969.

Smith, M. B. *Social psychology and human values*. Chicago: Aldine, 1969.

Suls, J., & Sanders, G. S. Self-evaluation via social comparison: A developmental analysis. In L. Wheeler (Ed.), *Review of personality and social psychology* (Vol. 3), in press.

Veroff, J. Social comparison and the development of achievement motivation. In C. P. Smith (Ed.), *Achievement-related motives in children*. New York: Russell Sage, 1969.

Weiner, B. *Theories of motivation: From mechanism to cognition*. Chicago: Markham, 1972.

Weiner, B., & Kun, A. *The development of causal attributions and the growth of achievement and social motivation*. Unpublished manuscript, Los Angeles, CA: University of California, 1976.

Weisz, J. R., & Stipek, D. J. Competence, contingency, and the development of perceived control. *Human Development*, 1982, *25*, 250–281.

White, R. W. Motivation reconsidered: The concept of competence. *Psychological Review*, 1959, *66*, 297–333.

White, R. W. The concept of healthy personality: What do we really mean? *The Counseling Psychologist*, 1973, *4*(2), 3–12.

EMERGENT ACHIEVEMENT BEHAVIOR:

SOME EARLY DEVELOPMENTS

Heinz Heckhausen

This chapter gives me the opportunity to report how we at our Bochum laboratory have tried, and continue to try, to convert ourselves into developmentalists. In our research on achievement motivation we typically have considered our subjects to be ageless individuals, be they adult students or even school children. We have equipped these ageless individuals with so many constructs and processes that sometimes we could not help but wonder how all this equipment might have developed and whether the tracing of developmental sequences would provide critical clues that confirm or disconfirm the nature of the equipment we have envisaged.

Suppose you want to look for a developmental sequence of achievement-related behavior. You could choose between two opposite lines of research: tracing forward or tracing backward. If you decide to trace forward, you have to

Advances in Motivation and Achievement, vol. 3, pages 1–32
ISBN 0-89232-289-6

start with some understanding of what constitutes an achievement–related act. You then must immerse yourself in the observation of infants producing out-comes in their manifold activities and of the way this production of outcomes changes as infants age into preschoolers and so on. I will not argue with the merits of such a procedure, but if you are not a Piaget *en miniature,* you may get lost.

We, instead, preferred tracing backward and tried to make our narrow-mind-edness a virtue. We started with statements of achievement motivation theory designed for ageless individuals. Then, we simply attempted to discover the lowest age for which these descriptions were applicable (Heckhausen, 1982). In what follows I focus on two statements of what achievement motivation is all about, and examine their respective precursors. The first statement is the initial definition of achievement motivation as "the competition with a standard of excellence" (McClelland, Atkinson, Clark & Lowell, 1953). The second state-ment refers to a later conception in achievement motivation research; to the risk-taking model (Atkinson, 1957).

TRACING BACKWARD: "COMPETITION WITH A STANDARD OF EXCELLENCE"

The conception of achievement-motivated acts in terms of a competition with a standard of excellence is a rather general one. The definition presupposes that the child intends by his or her own activity to produce an outcome that he or she will evaluate according to some standard of excellence. Intentions, of course, are hard to judge, but spontaneous and evaluative reactions to a simple standard, can be observed in expressive behavior.

How, though, can such observable responses be elicited? In a first attempt, nearly twenty years ago, we arrived finally at a simple tower stacking task (Heckhausen & Roelofsen, 1962). The child had to place twelve rings on a rack as quickly as possible. A standard of excellence was presented by having a simultaneously competing adult finish her tower earlier or later than the child. Of course, such a standard presupposes that the child is already able to judge correctly the temporal order of two events. A few two-year-olds master this cognitive prerequisite and by age 3½ most children do.

Initially we were mainly interested in seeing when, at the earliest, children reacted differentially to objective success and failure outcomes induced in the above manner. They clearly did so as soon as they could perceive that they had won or lost, namely between the ages of 2½ and 3½. After success the children raise their eyes from their own work and look triumphantly at the loser. The body stretches, the hands are often thrown high. The self, as it were, appears enhanced and becomes the central point in a widened psychological field of attention. Upon failure, however, the body collapses, is bent down, the head tilted to the side, the eyes and hands do not stray from one's own work; the psychological field narrows (for a film documentation see Heckhausen, Ertel & Kiekheben-

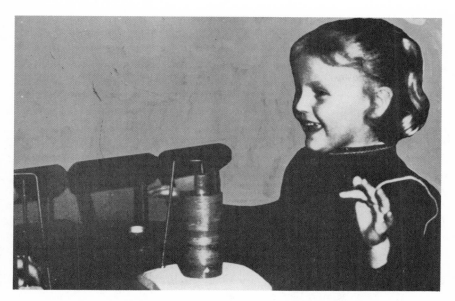

Figure 1. Prototypical expressions of pride (a) and shame (b) after success and failure, respectively, in a girl 4½ years of age.

Source: H. Heckhausen & I. Roelofsen, Anfänge und Entwicklung der Leistungsmotivation: (I.) im Wetteifer des Kleinkindes. *Psychol. Forschung*, 1962, *26*, 313–397. Abb. 6 (s. 325). Reprinted with permission.

Roelofsen, 1966). These reaction patterns appear to be prototypical expressions of pride and shame, respectively. They indicate self-evaluation in terms of standards of excellence. The first two pictures (Figure 1) give you an impression of characteristic, though tempered, success and failure reactions of a 4½ year old girl.

In our laboratory, Halisch and Halisch (1980) have replicated our original study. They carefully observed the success and failure reactions of 62 children between 28 and 44 months of age. Within this age group they looked for children whose reactions to success and failure (manipulated as above) differed in a fashion that indicated pride vs. shame. Pride and shame, indicating use of standards of excellence were judged present when the failure reaction differed, on at least three of the following criteria, from success reactions: no eye contact, embarrassed smile, body bent down, high-tension posture, verbal statement of failure. According to this rule, all failure reactions were rated as to whether their expressive characteristics showed a "clear," "not clear," or "no difference" to the respective reactions to (objective) success. The results are shown in Table 1.

We repeated this study with retarded children between the chronological ages of 6 and 14, whose mental ages varied between 3 and 6 years (Heckhausen & Wasna, 1965). Whenever their mental age was not below 3½ years they showed the same differences between success and failure expressions as the younger normal children did although in more drastic extremes of body posture, as the

Table 1. Numbers of Children in Subsequent Age Groups Who, After (Objective) Failure, Showed a Clear, an Unclear, or No Difference in Their Expressive Reaction as Compared to Their Reaction to (Objective) Success

		Reactions to Success and Failure		
Age in Months	N	Clearly Different	Not Clearly Different	Clearly Not Different
28–30	4			4
31–32	6			6
33–34	3		2	1
35–36	6		4	2
37–38	11	1	2	8
39–40	6	3	3	—
41–42	16	8	3	5
43–44	10	8	1	1
N	62	20	15	27

Source: C. Halisch & F. Halisch, Kognitive Voraussetzungen frühkindlicher Selbstbewertungsreaktionen nach Erfolg un Mißerfold, 2EPP, 1980, 12, 193–212. Reprinted with permission.

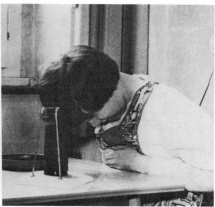

Figure 2. Expressive reactions to success (left) and failure (right) of a mentally
retarded girl of fourteen years and a mental age of 4½.
Source: H. Heckhausen & M. Wasna, Erfolg and Mißerfolg im Leistungswetteifer des imbezillen Kindes. *Psychol. Forschung,* 1975, *28,* 391–421,
Abb. 15u. 16 (s. 411). Reprinted with permission.

next two pictures (Figure 2) of a fourteen-year-old girl with a mental age of 4½
demonstrate.

But what about the youngest children who were not yet capable of comparing
times of completion? Whenever they had stacked all the rings, their expressive
behavior was centered joyfully on their tower. For instance, they raised their
hands in an admiring gesture and smiled at the completed outcome. They merely
took pleasure in the outcome as is shown by the boy of two years and nine
months in Figure 3. In contrast to older children who reacted in a self-centered
and self-evaluative way, they did not detach themselves immediately from their
work and did not look with an approval-seeking manner at the experimenter. The
thesis that these reactions reflect pleasure with the product rather than pride or
self-evaluation is supported by another observational study. A performance outcome, such as flashing of an electric bulb, was greeted with equal joy whether
the child or the mother had caused the effect (Heckhausen et al., 1966).

As to the effect of failure on children who do not yet react in a self-evaluative
way, several studies of task choice have reported observations confirming a
preperiod of emotional but not self-centered reactions to objective success and
failure (Heckhausen & Wagner, 1965; Wagner, 1969; Wasna, 1970). In these
studies, five levels of task difficulty were presented; e.g., weights that could be
lifted on a pulley and at the highest point (success) held in place by a latch. Most
of the children between 2 and 3½ years of age simply noted success or failure.
The others reacted to success with amazement or joy (i.e., pleasure in the

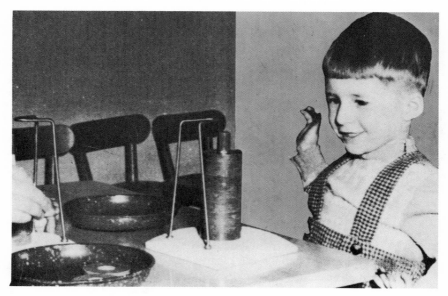

Figure 3.   "Pleasure in the outcome" without self-centered expression of pride after completion of a tower in a boy of two years and nine months.
Source: H. Heckhausen & I. Roelofsen, Anfänge und Entwicklung der Leistungsmotivation: (I.) im Wetteifer des Kleinkindes. *Psychol. Forschung,* 1972, *26,* 313–397. Abb. 6 (s. 325). Reprinted with permission.

outcome), or were satisfied at having overcome the difficulty presented by the task. Failures were registered with regret, anger, or rage, although these responses did not lastingly affect their mood. The first indications of self-centered evaluative reactions appeared after success rather than failure. In such cases, the child no longer simply demonstrated pleasure in the outcome, but rejoiced in her or his power. Obviously, such children experience a feeling of efficacy (White, 1959).

From all this we concluded that mere pleasure in the accomplished outcome is not a sufficient index of the presence of an achievement–motivated act. The crucial developmental mediator of an achievement–motivated act appeared to be the ability to attribute the achieved outcome to the self as the originator of that outcome. This development becomes apparent in children's expressive behavior when, for the first time, they reveal the experience of pride or shame contingent on attainment or nonattainment of a simple standard of excellence. Thus, in the 1960s, we believed we had discovered the origin of achievement motivation in an early accomplishment of causal attributional development. Namely, the first attribution of an action outcome to the self as the originator.

We did not pursue this line of research for many years, perhaps because the analysis of expressive behavior in order to infer the inner workings of young minds was not as respectable as it has since become. Foolishly, or at least prematurely, we joined the then popular socialization research. With some modest success we attempted, for instance, to trace back present individual achievement motive differences in middle childhood to antecedents of maternal independence training (Heckhausen, 1972). Recently, however, we have resumed our early research on developmental change in the nature of achievement-related acts. This work has involved a lot of videotaping and included children in the younger age brackets of one and two years of age. We are setting up a coding system for distinguishing between success and failure reactions in body posture and gestures, gaze contact, and diverse areas of facial expression as well as their developments.

Furthermore, we are pushing our inquiry still further backward into the "darkness" of earlier developments. We now have several reasons to question our initial conclusion that the origin of achievement-related acts coincides with the origin of the causal attribution of an action outcome to the self. We have come to realize the need for more careful consideration of the questions what do "action outcome" and "self" mean?

As to action outcomes or perception of success and failure, we now distinguish different pre-forms in a developmental order. The earliest form is the infant's awareness of a contingency between one's own activity and a responsive environment, particularly in natural social interactions with a caretaker (Papoušek & Papoušek, 1980). Already within the first three months of life, contingency awareness can be inferred from expressive behavior. If a stimulus-elicited head movement (Papoušek, 1967), or an eye contact with a certain object (Watson, 1966) is followed several times by a physical event (artificially mediated by the adult), infants not only perceive a reaction-outcome contingency—without any reduction of a primary need being necessary—they also rejoice in the contingency.

Later forms involve recognition of action-outcome contingency on tasks with continuous rather than discrete outcomes, for instance, pulling a waddling toy duck. Finally comes the lasting state of a "work" outcome such as a tower of blocks which has been produced by a coordinated set of outcome-oriented action steps. The ability to conceive or understand the latter type of outcome appears to be a prerequisite of most, if not all, achievement-related acts.

When building with blocks, 1½ year olds are the youngest children who sometimes stop their play activity in order to regard a work outcome that turned out particularly well or not at all. For example, they obviously noted when all their blocks had been made into a tower, or toppled over a short time before. This all went unnoticed in younger children (Hetzer, 1931) and illustrates the last mentioned development, i.e. to perceive the lasting state of an outcome of one's activity as an accomplishment.

However, successes do not always take the form of a concrete work outcome. New motor accomplishments are a prototypical form of achievement in the toddler age. An example is the girl in Figure 4, 1½ years of age. She has just climbed a low table for the first time, now stops and enjoys her elevated position.

For the "self," the middle of the second year also marks a veritable milestone. At about this time, children begin to react vehemently when a familiar adult thwarts ongoing action (Goodenough, 1931; Kemmler, 1957). The full-blown reaction to thwarting is a temper tantrum as represented in Rembrandt's drawing of "the naughty boy" (Figure 5). This development suggests that the self is now inextricably involved in children's motivation to act, or in the so-called effectance motivation (Harter, 1978; White, 1959). In the terms of Lewis

Figure 4.   In post-toddler age, new motor accomplishments are noticed with joy. This girl, 1½ years of age, has just climbed a low table for the first time. She stops and enjoys her elevated position.

Figure 5. A full-blown temper tantrum in the middle of the second year of age, as represented in Rembrandt's drawing ''the naughty boy.''

and Brooks-Gunn (1979), by age 1½, children have developed simplest forms of a "categorial self." This is an advance on an earlier-appearing "existential self." Both levels in the development of the self are inferred from self-recognition behavior in front of a mirror. As soon as there are behavioral indices of self-recognition, the child must already possess a memory image of his or her outer appearance, i.e., of a rudimentary form of a self-as-object, of a "categorial self." The more primitive precursor or self-as-object is the experience of a self-as-subject, or an "existential self." Such an experience is indicated by a lack of self-recognition but a preference for the mirror images of one's own movements because the mirror images are contingent (parallel in time) with the movements one executes and feels being executed.

In present studies in our laboratory of the "Wanting to do it oneself" phenomenon, Geppert and Küster (1983) have inferred the presence of a categorial self by two tests and gone on to examine the behavioral and affective correlates of this cognitive accomplishment. In the blanket test, the child was placed upon a blanket and asked to present the blanket to the mother. This test was modeled after an original observation by Piaget (1952, observation No. 168) that indicates the fifth stage of tertiary circular reactions. The blanket test was judged to be a first positive index of a categorial self if the child understood that he or she must first step off the blanket to be able to present it. In the other test, the well-known rouge test (Gallup, 1970), it was observed whether the children touched their noses that had, without their knowledge, been marked with rouge. According to Bertenthal and Fischer (1978), the rouge indicates the sixth stage of secondary circular reactions. By the age of 1½ and a few months below, children mastered only the blanket test, but children from one year and seven months on passed the rouge test too. Whereas the blanket test only requires an awareness of the present position of one's body when it impedes goal attainment, the rouge test demands an ability to coordinate a mirror image with the child's schema for what his or her nose looks like in a mirror.

The children were then involved in attractive play activities during which the experimenter repeatedly interrupted the children with several kinds of intervention, such as requesting turn-taking, or offering unrequested help. Children who had neither passed the blanket nor the rouge test accepted all kinds of intervention without any protest. Children who had passed only the blanket test accepted any mode of help that was offered or performed. However, they rejected forcefully any attempt or announcement of intent by the adult to take over the task, particularly the action at hand.

Those who had passed both tests (and were yet not older than 2½) also protested against taking-over. These protests were, for these children, particularly strong when the very last step of an action sequence was interfered with, presumably because at this point the intrusion undermines the attractiveness of the impending goal attainment. Interestingly, these were also the youngest children who uttered in their verbal protest their first names or the personal pronoun

"I" in order to stress their insistence on doing it alone (see also Klamma, 1957; Müller, 1958).

Since children of this age are already able to attribute action outcomes to the self, they also have the understanding we initially argued was necessary for the first appearance of achievement-motivated acts. Within this age group of 1½ to 2½ years, however, children do not yet show the prototypical expressive behavior associated with success and failure experiences we found in the original ring-stacking studies described previously.

The earliest appearance of such success and failure expressions was observed in a few 2½-year-olds. Interestingly 2½-year-olds were the youngest children in the intrusion studies of Geppert and Küster whose verbal protests clearly implied the feeling that they *can do* it and, thereby, revealed a categorization of themselves as competent. In most cases they accepted the experimenter's attempts to take over the task, but they vehemently protested against announced or extended help as if help would undermine their newly acquired self-categorization of competence.

Note that with increasing differentiation of the self, children reacted differently to the same interventions. The youngest children up to 1½ years who failed both tests of self-development invariably accepted all kinds of intervention. Older children between 1½ and 2½ years who passed both tests (or, at least the blanket test) accepted help but rejected taking-over. In their rejection they demonstrated awareness of being the originators of their action outcomes. In the oldest age group, from 2½ years up and with the appearance of the self-category of competence, children accepted taking-over but now rejected help. Even in the face of difficulties they refused help and instead, increased their efforts.

To conclude, in the light of this evidence concerning children's acquisition of self, their reactions to thwarting, intrusion or unrequested help, and their developing modes insisting on doing it alone, we now regard our initial conclusion from the ring-stacking studies to be wrong. The mere attribution of an action outcome to the self as the originator is a necessary, but not as initially thought, a sufficient prerequisite for the origin of self-evaluation in terms of standards of excellence. If the initial conclusion was correct, we would now have to predate the first appearance of such self-evaluations to age 1½. What is necessary, in addition, is the attribution of an action outcome to personal competence, an early category of the self which emerges after the age of two years at the earliest.

Finally, another line of investigation focused on an even simpler standard of excellence than that revealed in the task of competitive ring-stacking. In their replication of our original study, Halisch and Halisch (1980) assessed independently their subjects' ability for temporal judgements of earlier vs. later task completion. They found that those children capable of temporal judgement also competed in the ring-stacking task and showed the prototypical success and failure expressions. This indicates that the experience of success vs. failure presupposes a standard of excellence, i.e., the ability to make a comparative temporal judgement in our competition task. However, the authors also discovered several younger children who, although not yet capable of temporal judgement and not displaying competitive behavior, nonetheless showed a full-blown success experience in each trial after they had completed their tower, and who did not merely take pleasure in the effect as did the other younger subjects. These children presumably set their own standard of excellence, namely, the mere completion of the tower. They were between 2½ and 3½ years of age, that is, old enough to pursue as outcome of their activity the completion of a task.

The mere completion of the tower as a task-inherent standard of excellence does not appear likely to lead to clear failure experiences. Therefore, we invented further methods of inducing the experience of failure in younger children. Our first technique made the uncompleted tower suddenly disappear down into a box. After an initial startle reaction, however, this trick only produced curiosity and diverted the child's interest from completion of the tower. Our next trick employed a built-in bottom plate that carried the lowest block. A hidden button-push, controlled by the experimenter, tilted the bottom plate for a moment so that the tower toppled over. But, our subjects took this as a transient setback and began at once to restack the blocks. After all this we resorted to letting the toppling blocks irretrievably disappear through a hole in the table top so that the tower could not possibly be completed. Even this failed to produce a failure experience for our two-year-olds.

At first we attributed our failure to induce a failure experience to our lack of inventiveness. Now, however, we suspect that the experiences of success and failure may not be symmetrical events that appear at the same point in development. This is in line with observations in task-choice studies reported above (Heckhausen & Wagner, 1965). Children between 2 and 3½ years showed the first signs of self-centered reactions only after success. At any rate, it would be a fascinating peculiarity of human nature if the experience of success should occur before the experience of failure, and that it takes some period of warming up before achievement strivings become double-edged with the experience of failure as the ultimate alternative to success.

We have traced back a developing concern with standards of excellence to points from where we can start forward-tracing longitudinal studies. Because our results have been somewhat complex it might be useful to summarize them.

Evaluation of the outcome of one's own activity in terms of a standard of excellence was thought to be the immediate prerequisite for the emergence of achievement-motivated acts in early childhood. Of course, such an immediate prerequisite of achievement-motivated acts presupposes, in turn, other accomplishments.

At a rather fundamental level, children have to be able to stop their ongoing activity in order to regard the results as an outcome of that activity, as their "work." This accomplishment, at least in building blocks, has first been observed in 1½-year-olds. A precursor to experiencing an outcome of one's own activity as a self-produced "work" is the awareness of a contingency between one's own action and a certain effect in the environment. Contingency awareness can already be observed in infants.

The age of 1½ years is a first developmental milestone. Besides regarding the outcome of their activities and besides their ability to attribute the outcome to themselves as originators, they enjoy effects of their activities and are discontented or angry if pursued effects do not ensue. The developing self concept appears to play a decisive role, as was highlighted by studies on self-recognition and on "wanting to do it alone" as well as by observations about the earliest temper tantrums. By the age of 1½, children also begin (1) to take account of the position of their bodies when it impedes the attainment of a goal, (2) to recognize themselves in a mirror ("categorial self") and (3) to reject interventions into their ongoing activity, sometimes in the form of a temper tantrum. Rejection of interventions as first signs of wanting to do it alone appears to presuppose the emergence of early forms of a categorial self as indicated by tests for the above mentioned accomplishments (1) or (1) and (2).

The age of 2½ years brings a second developmental milestone. By this age, children have acquired a rudimentary self-concept of competence, beyond a sense of pure efficacy. They are able to attribute an outcome of their activity not only to themselves as originators, but to their personal competence, as an early category of the self-concept. At this point, they reject help because they can and want to do it alone, a feeling they now express verbally and explicitly. Moreover, the prototypical reactions of pride and shame to success or failure, respectively, can now be observed in some children especially when the standard of excellence for evaluating the outcome is rather simple.

As a simple standard for inducing perception of success and failure, a competitive ring-stacking game was used. Children competed with the experimenter as soon as they were able to understand what it means to finish earlier vs. later than the competitor. By age 3½, almost all children were able to understand the standard and competed. The youngest ones doing so were 2½. Most of the children who competed reacted also with self-evaluative expressive behavior to the attained outcome. The expressive reactions to success and failure are different and prototypes of the emotions of pride and shame, respectively.

Within the transition period between 2½ and 3½ years, some younger children behaved in an achievement-motivated way even before they could understand the competitive standard. They were concerned with a still simpler standard of excellence, namely, the mere completion of the work. Because the completion standard did not lend itself to failure, these children always experienced success. Several experimental attempts to induce failure experiences by blocking completion were not successful. It was concluded, therefore, that achievement-motivated acts emerge earlier as a success-oriented experience than as a failure-oriented one. This conclusion is corroborated by observations in task-choice studies. Among the youngest children between 2 and 3½ years, the first signs of self-centered reactions appeared only after success.

It is concluded that achievement-motivated acts emerge when two developmental prerequisites have been acquired. The first prerequisite consists of a rudimentary self-concept of competence. The second prerequisite consists of the abilities to meet the cognitive demands for understanding the standard of excellence of a given action outcome. If such demands are as low as possible, achievement-motivated acts can be observed in children between 2½ and 3½ years of age, i.e., inferred from self-evaluative reactions to the outcomes of their actions.

TRACING BACKWARD THE TERMS OF THE RISK-TAKING MODEL

I come now to the later and more refined manifestation of achievement motivation encompassed by the risk-taking model. The simple structure of the risk-taking model, that is, leaving aside individual difference parameters, boils down to a basic expectancy-value theory. This theory predicts which action goal is preferred when one can choose between alternative goals and with what intensity the preferred goal is pursued. The goal with the maximal product of incentive value and expectancy will be chosen and the magnitude of the product is considered to represent the strength of the respective tendency to act.

The theory is based on two assumptions. First, the incentive of success increases with the difficulty of the task, i.e., it is an inverse function of the probability of success. Second, the tendency to approach a certain task is the product of the incentive value and the expectancy (probability of success) of that task. That is, a task whose success incentive is very high because of its high difficulty, elicits only a weak approach tendency because the high incentive value is multiplied by a probability value of nearly zero. The product is maximal when incentive and probability are of intermediate magnitude, i.e., when the perceived difficulty is intermediate. It has often been shown in adults that tasks of intermediate difficulty elicit maximal motivational tendencies (see Heckhausen, 1977).

The risk-taking model contains three elements: the terms expectancy and incentive and the connection between the two terms. I will briefly take up these three elements. They are discussed elsewhere in greater detail (see Heckhausen, 1982).

Expectancy

With respect to the three dimensions in Kelley's (1967) attribution cube, expectancy is mainly based on consistency information (i.e., success or failure in successive attempts), sometimes on distinctiveness (i.e., different task properties) and rarely on consensus (i.e., social comparison). In early preschoolers, expectancies appear relatively unaffected by consistency cues. In our ring-stacking study, with an objective rate of 50% success, subjects had the opportunity to integrate consistency information. However, when asked who will win the next time, children under 4½ remained quite confident that they would win next time. Other evidence of such optimism in young children is reviewed elsewhere in this volume (Stipek).

However, we were interested in finding out whether, despite this optimism, young children do weigh their chances of success versus failure. Using the ring-stacking task, Eckhardt (1968) varied consistency information and investigated how this influences the confidence of prediction and postdiction in younger and older preschoolers. Children had 8 trials of ring-stacking with either 25, 50, or 75 percent success before they got 4 new trials with the same success rate as they had had before. Now, the tower of the competitor was hidden behind a screen so that after task competition, and in the presence of a third person as arbitrator, the child could postdict who had finished first. While the child was asked to predict or postdict the outcome of the game, manifestations of conflict and uncertainty in expressive behavior, such as silence, hesitation and evasion were recorded.

Table 2 contains the results. In the younger preschoolers, between 3½ and 4½ years, the frequency of expectancy conflicts did not peak at equal rates of success and failure, but rose with a higher rate of failure, i.e., with the consistency of failure outcomes. Obviously, 3- and 4-year olds do make some use of past performance information. With increasing probability of failure, the expectancy conflict became more frequent. For the older preschoolers between 4½ and 5½ years, however, expectancy conflict was most frequent at equal rates of success and failure. That is, the uncertainty of the outcome, and no longer the certainty of an undesirable outcome, has now become the source of conflict.

Table 2. Percentages of Subjects within Two Age Groups after One of Three Success Rates in a Competition Game, Manifesting Conflict while Predicting or Postdicting a New Trial

	Success Rate		
Age Group	75%	50%	25%
3;6–4;6 years	25	47[a]	80
(N = 43)	(N = 16)	(N = 17)	(N = 10)
4;7–5;6 years	67	90	65
(N = 54)	(N = 18)	(N = 19)	(N = 17)

[a]If one splits this age group, then from 9 younger children (3;8–4;2) only one shows conflict while from the 8 older children (4;3–4;6) seven manifest conflict (p < 01, Binomial test).
Source: Adapted from Eckhardt, 1968, p. 20.

Eckhardt only reported the incidence of conflict, not what had been predicted and postdicted. Fortunately, we know from other studies that, even in the fact of repeated failure, preschoolers remain optimistic and expect success (Parsons & Ruble, 1977; Shaklee & Tucker, 1979; Stipek & Hoffman, 1980; Stipek, in this volume). The younger they are, the more they are unaffected by consistency cues. However, even the 3- and 4-year–olds are not unable to integrate consistency information, as becomes evident when they have to predict the success of another child. Then, they use consistency information quite logically (Stipek & Hoffman, 1980). From 5 years on, preschoolers not only took increasing account of their past performance when predicting their success, they made also the same predictions for their own and the other child's performance.

These data from the study of Stipek and Hoffman (1980) fit into Eckhardt's conflict findings. Consideration of the results of both studies suggests the following interpretation. Young preschoolers are already aware of and can consider their past performance when predicting future performance. However, they have great difficulty distinguishing what is likely from what is desirable. In other words, they do not yet clearly distinguish between expectancy and value of outcomes. Eckhardt's conflict data (Table 2) indicates that this distinction becomes apparent in her children of 4½ to 5½ years. From this age on, predictions of future performance are increasingly based on rates of positive and negative past outcomes (consistency information) and become more and more independent of the desirability of the outcomes.

Expectancy may not only be based on sheer consistency information about past performance, but also on the causal attribution of these past outcomes (e.g., McMahan, 1973). Among possible causal attribution factors, the developing self-concept of competence will perhaps have the greatest influence on the prediction of one's future success. The early concept of competence is, intraindividually, a rather elastic notion and, therefore, lends itself to wishful thinking when one's future performance has to be predicted. For competence, among preschoolers, is still seen as dependent on the amount of effort the child will put out, or has put out at a task.

The effort-dependent elasticity of perceived competence is noteworthy. Studies on the development of causal schemata by Kun (1977), Surber (1980) and, in our laboratory, by Tweer (1976) have shown that preschoolers—and to some extent even elementary school children—when they have to infer ability or effort from information about the other one of the two factors and the magnitude of outcome, rate their ability as a covariate of the amount of effort given, but not, conversely, their effort as a covariate of the given degree of ability. To what extent overoptimistic expectations may be based on an effort-dependent notion of competence is still unclear. Presumably, the child may be more optimistic if the task is perceived as requiring less effort and less if it has already been practised. Incidentally, the coupling of ability estimates to perceived expenditure of effort protects young children, particularly, those of low ability, against otherwise depressing inferences when they have to compensate insufficient ability through increased effort and persistence. For, on the contrary, they still feel the more competent, the more effort they have exerted. It is, therefore, difficult to make young children helpless or doubtful about their competence (Rholes, Blackwell, Jordan, & Walters, 1980). This protection against an early and dim realism looks, as one might speculate, like a craft of evolution with some survival value for the human race.

Incentive Value

The second term of the risk-taking model, incentive value, refers to the anticipated emotional reaction to a success or failure outcome. In adults, incentive value is dependent on expectancy. With increasing task difficulty, the incentive value of success increases and the incentive value of failure decreases. This relationship between task difficulty and incentive value presupposes the development of several cognitive accomplishments besides the distinction between degrees of task difficulty. First, there has to be some notion of one's own competence. Second, an attained outcome can be, and is, attributed to one's own competence. Third, the understanding that the more difficult the task is, the more does a successful outcome presuppose a higher degree of competence. This implies mastery of the causal schema of simple covariation between competence and outcome magnitude as a direct index of task difficulty; or, at least, of the schema of multiple sufficient causes according to which task ease or competence is a sufficient cause for success. Fourth, the generation of a positive self-evaluative affect as a direct function of the inferred degree of one's own competence. Fifth, since in the failure case, incentive is inversely related to task difficulty, the child has to be able to construct negative correlations.

The child's mastery of these prerequisites can be inferred directly by asking the child several questions whose correct answers are a strict function of task difficulty. We followed a procedure introduced by Nicholls (1978). Children were shown an array of four tasks of the same type (more details below), of readily observed increasing degrees of difficulty. Each child was first asked which task was very easy and which was very hard; second, which task one would have to be very competent to complete; third, on which task would success please the child most; and fourth, on which task would failure most displease the child. In this way we gained deviation scores from correct answers to each of four achievement-related functions: perceived task difficulty, competence required, success incentive, and failure incentive. Expectancies are presumed to be based on perceived task difficulty and competence required. Understanding of incentive value was presumed to require these two functions.

The four functions were found to develop in the above order indicating an order of logical prerequisites. Cross-sectional data from 4- to 6-year-olds, retested after 6 months are shown in Figure 6. It shows the percentages of subjects

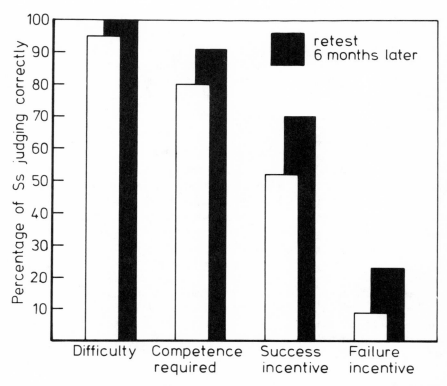

Figure 6. Percentages of 4- to 6-year olds (N = 64), retested 6 months later, who correctly judged the different achievement-related functions.

with correct judgements for each achievement-related function. Note that failure incentive, implying an inverse relationship, has for most children up to age 6, its peak at the difficult rather than the easy end of the task set.

Of course, the deviation scores decreased significantly with age. Interestingly, they vary quite a bit, intraindividually, according to the type of task and the cues indicating levels of difficulty. Each four-item set of each task type was visibly graded in an ascending order of difficulty. Figure 7 shows that type of task is a substantial source of intraindividual variation. These scores, averaged across all four achievement-related functions, give what we call a general ''maturity index'' for the two terms of the risk-taking model, expectancy and incentive. The children attained their best scores when confronted with a physical task (''elevator''), their second best with an intellectual task (''dog's kennel'') and their lowest scores with equal-sized puzzle boxes, distinguished only by visually displayed social comparison norms.

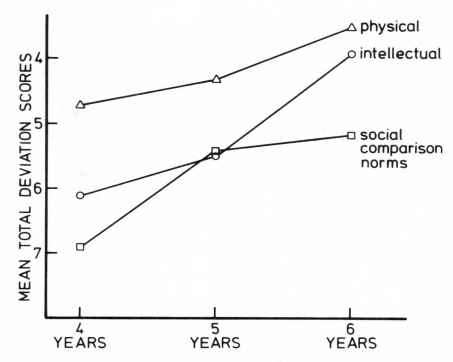

Figure 7. Mean index of achievement-related "maturity" as a function of age and type of task. ("Maturity" is defined as the mean total deviation score from correctly judging the four achievement-related functions).

In the physical task the child had to strike an air cushion as strongly as possible whereupon an "elevator" went up to a more or less high position (Figure 8). Actually, the child's action only triggered the movement of the elevator up to a preestablished level. In the two smaller houses the elevator went up to the highest position ("where some friends were playing"), in the two taller houses the elevator always got stuck at an intermediate level. In each case (also in the other task, "dog's kennel") the easier versions of a task could always be solved, but the two more difficult versions could not. In the intellectual task, a girl's dog had to learn to find its way through a maze to its kennel. Difficulty was varied by having an increasing number of other people's dogs, each with trails to their kennels (Figure 9).

Finally, the puzzle boxes used to assess understanding of social comparison cues were differentiated by cards. Each card had 20 schematic faces drawn on it of which either 4, 8, 12, or 16 faces were crossed indicating the number of children who had not been able to solve the respective puzzle. Here, the puzzles

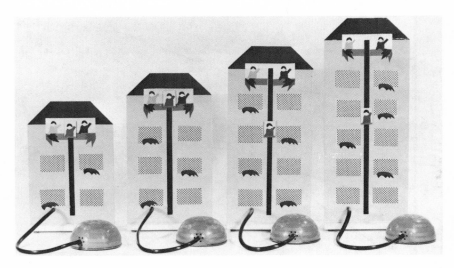

Figure 8.   The "elevator task" in a task-choice setting (see text).

remained in their boxes and were not visible. Subjects only chose that puzzle they would like most to perform. A majority of our five-year-olds were capable of integrating such consensus information to correctly judge difficulty, competence required, and the incentive value of success. Understanding of social comparison cues was also found to depend on the type of visual stimuli used. We had initially used the faces not crossed but colored yellow, as Nicholls (1978)

Figure 9.   The "dog's kennel" in a task choice setting: the easiest (left) and the most difficult version (right; see text).

had done. In accordance with the results of his study, most of our six-year-olds confused the implications of the colored faces for ability and incentive value. With crossed faces, however, the majority of our five-year-olds judged correctly throughout (Figure 10).

To sum up, there is a developing tendency among preschoolers to base incentive values of achievement outcomes on perceived difficulty. Success at a more difficult task pleases more, but the respective inverse relationship of failure incentive to task difficulty is not yet mastered. Most six-year-olds were still more displeased by failure at a more difficult task. As presumed, correct distinctions between easy and difficult tasks, as well as between difficulty levels requiring high versus low competence, developed in that order. Both perceived task difficulty and competence required appear to be logical prerequisites for correct judgements about incentive value of success, because they are the determinants of expectancies.

There is some intraindividual variability in preschoolers' correct judgements about task difficulty, competence required and incentive values, depending on the type of task and the cues indicating levels of difficulty. Children attained better scores at physical than at intellectual tasks, and when levels of difficulty were directly displayed by the task itself and not by visually displayed social comparison norms.

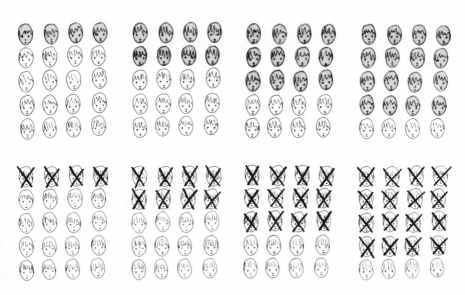

Figure 10. Two kinds of visual stimuli for social comparison cues: colored (above) versus crossed faces (below) indicating children who have failed.

Coordination of Expectancy and Incentive

So far, I have been setting the stage for consideration of the third element of the risk-taking model: the connection between expectancy and incentive in determining level of risk. In actual risk-taking, one has to resolve a dilemma. Two opposite tendencies, one of them expectancy-based, the other incentive-based have to be brought into a compromise. First, the possibility of success is maximized by choice of easy tasks. These, however, have low incentive value of success. Second, to maximize the success incentive, one would choose difficult tasks. With these tasks, however, one runs the greatest risk of failure. As noted earlier, adults usually resolve this dilemma by selecting tasks on which they have intermediate probabilities of success. How do young children grapple with the two opposing tendencies?

Scanning the literature I ran into a paradox of contradictory results. The contradiction occured systematically. There are two paradigms for assessing level of aspiration or risk-taking. One of them is task choice, the other is goal-setting. In task choice, a task is presented in a series of difficulty levels ranked in ascending level of difficulty. The subject has to choose one of the difficulty levels. In "repetition choice," a specific form of task choice, the subject repeatedly attempts tasks at increasing levels of difficulty. The first levels can be done easily, the last not at all. The subject is then given the choice of repeating one of the difficulty levels. Ever since the early studies by Rosenzweig (1933; 1945) most preschoolers, and also first and second graders, were found to prefer easy tasks, that is, difficulty levels they have already mastered (Crandall & Rabson, 1960; Heckhausen & Oswald, 1969; Reutenbach, 1968; Ruhland & Feld, 1977; Veroff, 1969).

However, in the rarer studies that used the other paradigm, goal-setting, the opposite is true (McClelland, 1958; Müller, 1958). When there is one task such as the classic ring-toss, at which difficulty and, therefore, performance can vary on a continuum, preschoolers tend to set goals at a difficulty level they have not yet mastered. That is, they select as their goal a level of performance beyond their previous level.

What we have, then, is a preference for easy tasks in repetition choice, and for rather difficult tasks in goal-setting; a combination that, henceforth, I will call the "easy-difficult pattern." The first explanation I entertained was that properties of the two risk-taking paradigms might lure the child into an one-sided centering on either the expectancy or the incentive dimension, depending on whether the task presents distinctiveness or consistency information, respectively. In short, my centering hypothesis assumes that, in task choice, the child centers on probabilities of success or failure. Because graded levels of difficulty are very salient in a series of distinct tasks, children should center on what appears possible and prefer tasks they know to be manageable. In contrast, the goal-setting paradigm appeared to focus attention on the last and highest goal.

Here, a centering on the attractiveness of success of the difficult task may be facilitated because there is no discrete, easier alternative task to select.

Pilot Studies

We have run pilot studies with two samples of 116 and 50 four- to six-year olds. In a single session, two trials of each risk-taking paradigm were presented to each child (i.e., two task choices and two goal-settings, respectively). We used two tasks: in the larger sample the "dog's kennel;" in the smaller sample we added a physical task, the "elevator." I will first report on the results with the intellectual task, "dog's kennel." Figure 11 represents the goal-setting version of the elevator task, and Figure 12 the goal-setting version of the dog's kennel. In both cases, a performance level of about two-thirds of the performance continuum could be attained. The elevator was stopped by a mechanical device in the apparatus and the path to the dog's kennel was interrupted by the experimenter's remark that the child has now lost her or his way. For the task-choice settings of both tasks, see Figures 8 and 9.

As to risk-taking, the majority of all children preferred, as expected, easy tasks (ones they had succeeded on) in task choice and difficult tasks performance levels (not yet mastered) in goal-setting. The respective percentages for both samples in the first trial, are 72 and 60 for easy task choice, and 72 and 84 for difficult goal-setting. In both samples, 50 and 53 percent showed the easy-difficult pattern. In the larger sample, the frequency of this pattern was highest among five-year-olds (70 percent) and lower among both four- and six-year-olds (46 and 41 percent, respectively). Thus, we replicated the paradoxical asymmetry of risk-taking in a within-subject design. This indicates that the paradox is not an artifact of differences in the samples and tasks of the studies cited above.

Initial though weak support for the centering explanation for the paradox came from differences between the two risk-taking paradigms in the maturity of understanding of difficulty and incentive value which the child was confronted with in the same session. Vis-à-vis task choice, all children of one subsample (N = 64; a subgroup of the original sample of 116 children, retested after half a year) mastered the expectancy function; that is, they answered correctly when asked which task was most difficult. But, 10 percent of them were unable to do so on goal-setting task ("where would it be most difficult to get to"). Conversely, the success incentive function was mastered by more children for goal-setting than for task choice. In goal-setting, 90 percent of the children judged that the most pleasure goes with success at the highest difficulty level whereas only 70 percent did so when confronted with task choice.

In Figure 13, the maturity of the incentive functions for success (joy) and for failure (anger) is differentiated according to whether children were asked where most "joy" or "anger" would be experienced in the task choice, or the goal-

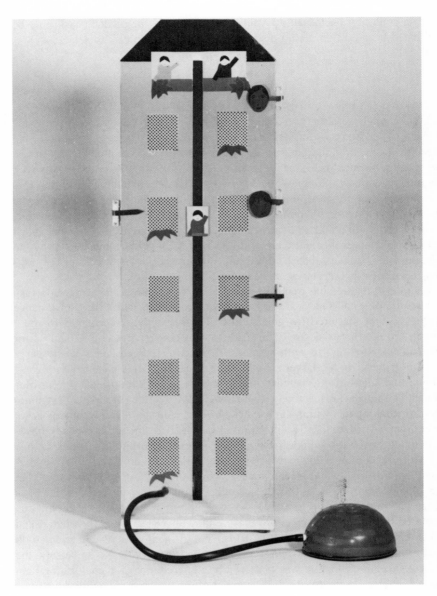

Figure 11.   Elevator as a goal-setting task.

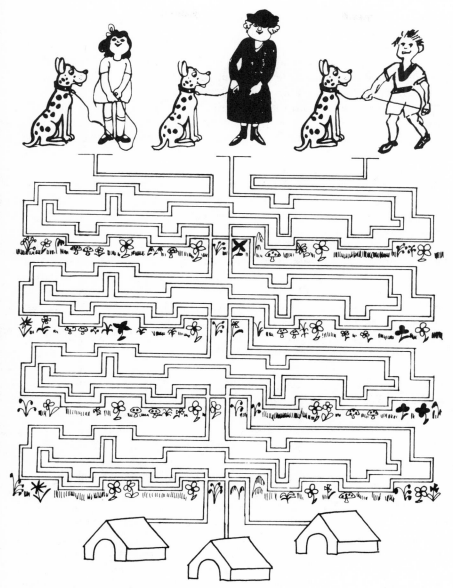

Figure 12. Dog's kennel as a goal-setting task.

setting version of the dog's kennel. As is shown, subjects of all three age groups gave more mature answers concerning success incentive when asked in the context of goal-setting. In the case of failure incentive, the same holds for the older groups. Thus, there is support for the hypothesis that in the task choice paradigm, children tend to center on probabilities of success or failure whereas in goal-setting, they center on incentive of success.

The peaking of the easy-difficult pattern at age five may indicate a developmental transition at this age. Perhaps, the degree of cognitive mastery of the expectancy and incentive functions influences the way the dilemma of risk-taking is solved. Children who master the expectancy function, that is, judge task difficulty, but not the success incentive function correctly, should prefer easy tasks in each of the two risk-taking paradigms. To test this hypothesis, we divided our sample into two maturity groups, one mastering only the expectancy function (task difficulty), and the other mastering both functions, expectancy as well as success incentive.

If we first look at the goal-setting paradigm, we find no difference between the two maturity groups in preference for low and high risks. In both groups, about 85 percent preferred high risks on the first trial. This result clearly disconfirms our hypothesis because children who did not master the success incentive function correctly, preferred high risks when confronted with the goal-setting paradigm for the first time.

In the second trial, however, after the high risk-takers had not attained their goal levels, about 50 percent of the subjects of both maturity groups set goals at or below the attained level. That is, with repeated feedback (consistency information) the centering on success incentive attenuated, and expectancy was taken account of. We may conclude that many children between 4 and 6 years of age already attempted to resolve the dilemma between the two opposing tendencies based on expectancy and on success incentive by selecting moderate probabilities of success. That is, all these children acted like more mature individuals.

We face another picture with the task choice paradigm. Here, maturity scores did make a difference. Within the low-maturity group—those who mastered only the expectancy function—about 80 percent of both samples preferred easy tasks, whereas only 50 to 60 percent did in the high–maturity group who had mastered the success-incentive function. That is, those who understood the incentive function were more drawn to difficult tasks. In the second trial, when distinctiveness is supplemented by consistency information, the low-maturity group kept preferring easy tasks, whereas in the high-maturity group the number of subjects choosing easy tasks rose to nearly 80 percent. In contrast to goal-setting, nonattainment of a chosen level of difficulty in task choice caused those preschoolers, who were already cognizant of the success-incentive function and had chosen a difficult task, to take a better account of success probabilities.

In sum, these results give only weak support to our hypothesis that the degree

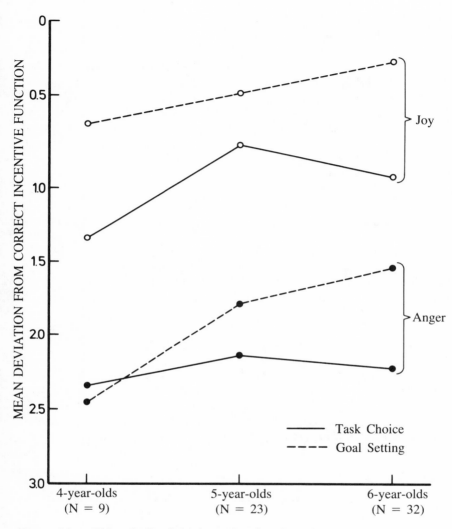

Figure 13. "Maturity" of the incentive functions for success (joy) and for failure (anger) as a function of age and of the risk-taking paradigm (task choice versus goal-setting). ("Maturity" is defined as the mean total deviation score from correctly judging the success incentive or the failure incentive function, respectively.)

of cognitive mastery of the expectancy and incentive functions might interact with the two risk-taking paradigms.

It remained possible that the preference for easy tasks at the choice paradigm was partly an artifact of a serial order effect. If subjects try to solve each task successively from the easy to the difficult end, they may tend to start anew with the easy end when it comes to choice. To check on this possibility, we reversed the order of practising for one half of the children in one sample. There was a significant order effect only in the first trial of the dog's kennel (not the elevator) task, $\chi^2(1) = 4,75$, $p < .05$, and $\chi^2(1) = 2,85$, $p < .10$, in the second trial. In other words, our results cannot be reduced to a serial order effect.

Finally, we wanted to test whether distinctiveness per se (that is, a graded array of difficulty levels) might cause the tendency to prefer easy tasks in the task choice paradigm. We presented a set of distinct tasks, but each of them with particular properties of a goal-setting task: a uniform continuum of possible performance levels approaching an ultimate goal. Such properties are best represented by our elevator task in which the elevator may eventually arrive at the uppermost floor. And, in fact, the results deviated from the usual preference for low difficulty found with other tasks like the "dog's kennel" where each task in the series appears to be self-contained and distinct from the other ones. The majority of our children chose the unsolved tasks, i.e., the tallest houses for pushing up the elevator. This was done by 82 percent of the high-maturity children, but only by 55 percent of the low-maturity children (who had not mastered the success incentive function on this particular task).

In short, the accentuated goal-setting properties in each distinct unit of the task set did override the distinctiveness cues of graded difficulty levels and reversed the usual preference for low difficulties in task choice. But note that many of the high-maturity children preferred the more daring risk under this mixed condition for the facilitation of high risk (goal-setting properties but distinct task units).

Summary

Let me sum up the tentative conclusions from our backward–tracing studies on early risk-taking. We have started out with the seeming paradox that children at task choice prefer low risks and at goal-setting high risks as if they would center either on expectancy or on success incentive, respectively. This paradox made us wonder in which sequence children acquire the expectancy and the incentive function, as well as when and how, eventually, they coordinate both functions. This last accomplishment is necessary for mature, i.e., realistic risk-taking. Our results can be summarized as follows.

First, an understanding of probabilities and incentive values of outcomes as being based on levels of objective difficulty, develops in an invariant sequence, with the understanding of competence required appearing to be the mediating link between expectancies and incentive values of success. That is, higher difficulty requires more competence, and more competence required for a success justifies more pride or greater incentive value of success. (See also, Nicholls & Miller, this volume.) The mastery of the inverse function of failure incentive (failure incentive increases with decreasing task difficulty) is still rare among preschoolers.

Second, the task choice paradigm, based on a set of distinct versions of a task varying in difficulty level, biases preschoolers toward appraisal of the situation in terms of probabilities of success and, therewith, to preference for easy tasks. This tendency is particularly strong when the success incentive function is not yet fully mastered.

Third, the goal-setting paradigm, based on consistency information on a continuum of possible performance levels, favors a focus on the incentive value of success rather than probability of success and, therewith, a tendency to set unrealistically high goals. This tendency appears to be rather independent of whether the success incentive function is already understood if the task cues accentuate an unattained difficult goal level.

Fourth, if the task choice paradigm is a set of tasks, each of which stresses a uniform continuum approaching a goal region, the usual preference at task choice for already solved difficulties reverses in a favor of difficulty levels not yet solved; particularly, when the success incentive function is already mastered.

Fifth, according to the distribution of cognitive maturity levels within a cross-sectional sample of preschoolers, as well as to the properties of distinctiveness in the task choice paradigm, an easy-difficult pattern of risk-taking results at the first trial of task choice and goal-setting, respectively.

Sixth, with repeated risk-taking and feedback, expectancy is increasingly taken into consideration; particularly by high risk-takers in goal-setting, whatever their cognitive maturity level might be.

In general, I tend to explain the initial paradox as follows. Preschoolers' risk-taking is initially heavily influenced by salient features of the task-setting. For instance, they tend to focus on the highest level of performance in goal-setting because, on a continuum, there is no discrete easier alternative level to select. Second, they tend to insure success by low risk-taking as soon as they have received success and failure feedback. Third, the understanding of the success incentive function makes the more mature children more daring, particularly at task choice. But after repeated failure they, too, choose a more realistic goal. (These are those who actually can center on either success incentive or expectancy.) The less mature children who do not yet understand the success incentive function center only on easy tasks. When they choose a difficult task it is because of salient task features.

At what age and under what conditions children coordinate expectancy and incentive to reliably arrive at a realistic risk-taking is still unclear. After having traced backward into early forms and conditions of risk-taking we are now in a better position to move with the process of development. We can now trace forward in a longitudinal study from three or four years of age up. We will observe how risk-taking unfolds: when and under which conditions a more balanced account of both expectancy and incentive is attained.

Hopefully, we will even discover when individual differences in the development of risk-taking originate. For we do know that adolescents and adults are far from uniform in the way they resolve the motivational dilemma posed by expectancy and incentive. Some people tend to weight expectancy more than incentive, others do the reverse. I believe that more knowledge of the course of motivational development will disclose where students of motivation should focus their attention in future research—even if they are only interested in individual differences of ageless individuals.

ACKNOWLEDGMENT

This chapter is an elaborated version of an invited address to the Sixth Biennial Meeting of the International Society for the Study of Behavioral Development, 17–21 August 1981, Toronto, Canada.

REFERENCES

Atkinson, J. W. Motivational determinants of risk-taking behavior. *Psychological Review*, 1957, *64*, 359–372.

Bertenthal, B. I., & Fischer, K. W. Development of self-recognition in the infant. *Developmental Psychology*, 1978, *14*, 44–50.

Gallup, G. G., Jr. Chimpanzees: Self-recognition. *Science*, 1970, *167*, 86–87.

Geppert, U., & Küster, U. The emergence of 'wanting to do it oneself': A precursor of achievement motivation. *International Journal of Behavioral Development*, 1983, *6*, 355–369.

Goodenough, F. L. Anger in young children. *University of Minnesota Institute of Child Welfare Monographs*, 1931, No. 9.

Halisch, C., & Halisch, F. Kognitive Voraussetzungen frühkindlicher Selbstbewertungsreaktionen nach Erfolg und Mißerfolg. *Zeitschrift für Entwicklungspsychologie und Pädagogische Psychologie*, 1980, *12*, 193–212.

Harter, S. Effectance motivation reconsidered. *Human Development*, 1978, *21*, 34–64.

Heckhausen, H. Die Interaktion der Sozialisationsvariablen in der Genese des Leistungsmotivs. In C. F. Graumann (Ed.), *Handbuch der Psychologie* (Vol. 7/2). Göttingen: Hogrefe, 1972.

Heckhausen, H. Achievement motivation and its constructs: A cognitive model. *Motivation and Emotion*, 1977, *1*, 283–329.

Heckhausen, H. The development of achievement motivation. In W. W. Hartup (Ed.), *Review of Child Development Research* (Vol. 6). Chicago: University of Chicago Press, 1982, 600–668.

Heckhausen, H., Ertel, S., & Kiekheben-Roelofsen, I. *Die Anfänge der Leistungsmotivation im Wetteifer des Kleinkindes*. Göttingen: Institut für den Wissenschaftlichen Film, 1966. (Sound Film)

Heckhausen, H., & Oswald, A. Erziehungspraktiken der Mutter und Leistungsverhalten des normalen und gliedmaßengeschädigten Kindes. *Archiv für die gesamte Psychologie*, 1969, *121*, 1–30.

Heckhausen, H., & Roelofsen, I. Anfänge und Entwicklung der Leistungsmotivation: (I) Im Wetteifer des Kleinkindes. *Psychologische Forschung*, 1962, *26*, 313–397.

Heckhausen, H., & Wagner, I. Anfänge der Entwicklung der Leistungsmotivation: (II) In der Zielsetzung des Kleinkindes. *Psychologische Forschung,* 1965, *28,* 179–245.

Heckhausen, H., & Wasna, M. Erfolg und Mißerfolg im Leistungswetteifer des imbezillen Kindes. *Psychologische Forschung,* 1965, *28,* 391–421.

Hetzer, H. *Kind und Schaffen.* Jena: Gustav Fischer, 1931.

Kelley, H. H. Attributional theory in social psychology. In D. Levine (Ed.), *Nebraska Symposium on Motivation.* Lincoln: University of Nebraska Press, 1967.

Kemmler, L. Untersuchung über den frühkindlichen Trotz. *Psychologische Forschung,* 1957, *25,* 279–338.

Klamma, M. *Über das Selbermachenwollen und Ablehnen von Hilfen bei Kleinkindern.* Vordiplomarbeit, Psychologisches Institut der Universität Münster, 1957.

Kun, A. Development of the magnitude-covariation and compensation schemata in ability and effort attributions of performance. *Child Development,* 1977, *48,* 862–873.

Lewis, M., & Brooks-Gunn, J. *Social cognition and the acquisition of self.* New York: Plenum, 1979.

McClelland, D. C. Risk-taking in children with high and low need for achievement. In J. W. Atkinson (Ed.), *Motives in fantasy, action, and society.* Princeton, N.J.: Van Nostrand, 1958.

McClelland, D. C., Atkinson, J. W., Clark, R. A., & Lowell, E. L. *The achievement motive.* New York: Appleton–Century–Crofts, 1953.

McMahan, I. D. Relationships between causal attributions and expectancy of success. *Journal of Personality and Social Psychology,* 1973, *28,* 108–114.

Müller, A. Über die Entwicklung des Leistungsanspruchsniveaus. *Zeitschrift für Psychologie,* 1958, *162,* 238–253.

Nicholls, J. G. The development of the concepts of effort and ability, perception of academic attainment, and the understanding that difficult tasks require more ability. *Child Development,* 1978, *49,* 800–814.

Papoušek, H. Experimental studies of appetitional behavior in human newborns and infants. In H. W. Stevenson, E. H. Hess & H. L. Rheingold (Eds.), *Early behavior: Comparative and developmental approaches.* New York: Wiley, 1967.

Papoušek, H., & Papoušek, M. Early ontogeny of human social interaction: Its biological roots and social dimensions. In M. von Cranach, K. Foppa, W. Lepenies & D. Ploog (Eds.), *Human ethology: Claims and limits of a new discipline.* Cambridge: Cambridge University Press, 1980.

Parsons, J. E., & Ruble, D. N. The development of achievement-related expectancies. *Child Development,* 1977, *48,* 1075–1079.

Piaget, J. *The origins of intelligence in children.* New York: International University Press, 1952.

Reutenbach, A. *Anspruchsniveausetzung von Erstklässlern in Abhängigkeit von einer gegebenen Leistungsnorm und Wiederaufnahme gelöster und ungelöster Aufgaben bei Belohnung und Nichtbelohnung.* Diplomarbeit, Psychologisches Institut, Ruhr-Universität, Bochum, 1968.

Rholes, W. S., Blackwell, J., Jordan, C., & Walters, C. A. A developmental study of learned helplessness. *Developmental Psychology,* 1980, *16,* 616–624.

Rosenzweig, S. Preference in the repetition of successful and unsuccessful activities as a function of age and personality. *Journal of Genetic Psychology,* 1933, *42,* 423–440.

Rosenzweig, S. Further comparative data on repetition choice after success and failure as related to frustration tolerance. *Journal of Genetic Psychology,* 1945, *66,* 75–81.

Ruhland, D., & Feld, S. The development of achievement motivation in black and white children. *Child Development,* 1977, *48,* 1362–1368.

Shaklee, H., & Tucker, D. Cognitive bases of development in inferences of ability. *Child Development,* 1979, *50,* 904–907.

Stipek, D., & Hoffman, J. Development of children's performance–related judgements. *Child Development,* 1980, *51,* 912–914.

Surber, C. F. The development of reversible operations in judgements of ability, effort, and performance. *Child Development,* 1980, *51,* 1018–1029.

Tweer, R. *Das Ökonomieprinzip in der Anstrengungskalkulation: Eine entwicklungspsychologische Untersuchung.* Diplomarbeit, Psychologisches Institut, Ruhr-Universität. Bochum, 1976.

Veroff, J. Social comparison and the development of achievement motivation. In C. P. Smith (Ed.), *Achievement-related motives in children.* New York: Russell Sage, 1969, pp. 46–101.

Wagner, I. Das Zielsetzungsverhalten von vier ausgewählten Gruppen normaler Kleinkinder in Einzel- und Paarsituationen. Unpublished dissertation, Ruhr-Universität, Bochum, 1969.

Wasna, M. *Die Entwicklung der Leistungsmotivation.* München: Ernst Reinhardt, 1970.

Watson, J. S. The development and generalization of "contingency awareness" in early infancy: Some hypotheses. *Merrill-Palmer Quarterly,* 1966, *12,* 123–135.

White, R. W. Motivation reconsidered: The concept of competence. *Psychological Review,* 1959, *66,* 297–333.

YOUNG CHILDREN'S PERFORMANCE EXPECTATIONS:
LOGICAL ANALYSIS OR WISHFUL THINKING?

Deborah J. Stipek

Observations of nearly any upper-elementary-school classroom will reveal a few children engaging in failure-avoidance behaviors which serve only to impede learning and confirm their already low expectations for success (Covington & Beery, 1976). They exert little effort, give up easily, and sometimes avoid achievement tasks altogether. This behavior has been conceptualized in a "learned helplessness" framework (Dweck & Goetz, 1978; Seligman, 1975). Consistent failure is presumed to cause some children to believe that performance outcomes are unrelated to their own efforts. Believing that their efforts are not likely to be effective, they have no reason to try hard, to persist at difficult tasks, or to seek achievement situations. Learned helpless behaviors may be especially common among retarded children, presumably because they have experienced a great deal of failure in school (Weisz, 1979).

Advances in Motivation and Achievement, vol. 3, pages 33–56
Copyright © 1984 by JAI Press Inc.
All rights of reproduction in any form reserved.
ISBN 0-89232-289-6

Experimental studies on the development of learned helplessness suggest that young children are less susceptible to the behavioral effects of failure than are older children (Rholes, Blackwell, Jordan & Walters, 1980). Thus, in contrast to older children, preschool children and, to some degree, children in the first few grades in school, tend to approach achievement tasks eagerly and confidently, exhibiting in only rare cases this failure-avoidance syndrome described by Covington and Beery (1976) and other discerning classroom observers.

Why would learned helplessness be relatively rare in young children? Cognitions believed to mediate the effects of failure on achievement behavior may be the key. Until about the second grade, children are apparently inclined to expect success in achievement situations and to evaluate their competence favorably, even in the face of what adults would consider compelling contrary evidence. Their persistent optimism may explain why several years of school are usually required for children's behavior to be noticeably impaired by failure (Weisz, 1979).

Perhaps developmental psychologists and educational researchers should be cheered that failure does not take its toll until the middle elementary school years and leave well enough alone. On the other hand, a better understanding of younger children's apparently unyielding optimism regarding their chances of success and of their usual eagerness in learning situations may have some practical value. It may, for example, enhance our understanding of factors producing eventual decline in some children's expectations for success. Furthermore, an investigation of the reasons for young children's unrealistically high expectations should inform us about their ability and inclination to process and interpret information relevant to their skills.

Before considering possible explanations for age differences in performance expectancies, diverse evidence suggesting that the decline is reliable and meaningful will be reviewed. Then, in an attempt to explain this phenomenon, we will consider the development of cognitive and motivational factors related to processing evaluative feedback.

DECLINING EXPECTATIONS

In one nonexperimental study of children's expectations for success, Entwisle and Hayduk (1978) asked children entering first and second grade to predict the grades they would receive in math and reading. Both middle- and working-class children began first grade expecting A's (although in both cases expectations were slightly higher for reading than for math). The middle-class children's expectations declined only slightly as a function of receiving lower grades in first grade and the working-class children's expectations seemed unaffected by the actual grades they received. In general, first-grade children maintained high expectations despite teachers' and parents' lower expectations and despite grades indicating lower performance than they had predicted. Not until the end of the second grade did children's expected grades correlate fairly well with their actual performance.

Experimental studies have produced further evidence suggesting that young children typically overestimate their future performance and that performance predictions decrease with age. Phillips (1963), for example, found that more third- than sixth-graders expected to "do much better" on the next trial of a psychomotor task (putting X's in squares.) Goss (1968) found in a study of children in grades 3, 6, 9, and 12 that estimates of strength and performance on a hand-dynamometer task decreased with age.

In a study by Clifford (1975) nearly all children in grades one, three, and five who had experienced relative failure on a task (2 or 3 correct solutions out of 10), predicted future performance higher than their past performance. However, raw expectation scores for success and failure conditions combined decreased with age, suggesting that the younger children were typically more optimistic than were older children, whatever their past performance. Even following relative success (7 or 8 correct solutions out of 10), many younger children but only a few older children predicted improved scores.

In a second study (Clifford, 1978), first and third graders predicted future performance on a puzzle task. Both age groups tended (to about the same degree) to expect their performance to improve. However, providing a salient, visual reminder of past performance had the effect of lowering predictions so that they more closely approximated past performance; this effect was more pronounced for the third graders than for the first graders.

Parsons and Ruble (1972) also observed that younger children maintained higher expectations than older children after both success and failure. Using the Matching Familiar Figures Test, they found that the difference between expectations after four failure and four success experiences was about the same for 6, 8, and 10-year-olds; for all age groups, expectations were lower after failure than they were after success. However, in both the success and failure conditions, the 6-year-olds had significantly higher expectations than the 8-year-olds. Thus, all age groups modified their expectancies to about the same degree as a function of previous outcomes, but the younger children tended to be more optimistic, regardless of their past performance.

In all of these studies of children first grade and older, the expectations of even the youngest children were somewhat lower following failure than they were following success. The evidence on whether preschool-age children significantly modify their expectations as a function of past performance, however, is inconsistent.

In a study including preschool-age children, Parsons and Ruble (1977) found, as they had in the earlier study described above, that the youngest children tended to have higher expectations after both success and failure than the older children. Moreover, repeated failure compared to success on the experimental task (a series of puzzles) did not systematically lower preschool-age children's expectations for success, as it did for children aged 6½ to 11.

Stipek and Hoffman (1980) found that after success, preschool-age children's expectations for their own performance were no higher than the expectations of children 5- to 8-years-old. However, consistent with Parsons and Ruble's (1977) finding, preschool-age children's expectations were not significantly affected by previous failure experiences; they had essentially the same high expectations for their future performance after four failure experiences as they had after four success experiences.

The results of two other studies suggest that preschool-age children do not ignore past failure experiences altogether. Using again a figure matching task, Parsons, Moses, and Yulish-Muszynski (Note 1) found that preschool-age children's expectations after success were somewhat higher than older children's. However, the younger children's expectations declined as a function of failure experiences, although the decline was not nearly as steep as it was for 6–8 and 9–12-year-olds.

Eckhardt (described by Heckhausen, this volume) found that children as young as 3½-years-old modified their expectations for a ring-stacking game following an extremely low (25%) success rate. However, the preschool children expected to win after an objective success rate of only 50%, suggesting some unrealistic optimism in their judgments. (See also Schneider, this volume.)

This same tendency to overrate one's competence is also apparent in studies on children's metamemory. Young children's typically inaccurate estimates of how well they will perform in a memory task are biased toward overestimation. Flavell, Friedrichs and Hoyt (1970) asked children to estimate the longest list of picture names that they could recall; then each child's actual memory span was tested on an analogous task. All children, from preschool-age to fourth grade tended to predict a higher level of recall than their previous performance. However, in part because actual memory increased with age, the degree of over-prediction declined with age. A much larger percentage of the preschoolers and kindergarteners than older children made the unrealistic prediction that they could recall all 10 items.

Yussen and Berman (1981) also found that accuracy in predicting the number of words and sentences that would be recalled increased with age from first to fifth grade. At every grade level, children tended to overestimate their performance. The increased accuracy occurred primarily because the older children actually performed better and, consequently, closer to their predicted performance.

Yussen and Levy (1975) expanded on the Flavell et al. (1970) study, varying subjects' experience on the pretrials. Some subjects made predictions following two successful trials (as in the Flavell et al. study) and some subjects made predictions following failure. Again, predicted memory decreased with age while memory accuracy increased. Pretrial outcomes (success or failure) did not significantly affect predictions for any age-group. The author's description of their surprise at the children's optimism corresponds to the response of many researchers studying preschool-age children's performance expectations:

> The authors were amazed by the several preschoolers who actually predicted that they could recall 10 or 9 items after just being shown that they could not recall this many in the . . . practice sequence. The preschoolers were aware of their failure but said things like: "If you gave me a different list like that, I could do it." (p. 507)

Related to children's declining performance expectations is research showing that children's estimates of their relative ability or attainment in school-related subjects also declines with age and does not begin to correlate significantly with their actual performance until at least the second grade (Eshel & Klein, 1981; Nicholls, 1978, 1979; Stipek & Tannatt, in press; Stipek, 1981). Results of experimental studies suggest further that younger children's own ability ratings are not significantly influenced by success or failure experiences as are older children's (Ruble, Parsons, & Ross, 1976). Younger children are not just inaccurate, they typically overestimate their ability or performance level. Children's estimates of their popularity with peers also declines with age (Ausubel, Schiff, & Glasser, 1952).

Thus, there is consistent evidence from different children in different circumstances suggesting that young children, regardless of their past performance, are more optimistic about their future performance on a task than are older children and that they generally overrate their competence. Particularly impressive is the diversity of tasks and contexts in which this positive, optimistic bias has been found: Young children's estimates of their competence or expectations for success have been shown to be unrealistically high on psychomotor, hand-dynamometer, puzzles, matching familiar figures, and metamemory tasks; in experimental and nonexperimental settings; and with or without previous performance feedback. They overestimate their popularity as well as their competence and probability of success on tasks.

The evidence on whether preschool-age children modify their expectations as a function of failure experiences is inconsistent. It is clear, however, that they lower their expectations when they experience failure less than do older children.

The consistency of the evidence for an optimistic bias across tasks and situations suggests that young children's overconfidence is not an artifact of a given experimental situation. Apparently, unrealistic though their expectations are, they really are their expectations. (See Schneider, this volume, for evidence on behavioral measures of expectations.)

There are undoubtedly many factors that contribute to young children's optimistic performance-related judgments. For example, the age-related changes in the kind of performance feedback children receive reviewed by Eccles et al. (this volume) surely contribute to the decline in children's optimism (see also Stipek, in press). This chapter focuses on developmental change in children's interpretations of performance feedback. Preoperational children are believed to be deficient in a number of cognitive skills that seem necessary for processing feedback and understanding the implications of that feedback for future performance and they seem inattentive to some kinds of feedback. We will examine information processing skills and attention to evaluative feedback as factors affecting children's performance-related judgments. Specifically, we will address the question of why young children systematically *over*estimate rather than merely inaccurately estimate their competence and chances of success.

COMPETENCE FEEDBACK

It is assumed that children receive considerable information regarding their competencies. Teachers and parents may rarely tell children outright that they are stupid (although they may tell them that they are smart), but children observe the outcomes of their achievement efforts and they receive information on which to base performance expectations. Teachers, for example, give ample feedback on the correctness of children's responses (Blumenfeld et al., Note 2). Also, even preschool-age children usually have peers available with whom they can compare their performance. Finally, children receive from parents and teachers evaluative feedback, either explicitly in the form of social reinforcement or implicitly by adult's behavioral response toward children in achievement settings. Age changes in children's attention to and interpretation of these kinds of competence feedback are discussed below. The question posed is, could changes in the way children attend to and interpret such feedback account for the changes in expectations and judgments of their own competence?

Objective Feedback

Consider first objective feedback that is available even to very young children. Children can observe the outcome of their achievement efforts (e.g., the puzzle is completed or not; the tower stands or falls) and teachers often indicate whether a response was correct or incorrect. But young children may not process or interpret this feedback in the same way as do older children or adults. Performance feedback may also have different implications (i.e., for future performance) for younger children than older children.

The meaning of failure. While it is generally assumed in research that children interpret "objective" failure like adults, recently several developmental theorists have noted the subjective nature of success and failure and stressed the importance of considering failure in both a cultural and a developmental framework (Frieze, in press; Maehr & Nicholls, 1980; Ruble, 1980). Developmental considerations regarding the meaning of failure have important implications for children's performance expectations and self-perceptions of competence. While it is true that children receive objective feedback relevant to their competencies, this feedback may not have the same meaning to them that it has for older children and, as a consequence, it may not be perceived to have the same implications for their future performance and competence.

Bialer (1961), for example, claims that goal achievement or non-achievement is not necessarily interpreted by young children as success or failure. He suggests that, while non-attainment of a goal leads to displeasure, it is not experienced as a failure and consequently does not influence children's future expectations or self-perceptions of ability. His explanation is that young children do not recognize their own responsibility in goal attainment or non-attainment. The evidence for the claim that young children do not accept personal responsibility for outcomes is not all that convincing. To the contrary, some evidence suggests that young children exaggerate the contingency of events on their behavior (Weisz & Stipek, 1982; Weisz, this volume). However, Bialer's explanation does not invalidate his observation that unattained goals are not necessarily regarded by the child as failures having implications for future performance.

Harter (1975) provides an example of an experimental task in which younger and older children apparently defined the task, and perhaps also the criterion for success, differently. Four- and 10-year-olds engaged in a probability problem-solving task, an automated box with two Plexiglas disks which could be lighted red and green and with a tray into which marbles were dispensed. When a disk was pushed, the lights turned off and, for a "correct" response a marble was released. The two age groups persisted for about the same amount of time in a situation in which 100% success was attainable. But responses to open-ended questions about the task suggested that the younger children persisted on the task because it produced an enjoyable sensory event (colored lights) whereas the older children persisted to solve the problem (to achieve 100% success for pushing the correct lighted disk). Thus, older children's failure to achieve 100% success was probably interpreted by them as failure. Because younger children focused on the sensory events which occurred regardless of whether the "correct" disk was pushed, they may not have interpreted their inability to achieve 100% success as failure.

Cognitive processing. Cognitive deficiencies of preoperational thinking are usually proposed as explanations for young children's failure to use objective past outcome information systematically in their expectancy judgments (e.g., Parsons & Ruble, 1977; Surber, this volume). Experimental studies suggest that poor memory of serial information may contribute to inaccurate predictions. In two studies, preschool-age children's ability and task-difficulty judgments (Shaklee, 1976) and their expectancy judgments (Stipek & Hoffman, 1980) were unrelated to past performance information even when they were reminded of past outcomes before their judgments were requested. Shaklee and Tucker (1979) found that only children who accurately recalled past performance made ability judgments that were differentiated according to the outcome, but many of the children who recalled past performance did not make outcome-differentiated ability judgments. This pattern of findings suggests that memory is necessary but insufficient for "accurate" ability judgments. Shaklee and Tucker (1979) propose that failure to integrate the past performance information may explain why some children remembered past outcomes but did not make outcome-differentiated ability judgments. (See Surber, this volume, for a discussion of children's integration skills.)

Another cognitive explanation for children's optimism despite objective evidence to the contrary concerns their understanding of the relationship between past and future performance. An association between past and future failure may simply be too weak for children to make realistic (adult-like) predictions. After all, for young children with rapidly developing competencies, failure is often followed by success.

There is also considerable evidence suggesting that young children do not attribute past performance to stable causes over which they have no control. Consequently, they can logically expect success to follow failure. Dweck (in press) suggests that young children have an "incremental" view of ability; they assume that ability is unstable and, to some degree, influenced by practice and effort. Consistent with Dweck's conceptualization is research suggesting that children infer that ability and effort are positively correlated given constant levels of success (Karabenick & Heller, 1976; Kun, 1977; Nicholls, 1978).

Interviews of young children provide further evidence of an "incremental" view of competence. When I asked children to explain their assessments of their own ability in school, 28% of the kindergarten and first graders discussed their work habits, including effort (Stipek, 1981). Anecdotal evidence from this study was, for me, even more persuasive. A few of the children who referred to competence or ability in their explanations of a peer's poor performance (e.g., "He's not very smart in reading") hastened to add, "If he practices he'll be smarter." Harter and Chao (reported in Harter, 1981) similarly found that 4- and 5-year-olds typically explained that the unsuccessful child merely needed to practice the skill to improve performance. One second grader's comment in a study by Harari and Covington (1981) also illustrates young children's view of the relationship between ability and effort: "If you study, it helps the brain and you get smarter" (p. 25).

Together these studies indicate that young children are not likely to attribute failure to a stable factor which limits the potential effectiveness of effort. Some preschool-age children may not even be able to remember and integrate past performance information. Memory and integration deficiencies and children's apparent tendency to attribute failure to controllable unstable causes seem to provide rather good explanations for why young children often expect success, even after repeated "objective" failure experiences. However, further evidence (discussed later) suggests that other factors are also at work.

Social Comparison

Performance feedback in the form of normative evaluation is also unlikely to lower young children's performance expectations or self-evaluations. Older children and adults usually interpret an outcome as success or failure in terms of how their performance compares to others. While even preschool-age children seem to be able to make social comparisons (Mosatache & Bragonier, 1981; Ruble, Feldman, & Boggiano, 1976), children tend not to compare their performance with other children until at least the second grade (Boggiano & Ruble, 1979; Ruble et al., 1980; Veroff, 1969). Moreover, their self-evaluations are relatively unaffected by normative information regarding their performance (Ruble, Parsons, & Ross, 1976; Ruble, Boggiano, Feldman, & Loebl, 1980).

Further evidence suggesting that young children do not consider normative information in their self-evaluations comes from a study we did in which children were asked to explain their self-ability rating (Stipek & Tannatt, in press). Preschool-age children often discussed their absolute level of mastery, usually giving an example of something they could do (e.g., "I can count to 10"). Not until the second and third grade did children explain their ability rating by making some reference to their competence or performance relative to peers ("I'm in the highest reading group," "I'm always the first one to finish my work"). (See also Heckhausen and Nicholls & Miller, this volume.)

It is usually easier for young children to surpass their own past performance level and elicit positive reinforcement from adults than it is for them to surpass the performance level of peers. By failing to compare their performance to other children, young children are spared one potential source of information indicating low competence. Whether children tend not to compare their performance to other children because they are cognitively unable to process comparative information, or because they simply are not motivated to obtain comparative information is an important question for developmentalists. However, whatever the reason, the relative lack of interest in comparing performance and in normative information may explain, in part, why they are able to maintain high expectations and a positive view of their competencies even when their performance is poor, relative to their peers.

Social Reinforcement

Spear and Armstrong (1978) found that, compared to older elementary school children, kindergarten and first-grade children's performance on motor and learning tasks was relatively more affected by social reinforcement statements made by adults than by peer comparisons. There is additional evidence suggesting that young children attend to and respond more to social reinforcement than to "objective" (e.g., correctness) feedback (Lewis et al., 1963; Meid, Note 3).

In a dissertation by Meid (Note 3, described in Harter, 1978), for example, 6-

and 10-year-olds were each given one of three levels of objective feedback (high, medium and low) regarding their past performance, and one kind of adult verbal feedback (praise, no comment, or mildly negative comments). The younger children's expectations for performance on a subsequent task were based entirely on the social feedback, even when the social feedback conflicted with the objective feedback. The older children took both objective feedback and social feedback into account in their expectancy statements.

Young children's concentration on social reinforcement may provide another explanation for why some children can consistently perform poorly in school by either a normative or an absolute standard, but maintain high expectations and self-evaluations. Perhaps regardless of children's "objective" or relative performance, as long as the teachers provide positive social reinforcement, children maintain a positive view of their competencies.

CHILDREN'S JUDGMENTS ABOUT THEIR OWN VERSUS ANOTHER CHILD'S PERFORMANCE

Four explanations for young children's typically high expectations have been discussed: First, the claim was made that preoperational children lack the cognitive capacities to remember and integrate a series of objective past performance feedback. Second, it was suggested that young children assume that performance outcomes are primarily a function of effort; if they intend to exert sufficient effort in the future they can logically expect to succeed. Third, evidence was cited suggesting that young children ignore social comparative feedback and are thus spared one source of negative information about their abilities and the probability of future success. Fourth, it was proposed that young children rely more on social reinforcement (which may be especially positive and plentiful in the early grades) in their ability and expectancy judgments than on "objective" or normative information.

The research program discussed below was designed to investigate the first explanation for unrealistic expectations—that preoperational children lack the cognitive capacities to remember and integrate a series of objective past performance feedback. We reasoned that if overly optimistic expectations for success are entirely explained by these or other cognitive deficiencies, then young children should have high expectations for other children's performance as much as for their own performance. To test this hypothesis, Joel Hoffman and I examined children's expectancy judgments for themselves and another child (Stipek & Hoffman, 1980).

The task consisted of a tower with graduated markings on both sides indicating scores from 0 to 100 in color-coded intervals of 10. The child pulled a string which, via a pulley, lifted a cart on which a ball was balanced. The ball was actually kept on the cart by a magnet that could be turned off surreptitiously by the experimenter when the cart was raised to a predetermined level. The point where the ball fell off on each of the four trials depended on the outcome condition to which the child had been randomly assigned: Failure (15, 20, 10, 15); ascending (15, 24, 36, 45); or success (100, 100, 100, 100).

In the "self" condition, children actually played "the game." After the four trials were completed, children were asked to predict performance on the next trial. When making performance judgments for another child, children in all three outcome groups were shown drawings illustrating a child (of the same gender) whose performance was the same as theirs and asked an identical series of questions. For every child the experimenter placed tacks on the balance marking the place where the ball had fallen off and the child's attention was drawn to these tacks before he or she was asked to make performance judgments.

Figure 1 shows that the 3- and 4-year-olds' predictions regarding their own performance were relatively unaffected by their past performance on the task. The differences between their mean expectations for the three performance outcomes for self were not significant. However, they used the information on the "other" child's performance quite logically.

In contrast to the preschool-age children, the outcome information influenced the older children's judgments about their own performance and the performance of another child equally. Comparing age-groups in the failure condition alone, children's expectations for their own performance declined monotonically with age (Figure 2) whereas expectations for the other child did not. Thus, the 3- and

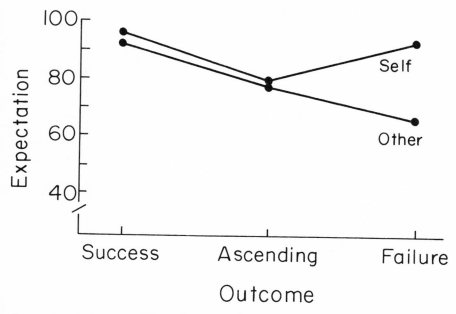

Figure 1. Mean expectations for self and other by outcome: 3- and 4-year-olds.

4-year-olds' expectancies resembled the older children's expectancies regarding another child's performance, but were higher than the older children's when their own performance was concerned. There were no significant age-group differences in expectations in the ascending and success conditions for either self or other.

These results suggest that preschool-age children used past-performance information and made performance-related judgments in an adultlike, logical fashion when judging others (i.e., their expectations declined as a function of past failure), but not when judging their own performance. Their use of past performance information in their judgments about another child's performance suggests that cognitive deficiencies in memory or in integrating a series of past outcomes cannot entirely explain their failure to incorporate past failure in their expectancy judgments regarding their own performance.

A second study found a difference between older children's judgments about their own and other children's competence that is analogous to the results of the expectation study; kindergarteners and first graders apparently used negative ability-related feedback in judgments about other children's competence but not in judgments about their own competence (Stipek, 1981).

Sixty-four children from kindergarten through third grade rated their own and each of their classmate's "smartness" on a scale from 1 to 5. The mean self-rating of the kindergarteners and the first graders combined was 4.69. In other words, nearly all of these younger children claimed to be "one of the smartest in

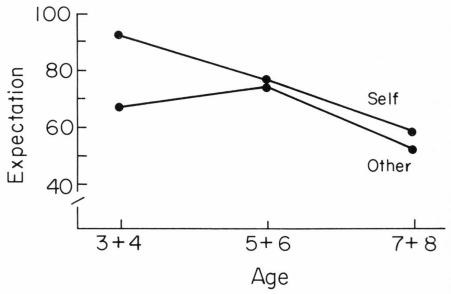

Figure 2.   Mean expectations for self and other by age group: Failure condition.

their class." Furthermore, their own competence ratings were not significantly correlated with teachers' or peers' ratings. Not until the second and third grade were children's perceptions of their own ability significantly correlated with the ratings they received from their teacher and classmates. However, even the kindergarteners' and first-graders' ratings of their *classmates* significantly reflected the teachers' assessment of their classmates' academic performance. Kindergarteners and first graders whom teachers claimed were in the bottom of their class academically received from their classmates a mean "smartness" rating of 2.78, compared to a mean rating of 3.83 received by the kindergarteners and first graders reportedly in the top third of their class. Again, children seemed to attend to and process negative ability-related cues about other children earlier than they did in judgments of their own ability. Why would children be less inclined to use the information-processing skills they possess when making judgments about their own performance than when judging others?

Attribution research has found that individuals predict future performance that is consistent with past performance (e.g., failure is predicted following failure) when the past performance is attributed to stable causes, but not when it is attributed to unstable causes (Weiner, 1979). Accordingly, one possible explanation for the self-other difference in the expectation study was that the preschool-age children attributed their own failure to unstable causes and the other child's failure to stable causes. This was tested in that study by using the method of paired comparisons (opposing all possible combinations of four causal factors: ability, effort, task difficulty, and luck). Attribution scores were derived by assigning 1 point to a factor for each time it was selected; the score for each factor could thus range from 0 to 3. Comparisons of the four attribution scores for self and other revealed no significant differences in the causal schemes children applied to their own and the other child's failure. However, this does not rule out the possibility that the assumed cause was perceived by the children to have different implications for their own and the other child's future performance. For example, children attributing past failure primarily to lack of effort may have intended to exert the necessary effort and thereby succeed on the next trial. They may not, however, have been confident that the other child would exert sufficient effort. Unfortunately, this interpretation cannot be tested with the data from this study.

The studies discussed below were designed to test alternative explanations for this self-other bias. The first explanation, inspired by Piaget, concerned preschool-age children's exaggerated perceptions of personal efficacy. We tested the possibility that, under some conditions, preoperational children's expectations reflect their wishes rather than a cognitive analysis of information relevant to the probability of future success. The second explanation is conceptualized in an information-processing framework; we tested the hypothesis that the different visual perspective children have on their own and another child's past performance outcomes results in different expectations for future performance.

WISHFUL THINKING

According to Piaget (1925, 1930), preschool-age children often do not differentiate between their wishes and their expectations. From studies of children's understanding of physical causality, he concludes that preoperational children regard their "desires as efficacious in themselves" (1930, p. 261). Piaget likens preoperational children's causal understanding of events or outcomes to infants' understanding of the causes of their own body movements. He gives an example of an infant discovering "that a desire to suck an object noticed by chance is immediately gratified with the help of his own hand seizing the object and bringing it to his mouth" (Piaget, 1925, p. 63, my translation). From the contiguity between desire and satisfaction infants derive a scheme linking their own desires with attainment, but they fail to distinguish between their desires and the intermediating actions, i.e., the hand bringing the object to the mouth. Piaget defines this scheme linking desires and outcomes as "efficacy."

There are certainly many situations in which infants' desires are fulfilled apart from their own actions. Sometimes, for example, an infant's hunger pains are relieved or uncomfortable wet diapers are changed by the good parent who anticipates the baby's needs. According to Piaget, this contiguity between desire and fulfillment deceives infants into thinking that they caused the outcome by simply desiring it.

Preoperational children, like infants, often do not have a sufficiently well developed understanding of physical causality to attribute some outcomes to anything other than their personal desires or efficacy. According to Piaget (1925), both the infant's and the preoperational child's perceptions of causality are based on contiguity. An understanding of the nature, or the "how" of many causal relationships comes later. Thus, "whenever the contiguous events are in harmony with the child's desire, this desire is perceived as the total or partial cause" (p. 64, my translation). Also, when children observe the contiguity between their own behavior and natural phenomena or events, in the absence of an "objective" explanation for the phenomena, they assume personal causation. Thus, Piaget (1930) reports that some preoperational children believe that they are responsible for the movement of the moon, the stars, and the clouds.

Piaget's concept of efficacy is somewhat different from Bandura's (1977), in which efficacy refers to the individual's belief that he or she can "successfully execute the behavior required to produce the outcomes" (p. 193). According to Piaget, young children often do not understand the instrumental behaviors, but they nonetheless believe they have the capacity to attain the desired outcome through their desires alone. Piaget claims that belief in the efficacy of their desires is strongest at about the age of four and declines thereafter. Children's perceptions of competence in Bandura's sense of a capacity to execute instrumental behaviors may follow a different developmental course (Weisz & Stipek, 1982).

What accounts for the decline in the preoperational child's exaggerated feelings of efficacy? According to Piaget (1925), the development of the child's sense of self separate from other individuals (associated with a decline in egocentrism) undermines feelings of personal efficacy. This objective self-awareness "is a product of the social environment and is attained by comparisons and conflict with other 'selves' " (p. 62, my translation). In conflict situations children discover limitations in their control over events. In addition, "objective" explanations for events learned through experience in the world supplant children's beliefs in personal causation. One might predict from this analysis that preoperational children would be most likely to have exaggerated perceptions of self-efficacy, and, consequently, unrealistic performance expectations in situations where they have experienced relatively little failure in achieving their goal (i.e., the contiguity between desire and outcome remains strong) and where they have no "objective" explanation for the outcome (e.g., in a novel experimental task).

Perhaps when making judgments about their own future performance, children confuse their desires with their "objective" judgment (i.e., they believe that their desires for success are sufficient to bring it about) whereas, when another child's performance is judged there is no personal inclination to interfere with processing the objective evidence.

The "wishful thinking" hypothesis being proposed is related to the motivational "intrusion" view of judgments proposed by a few social psychologists (e.g., Heider, 1958; McGuire, 1960) and personality theorists (e.g., Sullivan, 1947). According to this view, personal desires or ego needs "intrude upon" cognitive judgments. There is, in fact, evidence that older children's and adults' performance expectations are affected by their preferred outcome (Irwin, 1944; Marks, 1951). Our hypothesis is slightly different from the intrusion view in that we consider a strict differentiation between motivational and cognitive influences on judgments unnecessary. Our position therefore is closer to Piaget's (1981) claim that affect and cognition are indissociable. We are proposing, for example, a certain logic in young children's "confusion" between desires and expectations. If they perceive a causal relationship between desires and outcomes, as Piaget suggests, then expecting success following past failures is not illogical. The study described below tests the wishful thinking hypothesis (Stipek, Roberts, & Sanborn, in press).

A second hypothesis was also tested, that the effect of desires on children's processing of past performance information can be overcome by making past performance information especially salient. In a study by Clifford (1978), first and third graders' predictions of future performance on a puzzle task more closely approximated past performance when a salient visual reminder of past performance had been provided. Preschool-age children might also apply past performance information in their expectancy judgments if their attention is called to their previous failures by such a reminder.

If the wishful thinking hypothesis is correct, if children have higher expectations for their own performance than for the performance of another child because they have a stronger desire for their own success, then we should be able to raise children's expectations for another child by making the other child's success desirable to them. We assumed that children would desire another child's success more if they received a reward contingent on it. Thus we examined the effect of desires on performance expectations by manipulating the incentive value of performance outcomes. Specifically we hypothesized that 4-year-old children would have high expectations for another child if their own reward is contingent upon the other child's performance; their expectations for the other child should be relatively low if they have no desire (receive no reward) for the other child's success. Subjects' expectations for themselves should be high whether or not a reward is made contingent on their own performance, since presumably they desire success for themselves regardless of whether a tangible reward is offered.

Our second hypothesis, that the effect of desires on children's expectations for their own performance could be overcome by making past performance especially salient, was tested by providing a visual and auditory representation of each outcome. This condition was assumed to focus children's attention on past outcomes, rather than on the highest level of success, and, as a consequence, to lower expectations for children's own performance. Specifically, we hypothesized that subjects' expectations for themselves would be lower when past performance outcomes were made salient than when their attention was not called to the specific level of past performance they had achieved.

We used the tower task used in the previous expectancy study (Stipek & Hoffman, 1980). The only modification was that there were six color-coded intervals rather than ten. Sixty 4-year-olds were randomly assigned to six different conditions. Half of the children made predictions about their own performance ("self" conditions) and half made predictions about the performance of another child ("other" conditions). Within each of the self and other conditions, 10 children were offered a reward (a bag of marbles) for perfect success ("incentive" condition), 10 were provided a tangible representation of their previous performance (marbles were dropped noisily, one at a time for every interval the cart passed without the ball falling off, into a clear glass dish placed in front of the child; "salient outcome" condition), and 10 served as a control group (i.e., they were not offered a reward, nor were they given a tangible representation of their previous performance).

To render the "other" conditions realistic, we used a videotape of a real child the same age and gender rather than pictures. In all conditions the sequence of outcomes was the same: 1, 3, 1, 2, 1. Before any feedback and before the fourth, fifth, and sixth trials, children were asked for their performance expectations.

A 2 (self vs. other) by 3 (incentive vs. salient outcome vs. control condition) repeated measures analysis of variance (ANOVA) on predictions for the fourth, fifth, and sixth trials resulted in a near-significant self-other by experimental condition effect, $F(2, 54) = 3.10, p < .053$. The results were consistent with our hypothesis that the reward offered for getting the cart to the top would make the other child's success more desirable and would consequently raise expectations for the other child's performance. Predictions for the other child were higher ($p < .01$) in the incentive condition ($\bar{X} = 6.03$) than in the control condition ($\bar{X} = 4.63$).

The results were also consistent with our hypothesis that children's predictions of their own performance would be relatively low when they were provided a salient representation of their past performance: Subjects in the salient outcome condition made consistently low predictions ($\bar{X} = 4.63$) of their own performance, significantly ($p < .05$) lower than control subjects ($\bar{X} = 5.73$). (See Figure 3 for mean prediction for all of the experimental groups.)

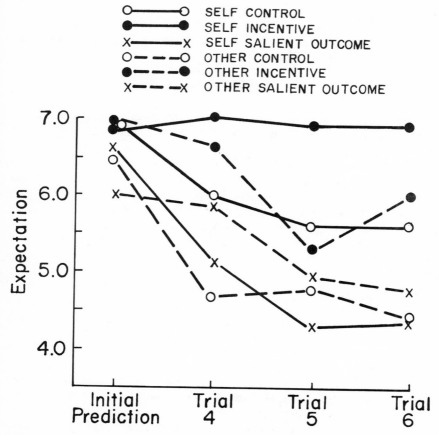

Figure 3. Mean expectations for self and other by experimental condition.

Having an investment in the other child's success apparently resulted in relatively higher expectations. This result supports our hypothesis that young children confuse their desires with their expectancy judgments. It also provides a possible explanation for the previous finding (replicated in the present study), that children had higher expectations for their own performance than for the unrewarded performance of another child (Stipek & Hoffman, 1980). Children may desire their own success more than they desire the success of another child, and this desire interferes with their processing of objective failure feedback.

However, the results of this study also suggest that desires do not necessarily predominate in young children's expectancy judgments. Children adjusted their future expectations to reflect their own past performance when their past failures were made especially salient. Apparently under some conditions, desires are not the primary factor in expectancy judgments.

There are probably other conditions under which young children use past performance failure feedback in judgments of their own future success. We extended the study described above to test the effect of one other variable on children's use of objective past performance information—the perspective they have on the performance feedback.

PERSPECTIVE

Children's perspective on performance outcomes might affect their use of performance feedback. For example, we hypothesized that children have a different visual perspective on the performance of another child than on their own performance. Performance judgments about another child, which are based on observations of the child *and* the outcome, might result in a strong association between the child and the outcome. In contrast, judgments about one's own performance may be based on observations of the outcome alone, resulting in a weaker person-outcome link. Our hypothesis is related to observations of adults indicating that actors tend to attribute their own actions to situational factors, whereas observers tend to attribute the same actions to stable personal dispositions (Jones & Nisbett, 1971).

To test this hypothesis, we added a condition to the self-other study just described (Stipek, Note 4). Children were videotaped while they were doing the task and shown the videotape of themselves performing the task before each expectancy statement was requested. Expectancies of children in this "self-video" condition were compared to expectancies of children in the "self" and "other" control conditions in the previously described study. Children in all conditions came from the same schools, and care was taken to equalize the amount of performance feedback given in all conditions. Our hypothesis was that children who saw themselves doing the task on the video would have lower expectations than children who were not provided with this "objective" perspective on their own performance; these children were also expected to have the same expectations as children judging another child's performance.

The results were in the right direction, but not significant even though the same numbers of children were included in each condition of this study as in the previous study. On all three predictions following failure, the 4-year-old children who observed themselves on the video made, on the average, expectancy statements almost identical to those made by children predicting another child's performance. Also on all three trials, the children who did not see themselves on the video had higher expectations than the other two groups. However, the differences were not significant, primarily because there was a good deal of variance within each treatment group. The results suggest that the video treatment may have the hypothesized effect of lowering children's expectations for themselves, but that the effect is weak compared to other factors influencing expectations.

CONCLUSION

At the beginning of this chapter it was proposed that young children's typically high expectations for success explain, at least in part, why they are apparently less susceptible to the behavioral effects of failure than are older children. The evidence reviewed from studies of children's performance expectations consistently showed that preschool-age children's expectations do not decline with cumulative failure as much as do older children's or adults' expectations. Thus, younger children are not only inaccurate (or "illogical" if we take the adults' response to failure as the standard), they are biased toward unrealistic optimism.

Young children's reliance on social reinforcement and their inattention to social comparative feedback were proposed as two factors contributing to positive self-perceptions of competence and unrealistically high expectations. Their tendency to assume that practice and effort inevitably lead to success was offered as a third explanation for young children's optimism. Cognitive deficiencies in remembering temporally separate events and applying past performance information to judgments about future performance were discussed as a fourth explanation for preschool-age children's failure to adjust future expectancies as a function of objective past performance (e.g., Parsons & Ruble, 1977). However, several sets of findings indicating that under certain circumstances preschool-age children do make adult-like, realistic predictions based on previous performance, suggest that these cognitive deficiencies do not explain children's optimism.

A few studies found that even though preschool-age children typically had higher expectations than older children, they lowered their expectations, at least to some degree, after multiple failure experiences (Eckhardt, 1968; Parsons et al., Note 1). Our studies suggest further that children use past performance realistically when judging another child's performance or when their own performance outcomes are made particularly salient.

Explanations for why preschool-age children use negative past performance information in judgments about another's performance but not in judgments about their own performance were explored. One proposed explanation concerned the different visual perspectives children have on others' versus their own performance. The results of our study described above provide no real support for the hypothesis that a stronger link between performance and the person is made when both are observed "objectively." However, there are other aspects of perspective which may have important implications for children's use of performance feedback. Perhaps because children are not distracted by their own participation when they observe another child, they have a better memory for the other child's performance history, or their greater concentration may allow them to perceive consistency in other children's feedback earlier than they are aware of that consistency in their own feedback. These potential explanations related to perspective merit further study.

A second explanation for children's more realistic judgments about other children (for which no evidence is available and research needs to be done) concerns young children's apparent failure to differentiate between effort and ability and their tendency to assume that practice and effort inevitably lead to success. Having access to their own, but not the other child's motivational state, the preschool-age children may have been confident that they would try hard on the next trial and consequently would succeed, but not confident that the other child would try sufficiently hard.

Support was provided for a third explanation for the self-other difference. This explanation is related to Piaget's (1925) claim that preschool-age children confuse their desires and their expectations. When their own reward was made contingent on the other child's achieving the highest level of success (i.e., when they had some personal investment in the other child's performance), children's expectations for the other child were raised to about the same level as their expectations for their own unrewarded performance. Having an investment in the other child's success apparently resulted in relatively higher expectations.

Is this "confusion" between desires and expectancies a cognitive or a motivational bias? Piaget would surely argue that cognitive and motivational variables are not distinguishable. Nevertheless, deficiencies in memory or integration of past information seem to be quite different from a tendency to expect the outcome one desires. In the former case, the child actually lacks the capacity to use past performance information as an adult would; in the latter case, the child has the capacity, but another variable, desires, interferes with the "logical" analysis. Let us, in the true spirit of Piaget, refer to "wishful thinking" as a cognitive-motivational factor.

Note that we are all, to some degree, susceptible to the "wishful thinking" illusion described by Piaget. Putting adults' wishful thinking into a theoretical framework, Irwin (1944) proposed several decades ago that adults' expectations can be distributed along a "realism-unrealism" continuum, the realistic expectations being independent of the individual's wants, and the unrealistic ones varying according to the individual's desires.

There is some evidence for the effect of desirability on expectations for older-elementary-school children and college students. Marks (1951) asked fifth and sixth graders to predict whether they would select a "picture card" out of a deck of cards in a series of trials. Subjects were significantly more likely to predict a picture card if they were told that they gained a point, than if they were told that they lost a point for each picture card drawn. Thus, they were more likely to predict the occurrence of the desirable than of the undesirable outcome. Irwin (1953) replicated this finding with college students, although the effect of desire on expectations was smaller than Marks had found for children. Studies by Crandall, Solomon, and Kelleway (1955) and by Pruitt and Hoge (1965) provide further evidence that adults' desires influence their subjective probability statements.

Though all the bases for young children's extraordinarily high level of confidence remain uncertain, that this confidence is especially marked when they, themselves are involved is not in question. This fact has important implications for achievement behavior. Indeed, there may even be survival benefits to being naturally endowed with a basic confidence in one's own efficacy.

Perhaps humans are naturally disposed to expect success unless there is evidence to the contrary. What constitutes "evidence to the contrary" or how much evidence is necessary to noticeably lower expectations may be the variables distinguishing young children from older children and adults. For all of the reasons discussed above regarding young children's attention to and interpretation of performance feedback, they may find it easy to maintain relatively high expectations in task situations; they may require more powerful and less ambiguous failure feedback than older children to relinquish their wishful thinking bias. The evidence against success may need to be all the more powerful, given their tendency to perceive effort and practice as the cause of failure. The lower expectations that we found when we provided a salient representation of performance feedback supports this view that young children use failure feedback if it is powerful. Apparently wishful thinking can, under some circumstances, be replaced by adult-like realism. Despite its potential survival value, optimism, even in young children, is evidently fragile—less fragile than in older children, but fragile, nonetheless.

It is perhaps unfortunate that children's naive optimism declines so soon after they enter school. To some degree, the development of more realistic expectations is unavoidable and even desirable. However, if success was defined in mastery rather than in normative terms and if children were given only tasks on which they could succeed with some effort, continually high expectations for success and the adaptive behaviors that are associated with high expectations might be maintained throughout the school years. Rather than lament young children's unrealistic judgments about their competencies, perhaps we should try harder to design educational environments which maintain their optimism and eagerness.

ACKNOWLEDGMENT

The author is grateful to David O. Sears and John R. Weisz for many helpful comments on earlier drafts of this chapter.

REFERENCE NOTES

1.   Parsons, J., Moses, L. & Yulish-Muszynski, S. The development of attributions, expectancies and persistence. Paper presented at the Annual meeting of the American Psychological Association, San Francisco, 1977.
2.   Blumenfeld, P., Wessels, K., Pintrich, P., & Meece, J. Age and sex differences in the impact of teacher communications on self-perceptions. Paper presented at the Biennial meeting of the Society for Research in Child Development, Boston, 1981.
3.   Meid, E. The effects of two types of success and failure on children's discrimination learning and evaluation of performance, Unpublished manuscript, Yale University, 1971.
4.   Stipek, D. Children's use of past performance information in ability and expectancy judgments. Presented as part of a symposium at the biennial meeting of the International Society for the Study of Behavioural Development, Toronto, 1981.

REFERENCES

Ausubel, D., Schiff, H., & Glasser, E. A preliminary study of the developmental trends in sociempathy: Accuracy of perception of own and others' sociometric status. *Child Development*, 1952, *23*, 111–128.
Bandura, A. Self-efficacy: Toward an underlying theory of behavioral change. *Psychological Review*, 1977, *84*, 191–215.
Bialer, I. Conceptualization of success and failure in mentally retarded and normal children. *Journal of Personality*, 1961, *29*, 303–320.
Boggiano, A. & Ruble, D. Competence and the overjustification effect: A developmental study. *Journal of Personality and Social Psychology*, 1979, *37*, 1462–1468.
Clifford, M. Validity of expectation: A developmental function. *Alberta Journal of Educational Research*, 1975, *21*, 11–17.
Clifford, M. The effects of quantitative feedback on children's expectations of success. *British Journal of Educational Psychology*, 1978, *48*, 220–226.
Covington, M. & Beery, R. *Self-worth and school learning*. New York: Holt, Rinehart and Winston, 1976.
Crandall, V., Solomon, D., & Kelleway, R. Expectancy statements and decision times as functions of objective probabilities and reinforcement values. *Journal of Personality*, 1955, *24*, 192–203.
Dweck, C. Theories of intelligence and achievement motivation. In S. Paris, G. Olson, & H. Stevenson (Eds.), *Learning and motivation in the classroom*. Hillsdale, NJ: Erlbaum, (in press).
Dweck, C., & Goetz, T. Attributions and learned helplessness. In J. Harvey, W. Ickes, & R. Kidd (Eds.), *New directions in attribution research* (Vol. 2). Hillsdale, N.J.: Erlbaum, 1978.
Entwisle, D., & Hayduk, L. *Too great expectations: The academic outlook of young children*. Baltimore, Md.: The John Hopkins University Press, 1978.
Eshel, Y., & Klein, Z. Development of academic self-concept of lower-class and middle-class primary school children. *Journal of Educational Psychology*, 1981, *73*, 287–293.
Flavell, J., Friedrichs, A., & Hoyt, J. Developmental changes in memorization processes. *Cognitive Psychology*, 1970, *1*, 324–340.

Frieze, I. Beliefs about success and failure in the classroom. In J. MacMillan (Ed.), *The social psychology of school learning*, New York: Academic Press. (in press)

Goss, A. Estimated versus actual physical strength in three ethnic groups. *Child Development*, 1968, *39*, 283–290.

Harari, O., & Covington, M. Reactions to achievement from a teacher and student perspective: A developmental analysis. *American Educational Research Journal*, 1981, *18*, 15–28.

Harter, S. Developmental differences in the manifestations of mastery motivation on problem-solving tasks. *Child Development*, 1975, *46*, 370–378.

Harter, S. Effectance motivation reconsidered: Toward a developmental model. *Human Development*, 1978, *21*, 34–64.

Harter, S. A model of mastery motivation in children: Individual differences and developmental change. In A. Pick (Ed.), *Minnesota Symposium on Child Psychology (Vol. 14)*. Hillsdale, New Jersey: Erlbaum, 1981.

Heider, F. *The psychology of interpersonal relations*. New York: Wiley, 1958.

Irwin, F. The realism of expectations. *Psychological Review*, 1944, *51*, 120–126.

Irwin, F. Stated expectations as functions of probability and desirability of outcomes. *Journal of Personality*, 1953, *21*, 329–335.

Jones, E., & Nisbett, R. The actor and the observer: Divergent perceptions of the causes of behavior. In E. Jones, D. Kanouse, H. Kelley, R. Nisbett, S. Valins, & B. Weiner (Eds.), *Attribution: Perceiving the causes of behavior*. Morristown, NJ: General Learning Press, 1971.

Karabenick, J., & Heller, K. A developmental study of effort and ability attributions. *Developmental Psychology*, 1976, *12*, 559–560.

Kun, A. Development of the magnitude-covariation and compensation schemata in ability and effort attributions of performance. *Child Development*, 1977, *48*, 862–873.

Lewis, M., Wall, M. & Aronfreed, J. Developmental change in the relative values of social and nonsocial reinforcement. *Journal of Experimental Psychology*, 1963, *66*, 133–137.

Maehr, M., & Nicholls, J. Culture and achievement motivation: A second look. In N. Warren (Ed.) *Studies in cross-cultural psychology*, Vol. 2, New York: Academic Press, 1980.

Marks, R. The effect of probability, desirability, and "privilege" on the stated expectations of children. *Journal of Personality*, 1951, *19*, 332–351.

McGuire, W. A syllogistic analysis of cognitive relationships. In M. Rosenberg, C. Hovland, W. McGuire, R. Abelson, & J. Brehm (Eds.), *Attitude organization and change*. New Haven, CT: Yale University Press, 1960.

Mosatche, H. & Bragonier, P. An observational study of social comparison in preschoolers. *Child Development*, 1981, *52*, 376–378.

Nicholls, J. The development of the concepts of effort and ability, perceptions of academic attainment and the understanding that difficult tasks require more ability. *Child Development*, 1978, *49*, 800–814.

Nicholls, J. The development of perception of own attainment and causal attributions for success and failure in reading. *Journal of Educational Psychology*, 1979, *71*, 94–99.

Parsons, J., & Ruble, D. Attributional processes related to the development of achievement-related affect and expectancy. *Proceedings of the 80th Annual Convention of the American Psychological Association*, 1972, *7*, 105–106.

Parsons, J., & Ruble, D. The development of achievement-related expectancies. *Child Development*, 1977, *48*, 1075–1079.

Phillips, B. Age changes in accuracy of self-perceptions. *Child Development*, 1963, *34*, 1041–1046.

Piaget, J. De quelques formes primitives de causalité chez l'enfant. *L'Année Psychologie*, 1925, *26*, 31–71.

Piaget, J. *The child's conception of physical causality*. London: Routledge & Kegan Paul, 1930.

Piaget, J. *Intelligence and affectivity: Their relationship during child development* (Annual Reviews monograph). Palo Alto, CA: Annual Reviews, Inc., 1981.

56   DEBORAH J. STIPEK

Pruitt, D., & Hoge, R. Strength of the relationship between the value of an event and its subjective probability as a function of method of measurement. *Journal of Experimental Psychology*, 1965, *69*, 483–489.

Rholes. W., Blackwell, J., Jordan, C., & Walters, C. A developmental study of learned helplessness. *Developmental Psychology*, 1980, *16*, 616–624.

Ruble, D. A developmental perspective on the theories of achievement motivation. In L. Fyans, Jr. (Ed.), *Achievement motivation: Recent trends in theory and research*. New York: Plenum Press, 1980.

Ruble, D., Boggiano, A., Feldman, N. & Loebl, J. Developmental analysis of the role of social comparison in self-evaluation. *Developmental Psychology*, 1980, *16*, 105–115.

Ruble, D., Feldman, N., & Boggiano, A. Social comparison between young children in achievement situations. *Developmental Psychology*, 1976, *12*, 192–197.

Ruble, D. Parsons, J. & Ross, J. Self-evaluative responses of children in an achievement setting. *Child Development*, 1976, *47*, 990–997.

Seligman, M. *Helplessness: On depression, development, and death*. San Francisco, CA: Freeman, 1975.

Shaklee, H. Development in inferences of ability and task difficulty. *Child Development*, 1976, *47*, 1051–1057.

Shaklee, H. & Tucker, D. Cognitive bases of development in inferences of ability. *Child Development*, 1979, *50*, 904–907.

Spear, P. S., & Armstrong, S. Effects of performance expectancies created by peer comparison as related to social reinforcement, task difficulty and age of child. *Journal of Experimental Child Psychology*, 1978, *25*, 254–266.

Stipek, D. Children's perceptions of their own and their classmates' ability. *Journal of Educational Psychology*, 1981, *73*, 404–410.

Stipek, D. The development of achievement motivation. In R. Ames & C. Ames (Eds.), *Research on motivation in education: Vol. I. Student motivation*. New York: Academic Press. (in press)

Stipek, D., & Hoffman, J. Development of children's performance-related judgments. *Child Development*, 1980, *51*, 912–914.

Stipek, D., Roberts, T., & Sanborn, M. Preschool-age children's performance expectations for themselves and another child as a function of the incentive value of success and the salience of past performance. *Child Development* (in press).

Stipek, D., & Tannatt, L. Children's judgments of their own and their peers' academic competence. *Journal of Educational Psychology*. (in press)

Sullivan, H. (1947). *Conceptions of modern psychiatry*. Washington, DC: William Alanson White Psychiatric Foundation.

Veroff, J. Social comparison and the development of achievement motivation. In C. Smith (Ed.), *Achievement-related motives in children*. New York: Russesl Sage Foundation, 1969.

Weiner, B. A theory of motivation for some classroom experiences. *Journal of Educational Psychology*, 1979, *71*, 3–25.

Weisz, J. R. Perceived Control and learned helplessness among mentally retarded and nonretarded children: A developmental analysis. *Developmental Psychology*, 1979, *15*, 311–319.

Weisz, J., & Stipek, D. Competence, contingency and the development of perceived control. *Human Development*, 1982, *25*, 250–281.

White, R. Motivation reconsidered: The concept of competence. *Psychological Review*, 1959, *66*, 297–333.

Yussen, S., & Berman, L. Memory predictions for recall and recognition in first, third, and fifth-grade children. *Developmental Psychology*, 1981, *17*, 224–229.

Yussen, S., & Levy, V. Developmental changes in predicting one's own span of short-term memory. *Journal of Experimental Child Psychology*, 1975, *19*, 502–508.

THE COGNITIVE BASIS OF TASK CHOICE IN PRESCHOOL CHILDREN

Klaus Schneider

After nearly a quarter of a century of tracing the origins of achievement motivation, no coherent developmental theory has emerged (cf. reviews by Heckhausen, 1982; Ruble, 1980; Trudewind, 1982). The traditional approach in this area has been the individual differences approach, i.e. the study of the determinants of individual differences in the motives to seek success and to avoid failure.

However, an alternative approach, focussing on age-related changes of achievement behavior and the mediating cognitions and emotions, has always had its advocates (Heckhausen & Roelofsen, 1962; Heckhausen & Wagner, 1965; Heckhausen & Wasna, 1965; Smith, 1969; Wagner, 1969; Wasna, 1970). In recent years there has been a renewed interest in the documentation of the developmental change in components of achievement oriented behavior such as task choice and level of aspiration setting and the related change in the understanding of subjective probabilities, the self perception of competence and the

Advances in Motivation and Achievement, vol. 3, pages 57–72
Copyright © 1984 by JAI Press Inc.
All rights of reproduction in any form reserved.
ISBN 0-89232-289-6

perception of causation of one's action outcomes (cf. Heckhausen, 1982; Nicholls, 1978, 1980; Ruble, 1980).

RISK-TAKING IN ACHIEVEMENT SITUATIONS: BASIC PHENOMENA AND ATKINSON'S MODEL

Since Hoppe's (1930) and Dembo's (1931) original studies, choice behavior (risk-taking) and goal setting has probably been the most studied phenomenon in achievement-oriented contexts. Most subjects have preferred task levels of intermediate difficulty (risk-taking) or have set goals a little higher than what they achieved before. However, there are subjects with an apparent defensive strategy, who choose either difficulty levels too high or too low in respect to their competence level or who state goals which are far above or below their last result.

The little empirical evidence we have so far shows that even preschoolers prefer challenging or intermediate difficulty levels when they are faced with concrete difficulty levels which they have had a chance to practice on (Heckhausen, 1967). McClelland (1958), who demonstrated this phenomenon with 5 year-old boys, used a ring-toss game. With a similar task and a similar procedure we made the same observations. Figure 1 illustrates the pooled choices of three distances in a ball task of 30 preschoolers between 4;6 and 6;6 years old. Children preferred the intermediate distance where they hit a basket with a tennis ball in about 42% of all trials.

The most popular explanation of this preference for intermediate difficulty levels is a variant of an expectancy-value-model of task choice. For more than two decades, research on risk-taking and goal-setting has been guided by Lewin's (cf. Lewin, Dembo, Festinger, & Sears, 1944) and Atkinson's (1957) affect-maximization-minimization model. In Atkinson's model, which was developed in research with adults, it is assumed that individuals try to maximize the positive affect consequent on success and to minimize the negative affect consequent on failure. Atkinson followed Escalona (1940), Festinger (1942) and Lewin et al. (1944) in their intuitive notion that more positive affect ("pride" and "joy") is experienced when a person succeeds at a difficult task than at an easy one, and more negative affect is experienced when a person fails at an easy task than at a difficult one. Therefore linear relationships are assumed between perceived difficulty, reflected in subjective probability estimates, and the incentive values of success and failure (anticipated affect associated with success and failure) at different levels of difficulty.

Atkinson's model combined both variables—subjective probabilities and incentives of success and failure—by multiplication. Therefore, affect associated with success and failure was predicted to be maximal at intermediate difficulty levels where subjective probability of success (P_s) is .50. Consequently, suc-

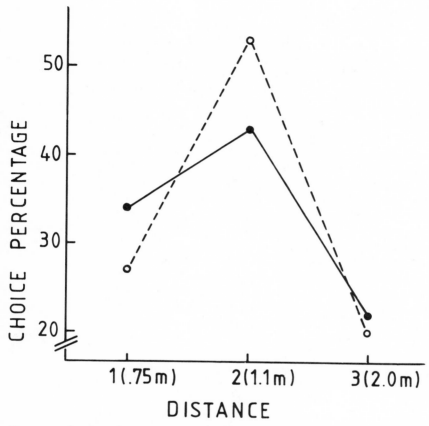

Figure 1.   Distribution of chosen difficultty levels of 30 preschoolers (15 girls and 15 boys) in a ball throwing game. Children were 4;6 to 6;6 years old. The difficulty levels 1 to 3 are defined by the distances (in meters) from which subjects tried to throw a tennis ball into a basket. Choices were pooled over all subjects. Each subject had at least 8 choices and was interrupted after a maximum of 15 choices. The solid line shows the distribution of all choices; the dashed line the distribution of the first choice. The objective success probabilities at these distances were: 1. (64%); 2. (42%); 3. (20%).

cess-oriented subjects were predicted to prefer this difficulty level, whereas anxious or failure-avoidant individuals were predicted to prefer avoiding it.

Atkinson's model was fairly successful in the prediction of relative differences in the preference for task difficulty levels between success- and failure-oriented subjects. However, only a few studies demonstrated the predicted preference for very difficult or very easy tasks in failure-oriented subjects. In most studies, failure-oriented subjects, compared with success-oriented subjects, showed only a reduced preference for intermediate task difficulty levels. In other words, in general, mature individuals prefer tasks of intermediate difficulty. Only under very special conditions will failure-oriented subjects choose extreme difficulty levels (cf. Heckhausen, Schmalt, & Schneider, in prep., Chapt. 3).

Can we explain the intermediate task difficulty choices of preschool children with the Atkinson theory? The answer seems to be negative, because children at this age may not be able to process task information in the way assumed by the model:

1. Even a sizable proportion of 6-year-olds do not perceive the relationship between normative task difficulty and incentive value of success in the way predicted by the model (Nicholls, 1978; 1980).
2. Children at this age may not even be able to correctly estimate success probabilities on the basis of a series of experienced successes and failures (Parsons & Ruble, 1977; Stipek, this volume).
3. Preschool children normally do not combine values of outcomes and probabilities of achieving these outcomes in decision situations; they focus on one parameter, predominantly the value parameter (Schmidt, 1966).

Thus, there appears to be a need for an alternative theory in which fewer assumptions concerning the necessary steps in information processing are made.

RISK-TAKING AND SEARCH FOR COMPETENCE INFORMATION

An information-maximization principle has been proposed as an alternative to Atkinson's affect-maximization model (Meyer, 1973; Schneider, 1973, 1974; Weiner, Frieze, Kukla, Reed, Rest, & Rosenbaum, 1971). Meyer, Weiner and associates and Schneider assume that the preference for intermediate difficulty levels reflects the search for competence information.

Our own approach to the study of task choice in achievement situations (Schneider, 1973, 1974) makes use of the logic of information theory. In this view, success at a high difficulty level of a given task indicates one can succeed at lower difficulty levels of the same task, whereas a failure at an easy task indicates one will fail at more difficult tasks. Thus more information of competence should be revealed by a success at a high difficulty level, and more information of a lack of competence by a failure at a low difficulty level.

The same logic is inherent in the formal definition of the information value of an uncertain event as a logarithmic function of the reciprocal of the a priori probability of that event (Shannon, 1948). Thus the calculus of information theory can be used to infer the expected information value of a performance outcome at a given task. It is, however, unlikely that children are able to relate competence information to task difficulty, in the way assumed by information theory, because they are unable to associate greater incentives of success with more difficult tasks.

In information theory, however, the averaged expected information over a set of outcomes is identical with the uncertainty of that set of outcomes. This assumption seems to be valid for the psychological phenomenon of subjective uncertainty as well (Cohen, Hansel, & Walker, 1960; Schmidt & Zarn, 1964).

In task choice studies with adults, we have found that subjective uncertainty of outcome is maximal at intermediate difficulty levels, where the objective success probability is about 30%, and predicts choice behavior (at least the group preference functions) better than Atkinson's original model (Schneider, 1973, 1974; cf. Schneider & Heckhausen, 1981). In these studies, subjective uncertainty has been assessed behaviorally by measuring the decision times taken by students when asked to predict whether they would succeed or fail and by having them judge their confidence in their predictions.

We assumed that subjects chose intermediate difficulty levels in achievement situations in order to receive maximal competence information (ultimate goal), but that their actual choice behavior was guided by states of subjective uncertainty. Therefore, the proximal goal of subjects in task choice situations seems to be the creation and resolution of a maximum of subjective uncertainty. This is achieved by the choice of a moderate difficulty level and by subsequent performance feedback.

Berlyne (1960, 1966) has proposed a similar theory for the explanation of exploratory behavior. Specific exploration is instigated by states of subjective uncertainty, caused by objects with specified qualities like complexity, ambiguity etc. Exploratory behavior, then, has as its goal the reduction of this state of uncertainty. To explain both task choice in achievement situations and exploratory behavior with the same theoretical concept seemed to us to open a promising approach to the study of competence motivation in preschool children, as both behavioral systems are presumed to have a common origin—ontogenetically and phylogenetically (Lorenz, 1969; White, 1959). The more immediate advantage of subjective uncertainty as an explanatory concept in preschoolers competence motivation seems to be the fact that this experiental variable can be measured with non-verbal methods.

SUBJECTIVE UNCERTAINTY IN VISUAL INVESTIGATION (STUDY I)

In our first study we examined the value of the concept of subjective uncertainty for the explanation of preschoolers' choice behavior in a curiosity paradigm. Our hypothesis was that re–examination of briefly exposed figures would be a function of the individual's state of subjective uncertainty about what the figures represented (cf. Schneider, Barthelmey, & Herrmann, 1981).

According to Berlyne (1966) a state of uncertainty about the meaning of an object or stimulus should motivate the actor to seek further information by visual inspection, manipulation, question asking etc. Berlyne and associates have demonstrated this phenomenon in studies with adults (Berlyne, 1960, 1966, 1974). We asked therefore (a) if decision time is a valid indicator of subjective uncertainty in preschool children in a curiosity-oriented situation and (b) if subjective uncertainty predicts visual exploratory behavior at this age?

Subjects were 39 boys and 42 girls between 3½- and 6½-years-old. They were shown two series of slides (animals: horse, cat, dog; toys: truck, doll, spinning top) at three exposure times: 20 msec, 60 msec and 120 msec in three different boxes arranged in a semi-circle. Children were asked if they had recognized the displayed object and the time needed for the answer, decision time, was measured. Objective recognition probabilities for the three exposure times were in the range of 0%, 50% and 100%. Later all subjects were given a chance to see all slides again in the order of their choice. We took the rank order of this choice, the subject's preference function, as the indicator of the amount of curiosity in respect to the different exposure times.

Figure 2 shows the recognition frequencies (in %) for the two picture series in the three age groups as a function of 3 predetermined exposure times. An intermediate time of 60 msec was chosen on the basis of pilot work in order that approximately 50% of all children should recognize the displayed object. The percentages of recognition are highly similar for the two series, toys and animals, and for the three age groups. From these objective performance data objective uncertainty values, using Shannon's formula, could be calculated (Figure 2b).

Averaged decision times, our behavioral measure of subjective uncertainty, reflect the objective uncertainty values of the exposure times perfectly in the middle and oldest group, but not in the youngest group of children between 3 years; 6 months and 4 years; 5 months old.

An analysis of variance of the decision times showed, besides the highly significant main effect for exposure time (F (2, 243)=28.8, $p <$ .001), a significant interaction: age × exposure time (F (4, 243)=9.49, $p <$ .001). Exposure time apparently has no effect on the decision time of the youngest children but influences decision time in the way predicted by the information theory model for children from 4½ years on. The computation of simple main effects for each group confirms this: the effect of objective uncertainty (exposure time) is significant ($p <$ .001) in the second and third age groups, not in the first.

In order to examine the relationship between subjective uncertainty and the preference for the order of a second inspection of the different presentations, Kendall rank correlations were computed for each subject between the rank order of subjective uncertainty (decision time) and the preference over the three exposure times for the sequence of a second inspection. The averaged Kendall

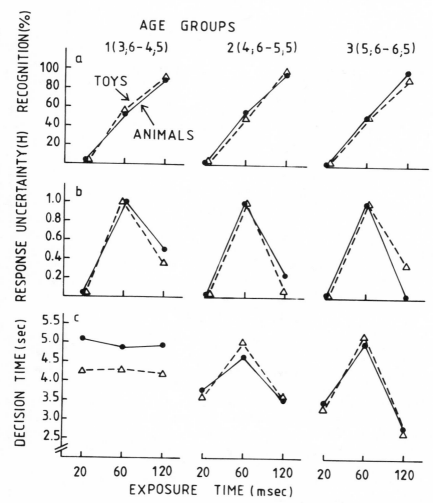

Figure 2. Mean recognition of the different figures (in %) at each exposure time (Fig. 2a) and corresponding mean objective uncertainty values and decision times (Figures 2b and 2c) of the three age groups. There are 13 boys and girls in each age group; 4 years (1), 5 years (2) and 6 years old (3).

coefficients are shown in Table 1. Only in the oldest group, children from 5 years, 6 months - 6 years; 5 months old, can the preference rank order for a further inspection validly be predicted on the basis of subjective uncertainty data. In the case of animals as stimulus material this relation is quite impressive. From among 27 subjects in this age group, only 3 subjects have a negative relation

Table 1. Averaged Kendall Rank Correlations Between Individual Preference Functions and Subjective Uncertainty (Decision Times) for Three Picture Exposure Times.

	Age Groups		
	1 (3;6–4;5)	2 (4;6–5;5)	3 (5;6–6;5)
$\bar{\tau}$	−.14	−.21	.58
z - values	−1.08	−1.44	3.75 ($p < .0001$)[a]
	($p < .0001$)[b]		($p = .0001$)[b]
$\bar{\tau}$	−.06	−.14	.21
z - values	.42	1.25	1.39 ($p < .10$)[a]
		($p < .05$)[b]	
		($p < .01$)[b] (one-sided tests)	
N	27	27	27

Notes:
[a]Test for the significance of the relationship between the two variables (WILCOXON-test).
[b]Comparison of the degree of the relationship between the two variables in a different age groups (U-test).

between subjective uncertainty and preference and 14 have a perfect correlation of 1.0.

The results of this study show (1) that it is possible to assess states of subjective uncertainty in preschool children above approximately 4 years with the nonverbal method and that (2) such states of uncertainty are related to the preference for a further presentation of briefly exposed photographs. Thus the motivation to explore an object in the world seems to be a function of the state of subjective uncertainty created by that object (in this case by a figural presentation) in this age group as well as in adults. The goal of the following study was to establish whether states of subjective certainty/uncertainty can also be assessed in preschool children in achievement situations and whether they are related to task choice as found with adults (Schneider, 1973).

SUBJECTIVE UNCERTAINTY AND SUBJECTIVE PROBABILITIES OF SUCCESS IN ACHIEVEMENT SITUATIONS IN PRESCHOOLERS (STUDIES II, III, IV AND V)

Study II

A marble game in which the subject had to roll marbles through gates of three different widths at the end of a table was used in this study. The gate could be hidden with a screen and suddenly exposed. After 6 practice trials with each gate, the screen was lowered before the gate area. The subject was then shown, by raising the screen, one of the gates. Children were then asked to predict by saying "yes" or "no," whether or not they would get through on the next trial. Time to respond was taken as an index of subjective uncertainty in respect to action outcome. All 3 gates were shown in a random sequence. Children also estimated their chances of success for each gate. For this purpose they were asked to push the number of marbles (out of six) they thought they might succeed with from the left to the right of a rod. This provided a behavioral index of outcome expectancy.

Ninety-three children (50 girls and 43 boys) took part in this study and were divided into two age groups: 3;6 to 4;5 and 4;6 to 5;5. During the six practice trials at each difficulty level the four year old children succeeded on 23%, 47% and 67% of all the practice trials, the 5 year olds on 25%, 50% and 75%. Our assumption was that on the basis of such an extensive success/failure feedback even preschool children might be able to assess their success chances at the different difficulty levels. In Figure 3, the subjective probabilities of success, the proportions of success predictions (yes-percent), and the means of the related decision times are shown.

The behaviorally assessed subjective probabilities of success (see Figure 3b) are generally higher than the objective probabilities of success based on the results of the children in the practice period. However, even the younger children

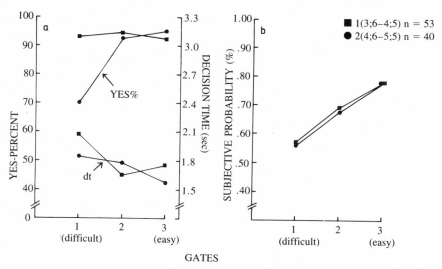

Figure 3. Percentages of success prediction (yes %) and related means of decision times (dt) (Fig. 3a) and subjective probabilities of success (Fig. 3b). Subjects are divided into 4-year-olds (1) and 5-year-olds (2).

demonstrate appreciable responsiveness to the actual probabilities. The main effect of difficulty levels is highly significant (F (2, 178) = 20.6, $p <$ .001) and there are no effects of the age factor.

Yet in contrast to the understanding manifested in this assessment procedure, children seemed unwarrantedly optimistic in their predictions of success by saying "yes" at each difficulty level to the experimenter's question as to whether they would pass the gate or not (see Figure 3a). Only in the group of 5-year-old children did the percentage of success predictions drop to 70% at the highest difficulty level (gate 1), whereas the younger children predicted success in 93% of all cases. This difference is significant ($p <$ .05). It seems that children in this situation answered the experimenter's question without due consideration of the realities of the task and their own achievement.

This is confirmed by the fact that the average decision times needed to answer this question do not discriminate between the three difficulty levels (F (2, 178) = 1.2, n.s.). The average decision time of 1.7 sec at the intermediate gate is (in addition) rather short compared with the 2 to 3 times longer period adult subjects needed to predict a success or failure at an intermediate difficulty level of a similar psychomotor task (Schneider, 1973, 1974).

Therefore, we have to conclude that preschool children are unwarrantedly optimistic when asked to predict a success or failure for a single trial at such a task. They decide quickly without considering the information they have. They are, however, able to do better. Their nonverbal probability estimates indicate that they process success and failure feedback in a meaningful way and make clear discriminations between the different difficulty levels. Thus, one might significantly underestimate young children's responsiveness to task difficulty cues and past performance if one relied on verbal statements of success expectancies. The more concrete index of expectancy suggests that these children do make sufficiently veridical assessments of chances of success to mediate realistic, moderate risk-taking.

The present finding of more realistic assessments of success probabilities with the concrete measurement procedure we used is also at variance with findings reported by other workers using questioning techniques (e.g. Parsons & Ruble, 1977). It seemed to us that the contradictory results in this area of research (Stipek, this volume) may be a consequence of different measurement procedures. To examine this question further, two more studies were conducted to examine the reliability of our finding that, when measured non-verbally, preschoolers' performance expectancies reflect the performance feedback received.

Study III and IV

In these two experiments we used a ball-throwing game. A tennis ball had to be thrown into a box or a basket from three different distances. Samples of 60 (Study III) and 39 (Study IV) preschoolers were tested. First children had a chance to throw tennis balls 15 times (Study III), or 10 times (Study IV) from 3 predetermined distances into a box. Afterwards children were asked, at every distance, beginning with the farthest, to separate 6 tennis balls into two little boxes (Study III) or into two glass cylinders (Study IV). The balls placed in one box (cylinder) should represent the ones they expected to hit, the others they expected to miss. The left vs. right positions of the hit- and miss-boxes were alternated over children. The average probability estimates are shown in Figure 4.

Children were divided into three age groups. Numbers of girls and boys did not differ by more than 2 in each age group. Results for the larger sample (Study III) show that even the youngest children (3;6 to 4;5) have some understanding of the variation in difficulty and of their chances of success at each difficulty level. Their nonverbal probability estimates reflect the objective success probabilities at the three distances.

For the probability estimates, there is an effect for difficulty level ($F(2, 108)$ = 38.5, $p < .001$) and a difficulty $\times$ age interaction ($F(4, 108) = 6.67$, $p < .001$). Although the overall difficulty effect was significant ($p < .05$) for each group, simple main effect tests showed that the three groups differed significantly at the greatest distance ($p < .01$). The youngest children (3½- to 4½-years-old) overestimated their success chances here more than did the older children.

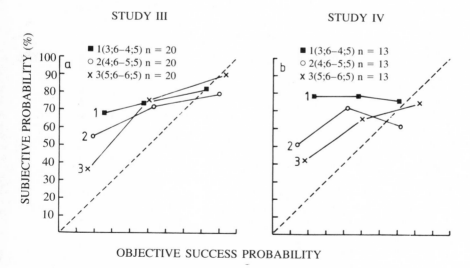

Figure 4. Mean probability estimates in Studies III and IV. Probability estimates are shown as functions of the objective success probabilities at the three distances. The dashed fline represents a perfect association between objective and subjective success probabilities. Age groups are 4 (1), 5 (2) annd 6 years (3).

The results of study IV confirm the general tendency of these findings. However, here the youngest group and to a certain degree also the children between 4½- and 5½-years-old did not demonstrate responsiveness to the objective success probabilities. There was a main effect for difficulty levels ($F(2, 64) = 6.41$, $p < .05$). Testing each group separately showed the difficulty level effect to be significant ($p < .01$) only in the group of the oldest children.

Generally, the results with the behavioral assessment procedure of subjective probability of success of three studies show that even preschool children from 3½ years on can have appreciable awareness of their probabilities of success on skill tasks. There is the same bias found in older subjects: a general overestimation of chances, especially where objective chances are low. This effect is most marked in the youngest children. The amount of realism demonstrated by preschool children is, however, dependent on the assessment procedure used. When asked by the experimenter whether they will hit a certain gate or not (Study II) children seem less restrained in their general tendency to be optimistic (see Stipek, this volume) than in predicting the expected hits in 6 trials with a nonverbal procedure (Study II, III and IV).

One possible explanation for the different findings might be that children will usually predict success for the very next trial in an achievement task, especially when asked by an other person. They may assess their chances more realistically in the long run, i.e. in respect to a certain number of trials. Such an effect of the assessment procedure was observed already in adult subjects (Schneider, 1972). Thus, although children might experience different states of uncertainty when considering their chances at varying difficulty levels of an achievement task, these states may not manifest themselves during the actual response to the experimenters question, because of the children's general optimism.

Decision time, measured in the way we did it here, seems an inappropriate index of subjective uncertainty in an achievement situation in this age group, at least for the tasks and the method of presentation of task difficulty levels used so far. Decision time, however, proved to be a useful index of uncertainty in a curiosity-oriented situation for children from 4½ years on (Study I). Accordingly, we made one more study of decision time on an achievement task. This time, with a different task and with a simultaneous presentation of task difficulty levels, we found a strong relationship between decision time for predicting success or failure, an index of uncertainty, and of objective difficulty level (Unzner & Schneider, 1983).

Study V

Subjects were 30 preschool children, 3 to 6 years of age. The tasks used were 5 wooden boxes, differently coloured and of different sizes. The boxes were arranged in a semi-circle around the child. The sizes of the boxes were 1: 10 ×

10 cm; 2: 13 × 13 cm; 3: 22 × 22 cm; 4: 53 × 53 cm and 5: 60 × 60 cm. The female experimenter pointed to a randomly chosen box and the child was asked if she or he would be able to lift the box. Children answered by saying "yes," or "I don't know" or by nodding or turning the head. Video recordings of the children were made. From these, decision times and the number of eye fixations in the decision period were measured or counted respectively. (Typically children looked from one box to the other or from the box pointed to by the experimenter to the experimenter.)

Medians of the decision times for the 5 boxes, means of the number of eye fixations and answers to the question "Can you lift this one?" are given in Figure 5. As the figure reveals, decision time and number of eye movements

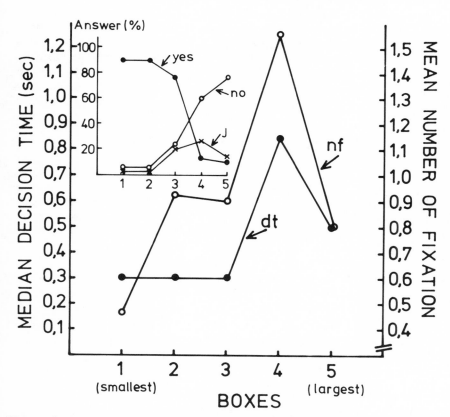

Figure 5. Medians of decision times (dt) in predicting success (lifting) or failure (not lifting) for the 5 boxes; mean numbers of eye fixations (nf) in the decision period; and percentages of success ("yes"), failure ("no") and "I don't know" answers (I; insert).

were both highest for box 4, where the distribution of yes-, no-, and I don't know-answers indicate strongest uncertainty. The differences between the 5 boxes were significant for decision time ($\chi^2 = 9.53$, p < .05) and for number of eye fixations ($\chi^2 = 19.89$, p < .001; Friedeman-analysis in both cases). Either the more concrete nature of this task—lifting boxes compared to rolling metal balls through a gate—or the simultaneous presentation of all difficulty levels—as opposed to the consecutive presentation of gates as in experiment II—may have facilitated the experience of uncertainty in predicting a success or failure for this task and its expression in the assessed behavioral indices.

In conclusion, the results with the behavioral assessment procedure of subjective probabilities of success in Studies II, III and IV and the decision time and eye-movement data of the last study show that preschool children are responsive to variations in the difficulty of concrete physical skill tasks. Further, they are able to assess these probabilities quite realistically. In other words their feelings of more or less uncertainty of being able to master tasks reflect their actual probabilities of mastery quite well. Therefore, they can and do choose difficulty levels that are neither too easy nor too difficult for them. Thus they are able to explore the environment and to select tasks that enable them to increase their competence in an efficient way.

ACKNOWLEDGMENTS

Studies III and IV reported in this chapter were done in cooperation with undergraduate psychology students of the Philipps-Universität Marburg: Berthold Huber, Christiane Lorch, Ulrike Meinhardt, Joachim Messer, Dieter Nispel and Gisela Rühl. Study II is part of an ongoing research project supported by the VW-Foundation. The assistance of the research assistants Dagmar Marx, Brigitte Prankel and Burgi Scheiblechner is gratefully acknowledged.

REFERENCES

Atkinson, J. W. Motivational determinants of risk taking behavior. *Psychological Review*, 1957, *64*, 359–372.

Berlyne, D. E. *Conflict, arousal, and curiosity*. New York: McGraw-Hill, 1960.

Berlyne, D. E. Curiosity and exploration. *Science*, 1966, *153*, 25–33.

Berlyne, D. E. (Ed.). *Studies in the new experimental aesthetics*. Washington, D.C.: Hemisphere, 1974.

Cohen, J., Hansel, C. E. M., & Walker, D. B. The time taken to decide as a measure of subjective probability. *Acta Psychologica*, 1960, *17*, 177–183.

Dembo, T. Der Ärger als dynamisches Problem. *Psychologische Forschung*, 1931, *15*, 1–144.

Escalona, S. K. The effect of success and failure upon the level of aspiration and behavior in manic-depressive psychoses. *University of Iowa studies in Child Welfare*, 1940, *16*, 199–302.

Festinger, L. A theoretical interpretation of shifts in level of aspiration. *Psychological Review*, 1942, *49*, 235–250.

Heckhausen, H. *The anatomy of achievement motivation*. New York: Academic Press, 1967.

Heckhausen, H. The Development of achievement motivation. In W. W. Hartup (Ed.), *Review of child development research* (Vol. 6). Chicago: University of Chicago Press, 1982.

Heckhausen, H., Schmalt, H. D., & Schneider, K. *Achievement motivation in perspective*. New York: Academic Press, in prep. (1984).

Heckhausen, H., & Roelofsen, I. Anfänge und Entwicklung der Leistungsmotivation: (I) im Wetteifer des Kleinkindes. *Psychologische Forschung*, 1962, *26*, 313–397.

Heckhausen, H., & Wagner, I. Anfänge und Entwicklung in der Leistungsmotivation: (I.) in der Zielsetzung des Kleinkindes. *Psychologische Forschung*, 1965, *28*, 179–245.

Heckhausen, H., & Wasna, M. Erfolg und Mißerfolg im Leistungswetteifer des imbezillen Kindes. *Psychologische Forschung*, 1965, *28*, 391–421.

Hoppe, F. Erfolg und Mißerfolg. *Psychologische Forschung*, 1930, *14*, 1–62.

Lewin, K., Dembo, T., Festinger, L., & Sears, P. S. Level of aspiration. In J. McV. Hunt (Ed.), *Personality and behavior disorders* (Vol. 1). New York: Ronald, 1944.

Lorenz, K. Innate bases of learning. In K. H. Pribram (Ed.), *On the biology of learning*. New York: Harcourt, 1969.

McClelland, D. C. Risk taking in children with high and low need for achievement. In J. W. Atkinson (Ed.), *Motives in fantasy, action, and society*. Princeton, NJ: Van Nostrand, 1958.

Meyer, W. U. Leistungsmotiv und Ursachenerklärung von Erfolg und Mißerfolg. Stuttgart: Klett, 1973.

Nicholls, J. G. The development of the concepts of effort and ability perception of academic attainment, and the understanding that difficult tasks require more ability. *Child Development*, 1978, *49*, 800–814.

Nicholls, J. G. The development of the concept of difficulty. *Merrill Palmer Quarterly*, 1980, *26*, 271–281.

Parsons, J., & Ruble, D. M. The development of achievement-related expectancies. *Child Development*, 1977, *48*, 1075–1079.

Ruble, D. M. A developmental perspective on theories of achievement motivation. In L. J. Fyans (Ed.), *Achievement motivation*. New York: Plenum, 1980.

Schmidt, H. D. *Leistungschance. Erfolgserwartung und Entscheidung*. Berlin: VEB Deutscher Verlag der Wissenschaften, 1966.

Schmidt, H. D., & Zam, R. Erfolg und Mißerfolg als Determinanten einiger Entscheidungsparameter. *Zeitschrift für Psychologie*, 1964, *169*, 18–34.

Schneider, K. The relationship between estimated probabilities and achievement motivation. *Acta Psychologica*, 1972, *36*, 408–416.

Schneider, K. *Motivation unter Erfolgsrisiko*. Göttingen: Hogrefe, 1973.

Schneider, K. Subjektive Unsicherheit und Aufgabenwahl. *Archiv für Psychologie*, 1974, *126*, 147–169.

Schneider, K., Barthelmey, E., & Herrmann, P. Subjektive Unsicherheit und visuelle Exploration bei Kindern im Vorschulalter. *Zeitschrift für Entwicklungspsychologie und Pädagogische Psychologie*, 1981, *13*, 106–115.

Schneider, K., & Heckhausen, H. Subjective uncertainty and task preference. In H. J. Day (Ed.), *Advances in intrinsic motivation and aesthetics*. New York: Plenum, 1981.

Shannon, C. E. A mathematical theory of communication. *Bell System Technical Journal*, 1948, *27*, 379–423, 623–656.

Smith, C. P. (Ed.), *Achievement related motives in children*. New York: Russell Sage Foundation, 1969.

Trudewind, C. Ecological determinants in the development of the achievement motive and its individual differences. In W. W. Hartup (Ed.), *Review of Child Development Research* (Vol. 6). Chicago: University of Chicago Press, 1982.

Unzner, L., & Schneider, K. Erlebte Schwierigkeit und subjektive Unsicherheit im Leistungshandeln: ihre Entwicklung im Vorschulalter. Manuscript in preparation. University of Marburg, 1983.

Wagner, J. Das Zielsetzungsverhalten von vier ausgewählten Gruppen normaler Kleinkinder in Einzel und Paarsituationen. Unpublished Doctoral Dissertation, Ruhr-Universität, Bochum, W. Germany, 1969.

Wasna, M. *Die Entwicklung der Leistungsmotivation.* München: Ernst Reinhard, 1970.

Weiner, B., Frieze, I., Kukla, A., Reed, L., Rest, S., & Rosenbaum, R. M. *Perceiving the causes of success and failure.* New York: General Learning Press, 1971.

White, R. W. Motivation reconsidered: The concept of competence. *Psychological Review,* 1959, *66,* 297–333.

OVERSUFFICIENT AND INSUFFICIENT JUSTIFICATION EFFECTS:

COGNITIVE AND BEHAVIORAL DEVELOPMENT

Saul M. Kassin and Mark R. Lepper

Imagine a child confronted with an intrinsically interesting activity, one that he or she might spontaneously choose to engage in for the sake of curiosity, enjoyment, or adventure. Now suppose that this child is offered an attractive reward for engaging in this activity and does so in anticipation of this windfall. How might this means-end contingency and the social messages it conveys affect the child's intrinsic motivation and behavior in a later situation in which the activity is available but the reward is not? Next, compare the response of this child with that of another who encounters this same fascinating activity and decides to

Advances in Motivation and Achievement, vol. 3, pages 73–106
Copyright © 1984 by JAI Press Inc.
All rights of reproduction in any form reserved.
ISBN 0-89232-289-6

engage in it without external pressures or inducements. How intrinsically interesting will these two children subsequently find this activity?

One obvious possibility is that children provided with both the intrinsic pleasures of the activity itself and some additional external reward would later find the activity more highly attractive, even if the external reward were no longer available. The positive affect potentially associated with the receipt of an additional reward might reinforce or generalize to engaging in the activity itself. Under many circumstances, however, one might also expect precisely the opposite effect to occur.

Attribution (Kelley, 1967, 1973) and self perception (Bem, 1967, 1972) theories, for example, predict that the imposition of a superfluous external inducement may often undermine a child's spontaneous interest in an object or activity. In operational terms, the previously rewarded child might no longer choose to initiate an activity once it is stripped of its prior instrumental value. This behavioral phenomenon, for reasons that will be elucidated shortly, has been labeled the "overjustification effect" (Lepper, Greene, & Nisbett, 1973). Theoretically, this effect is presumed to be mediated by a shift in perceptions of oneself from intrinsically motivated ("I did X because I like it") to extrinsically motivated ("I did X in order to get Y"). This shift, in turn, has been hypothesized to reflect the operation of a "discounting principle" (Kelley, 1973) where the perceived role of a given cause (e.g., one's intrinsic motivation toward an activity) in producing a given effect is diminished if other plausible causes (e.g., extrinsic factors such as a promise of reward or threat of punishment) are also present.

At what age do such overjustification effects and related self-perception and social-inference phenomena begin to emerge? As the title of this chapter implies, development in this domain is not a unitary process. Instead there appears to be an asynchrony between the cognitive and behavioral components, or manifestations, of these phenomena. On the one hand, research on intrinsic-extrinsic motivation has provided compelling evidence for the detrimental effects of superfluous rewards and other forms of social influence on the behavior of preschoolers as well as older children and adults. That is, preschoolers who are rewarded for engaging in an enjoyable activity will often subsequently lose interest in that activity. On the other hand, several studies of children's social inferences suggest that preschool-age children do not (and maybe cannot) use the discounting principle in their attributions. That is, they do not infer a decrease in intrinsic motivation from behavior that occurs in the presence of an extrinsic inducement. In short, young children fall prey to the overjustification effect in their behavior but do not exhibit use of the cognitive principle that is believed to mediate that effect.

Taken together, the behavioral and cognitive literatures on overjustification and discounting offer a paradox. How can overjustification and related behavioral phenomena in preschoolers be mediated by a cognitive schema that they apparently do not possess? Guided by this question, the present chapter was written with four goals in mind: (a) to provide a review of the relevant behavioral and cognitive literatures, (b) to compare these two research traditions and analyze the developmental discrepancies between them, (c) to propose an explanation for developmental asynchronies in different domains, and (d) to suggest useful avenues for future, integrative research in this area.

THE BEHAVIORAL LITERATURE

We begin, then, with the paradox that young children's actions appear to reflect an appreciation of inferential principles that they otherwise appear incapable of understanding. To make clear the precise nature of this paradox and to provide a basis for further analysis, it is necessary to consider more fully the sorts of data that have been used to justify these conflicting viewpoints. In the present section, therefore, we will examine the evidence suggesting that even young children respond to direct social influence attempts in a fashion that implies the operation of a discounting principle. In the following section, we will turn to the contrasting evidence on young children's social inferences that suggests that the use of a discounting principle is beyond their grasp.

Consider the behavioral evidence supporting the claim that children act in accord with a discounting principle. This evidence derives primarily from two basic experimental paradigms that have been employed extensively with young children. The first involves what have been termed "overjustification" effects, the second what have been termed "insufficient justification" effects. Both have been interpreted in terms of the attributional model proposed by Kelley (1967, 1973) and Bem (1967, 1972), accounts that presume the operation of the discounting principle.

In the context of attributions regarding motivation, this principle has two implications. When salient extrinsic incentives or constraints appear to provide a plausible and sufficient reason for a person's engaging in an activity, an observer (or actor) will be commensurately less likely to view that activity as intrinsically interesting to that person. Conversely, when external incentives and constraints appear insufficient to account for a person's engaging in an activity, one will be correspondingly more likely to view that activity as intrinsically attractive or interesting to that person. Conceptually analogous effects are predicted by this model, moreover, for situations involving social inferences (i.e., in which an observer is asked to make inferences about the motivation of another) and situations involving self-perceptions (i.e., in which the actor is asked or stimulated to reflect upon his or her own previous actions).

The "Overjustification" Paradigm

In a self-perception context, the first of these postulates implies the following specific hypothesis: If a person were induced to engage in an activity of initial high intrinsic interest, under conditions that made salient the instrumentality of that activity as a means of obtaining some salient extrinsic end, the person ought subsequently to find that activity to be of less intrinsic interest when extrinsic rewards are no longer available. Because the offer of extrinsic rewards for engagement in an activity of initial inherent interest involves the use of a functionally superfluous incentive, an overly sufficient justification, this proposition has been termed the "overjustification" hypothesis.

In the first examination of this hypothesis with young children, Lepper, Greene, and Nisbett (1973) compared the effects of three experimental procedures. During a baseline phase, preschool children were unobtrusively observed in their regular nursery school classrooms during free-play periods in which children had the opportunity to engage in a particular target activity—drawing pictures with colorful magic marker pens—or any of a variety of other interesting activities. Only those children who showed a high level of initial intrinsic interest in the drawing activity (i.e., those who chose to engage in this activity in preference to several dozen alternatives available) were selected as subjects for the study. During a subsequent treatment phase, these children were asked to undertake this target activity under one of three conditions. In the Expected Reward condition, children were first shown an attractive extrinsic reward—a Good Player Award—and were asked if they would like to draw some pictures with the magic markers in order to win this reward. In the Unexpected Reward condition, children were asked to engage in the same activity without mention of any extrinsic reward; but upon completion of the task, these children received the same reward and feedback as Expected Reward subjects. In the No Reward control condition, children were asked to engage in the same task without either promise or receipt of any tangible reward.

All children, therefore, were asked to engage in an activity that they had initially found to be intrinsically interesting. Only those in the Expected Reward condition, however, did so under conditions that made salient the instrumentality of engaging in this activity as a means of obtaining a functionally superfluous, "oversufficient," extrinsic reward. Two weeks later, children's subsequent intrinsic interest in the activity—in the absence of any further extrinsic rewards or constraints—was assessed through covert observations of children's spontaneous play with the target activity during additional free-choice periods in their regular classrooms. The results were consistent with the discounting principle that is suggested by an attributional model. Children in the Expected Reward condition showed a significant decline in intrinsic interest in the target activity. They played less with the magic markers than children in the Unexpected Reward and No Reward control conditions and they spent less time with this activity than they had during the baseline period.

Subsequent research suggests that these findings are quite robust, even with quite young children. A number of later studies have demonstrated analogous effects with preschool and kindergarten children (e.g., Anderson, Manoogian, &

Resnick, 1976; Birch, Birch, Marlin, & Kramer, in press; Boggiano & Ruble, 1979; Fazio, 1981; Greene & Lepper, 1974; Lepper & Greene, 1975; Lepper, Sagotsky, Dafoe, & Greene, 1982; Loveland & Olley, 1979; Ross, 1975; Wells & Shultz, 1980), as well as with children in the early elementary grades (e.g., Dollinger & Thelen, 1978; Karniol & Ross, 1977; Kruglanski, Alon, & Lewis, 1972; McLoyd, 1979; Morgan, 1981; Ross, Karniol, & Rothstein, 1976; Sorenson & Maehr, 1976; Swann & Pittman, 1977). Similar effects have also been demonstrated in other research with older children and adult subjects (cf. Deci, 1975; Deci & Ryan, 1980; Lepper & Greene, 1978a).

The results of this further research also provide additional support for an attributional analysis of the phenomena by demonstrating that the presence and magnitude of discounting effects vary systematically as predicted by an attributional account. Thus, the offer of superfluous extrinsic rewards appears likely to undermine children's later intrinsic interest only when (1) the extrinsic rewards are expected (Greene & Lepper, 1974; Lepper & Greene, 1975; Lepper et al., 1973; Lepper et al., 1982) and contingent upon task engagement (Ross et al., 1976; Swann & Pittman, 1977); (2) the instrumentality of task engagement is salient (Ross, 1975) but initial attitudes are not salient (Fazio, 1981) for the child; and (3) the activity is one of high initial intrinsic interest to the child (Loveland & Olley, 1979; McLoyd, 1979). In short, these effects seem to occur only, as predicted, under conditions in which the offer of superfluous extrinsic incentives provides a plausible and salient alternative attribution for engagement in an activity of initial intrinsic interest.

Other forms of salient social control, such as unnecessarily close adult surveillance, also appear capable of producing decrements in later intrinsic interest (Lepper & Greene, 1975) as an attributional model would predict. Indeed, in the limiting case, the simple imposition of a contingent "mean-ends" relationship between two activities of equivalent high initial interest (e.g., "In order to have a chance to do or get Y, you must first do X.") appears sufficient to decrease interest in the activity presented as a "means" to some external "end" (Lepper et al., 1982).

Taken together, these findings help to eliminate a number of possible alternative explanations of these "overjustification" effects (cf. Lepper, 1981). In so doing, they establish a behavioral paradigm in which children's overt actions, in response to a direct social influence attempt, appear to be governed by a discounting principle.

The "Insufficient Justification" Paradigm

In addition to these detrimental effects of overly sufficient extrinsic pressures on intrinsic interest, an attributional analysis also makes complementary predictions concerning the effects of psychologically insufficient justification on later motivation. The other side of Kelley's discounting principle suggests that in the absence of strong extrinsic pressures, high intrinsic motivation will be inferred. Suppose, for example, that external pressure were applied to induce a child to refrain from engaging in an activity that he or she would initially have found to be of high intrinsic interest. An attributional analysis would suggest that the less the external pressure applied, as long as the child does comply with the prohibition, the more intrinsically motivated the child should perceive his or her avoidance of the activity to be. As a result, avoiding the prohibited activity in the face of minimal external pressures should result in a subsequent derogation of the forbidden activity—a "sour grapes" effect.

In a first examination of this general proposition, Aronson and Carlsmith (1963) created a situation in which preschool children were asked not to play with a particularly attractive toy during a temptation period in which the experimenter left the room. First, the attractiveness of this toy was established by asking each child to rank a set of toys from most to least desirable. Next, the child was forbidden to play with this toy under one of two conditions at which point the experimenter left the room. In the Mild Threat condition, children were told that the experimenter would be "annoyed" if they played with the forbidden toy; in the Severe Threat condition, children were told that the experimenter would be "very angry" and would respond with a variety of punitive measures if they played with the forbidden toy. Following the temptation period, children's attitudes towards the previously forbidden toy were again assessed. As predicted, children in the mild threat condition showed significantly greater derogation of the forbidden activity than did those in the severe threat condition.

Again, subsequent research with children has established the replicability of this finding. Other work with preschool and kindergarten children (e.g., Carlsmith, Ebbesen, Lepper, Zanna, Joncas, & Abelson, 1969; Lepper, Zanna, & Abelson, 1970; Turner & Wright, 1965; Zanna, Lepper, & Abelson, 1973) and children in the early elementary grades (e.g., Freedman, 1965; Lepper, 1973; Pepitone, McCauley, & Hammond, 1967) has produced comparable findings across a variety of different threat procedures and specific activities. Moreover, children in the mild threat conditions in these later studies not only "reported" that the previously forbidden activity was less attractive to them; they were also likely to avoid that activity in the future, even when it was no longer prohibited, up to six weeks following the experimental sessions (cf. Freedman, 1965; Pepitone et al., 1967).

Most of these experiments, it should be noted, were initially derived not from an attributional model, but from Festinger's (1957) theory of cognitive dissonance. Thus, although there remains controversy concerning the extent to which the dissonance and attributional models can be empirically distinguished (e.g., Fazio, Zanna, & Cooper, 1977; Greenwald, 1975), these results provide some support for an attributional analysis. The convergence in findings between the "overjustification" and "insufficient justification" paradigms is worth attention, however, because it suggests the possibility that a discounting principle may underlie children's behavioral responses to social influence attempts in a variety of situations.

Developmental Issues

Because our primary focus in this chapter is on a developmental paradox, it is important to note that the foregoing studies do not speak directly to potential developmental changes in children's responses to social influence attempts. These studies do not demonstrate that attributional processes do not change with age. Instead, they simply demonstrate that the responses of even very young children, in the face of overt social influence attempts, appear consistent with an attributional model.

In fact, it is worth noting that almost no explicitly developmental research has been conducted in these areas, although recent studies by Boggiano and Ruble (1979) and Morgan (1981) are notable exceptions. Perhaps because some of the earliest research in each area (e.g., Aronson & Carlsmith, 1963; Lepper et al., 1973) appeared to demonstrate predicted effects with young children that appeared generally consistent with findings in analogous, or conceptually related, paradigms with adults, there seems to have been little impetus for further research comparing children's responses to such situations at different ages. With this caveat in mind, then, let us turn to the contrasting findings that have emerged from the developmental study of children's inferences about the motives of others—findings that have appeared to yield conclusions at variance with the attributional analysis offered above.

THE COGNITIVE LITERATURE

The overjustification hypothesis was derived partly within the framework of self perception theory (Bem, 1967, 1972) which predicted that people's true intrinsic motivation for an activity is partly a consequence of their perceived level of intrinsic motivation. The latter, in turn, represents the outcome of an attributional analysis. In Kelley's (1971, 1973) terminology, people are said to invoke a multiple sufficient cause (MSC) schema in which both intrinsic motivation and extrinsic inducements are perceived as sufficient causes of behavior. With regard to the overjustification and insufficient justification effects, this causal schema implies a discounting principle which suggests that people will perceive their own level of intrinsic motivation to be lower when their behavior is accompanied by a salient and sufficient extrinsic cause than when it is not. For Bem (1967), moreover, this self-perception process was viewed as involving the application of more general principles of social perception or social inference to the "special case" in which the self is the actor under scrutiny.

In an early attempt to understand children's intuitive theories about human behavior and motivation, Baldwin and Baldwin (1970) created conditions that were suitable for testing use of the discounting principle. These investigators presented adults and children of varying ages with a series of illustrated stories that depicted acts of kindness. Each story contained two identical behaviors—one performed in the presence, and the other in the absence, of a plausible external cause. Subjects then selected the picture in which the actor was "kinder" and explained that choice. In one story, for example, a child lets another use his wagon; in the second he does so after his brother offers a "bribe" in exchange for use of the wagon. Other forms of extrinsic cause included a parental command, an obligation to a guest, a trade, and the return of a favor. Overall, this study revealed that although fourth graders, older children and adults judged the unconstrained positive behaviors as kinder than those prompted by extrinsic circumstances, kindergarteners and second graders generally did not.[1]

Although the Baldwins' (1970) research was not specifically designed to assess children's use of a MSC schema, it had obvious relevance to the developmental attribution literature that was to follow. Indeed, their findings were subsequently supported by two experiments aimed directly at testing children's use of the discounting principle (Shultz, Butkowsky, Pierce, & Shanfield, 1975; Smith, 1975). Smith (1975), for example, presented kindergarteners, second graders, fourth graders, and adults with pairs of stories that compared two children who played with a particular toy: one in the presence of a situational constraint (i.e., a reward, command, or obligation) and the other without any type of external inducement. The following story-pair provides one example:

  1. Tom was at the playground and he saw two toys there: a hammer and a shovel. And he
     said that he wanted to play with the shovel.
  2. Joe was at the playground, and he saw two toys: a hammer and a shovel. Joe's mother
     was there, and she said that Joe could have some ice cream if he played with the
     shovel. And Joe said that he wanted to play with the shovel. (Smith, 1975, p. 740)

Following the presentation of each story and an accompanying picture, subjects chose the actor who they thought had wanted to play with the toy more. Overall, adults and fourth graders responded in a manner consistent with a discounting principle, ascribing less "want" to the actor who played with the toy in the overjustification condition. The kindergarten children, however, appeared to respond randomly, showing no signs of a discounting principle. Second graders fell between these two extremes. This general finding, that children do not begin to discount reliably until the fourth grade, was supported in other research conducted along the same lines (Shultz et al., 1975).

The foregoing research raised a very fundamental question, one whose answer had been assumed by proponents of the attributional interpretation of the overjustification and insufficient justification effects: "Do preschool-age children discount?" On the one hand, very young children had shown the same behavioral response as older children and adults when placed in overjustification and insufficient justification situations (Lepper et al., 1973; Aronson & Carlsmith,

1963). On the other hand, preschoolers consistently failed to discount another actor's intrinsic motivation in these initial social-perception studies (Baldwin & Baldwin, 1970; Smith, 1975; Shultz et al., 1975).

Impelled by this disparity, Karniol and Ross (1976) sought to improve upon previous research in two ways. First, they explicitly ensured that all subjects were able to recall the stimulus events before posing the attributional questions. Second, they employed two reward-constraint stories and two command-constraint stories per subject in order to determine the consistency with which individual subjects used the discounting principle. Kindergarteners, first graders, second graders, and adults were thus presented with a series of story-pairs adapted from Smith's (1975) study. The results showed that although most kindergarteners and first graders did not discount, they did not respond unsystematically either. Instead, many of them employed an additive principle, inferring *greater* intrinsic motivation on the part of the characters who acted in the presence of an extrinsic cause. Apparently, these younger children viewed a reward offer as an added incentive that actually increases one's intrinsic motivation. Interestingly, the command stories produced greater discounting and, correspondingly, less of a tendency to use an additive mode of logic.

In quite a different context, Kun (1977) also found evidence for an additive principle among young children. Subjects in the first, third, and fifth grades were read stories concerning boys' performances on a set of puzzles. Each story provided information about the outcome and the status of one facilitative cause—the actor's level of ability or effort. Subjects then judged the magnitude of the cause that was not specified in the story (effort or ability). As it turned out, the third and fifth graders used a discounting rule, assuming that if two persons performed equally well the one who had greater ability must have exerted less effort, and vice versa. First graders, however, inferred that the presence of one facilitative cause implied the presence of the other, leading Kun (1977) to suggest that young children maintain a primitive belief that "good things go together." At the same time, Kun's own data and those of other comparable projects (Karabenick & Heller, 1976; Surber, 1980) again suggest some inconsistencies in performance across different content areas—that children, for example, will discount an actor's effort at an earlier age than they do his or her ability.

The discovery that preschool-age children generally do not discount and, in fact, often employ a qualitatively different, additive principle has received quite a bit of empirical support from a variety of sources (Butzin, 1979; Cohen, Gelfand, & Hartmann, 1981; Costanzo, Grumet, & Brehm, 1974; Karniol & Ross, 1979; Kun, 1978; Leahy, 1979). Not expectedly, this research widened the gap between behavioral indices of discounting and the more direct attributional data. After all, classical self-perception theory had originally been cast in terms of a "radical behaviorist" model (Bem, 1967; 1972): self-perception processes, in this account, were derived from, and should therefore mirror, social-perception processes. From such a perspective, one would have to predict from preschoolers' use of an additive principle that their intrinsic interest in an activity should be enhanced rather than undermined by the activity's previous association with reward.

In any case, this paradox led investigators to question young childrens' cognitive competencies. Are preschoolers simply incapable of discounting due to some pivotal cognitive deficit? Kun (1977), for example, noted that discounting involves a formal process of inverse compensation which develops relatively late in the acquisition of concrete operations. Or can young children discount, but only in certain situations (cf. Kassin, Lowe, & Gibbons, 1980; Kassin & Gibbons, 1981; Karniol & Ross, 1979; Lepper et al., 1982; Shultz & Butkowsky, 1977; Surber, 1980; Wells & Shultz, 1980)? It will be seen later that recent research provides general support for this latter alternative.

A COMPARISON OF THE BEHAVIORAL AND COGNITIVE LITERATURES

These two research traditions, then, present discrepant views of young children's understanding or usage of a discounting principle. Let us turn, in this section, to a consideration of four possible resolutions of this discrepancy.

Non-Attributional Mediators of the Behavioral Effects

The first obvious possibility, of course, is that reward-induced decrements in intrinsic motivation are mediated by other (i.e., nonattributional) variables. Certainly, this could explain the different rates with which discounting phenomena develop in the behavioral and the cognitive domains.

One class of behaviorally-oriented alternative explanations is based on the assumption that the promise of an attractive, task-contingent reward evokes a set of "competing responses" characteristic of high drive states (Reiss & Sushinsky, 1975, 1976). Specific examples of such reactions include general excitement, evaluation anxiety, cognitive or perceptual distraction, and frustration resulting from the delay in receipt of the reward. According to this competing responses hypothesis, any one of these reactions may adversely affect the manner in which subjects approach the task and the enjoyment they derive from it during the experimental session. In short, subsequent interest in an activity is said to decrease because competing responses detract from task enjoyment and performance quality during the reward period.

Ross, Karniol, and Rothstein (1976) tested one version of the competing response hypothesis with first, second, and third grade children. In the overjustification paradigm, subjects are offered a reward but then do not receive it until they have completed the experimental activity. Conceivably, the frustration aroused by having to wait for the reward (or the distraction or excitement produced by the reward) becomes associated with the interpolated activity and thereby decreases task enjoyment. Ross et al. (1976) promised one group of children a prize for participating in an activity and a second group of children a prize simply for waiting a specified amount of time during which they happened, incidentally, to be engaged in the same activity. Relative to a nonrewarded control group, children in the task-contingent reward condition showed a decrement in subsequent intrinsic motivation. Children in the wait-contingent group—potentially frustrated, excited, or distracted, but unable to attribute their task engagement to the prize—showed no such decrement. Conceptually analogous results have been reported, with first through third grade children, by Swann and Pittman (1977).[2]

A second related, but potentially distinct, class of alternative explanations for this literature involves the general assumption that the effects of extrinsic rewards on subsequent intrinsic interest are mediated by differences in the actual performance of subjects during the prior treatment phase (e.g., Calder & Staw, 1975). Thus, the introduction of task-contingent rewards may cause the subject to increase his or her effort expenditure during the experimental session. As a result, rewarded subjects may become more fatigued or satiated with the task than nonrewarded subjects. Alternatively, the offer of extrinsic rewards may lead to more hurried and less competent performance that should yield less satisfaction. To date, however, the cumulative evidence does not provide support for these performance-based hypotheses. A number of investigators have observed decrements in subsequent intrinsic interest in the absence of differences in initial effort or performance; others have shown a lack of relationship between the effects of a particular contingency on measures of immediate performance versus subsequent intrinsic interest (Amabile, DeJong, & Lepper, 1976; Boggiano & Ruble, 1979; Calder & Staw, 1975; Dollinger & Thelen, 1978; Enzle & Ross, 1978; Harackiewicz, 1979; Lepper & Greene, 1975; Lepper et al., 1982; Lepper, Sagotsky, & Greene, 1981a, 1981b; Morgan, 1981; Ross, 1975; Ross et al., 1976; Smith & Pittman, 1978).

A third general alternative account of the overjustification literature takes a rather different tack, explaining the results obtained as a consequence of a ''contrast'' effect because the intrinsic value of an activity is perceived as lower when it is encountered in a context in which its inherent attractiveness may be contrasted with some more desirable extrinsic reward. Although a variety of additional assumptions are required to adapt this account so that it provides an explanation of the specificity of the overjustification effect to cases involving contingent and expected rewards, it remains a possible alternative for some of the experimental literature (cf. Greene, Sternberg, & Lepper, 1976). Such a position fails to account, however, for several sorts of experimental findings. First, a contrast model should predict equally powerful effects of extrinsic rewards, whether those rewards are presented as indicative of and contingent upon one's performance at the task or one's mere willingness to undertake the task; yet these two procedures have been consistently shown to have quite different effects on subsequent intrinsic interest (e.g., Boggiano & Ruble, 1979). Similarly, the contrast approach fails to account for the elimination of such effects under conditions of no choice (Folger et al., 1978). Finally, a contrast model does not explain the finding that the imposition of a means-end contingency between two activities of equal initial interest will produce a decrease in the later attractiveness of the activity undertaken as a means rather than an end (Lepper et al., 1982).

Overall, then, we must conclude that alternative explanations of the overjustification phenomenon have received little, if any, empirical support.[3] Moreover, none of these alternatives provides a suitable explanation for the conceptually related research on insufficient justification described earlier. An additional strength of the attributional model is, thus, its ability to provide a common framework for the consideration of both sets of findings. Still, rather than declare the self-perception/discounting explanation a ''winner'' by default, let us review briefly some additional research that provides more direct support for this account. In perhaps the most direct test, Pittman, Cooper, and Smith (1977) provided adult subjects, half of whom were performing a task in anticipation of reward, with bogus physiological feedback indicating that their arousal reflected ''interest in the game,'' ''interest in the money,'' or no feedback whatsoever. Subsequent interest in the game among Expected Reward subjects was greater in the intrinsic interest feedback condition than in the other two, although it remained lower than in the No Reward condition.

Similarly, Johnson, Greene, and Carroll (1981) compared the responses of adult subjects to an Expected Reward procedure in the face of a description of their task by the experimenter that highlighted either their potential intrinsic interest in the task or the extrinsic rewards they could obtain through task engagement. Focusing subjects' attention on their previous expressed interest in the task led to an elimination of the otherwise detrimental effect of expected rewards on later intrinsic interest.

These studies provide clear evidence for the potential importance of self-attributional processes in overjustification with adults. It is entirely possible, of course, that the same behavior in children is mediated by different events. Two highly suggestive studies with children are thus worth mentioning here. In the first, Kruglanski, Alon, and Lewis (1972) led a group of Unexpected Reward children to believe that they had in fact been promised an attractive extrinsic reward in advance. As it turned out, a significant negative effect was obtained, but this effect was accounted for almost entirely by the responses of those subjects who falsely reported themselves to have undertaken the target activity for the reward (i.e., those children who made an erroneous ''extrinsic'' attribution concerning their behavior). Moreover, since the reward manipulation did not take place until the activity was completed, subjects should not have approached the task or performed differently during the experimental phase. More recently, Fazio (1981) had young children participate in an activity with or without the promise of reward, but exposed half the subjects to a photograph of themselves freely participating in the activity at a previous time as a "reminder" of their intrinsic interest in the task. As predicted by an attributional hypothesis, presentation of this photograph—a self-perception cue for high, intrinsic interest—eliminated the adverse effect of the Expected Reward procedure.

At this point, we conclude that there is little empirical support for the idea that the overjustification phenomenon is mediated by nonattributional variables, and there is at least tentative evidence favoring the attributional viewpoint. That is, when subjects' attributions are experimentally manipulated, they produce the predicted results. As a consequence of this conclusion, the developmental paradox remains unresolved.

Methodological Vagaries of the Attribution Experiment

A second possible explanation for the overjustification paradox is that preschoolers' attributional prowess is underestimated in social discounting research and that the problem lies in the insensitivity of the experimental paradigm within which young children's attributions are assessed. Thus one might ask whether young children's failures to discount reflect their lack of *competence* and sophistication with the MSC schema or, instead, merely an experiment-specific *performance* deficit? Gelman (1978) has lamented the fact that preschoolers' general cognitive abilities are often underestimated because psychologists frequently operationalize a concept through a single task.

Kassin (1981) and Surber (1980) have argued that the discounting literature reviewed above is similarly limited because most findings are based on children's responses to hypothetical stories about interpersonal events. At the most basic level, it is entirely possible that preschool-age subjects have difficulty processing the causally relevant information in these experiments. After all, the material is linguistic and hence relatively abstract. Moreover, because the critical elements of the stories are, by necessity, presented in successive sentences or paragraphs after which children's inferences are assessed, story recall could prove difficult for younger subjects (e.g., Bryant & Trabasso, 1971). On a more conceptual level, there is evidence to suggest that the stories typically employed do not adequately convey to young children the causal-facilitative power of a reward contingency. Specifically, Karniol and Ross (1979) reported that kindergarten children do not interpret the reward offer in their stories as a "bribe" that is intended to elicit compliance.

Indeed, experiments that have been designed to "simplify" the discounting task by circumventing the foregoing problems have met with some success. Kassin and Gibbons (1981) and Kassin, Lowe, and Gibbons (1980), for example, had subjects watch a vivid "perceptual analog" of the discounting stories. Children of various age levels watched a brief, silent cartoon in which two animated objects moved simultaneously, from opposite directions, and with equal velocity toward a house. One "actor" was carried to its destination by a third object, while the other achieved the same goal without external assistance. When asked to choose the actor who was more intrinsically motivated—i.e., who "wanted to get to the house more" (Kassin et al., 1980) or "tried harder to get to the house" (Kassin & Gibbons, 1981)—both second graders (Kassin et al., 1980) and kindergarteners (Kassin & Gibbons, 1981) responded in line with a MSC schema. That is, they perceived greater intrinsic motivation in the character whose movements were not extrinsically facilitated.

Along related lines, Shultz and Butkowsky (1977) found that preschoolers discounted another child's intrinsic motivation when they viewed his or her behavior on videotape. Finally, Karniol and Ross (1979) and Lepper et al. (1982) have shown that preschoolers exhibit use of a discounting schema in social-perception contexts when they clearly appreciate the inducement value of the reward offered to the target person. Collectively, this most recent research suggests that, at the very least, preschool-age children have the cognitive "capacity" to invoke a discounting schema in their social perceptions. Whether they do, in fact, apply this knowledge in traditional overjustification and insufficient justification paradigms remains to be seen.

Self-Perception Versus Other Perception

In comparing the overjustification and discounting paradigms, one is also struck by a third possibility—that the developmental asynchrony between the two may be a function of the difference between the processes of self- and other-perception, respectively. In the adult attribution literature, findings of an actor-observer difference are commonplace (cf. Jones & Nisbett, 1971). After all, self- and other-attributors differ in their perceptual focus on attention, their empathic and motivational orientation, and their access to internal cues and historical information.

Monson and Snyder (1977) reviewed the extant literature and proposed that "actors should make more situational attributions than should observers about behavioral acts that are under situational control; by contrast, actors' perceptions of behaviors that are under dispositional control ought to be more dispositional than the perceptions of observers" (p. 96). A recent study by Small and Peterson (1981) supported this hypothesis. Tentatively, one might conclude that people are generally more "accurate" in their self attributions than in the causal inferences they make about others. In the domain of moral judgments, Piaget (1932) and, later, Keasey (1977) observed a conceptually analogous self-other difference. Specifically, they found that children distinguished between intentional and accidental acts in their own real-life behavior before they were able to apply this distinction to the behavior of others. Piaget's explanation for this difference is that preschool children, as observers, are unable to shift their attention from the salient, overt features of another person's behavior to underlying motives and intentions. We can envision at least two reasons why young children might show signs of a discounting schema in the self-perception over-justification studies but not in other-perception, attribution research.

First, subjects' level of task involvement is undoubtedly greater when they are personally engaged in a hedonically relevant activity than when they are asked to think about the motivations of a fictional character in a story. Indeed, there is some support for this involvement hypothesis. In an experiment with adults, Kassin and Hochreich (1977) found that subjects made more complex causal attributions when the importance of their task was emphasized. More germane to our current concern is a recent developmental study by Feldman (1979, cited in Feldman & Ruble, 1981). Research on the development of impression formation has consistently shown that until the ages of 7–8, children do not form inferences about other people (Flapan, 1968; Gollin, 1958; Livesley & Bromley, 1973; Peevers & Secord, 1973). That is, young children describe others almost ex-clusively in concrete terms, referring to physical appearance and overt acts, while making little reference to abstract traits or motives. As in the discounting literature, younger children's "failures" have typically been viewed as reflect-ing some cognitive deficit. Feldman (1979), however, found that preschoolers' use of abstract descriptors increased dramatically when the relevance of their task was heightened through an expected-interaction manipulation.

A second possible basis for the superiority of actors over observers is their differential focus of attention. Guttentag and Longfellow (1978) have pointed out that the overjustification effect depends on an over-attention to environmental causes at the expense of internal ones. Jones and Nisbett's (1971) actor-observer hypothesis, that actors attend to salient features of their behavioral situation whereas observers attend to the actor, appears to operate even among pre-schoolers (Curtis & Schildhaus, 1980). Taken together, one might speculate that young children in a self-perception context attend to environmental constraints in addition to the task, thereby accentuating the extrinsic causes of their behavior (cf. Ross, 1975). Recall Fazio's (1981) finding that when children perform a rewarded activity in the presence of a photograph of themselves previously engaging in the activity without external constraint, the overjustification effect disappears. For observers, in contrast, the actor is salient, so the discounting of intrinsic causes may be inhibited.

Judgmental Versus Behavioral Response Criteria

One final, but potentially critical, difference between the overjustification and discounting literatures lies in the response criteria that are used to evaluate the operation of a discounting schema. Put simply, what must a child do in order to convince a psychologist that he or she understands and/or uses the discounting principle? In general, three broad classes of responses can be measured: (1) overt behaviors that are presumed to be manifestations of an underlying attribution; (2)

attributional judgments that involve a prediction, choice, or rating; and (3) explanations that require subjects to articulate the reasons for their behavior or judgment.

A review of the developmental attribution literature (Kassin, 1981) reveals quite unambiguously that children behave as if they comprehend various principles before they can make the appropriate causal judgments—a pattern reminiscent of Piaget's (1932) observation that active moral behavior precedes verbal moral judgments. At the next level, children consistently make schema-consistent judgments long before they are able to explain the attributional logic that underlies them (Bullock, 1981; Kassin, 1981). Take, for example, the principle that causes and effects covary. The fact that infants can be classically conditioned to a neutral stimulus only if it consistently precedes an unconditioned stimulus (Lipsitt & Kaye, 1964) suggests that, at some level, they "understand" the principle of covariation. Yet attribution research in which subjects are required to make explicit causal judgments (e.g., Siegler, 1975) has shown that preschoolers have extreme difficulty demonstrating their knowledge of this cornerstone rule of logic.

The hypothesis that attribution-mediated behavior precedes attibutional judgments was recently supported by Wells and Shultz (1980). Preschool-age children were rewarded for playing with one of two available toys but not rewarded for playing with the other. Afterwards, these subjects predicted which toy they would choose to play with in the future (judgment), after which the actual time they spent playing with each toy was recorded (behavior). In addition to participating in this self-perception, real behavior situation, subjects also watched another child go through the same situation (other perception-real behavior), read a hypothetical story about themselves in that situation (self-hypothetical), and read a story about another child in that situation (other-hypothetical). Overall, the children showed no signs of a preference for either the rewarded or unrewarded toy in their predictions. They did, however, show a discounting effect in their behavior, spending more time playing with the unrewarded than the rewarded toy.

TOWARD A RESOLUTION OF THE PARADOX

To this point, then, our discussion has suggested the following tentative conclusions:

1.   There is an extensive experimental literature that documents the comparable effects on the later behavior of preschoolers, older children, and adults of direct social influence attempts that involve either psychologically "oversufficient" or psychologically "insufficient" justification. As predicted by an attributional model, young children (as well as older subjects) find initially interesting tasks undertaken in order to achieve some superfluous external goal to

be subsequently less intrinsically interesting. Similarly, even preschool children seem to develop more negative attitudes towards activities they have foregone in the face of minimal and psychologically insufficient external pressure.

2.   The possibility that these behavioral overjustification and insufficient-justification phenomena are mediated by alternative, nonattributional mechanisms has received little experimental support.

3.   Although older children and adults regularly discount the intrinsic motivation of actors who have been observed to respond in the presence of salient extrinsic constraints, preschoolers often do not make such causal inferences. Instead, in such social perception contexts, young children will often employ an opposite, "additive" model.

4.   Faced with the apparent paradox that preschool-age children behave as if they are discounting their own intrinsic motivation while showing an apparent inability to employ this principle in their attributions, three possible explanations were considered. First, the developmental attribution research paradigm may be simply insensitive to young children's inferential abilities; indeed the most recent research suggests that although they do not employ the discounting principle reliably, they are at least cognitively capable of doing so. Second, preschoolers may generally make more sophisticated inferences in a self-perception context than when asked to judge the behavior of another person. Third, children may generally demonstrate their underlying competencies in overt behavior, considerably before they show signs of comparable competencies in the domain of purely cognitive judgments.

Collectively, the foregoing conclusions form part of the basis for a resolution of the apparent paradox posed by these conflicting literatures. What remains is for us to articulate more clearly the alternative perspectives from which the acquisition of a discounting principle may be viewed. Only when we understand the process by which children acquire this causal inference rule and the levels at which they employ it can we then explain the disparity between the cognitive and behavioral data.

Acquisition of the Discounting Principle: Alternative Models

How might children come to learn a discounting principle or the application of such a principle to the domains of social interaction and social inference? What, indeed, is meant by "learning" a discounting principle? The present literature suggests three basic possibilities.

The "Cognitive-Developmental Stage" Approach

A first possibility is that suggested by a global-stage version of the cognitive-developmental approach—that children either do or do not "possess" an inverse compensation or multiple sufficient cause schema. From this perspective, acquisition of such a schema is seen as indicative of, and tied to, a particular "stage" of cognitive development. Learning to apply a discounting schema to particular social situations or specific attributions of motivation becomes an essentially "top-down" process. Once the child has advanced to a sufficiently high stage of cognitive development, he or she will be expected to apply the abstract reasoning abilities characteristic of that stage across the range of inferential tasks to which that competence is relevant.

This view implies that children will not discount until they are equipped with an abstract rule (or the ability to generate that rule), but that children who are so equipped will uniformly discount in all appropriate settings, provided only that the tasks and materials are clearly presented. It implies, in its strong form, great generality in performance across tasks in both the social and nonsocial domains. This conception—that children either have, or have not yet, acquired the relevant schema—is characteristic of many of the earlier investigations of the development of children's social inferential abilities (e.g., Kun, 1977; Shultz, Butkowsky, Pearce, & Shanfield, 1975; Smith, 1975).

Most recently, such a view has been put forward by Morgan (1981), on the basis of a further study that makes explicit the lack of congruence between children's apparent competence in behavioral and cognitive domains considered in the preceding situations. In particular, Morgan (1981) selected children who displayed different stages of causal-schematic development on a series of social-discounting stories and then exposed these children to a traditional overjustification procedure. He found that subjects offered an extrinsic reward for engaging in an initially interesting task showed a significant decrease in intrinsic interest in the task, independent of their level of cognitive sophistication, and concluded that "young children may not possess the cognitive structures postulated by the self-perception models" and that "it seems difficult to reconcile the complexity of the discounting principle with the demonstrated cognitive structures of pre-operational children" (p. 818). In short, Morgan (1981) implies that the absence of an abstract cognitive schema in preoperational children precludes their use of a discounting principle.

The "Social-Learning" Approach

At the other extreme from this version of a cognitive-stage approach lies a second possibility, derived from a social-learning analysis. In this view, children's understanding of discounting is seen as likely to develop on an inductive, and thus initially highly situation-specific, basis. That is, children are seen as likely to develop, from their own personal experiences and observations, a concrete understanding of particular instances when a discounting-like principle applies to specific social situations. Subsequent learning then involves a process of generalization and abstraction across functionally analogous experiences, ultimately resulting in the construction of an abstract rule. Learning to discount, within this approach, is a bottom-up, rather than a top-down, process.

Children may learn to expect an inverse relationship between the imposition of extrinsic pressures to induce a person to engage in a task and the likely inherent attractiveness of that task to the person, for example, by observing or themselves experiencing negative relationships of this sort in a variety of concrete social situations. At first, children's use of a discounting-like principle may be limited to specific contexts in which they have had frequent or consistent experiences with social constraints of this sort. Only gradually, as the child's range of social experiences increases, will the child begin to abstract more general principles of social inference that can be applied to novel situations.

Lepper and Greene (1978b), for example, have suggested that the development of inferential principles of this sort may be usefully viewed as a process of gradual acquisition and elaboration of cognitive scripts—i.e., cognitive representations of recurring or routinized event sequences (Abelson, 1981)—that may be learned through repeated observation or direct experience with related social situations. With development, the child progresses from initially concrete to more abstract and reflective social schemas or scripts (Abelson, 1976, 1981; Nelson, 1981). Lepper et al. (1982) describe such a process as follows:

> From this viewpoint, relatively hypothetical or categorical scripts embodying a ''discounting'' principle (e.g., ''When someone uses powerful incentives or sanctions to induce me to do something, the chances are that it is boring or unpleasant.'') are derived through the abstraction of common features from sets of relatively more concrete and episodic social scripts (e.g., ''When mom tells me I can't have my dessert until I clear my plate, what's left on my plate is usually yucky.'' or ''When dad says I have to finish some task before I can go out to play, that task is probably something I don't want to do.'') (p. 53).

Simultaneously, similar processes of abstraction and generalization may be occurring in the child's understanding of inverse compensation principles in other domains, such as causal attributions for achievement outcomes (e.g., ''When one has to work hard to succeed, one's ability at the task is low.'') Only at the culmination of this learning process will the child be likely to comprehend the manner in which principles of interaction and inference from each of these different domains can be viewed as instances of an even more general inverse compensation or discounting principle.

In contrast to the generality in the use or non-use of a discounting principle implied by the cognitive-developmental stage approach, the social-learning model implies situation-specificity in children's responses, at least through the early stages of development. Variation in children's responses across situations should be predictable, however, as a function of children's previous experiences in different settings. Thus, young children may generally respond in a more sophisticated fashion to direct social control attempts (e.g., commands) than to indirect attempts (e.g., feelings of obligation), since the former will typically be more closely tied to their own prior experiences. Similarly, they should show greater apparent sophistication in responding to social constraints with which they have had frequent and consistent prior experience, such as a "clean your plate before you can have dessert" contingency (Lepper et al., 1982) or a familiar physical inducement, like being carried to a goal (Kassin et al., 1980).

The "Social-Developmental" Approach

Between these two extreme positions lies a third, intermediate possibility that we will term a social-developmental approach. From this perspective, children's understanding and use of a discounting schema is presumed to be a joint function of their stage of cognitive development and their specific learning experiences in particular social contexts. This position accepts the "capacity" requirement of the cognitive stage model, but also maintains that children must learn to generalize the relevant judgment strategy to appropriate situations.

Surber (1980) suggests a specific version of this approach, postulating the following general sequence: "The acquisition of the discounting principle undergoes a developmental period during which it is inconsistently applied across judgmental dimensions. That is, some general cognitive skill behind the discounting principle may be somewhat unstable until, say, early formal operations." Such a view, obviously, implies situation-specificity of the sort predicted from a social-learning analysis at early stages of development, but generality across situations of the sort predicted by a cognitive-developmental approach at later stages of development. This approach is not inconsistent with Piaget's position. What remains for proponents of this approach, however, is to articulate the pattern of situation (and response) specificity expected among young children and to explain the process by which generality and abstraction are achieved.

AN INTEGRATIVE DEVELOPMENTAL MODEL

In the preceding two sections, we have considered two sets of issues regarding the seemingly contradictory results obtained in previous research relevant to children's use of a discounting principle. First, we examined a number of methodological features of prior research efforts that may have contributed to the differential findings obtained in the cognitive and the behavioral literatures. Second, we presented a set of alternative models regarding the ways in which children might acquire and learn to apply a discounting principle to social situations. We are now in a position to reconsider the apparent paradox in findings with which we began this chapter and to offer a more integrative model for understanding the results of prior research in both the behavioral and the cognitive domains.

The Cognitive-Behavioral Paradox Reconsidered

Recall our initial conundrum. Research on children's overt reactions to direct social influence attempts suggests that even young children act in accordance with a discounting schema, yet much of the research on young children's inferences about the motivation of others suggests that they do not possess the requisite cognitive capacities to employ such a discounting principle. In what ways are these findings truly in conflict?

In view of our subsequent discussion, it seems apparent that our experience of these findings as paradoxical depends on two strong, but typically implicit, assumptions: (1) the "radical behaviorist" assumption that principles of self-perception follow, and are derived from, an understanding of comparable principles in the larger domain of social perception; and (2) the "cognitive-developmental" assumption that acquisition of a discounting principle occurs in a highly generalizable stage-like fashion. If both were true, the results we have reviewed would indeed lead us to be concerned that young children in oversufficient and insufficient justification studies must be "thinking the unthinkable."

What we have tried to suggest in the preceding discussions, however, is that neither of these assumptions is necessarily warranted. From the available data, one would be hard put to argue either that principles of self-perception derive solely or primarily from an understanding of more general principles of social perception or that the acquisition of inferential principles such as discounting occurs as a unitary stage-like process. Nor is either of these assumptions necessary for the application of an attributional model to the behavioral and cognitive domains of interest. In the following section, we will examine a model for the development of self-perception and social-perception processes that rests on neither of these assumptions and provides one resolution of the apparent paradox with which we began.

A Social-Developmental Analysis

If the development of children's use of a discounting principle is not presumed to follow a simple, unitary stage model, what will determine children's use of such a principle in different contexts? Our discussion has suggested two sets of factors that should interact with age in determining a child's performance in different situations to which a discounting principle is potentially relevant. These involve, on the one hand, the nature of the response required of the child and, on the other hand, the nature of the stimulus situation in relation to the child's prior social learning history.

Response Factors

On the response side, we maintain that the question "does the child understand the discounting principle?" cannot be answered categorically in the affirmative or negative. Instead, we need to distinguish three levels of causal knowledge—(a) tacit, behavioral knowledge (the "as if" level), (b) self-report, judgmental knowledge, and (c) symbolic, explanatory, reflective knowledge (cf. Kassin, 1981). There is, moreover, widespread support for the proposition that these three levels of understanding represent a characteristic sequence in the development of social cognition in many areas (Flavell & Ross, 1981; Sedlak & Kurtz, 1981).

Within the specific literature on children's use of a discounting schema, examples of the importance of response mode are also apparent. Wells and Shultz (1980), for example, found that young children placed in an overjustification situation showed a decrease in their level of actual intrinsic motivation (overt behavior) but not in their predictions about their intrinsic motivation (judgments). At the next level, Kassin et al. (1980) found that young children make discounting judgments before they can articulate the attributional logic that they appear to employ (explanation).

Since these different levels—behavioral, judgmental, and explanatory—place increasing cognitive demands on the child, we would expect a child's performance across these measures to vary with age and general cognitive development. Presumably at a very young age, children will lack the capacity for understanding discounting or inverse compensation relationships at any level. Beyond this minimal level of cognitive capacity, however, we should expect to find children's performance in any specific context to follow a simple developmental sequence. At an initial level, children may act in a relatively sophisticated (i.e., adult-like) fashion but may not yet be able to translate their tacit knowledge into verbal judgments or explanations of their actions. At a second level, older children's actions and their explicit judgments may reflect the operation of a discounting principle, but they will remain unable to provide a compelling explanation or justification of their actions or judgments. Finally, at a third level, yet older children or adults will show a more consistent and sophisticated response across all three response modes.[4]

Situational Factors

At the same time that children's judgments within a particular domain are expected to vary developmentally as a function of response mode, a particular child's responses may also vary across situations as a function of the specific social learning history of that child. Once beyond the minimal level of cognitive competence necessary for any application of a discounting schema, children's use of a discounting principle is presumed to reflect a process of continuing abstraction and generalization from initially situation-specific response patterns. In line with the social-developmental model outlined earlier, we would expect the responses of young children to show high variability across situations, even when response modes are equivalent. Such variability may be expected because young children do not invoke a generalized discounting principle per se; rather, they are likely to draw appropriate inferences only when a situation resembles a previous instance in which they had personally experienced or observed inverse relationships between intrinsic and extrinsic motivation. For adults, at the other extreme, successive generalizations and abstractions of initially concrete and situation-specific knowledge should produce considerably higher levels of consistency across different stimulus situations.

What, then, should determine the young child's use of a discounting principle in some settings but not others? Most generally, our claim is that the sophistication of young children's responses will vary as a function of their ability to assimilate particular stimulus situations to "familiar" and concrete contexts in which they have previously learned to expect an inverse relationship between external pressures and internal attitudes and interests. This process, in turn, will depend on two general classes of factors.

The first of these involves features of the child's prior social-learning history that should influence his or her association of a discounting effect with particular familiar situations. These would include both the sheer frequency with which young children have experienced or observed concrete instances of an inverse relationship between external pressures and internal desires in a particular setting and the degree to which such inverse relationships have been consistently or uniquely associated with that setting. Lepper et al. (1982), for example, were able to identify one social script that seemed highly familiar to most preschoolers—the dinnertable rule that one can't have dessert until one has finished the less appetizing parts of the meal—and were able to show that preschool children confronted with comparable situations showed much greater use of a discounting principle than had been observed in prior research using less well-rehearsed social scripts. Similarly, Karniol and Ross (1976) found that children were more likely to employ a discounting principle in contexts involving a command rather than a reward. Because the use of commands, compared to the use of rewards, is uniquely associated with settings in which parents wish to induce compliance with disagreeable requests (Lepper, 1981), such findings make theoretical sense.

The second set of factors, by contrast, involves characteristics of new stimulus situations that are likely to influence the ease with which they can be assimilated to prior social scripts. These include the similarity of the present setting to past situations which evoke an inverse compensation script for the child and the manner of presentation of a new setting (e.g., whether the situation involves actual and concrete interactions or hypothetical and abstract presentations of social interactions). Thus, situations that are highly similar to settings in which the child has developed an appreciation of discounting and situations that are presented in a highly concrete fashion will evoke seemingly sophisticated actions and judgments from young children (Lepper & Greene, 1978b; Shultz & Butkowsky, 1977).

If one assumes that young children are more likely to encounter and recognize recurrent interaction patterns in their own direct social interactions with others than in their observations of interactions among others, this analysis would also lead to the expectation that young children will generally show greater sophistication in settings that involve self-perception, rather than social-perception processes. Were it possible to uncover natural settings in which this typical association did not hold, or to create experimentally conditions that violate this general premise, however, the model would predict a reversal of this pattern.

Thus, for young children, use of a discounting principle in a given setting should be highly dependent upon the relationship between that setting and other situations in which the child has had previous experience with a negative relationship between external pressure and internal motives. As children grow older, however, both their range of social experiences and their ability to view these experiences in terms of more general and abstract principles will increase. Eventually, older children and adults will be able to construct from their scripted experiences an abstract discounting schema that resembles Kelley's (1973) formal definition of this principle. Development of such an abstract attributional rule should permit them to discount causal possibilities even in novel and ambiguous circumstances.[5]

The Social-Developmental Model

Combining these situational and response factors, our expectations concerning the development of an understanding of discounting and its application to various settings are outlined schematically in Table 1. Along the left hand side of this Table is a rough characterization of subjects by age and presumed level of general cognitive development. Across the top is the dimension of ease of assimilation of the test situation to previous settings in which subjects have consistently experiences or observed discounting effects, and within each cell are predictions regarding the response modes in which children at a given age and in a particular type of situation are likely to show discounting effects. In this scheme, listing of a response mode implies a prediction of a discounting effect; the absence of a listing implies a prediction that discounting will not occur. Entries followed by a question mark represent potentially transitional cases.

Our expectations regarding the performance of preschool children across situations and response modes, then, are depicted in the first row of Table 1. From this table, it can be seen that preschool-age children should exhibit discounting-related *behavior* in a wide variety of constraint situations—an expectation that is consistent with the overwhelming evidence reviewed earlier on the effects of extrinsic constraints on intrinsic motivation (cf. Lepper, 1981).

It is next predicted that young children will make schema-consistent *judgments* only in self- or other-perception situations that are familiar and/or when they appreciate the causal power of the social or physical constraint. This qualification helps to explain much of the situation- and response-specific evidence for preschoolers' use of the discounting principle in social perception. For example, Baldwin and Baldwin (1970) reported that kindergarteners discounted the kindness of an actor whose generosity was prompted by obedience but not one whose

Table 1. A Social-Developmental Analysis of Children's Use of a Discounting Schema as a Function of Age of Child, Response Mode, and Stimulus Situation.

Subjects	Stimulus Situation		
	Highly familiar, concrete, scripted situations $\longrightarrow$		Novel situations, requiring generalization and abstraction
Preschoolers (pre-operational)	behavior judgment explanation (?)	behavior judgment (?) —	behavior (?) — —
Elementary-school children (concrete operations)	behavior judgment explanation	behavior judgment explanation (?)	behavior judgment (?) —
Adults (formal operations)	behavior judgment explanation	behavior judgment explanation	behavior judgment explanation (?)

Note: Entries in this matrix indicate cases in which evidence of a discounting effect is to be expected.

behavior was induced by a sense of obligation to a guest. Karniol and Ross similarly found that kindergarteners were more likely to (a) discount the intrinsic motivation of an actor who responds to a command than to a reward offer (1976), and (b) employ a discounting principle under conditions that make salient the manipulative intent of the adult making a request (1979). Finally, it appears that children discount effort expenditure at an earlier age than they do desire or intention (Kassin et al., 1981; Kassin & Gibbons, 1981) or ability (Karabenick & Heller, 1976; Kun, 1977; Surber, 1980). Consistent with our familiarity hypothesis, this discrepancy may occur because the concept of "trying" can be easily experienced personally (cf. Nicholls, 1978).

Finally, we would expect preschoolers to provide verbal *explanations* for their behavior/judgments only in concrete, specific, and highly scripted settings. In a relevant test of this hypothesis, Lepper et al. (1982) conducted two experiments in which preschoolers judged the attractiveness of two activities—one presented as a "means," the other as an "end." In one study, subjects were told a story about a familiar everyday situation they had repeatedly encountered personally in the past. This story involved a child who is given a choice of two foods that are presented in contingent fashion (i.e., if you eat food A, then you can have food B). In a second study, the same means-end contingency was presented in a substantially more novel context involving two art activities (i.e., if you play with activity A, then you can play with activity B). In both studies, children predicted that the actors preferred and would freely choose the food or activity presented as an end to that presented as a means. Only in the first, more familiar situation, however, did the preschoolers provide relevant reasons for their discounting judgments.

Our expectations for older children and adults are similarly diagrammed in the second and third rows of Table 1. Our general expectation, clearly, is an increased application of a discounting principle to less familiar and scripted stimulus settings and on more complex and reflective response measures with increasing age. Again, these expectations are generally consistent with the literature we have reviewed in this chapter.

Of course, the present model is largely postdictive at this point. It could be employed in future research, however, to derive more specific predictions of the conditions under which one would expect children to act, draw inferences, or explain actions in accord with a discounting principle by (a) independently identifying or experimentally manipulating the child's prior experiences in situations similar to a particular experimental context (cf. Lepper et al., 1982), and (b) assessing the behavioral, judgmental and symbolic components of the overjustification and insufficient justification effects on a within-subject basis (cf. Kassin, 1981; Wells & Shultz, 1980).

General Implications

Similar considerations may have relevance to a number of other research areas as well. Although our social-developmental model was specifically developed to organize and explain research concerned with children's use of a discounting principle in settings involving children's motives and their inferences about motives, we believe that it may also have more general implications for a variety of other literatures concerned with the development of social-cognitive principles and abilities.

As we examine the developmental literatures regarding other domains of social inference—whether moral judgments (e.g., Chandler, Greenspan, & Barenboim, 1973; Darley, Klosson, & Zanna, 1978; Lickona, 1976), attributions in the achievement domain (e.g., Nicholls, 1978; Weiner, 1974, 1979), or empathetic responsiveness (e.g., Hoffman, 1976), a common pattern seems to emerge. In each of these areas, as in the present case, three characteristics of young children's responses seem salient (cf. Sedlak & Kurtz, 1981). First, it appears that children frequently display a greater sophistication in their overt actions than in their social judgments and, in turn, their social explanations. Second, the sophistication of young children's responses appears to show relatively great variability across different stimulus situations within each of these literatures. Third, the relative sophistication of children's responses within a given setting appears to vary systematically as a function of the manner in which experimental stimuli are presented and children's responses are assessed.

Although it falls beyond the scope of the present chapter to explore these other literatures in detail, we suggest that the conceptual framework presented here may also prove useful in understanding the results of research in these other domains of social cognition. An interactive perspective that takes into account both the child's specific social-learning experiences and general advances in his or her conceptual abilities, in short, may prove generally useful as a strategy for understanding the development of children's social-cognitive competencies.

SUMMARY

Young children in social-psychological experiments characteristically behave in ways that suggest that their actions were governed by a social discounting principle. Yet research examining children's cognitive competencies suggests that these same children do not possess the conceptual mechanisms typically presumed to be required for understanding such a principle. In the present chapter, we have reviewed the evidence for both these claims and have examined a number of potential resolutions of this seeming paradox.

Our analysis led us to propose a theoretical alternative to both the cognitive-developmental stage approach and the radical-behaviorist position that have frequently been applied to this area. In this proposed social-developmental analysis, the relative sophistication of children's responses to situations to which a discounting principle may be applied is viewed as a joint function of the child's level of general cognitive development, his or her previous specific social-learning history, and the nature of the response required of the child as evidence of the use of a discounting principle.

In general, this model suggests that young children will initially be likely to respond in terms of a sophisticated discounting principle primarily in highly familiar, "scripted" situations and under conditions that permit the child to respond on the basis of tacit, rather than more generalized or reflective, social knowledge. Thus, Polanyi's (1958) argument that "We can know more than we can tell and we can tell nothing without relying on our awareness of things we may not be able to tell" may have special relevance to the case of the young child trying to construct and abstract the principles governing social interactions.

ACKNOWLEDGMENTS

Preparation of this chapter was supported in part by National Institute of Child Health and Human Development grant HD–MH–09814 and National Science Foundation grant BNS–79–14118 to the second author.

NOTES

1.   It should be noted that different types of facilitative circumstances elicited varying degrees of discounting among the young children. For example, 66% of the kindergarteners perceived an unconstrained positive act as kinder than one that was prompted by a trade offer. In contrast, only 39% discounted the kindness of an act that was extrinsically motivated by an obligation to a guest. The importance of these differential results will become clearer as our argument is developed further.

2.   Smith and Pittman (1978) tested the distraction variant of the competing response hypothesis with a population of adults. They reported that although the presence of reward stimuli decreased subsequent intrinsic motivation, the presence of a nonreward distractor did not. Again, it appeared that the perception of a contingency between one's own behavior and a reward is critical to the undermining of intrinsic motivation.

3.   Recently, Ransen (1980) proposed that the negative effects of extrinsic rewards on intrinsic interest have a control–motive basis. One of Ransen's interpretations was that the offer of extrinsic incentives for participating in an intrinsically interesting activity has the immediate effect of under-mining a child's perception of control over the decision to engage in the rewarded activity. This decline is perceived control, in turn, has a depressing effect on task involvement and intrinsic motivation. A second interpretation was based on psychological reactance theory (Brehm, 1966)—that people see the promise of reward as an encroachment on their freedom of choice. This reactance arousal then motivates individuals to avoid the rewarded activity in the future as an attempt to reassert their lost freedom. Using Bem and Funder's (1978) template-matching technique, Ransen (1980) identified children along the continua of perceived control (i.e., those who are happiest when engaging in activities that they perceive to be products of their own conscious choice) and reactance (i.e., those who have a strong need for autonomy) and then observed their behavior in the standard overjustification paradigm. His correlational data revealed that male children who enjoy con-trol/freedom and respond negatively to its loss showed the largest decrements in playtime measures of intrinsic motivation. This pattern did not hold for females.

Although these findings appear to provide an alternative explanation of the overjustification effect, the data are suggestive at best. First, because the results are correlational, they remain open to a variety of competing hypotheses. This is particularly problematic because this study does not include any relevant control condition. Second, these results are inconsistent with the extant literature in two respects. First, these correlations were found among boys but not girls, although sex differences are typically not obtained in overjustification studies. Second, these negative reactions to loss of control and freedom imply immediate performance differences, yet many investigators have found behav-ioral differences in the absence of such adverse effects (cf. Lepper & Gilovich, 1981).

Finally, neither Ransen's (1980) loss of control nor reactance explanations effectively resolve the developmental paradox at issue here. These explanations are virtually indistinguishable from an attributional account. They too rely on subjects' abilities to draw inferences concerning the manip-ulative intent of the agent offering rewards for task performance.

4.   In this context it may be both interesting and instructive to note that a number of investigators have reported strong overjustification effects on behavioral measures that have not been accompanied by comparable effects on self-report indices of intrinsic motivation even with *adult* actors (Deci, 1971; Folger, Rosenfield, & Hays, 1978; Smith & Pittman, 1978; Wilson, Hull, & Johnson, 1981), although other studies have found such effects with various self-report measures (e.g., Amabile, DeJong, & Lepper, 1976; Calder & Staw, 1975; Harackiewicz, 1979; Kruglanski et al., 1972; Kruglanski, Friedman, & Zeevi, 1971). Interpretation of such results remains controversial, but these and other related findings (Nisbett & Wilson, 1977) suggest that attributional processes underlying behavioral responses may frequently be relatively inaccessible even to cognitively sophisticated subjects (Wilson et al., 1981).

5.   It is also of some interest to consider the possible application of this analysis to differences in the accessibility of reflective social knowledge across different domains even among adult subjects.

Nisbett and Wilson (1977) and Wilson, Hull, and Johnson (1981), for example, have summarized data from a number of literatures that suggest that adults may often be unable to provide a clear account of the reasoning that led them to respond in accord with a discounting principle. Perhaps the most obvious exception to this analysis, however, occurs in the study of subjects' attributions regarding the causes of outcomes on achievement-related tasks. In this domain, subjects seem to be able to provide much more detailed explanations for their judgments in accord with a discounting principle (cf. Weiner, 1974, 1979). An obvious explanation of this difference, in terms of the present model, is that our shared experiences in school provide a setting in which each of us is given considerable direct experience in using such principles to evaluate our abilities and efforts relative to others confronted with comparable instruction and test situations—a type of concerted "training" rarely encountered in the domain of attributions regarding motives or emotions.

REFERENCES

Abelson, R. P. Script processing in attitude formation and decision-making. In J. S. Carroll & J. W. Payne (Eds.), *Cognition and social behavior*. Hillsdale, NJ: Lawrence Erlbaum Associates, 1976.

Abelson, R. P. Psychological status of the script concept. *American Psychologist*, 1981, *36*, 715–729.

Amabile, T. M., DeJong, W., & Lepper, M. R. Effects of externally-imposed deadlines on subsequent intrinsic motivation. *Journal of Personality and Social Psychology*, 1976, *34*, 92–98.

Anderson, R., Manoogian, S. T., & Reznick, J. S. The undermining and enhancing of intrinsic motivation in preschool children. *Journal of Personality and Social Psychology*, 1976, *34*, 915–922.

Aronson, E., & Carlsmith, J. M. The effect of the severity of threat on the devaluation of forbidden behavior. *Journal of Abnormal and Social Psychology*, 1963, *66*, 584–588.

Baldwin, C. P., & Baldwin, A. L. Children's judgments of kindness. *Child Development*, 1970, *41*, 29–47.

Bem, D. J. Self-perception: An alternative interpretation of cognitive dissonance phenomena. *Psychological Review*, 1967, *74*, 183–200.

Bem, D. J. Self-perception: The dependent variable of human performance. *Organizational Behavior and Human Performance*, 1967, *22*, 105–121.

Bem, D. J. Self-perception theory. In L. Berkowitz (Ed.), *Advances in experimental social psychology* (Vol. 6). New York: Academic Press, 1972.

Bem, D. J. & Funder, D. C. Predicting more of the people more of the time: Assessing the personality of situations. *Psychological Review*, 1978, *85*, 485–501.

Birch, L. L., Birch, D. M., Marlin, D. W., & Kramer, L. Effects of instrumental consumption on food preference: "Drink your milk and then you can...." Unpublished manuscript, University of Illinois, 1981.

Boggiano, A. K., & Ruble, D. N. Perception of competence and the overjustification effect: A developmental study. *Journal of Personality and Social Psychology*, 1979, *37*, 1462–1468.

Brehm, J. W. *A theory of psychological reactance*. New York: Academic Press, 1966.

Bryant, P. E., & Trabasso, T. Transitive inference and memory in young children. *Nature*, 1971, *232*, 456–458.

Bullock, M. Preschoolers' understanding of causal mechanism. Paper presented at the Biennial Convention of the *Society for Research in Child Development*, Boston, April 1981.

Butzin, C. Children's moral judgments of ulterior motives. Paper presented at the Biennial Convention of the *Society for Research in Child Development*, San Francisco, May 1979.

Calder, B. J., & Staw, B. M. Interaction of intrinsic and extrinsic motivation: Some methodological notes. *Journal of Personality and Social Psychology*, 1975, *31*, 76–80.

Calder, B. J., & Staw, B. M. Self–perception of intrinsic and extrinsic motivation. *Journal of Personality and Social Psychology,* 1975, *31,* 599–605.

Carlsmith, J. M., Ebbesen, E. G., Lepper, M. R., Zanna, M. P., Joncas, A. J., & Abelson, R. P. Dissonance reduction following forced attention to the dissonance. *Proceedings of the 77th Annual Convention of the American Psychological Association,* 1969, *4,* 321–322.

Chandler, J. M., Greenspan, S., & Barenboim, C. Judgments of intentionality in response to videotaped and verbally presented moral dilemmas: The medium is the message. *Child Development,* 1973, *44,* 315–320.

Cohen, E. A., Gelfand, D. M., & Hartmann, D. P. Causal reasoning as a function of behavioral consequences. *Child Development,* 1981, *52,* 514–522.

Costanzo, P. R., Grumet, J. F., & Brehm, S. S. The effects of choice and source of constraint on children's attributions of preference. *Journal of Experimental Social Psychology,* 1974, *10,* 352–264.

Curtis, R. C., & Schildhaus, J. Children's attributions to self and situation. *Journal of Social Psychology,* 1980, *110,* 109–114.

Darley, J. M., Klosson, E. C., & Zanna, M. P. Intentions and their contexts in the moral judgments of children and adults. *Child Development,* 1978, *49,* 66–74.

Deci, E. L. Effects of externally mediated rewards on intrinsic motivation. *Journal of Personality and Social Psychology,* 1971, *18,* 105–155.

Deci, E. L. *Intrinsic motivation.* New York: Plenum Press, 1975.

Deci, E. L. Notes on the theory and metatheory of intrinsic motivation. *Organizational Behavior and Human Performance,* 1975, *15,* 130–145.

Deci, E. L., & Ryan, R. M. The empirical exploration of intrinsic motivational processes. In L. Berkowitz (Ed.), *Advances in experimental social psychology* (Vol. 13). New York: Academic Press, 1980.

Dollinger, S. J., & Thelen, M. H. Overjustification and children's intrinsic motivation: Comparative effects of four rewards. *Journal of Personality and Social Psychology,* 1978, *36,* 1259–1269.

Enzle, M. E., & Ross, J. M. Increasing and decreasing intrinsic interest with contingent rewards: A test of cognitive evaluation theory. *Journal of Experimental Social Psychology,* 1978, *14,* 588–597.

Fazio, R. H. On the self-perception explanation of the overjustification effect: The role of the salience of initial attitude. *Journal of Experimental Social Psychology,* 1981, *17,* 417–426.

Fazio, R. H., Zanna, M. P., & Cooper, J. Dissonance vs. self-perception: An integrative view of each theory's proper domain of application. *Journal of Experimental Social Psychology,* 1977, *5,* 464–479.

Feldman, N. S., & Ruble, D. N. The development of person perception: Cognitive and social factors. In S. Brehm, S. Kassin, & F. Gibbons (Eds.), *Developmental social psychology: Theory and research.* New York: Oxford University Press, 1981.

Festinger, L. *A theory of cognitive dissonance.* Stanford, CA: Stanford Press, 1957.

Flapan, D. *Children's understanding of social interaction.* New York: Columbia University Teacher's College Press, 1968.

Flavell, J. H., & Ross, L. (Eds.), *Social cognitive development: Frontiers and possible futures.* Cambridge: Cambridge University Press, 1981.

Folger, R., Rosenfield, D., & Hays, R. P. Equity and intrinsic motivation: The role of choice. *Journal of Personality and Social Psychology,* 1978, *36,* 557–564.

Freedman, J. L. Long-term behavioral effects of cognitive dissonance. *Journal of Experimental Social Psychology,* 1965, *1,* 145–155.

Gelman, R. Cognitive development. *Annual Review of Psychology,* 1978, *29,* 297–332.

Gollin, E. Organizational characteristics of social judgments: A developmental investigation. *Journal of Personality,* 1958, *26,* 139–154.

Greene, D., & Lepper, M. R. Effects of extrinsic rewards on children's subsequent intrinsic interest. *Child Development*, 1974, *45*, 1141–1145.

Greene, D., Sternberg, B., & Lepper, M. R. Overjustification in a token economy. *Journal of Personality and Social Psychology*, 1976, *34*, 1219–1234.

Greenwald, A. G. On the inconclusiveness of "crucial" cognitive tests of dissonance versus self-perception theories. *Journal of Experimental Social Psychology*, 1975, *11*, 490–499.

Guttentag, M., & Longfellow, C. Children's social attributions: Development and change. In H. E. Howe, Jr. (Ed.), *Nebraska symposium on motivation* (Vol. 25). Lincoln: University of Nebraska Press, 1977.

Harackiewicz, J. M. The effects of reward contingency and performance feedback on intrinsic motivation. *Journal of Personality and Social Psychology*, 1979, *37*, 1352–1361.

Hoffman, M. L. Empathy, role-taking, guilt and the development of altruistic motives. In T. Lickona (Ed.), *Moral development and behavior*. New York: Holt, Rinehart & Winston, 1976.

Johnson, E. J., Greene, D., & Carroll, J. S. Overjustification and reasons: A test of the means-ends analysis. Unpublished manuscript, Carnegie–Mellon University, 1981.

Jones, E. E., & Nisbett, R. E. The actor and the observer: Divergent perceptions of the causes of behavior. In E. E. Jones, D. E. Kanouse, H. H. Kelley, R. E. Nisbett, S. Valins & B. Weiner (Eds.), *Attribution: Perceiving the causes of behavior*. Morristown, NJ: General Learning Press, 1971.

Jones, E. E., Kanouse, D. E., Kelley, H. H., Nisbett, R. E., Valins, S., & Weiner, B. (Eds.). *Attribution: Perceiving the causes of behavior*. Morristown, New Jersey: General Learning Press, 1971.

Karabenick, J. E., & Heller, K. A. A developmental study of effort and ability attributions. *Developmental Psychology*, 1976, *12*, 559–560.

Karniol, R., & Ross, M. The development of causal attributions in social perception. *Journal of Personality and Social Psychology*, 1976, *34*, 455–464.

Karniol, R., & Ross, M. The effect of performance-relevant and performance-irrelevant rewards on children's intrinsic motivation. *Child Development*, 1977, *48*, 482–487.

Karniol, R., & Ross, M. Children's use of a causal attribution schema and the inference of manipulative intentions. *Child Development*, 1979, *50*, 463–468.

Kassin, S. M. From laychild to "layman": Developmental causal attribution. In S. S. Brehm, S. M. Kassin, & F. X. Gibbons (Eds.), *Developmental social psychology: Theory and research*. New York: Oxford University Press, 1981.

Kassin, S. M., & Gibbons, F. X. Children's use of the discounting principle in their perceptions of exertion. *Child Development*, 1981, *52*, 741–744.

Kassin, S. M., & Hochreich, D. J. Instructional set: A neglected variable in attribution research? *Personality and Social Psychology Bulletin*, 1977, *3*, 620–623.

Kassin, S. M., Lowe, C. A., & Gibbons, F. X. Children's use of the discounting principle: A perceptual approach. *Journal of Personality and Social Psychology*, 1980, *39*, 719–728.

Keasey, C. B. Young children's attribution of intentionality to themselves and others. *Child Development*, 1977, *48*, 261–264.

Kelley, H. H. Attribution theory in social psychology. In D. Levine (Ed.), *Nebraska symposium on motivation* (Vol. 15). Lincoln, Nebraska: University of Nebraska Press, 1967.

Kelley, H. H. Attribution in social interaction. In E. E. Jones, D. E. Kanouse, H. H. Kelley, R. E. Nisbett, S. Valins & B. Weiner (Eds.), *Attribution: Perceiving the causes of behavior*. Morristown, NJ: General Learning Press, 1971.

Kelley, H. H. The processes of causal attribution. *American Psychologist*, 1973, *28*, 107–128.

Kruglanski, A. W., Alon, S., & Lewis, T. Retrospective misattribution and task enjoyment. *Journal of Experimental Social Psychology*, 1972, *8*, 493–501.

Kruglanski, A. W., Friedman, I., & Zeevi, G. The effects of extrinsic incentives on some qualitative aspects of task performance. *Journal of Personality*, 1971, *39*, 606–617.

Kun, A. Development of the magnitude–covariation and compensation schemata in ability and effort attributions of performance. *Child Development*, 1977, *48*, 862–873.

Kun, A. *Perceived additivity of intrinsic and extrinsic motivation in young children: Refutation of the "overjustification" hypothesis.* Paper presented to the Annual Convention of the American Psychological Association, Toronto, Canada, 1978.

Leahy, R. L. Development of conceptions of prosocial behavior: Information affecting rewards given for altruism and kindness. *Developmental Psychology*, 1979, *15*, 34–37.

Lepper, M. R. Dissonance, self–perception, and honesty in children. *Journal of Personality and Social Psychology*, 1973, *25*, 65–74.

Lepper, M. R. Intrinsic and extrinsic motivation in children: Detrimental effects of superfluous social controls. In W. A. Collins (Ed.), *Minnesota symposium on child psychology* (Vol. 14). Hillsdale, NJ: Lawrence Erlbaum Associates, 1981.

Lepper, M. R. Social control processes and the internalization of social values: An attributional perspective. In T. E. Higgins, D. N. Ruble & W. W. Hartup (Eds.), *Developmental social cognition: A sociocultural perspective*. New York: Cambridge University Press, in press.

Lepper, M. R., & Gilovich, T. The multiple functions of reward: A social-developmental perspective. In S. S. Brehm, S. M. Kassin, & F. X. Gibbons (Eds.), *Developmental social psychology: Theory and research*. New York: Oxford University Press, 1981.

Lepper, M. R., & Greene, D. Turning play into work: Effects of adult surveillance and extrinsic rewards on children's intrinsic motivation. *Journal of Personality and Social Psychology*, 1975, *31*, 479–486.

Lepper, M. R., & Greene, D. (Eds.). *The hidden costs of reward*. Hillsdale, NJ: Lawrence Erlbaum Associates, 1978. (a)

Lepper, M. R., & Greene, D. Overjustification research and beyond: Toward a means– ends analysis of intrinsic and extrinsic motivation. In M. R. Lepper & D. Greene (Eds.), *The hidden costs of reward*. Hillsdale, NJ: Lawrence Erlbaum Associates, 1978. (b)

Lepper, M. R., Greene, D., & Nisbett, R. E. Undermining children's intrinsic interest with extrinsic rewards: A test of the "overjustification" hypothesis. *Journal of Personality and Social Psychology*, 1973, *28*, 129–137.

Lepper, M. R., Sagotsky, G., Dafoe, J., & Greene, D. Consequences of superfluous social constraints: Effects of nominal contingencies on children's subsequent intrinsic interest. *Journal of Personality and Social Psychology*, 1982, *42*, 51–65.

Lepper, M. R., Sagotsky, G., & Greene, D. *Self determination, extrinsic rewards, and intrinsic interest in preschool children*. Unpublished manuscript, Stanford University, 1981. (a)

Lepper, M. R., Sagotsky, G., & Greene, D. *Overjustification effects following multiple–trial reinforcement procedures: Experimental evidence concerning the assessment of intrinsic interest*. Unpublished manuscript, Stanford University, 1981. (b)

Lepper, M. R., Zanna, M. P., & Abelson, R. P. Cognitive irreversibility in a dissonance-reduction situation. *Journal of Personality and Social Psychology*, 1970, *16*, 191–198.

Lickona, T. Research on Piaget's theory of moral development. In T. Lickona (Ed.), *Moral development and behavior*. New York: Holt, 1976.

Lipsitt, L. P., & Kaye, H. Conditioned sucking in the human newborn. *Psychonomic Science*, 1964, *1*, 29–30.

Livesley, W., & Bromley, D. *Person perception in childhood and adolescence*. London: Wiley, 1973.

Loveland, K. K., & Olley, J. G. The effect of external reward on interest and quality of task performance in children of high and low intrinsic motivation. *Child Development*, 1979, *50*, 1207–1210.

McLoyd, V. C. The effects of extrinsic rewards of differential value on high and low intrinsic interest. *Child Development*, 1979, *50*, 1010–1019.

Monson, T. C., & Snyder, M. Actors, observers, and the attribution process: Toward a reconceptualization. *Journal of Experimental Social Psychology*, 1977, *13*, 89–111.

Morgan, M. The overjustification effect: A developmental test of self–perception interpretations. *Journal of Personality and Social Psychology*, 1981, *40*, 809–821.

Nelson, K. Social cognition in a script framework. In J. H. Flavell & L. Ross (Eds.), *Social cognitive development: Frontiers and possible futures*. Cambridge: Cambridge University Press, 1981.

Nicholls, J. G. The development of the concepts of effort and ability, perception of academic attainment and the understanding that difficult tasks require more ability. 1978, *49*, 800–814.

Nisbett, R. E., & Wilson, T. D. Telling more than we can know: Verbal reports on mental processes. *Psychological Review*, 1977, *84*, 231–259.

Peevers, B. H., & Secord, P. F. Developmental changes in attribution of descriptive concepts to persons. *Journal of Personality and Social Psychology*, 1973, *27*, 120–128.

Pepitone, A., McCauley, C., & Hammond, P. Change in attractiveness of forbidden toys as a function of severity of threat. *Journal of Experimental Social Psychology*, 1967, *3*, 221–229.

Piaget, J. *The moral judgment of the child*. New York: Free Press, 1965. (Original translation, London: Routledge & Kegan Paul, 1932.)

Pittman, T. S., Cooper, E. E., & Smith, T. W. Attribution of causality and the overjustification effect. *Personality and Social Psychology Bulletin*, 1977, *3*, 280–283.

Polanyi, M. *Personal knowledge: Toward a post-critical philosophy*. New York: Harper & Row, 1958.

Ransen, D. L. The mediation of reward-induced motivation decrements in early and middle childhood: A template matching approach. *Journal of Personality and Social Psychology*, 1980, *39*, 1088–1100.

Reiss, S., & Sushinsky, L. W. Overjustification, competing responses, and the acquisition of intrinsic interest. *Journal of Personality and Social Psychology*, 1975, *31*, 1116–1125.

Reiss, S., & Sushinsky, L. W. Comment: Undermining *extrinsic* interest. *American Psychologist*, 1975, *31*, 782–783.

Reiss, S., & Sushinsky, L. W. The competing response hypothesis of decreased play effects: A reply to Lepper and Greene. *Journal of Personality and Social Psychology*, 1976, *33*, 233–244.

Ross, M. Salience of reward and intrinsic motivation. *Journal of Personality and Social Psychology*, 1975, *32*, 245–254.

Ross, M. Karniol, R., & Rothstein, M. Reward contingency and intrinsic motivation in children: A test of the delay of gratification hypothesis. *Journal of Personality and Social Psychology*, 1976, *33*, 442–447.

Sedlak, A. J., & Kurtz, S. T. A review of children's use of causal inference principles. *Child Development*, 1981, *52*, 759–784.

Shultz, T. R., & Butkowsky, I. Young children's use of the scheme for multiple sufficient causes in the attribution of real and hypothetical behavior. *Child Development*, 1977, *48*, 464–469.

Shultz, T. R., Butkowsky, L., Pearce, J. W., & Shanfield, H. Development of schemes for the attribution of multiple psychological causes. *Developmental Psychology*, 1975, *11*, 502–510.

Siegler, R. S. Defining the locus of developmental differences in children's causal reasoning. *Journal of Experimental Child Psychology*, 1975, *20*, 512–525.

Small, K. H., & Peterson, J. L. The divergent perceptions of actors and observers. *Journal of Social Psychology*, 1981, *113*, 123–132.

Smith, M. C. Children's use of the multiple sufficient cause schema in social perception. *Journal of Personality and Social Psychology*, 1975, *32*, 737–747.

Smith, T. W., & Pittman, T. S. Reward, distraction, and the overjustification effect. *Journal of Personality and Social Psychology*, 1978, *36*, 565–572.

Sorenson, R. L., & Maehr, M. L. Toward the experimental analysis of "continuing motivation." *Journal of Educational Research*, 1976, *69*, 319–322.

Surber, C. F. Developmental changes in inverse compensation in social and nonsocial attributions. In S. Yussen (Ed.), *The growth of reflection*. New York: Academic Press, 1980.

Swann, W. B., Jr., & Pittman, T. S. Initiating play activity of children: The moderating influence of verbal cues on intrinsic motivation. *Child Development,* 1977, *48,* 1125–1132.

Turner, E. A., & Wright, J. Effects of severity of threat and perceived availability on the attractiveness of objects. *Journal of Personality and Social Psychology,* 1965, *2,* 128–132.

Weiner, B. (Ed.). *Achievement motivation and attribution theory*. Morristown, NJ: General Learning Press, 1974.

Weiner, B. A theory of motivation for some classroom experiences. *Journal of Educational Psychology,* 1979, *71,* 3–25.

Wells, D., & Shultz, T. R. Developmental distinctions between behavior and judgment in the operation of the discounting principle. *Child Development,* 1980, *51,* 1307–1310.

Wilson, T. D., Hull, J. G., & Johnson, J. H. Awareness and self–perception: Verbal reports on internal states. *Journal of Personality and Social Psychology,* 1981, *40,* 53–71.

Zanna, M. P., Lepper, M. R., & Abelson, R. P. Attentional mechanisms in children's devaluation of a forbidden activity in a forced–compliance situation. *Journal of Personality and Social Psychology,* 1973, *28,* 355–359.

CONTINGENCY JUDGMENTS AND ACHIEVEMENT BEHAVIOR:
DECIDING WHAT IS CONTROLLABLE AND WHEN TO TRY

John R. Weisz

> "Practice makes perfect."
> "If at first you don't succeed, try, try again."
> "You'll do better when you get older."

With aphorisms like these, we parents and teachers encourage the youngsters in our lives to persevere, to persist in their efforts to achieve. Yet, these aphorisms, intended to inspire, may often confuse. The fact is, there are many situations where no amount of practice will make perfect, where trying and trying again will not lead to success, and where we do not improve with maturity. A number of such situations can be grouped under the umbrella term, *noncontingent events*.

Advances in Motivation and Achievement, vol. 3, pages 107–136
Copyright © 1984 by JAI Press Inc.
All rights of reproduction in any form reserved.
ISBN 0-89232-289-6

By this term I refer to events, or "outcomes," that do not covary with the quality or intensity of individuals' behavior. Chance events represent relatively pure instances of noncontingency. But many events that are not entirely chance-determined are nonetheless largely noncontingent. Most of us recognize the logical limitations of the handy aphorisms cited above. Yet, we continue to use them in their unqualified form when we are trying to encourage achievement behavior. In doing so, we implicitly emphasize the existence of contingency—perhaps for a very good reason: children's notions about how contingent their outcomes are may help determine how hard they try.

In general, achievement striving is apt to be stimulated when individuals believe that outcomes they care about are contingent upon the behavior of people like them (see Abramson, Seligman, & Teasdale, 1978). In contrast, achievement striving is apt to be undermined by the belief that achievement outcomes occur noncontingently (see Seligman, 1975). Let us suppose that two employees of the same corporation differ markedly in their contingency perceptions, with one believing that salary and promotion are highly contingent on the quality of worker performance and the other believing that salary and promotion results largely from caprice, bias, or "lucky breaks." All other things being equal, these two employees are likely to differ in the level of achievement behavior they show on the job. Similarly, a child who believes that her teacher assigns grades in accord with the quality of his students' work is apt to work harder than a child who thinks the teacher is unfair or arbitrary.

I want to emphasize one key point from the outset: a perception of contingency is neither inherently desirable nor inherently undesirable. There are certainly some work and school situations where a high level of contingency prevails, and where a perception of noncontingency can thus inappropriately undermine achievement behavior. On the other hand, all of us know of work situations where advancement does not correlate well with job performance and school situations where grades are not closely linked to the quality of students' work. In these latter cases, the most adaptive path for any individual may be to recognize the noncontingency that prevails, and seek out those true "achievement situations," where outcomes are better correlated with the individual behavior. People who mistakenly believe that outcomes are highly contingent may persist unreasonably in their efforts to achieve. These efforts may, in turn, culminate in frustration, disappointment, and inappropriate self-reproach for adverse outcomes that are, in fact, not the individual's "fault." In other words, faulty judgments about contingency can stimulate indiscriminate achievement behavior and inappropriate self-blame.

So, inaccurate perceptions of contingency, or of noncontingency, can have adverse effects in the achievement domain. This being the case, an important task of development is the acquisition of contingency-detection skills—a capacity to distinguish accurately between contingent and noncontingent events. It is the development of this capacity that we will consider in this chapter. First, we will examine developmental literature in this area prior to 1980. Then we will describe some recent research on perceived contingency conducted at the University of North Carolina. Finally, we will consider the implications of the findings for the development of achievement behavior.

DEVELOPMENTAL LITERATURE

The developmental literature on how people make judgments about contingency comes mostly from the Piagetian tradition. That literature suggests something very important about early contingency judgments. It suggests that early childhood is not characterized by a state of sheer confusion in which very young children make random errors; instead, it is a time when youngsters seem to repeatedly overestimate the pervasiveness of contingency in their world.

Let us first consider Piaget and Inhelder's (1975) developmental analysis of chance and probability concepts. There they argue that children only come to understand the noncontingency of random events when they develop a grasp of reversible operations. The outcome of a throw of the dice, for example, is not logically reversible. But its fortuitous nature can only be understood when it is contrasted with events that *can* be reversed by inverting a causal sequence— events such as turning on a radio and turning up the volume. The contrast between reversible and nonreversible events only begins to make sense during the elementary school years (the period of development Piaget calls concrete operations); and the contrast is not fully understood until adolescence (formal operations).

Because very young (pre-elementary) children do not really comprehend logical, reversible operations, they have no internalized standard representing truly contingent relations, against which to test new experience. One result is that events that occur by chance, both in games and in nature, are perceived as being contingent on potentially identifiable causes. Piaget and Inhelder (1975) see evidence of such a perception in many of the young child's *Why* questions. Questions such as, "Why isn't there a spring in our garden?" or "Why are you so tall and yet have small ears?" (1975, p. xviii), are said to reveal a key assumption of young children: the assumption that identifiable contingencies exist for what are actually chance events in nature. Piaget and Inhelder do not give examples drawn from games of chance; but in our own research we have encountered young children's questions about why dice fell into a certain pattern, and how a younger child could draw winning cards more often than an older child. These Why questions seem to reflect contingency assumptions similar to those discussed by Piaget and Inhelder.

Other examples of erroneous perceived contingency are given in Piaget's (1930) studies of causal reasoning *per se*. In one example, a child states that, "The moon gets bigger because we are growing bigger" (1930, p. 304). Adults might make such a statement in an analogical sense; but the young child, according to Piaget, "means that we actually make the moon grow bigger" (p. 304). Such errors seem to result from a failure to understand reversible operations (as discussed earlier) and from other difficulties in comprehending the relation between causes and effects (for a detailed discussion of these difficulties see Sedlack & Kurtz, 1981; for related evidence in the achievement domain see Nicholls, 1978). Whatever their causes, the kinds of illusory contingency described in the causality literature (e.g., Piaget, 1930) like those described in the literature on chance (Piaget & Inhelder, 1975), are depicted as declining during development, and as essentially disappearing with the emergence of formal operational thought.

A third body of Piagetian literature that seems relevant to the study of perceived contingency concerns "immanent justice." Early Piagetian research (e.g., Piaget, 1932) identified a tendency in young children to perceive noncontingent adverse events as contingent on people's misbehavior. For example, Piaget told children a story about a bridge that collapsed under a youngster who had just stolen something; young children often construed the collapse as a punishment, contingent on the youngster's misbehavior. Older children and adolescents, by contrast, were more likely to find plausible *naturalistic* explanations for such adverse events, explanations not invoking contingency between the adverse event and the human behavior.

So, Piagetian literature on the chance concept, on causal reasoning, and on immanent justice all seem to point to developmental declines in various forms of illusory contingency. On the other hand, the actual *data* offered by Piaget are rather limited and largely anecdotal. This is certainly true of Piaget and Inhelder's (1975) analysis of the *chance* concept. Most of their research evidence deals only with notions of randomness and rules of probability; the speculations that young children perceive chance events as contingent are supported almost entirely by a few examples Piaget and Inhelder use to illustrate their views. Piaget's discussions of *causal reasoning* have been criticized (e.g., as early as Huang, 1943) for emphasizing investigator-selected anecdotes and examples that do not reflect modal child responses. And recent research by Karniol (1980) on *immanent justice* responses by children has indicated that when carefully standardized interview methods are combined with detailed reporting of results, the kinds of developmental trends reported by Piaget may not be found.

There is another reason for uncertainty about the nature of developmental change in illusory contingency. It comes in the form of non-Piagetian evidence on *adults'* interpretations of random events. One line of evidence (reviewed by Lerner, 1977) concerns the "justice motive." Findings in this area indicate that even adults show a tendency (perhaps motivationally—rather than cognitively—based) to perceive noncontingent favorable and unfavorable outcomes as contingent consequences of people's good and bad behavior, respectively. Other research (e.g., Langer, 1975; Wortman, 1975) has been focused on adult's beliefs about chance outcomes independently of considerations of morality and justice. This research, too, points to a persistent belief that chance events are contingent on human attributes such as skill. In one study, for example, Langer (1975) had Yale students bet money against an opponent in a totally chance game, drawing for high card from a deck of 52. Students betting against an apparently awkward, diffident "schnook" (actually Langer's confederate) bet larger sums of money than did students betting against an apparently confident "dapper" opponent. This and other evidence (reviewed by Langer, 1977) shows that, in at least some situations, adults make contingency errors that are similar in theme to errors made by young children—i.e., believing that chance outcomes can be influenced by human characteristics or behavior.

It is certainly possible that adults who made such errors have the capacity to make accurate contingency judgments but fail to use that capacity in situations structured to induce an "illusion of control." (Langer's situations were so designed). Still, the findings of the adult research leave some uncertainty about the nature of developmental change. Other contributors to this uncertainty have been the relatively uncontrolled research methods used by Piaget and the fact that the various lines of evidence reviewed above have been focused on differing forms of illusory contingency. One means of clarifying our picture of developmental change may be to focus on one form of perceived contingency at a time, using methods that are more controlled than Piaget's and not designed specifically to induce a perception of contingency. This was the intent behind the series of studies I will describe next.

THE CONTINGENCY EXPERIMENTS

The studies dealt with people's judgments about the noncontingent outcomes of chance activities. A basic property of such noncontingent outcomes is that they do not covary with the behavior or characteristics of the actors who produce them; and it was this property upon which much of the research was focused. How does one go about studying children's contingency judgments? Obviously, young children cannot be expected to answer questions that involve terms like "contingency." However, both young children and adolescents can be asked to make performance predictions for actors who differ in characteristics that would influence competence—determined outcomes (e.g., older versus younger actors) and for actors who differ in behavior that would be relevant to competence—related outcomes (e.g., actors who try hard versus those who do not). The degree to which outcomes are perceived as contingent can then be inferred from the degree to which performance differences are predicted between older and younger actors, those who try hard and those who do not, etc.

This inferential process is illustrated in Figure 1. The figure also provides a visual representation of the concept of contingency/noncontingency. Suppose that we ask people to predict outcomes that others would obtain at some activity, say, a roulette game in which players can bet on either black or red. We indicate that the players each have five tries; the prediction task is to judge how many "wins" would be scored by a person who concentrates and "tries very hard" at the game, and how many wins would be scored by a person who "does not try very hard." As Figure 1 suggests, predictions that the person who tries hard would win as often as the person who does not try hard would imply a belief that outcomes in the game are noncontingent—not contingent, at least, on variations

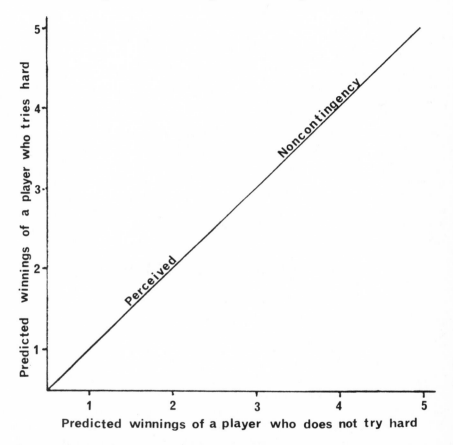

Figure 1. Pictorial representation of contingency/noncontingency. Predictions that lie along the diagonal reflect perceived noncontingency. Predictions that lie anywhere off the diagonal reflect perceived contingency. [See also Seligman, 1975]

Source: "Perceived contingency of skill and chance events: A developmental analysis." John C. Weisz, Keith Owen Yeates, Dan Robertson, and Jean C. Beckman. *Developmental Psychology,* copyright © 1982, vol. *18,* (6), 898–905. Reprinted with permission.

in effort. By contrast, predictions that fall anywhere off the diagonal in Figure 1 imply a belief that outcomes are influenced by variations in effort. Predictions that lie above the diagonal imply that effort enhances outcomes; predictions below the diagonal imply the view that effort is counterproductive. Both views are forms of perceived contingency. This sort of prediction task and this sort of inferential process provided the basis for the studies that will be described next.

Study 1: Chance Events in the Laboratory

In the first study (Weisz, 1980), kindergarteners and fourth-graders took part in a totally noncontingent guessing game. Twenty white 3 in. × 5 in. cards were spread out in front of the child. Ten had a blue spot on one side, ten had a yellow spot. The child counted out five yellows and five blues and the child and adult mixed these ten cards thoroughly. Asked how many yellows and how many blues were in this mixed stack, all children answered correctly. The experimenter lined five poker chips up in front of the child; she explained that the child would draw cards from the deck, would win a chip for each yellow card drawn (blue for half the children), and at the end would win a prize, "if you have won enough chips." After each draw the card was returned to the deck, and the deck shuffled.

After the child had had five trials at this task, the experimenter asked several questions. The child was asked to explain why another child who had played the game "didn't win even one chip" and why yet another child "won five chips—s/he got the right color *every* time." Responses to these relatively unstructured questions were categorized as either not codable (e.g., no answer, "I don't know"), or (1) *perceived noncontingency* (e.g., "It's just luck." "It just happened."), or (2) *perceived contingency* (e.g., "She tried real hard.") Using this scheme, two independent raters showed better than 90% concordance on both questions. As Table 1 shows, the two questions evoked striking effects of grade level. On both questions not one kindergartener's response reflected a belief in

Table 1. Perceived Contingency and Noncontingency on Two Minimally Structured Questions

Question A: Why did a (fictitious) child pick the *wrong* color every time?

	Kindergarteners	Fourth-Graders
Perceived noncontingency	0	11
Perceived contingency	9	6

Question B: Why did a (fictitious) child pick the *right* color every time?

	Kindergarteners	Fourth-Graders
Perceived noncontingency	0	15
Perceived contingency	12	3

Note: For both tables, $p < .01$ (two-tailed Fisher exact tests).

noncontingency. By contrast, most fourth graders gave noncontingency explanations.

Children also were asked to use two rows of five chips each to predict winnings for other children who would try five trials of the game. They predicted the winnings of: (1) "most kids older than you" and "most kids younger than you," (2) a child who "got to practice lots of times before trying to win chips" and one who "didn't get to practice picking the cards at all;" (3) a child who "was very careful and tried very hard to pick the yellow cards and win chips" and one who "didn't try very hard at all—s/he picked cards very quickly and didn't seem to care what color s/he got;" and (4) a child who "was very smart" and one who "was not very smart." The order of the questions was randomized across subjects.

Each of the four sets of paired predictions was subjected to a separate analysis of variance in which grade level (kindergarten versus fourth) was one factor, and contingency variable (e.g., practice vs. no practice) was treated as a repeated measure. The results of the analyses for the age variable, the practice variable, and the "smartness" variable, were quite similar. Kindergarteners expected that older, more practiced, and smarter children would win many more chips than would their younger, less practiced, and less intelligent counterparts. Fourth graders, by contrast, expected the three contingency variables to make very small and generally nonsignificant differences in task outcomes. The only exception to this pattern was that both kindergarteners and fourth graders predicted that children who tried hard would win substantially and significantly more than children who did not try hard (mean difference between "tried hard" and "did not try hard:" 1.7 for both groups). In general, these results suggest that, except for a lingering belief that trying hard would help, fourth graders were pretty advanced in their ability to recognize noncontingency.

Another look at the data will lead us to temper that conclusion somewhat. A precisely logical concept of noncontingency would lead a person to predict equal winnings for older and younger children, for those who are smart and those who are not, etc. Most fourth graders were unwilling to carry their perceived noncontingency quite that far. Even most fourth graders who had strongly asserted the chance-controlled nature of the task on unstructured questions proceeded to predict slightly higher winnings for children who were older, had practiced, were smarter, or had tried harder. In fact, of the 17 children who mentioned luck or chance as a determinant of outcomes on at least one of the unstructured questions, only one went on to predict equal winnings for both children in all four paired predictions.

Overall, the results suggested that change may take place between the kindergarten and fourth grade years and that the change looks like that described by Piaget. At the kindergarten level, our measures fairly consistently showed a belief that outcomes on this guessing game were highly contingent on behavior and characteristics of individual players. Fourth graders were generally able to identify the outcomes as noncontingent when we asked them for causal attributions. But even fourth graders showed two lapses in sophistication. First, they believed as strongly as did kindergarteners that variations in effort would influence these noncontingent outcomes. Second, they illogically predicted that variations in age, practice, and intelligence would have a slight influence on outcomes. This suggests the existence of a sort of illusory contingency, pronounced at the kindergarten level, and still lingering in weakened form at fourth grade.

Study 2: Chance Events at the State Fair

Study 1 was limited in its implications, however, because it relied on a single laboratory task designed specifically to make the chance-controlled nature of its outcomes clear to children. Many naturally occurring noncontingent outcomes in real life are not so designed, and may well evoke quite different reactions from children. Whether or not the support for Piaget's developmental prediction generated in Weisz (1980) is limited to such specially-simplified laboratory tasks remains unclear. Developmental patterns that emerge from such contrived circumstances can be credited with greater transcontextual validity if they can also be demonstrated in naturally-occurring settings (see Weisz, 1978). For this reason, the North Carolina State Fair was chosen as the setting for Study 2 (Weisz, 1981). There, children were interviewed following voluntary participation in games of chance along the fair midway. The children we interviewed ranged from 6 to 14 years of age. Each child was interviewed immediately after completing one of the following totally chance activities: an electronic horse race on which participants placed bets, a pond from which participants pulled plastic ducks with prize information painted underneath, a giant dice throw with months and holidays on the die faces, and a giant dice throw with various colors on the faces.

Children were first asked whether they had won the prize they wanted or not. Then they were asked, "Why do you think it turned out that way? What caused you *to win/not to win* the prize you wanted?" Raters later coded the responses as reflecting perceived contingency or noncontingency. When children were divided at the age median to form a younger group (6–10 yr.) and an older group (11–14 yr.), the significant age difference in codable responses to this question mirrored the results of Study 1. The majority of the younger group showed perceived contingency; the majority of older subjects perceived their outcomes as noncontingent.

Children were also asked to predict the winnings (out of five tries at their game of chance) of (1) an older and younger child, (2) a "smart" and a "not very smart" child, (3) a child who "tried really hard" and one who did not, and (4) a child who "got to practice all s/he wanted" and one who "did not get to practice at all." These questions on variations in grade, intelligence, effort, and practice, were randomly ordered for each child. Responses were analyzed as in Study 1;

the results showed age differences similar to, but even more consistent than those of Study 1. Our younger subjects predicted that children who were older, were smarter, tried harder, or had practiced, would win significantly more often than their younger, less intelligent, less effortful and unpracticed counterparts, respectively. Our older subjects predicted small, nonsignificant outcome differences as a function of age, intelligence, effort, and practice. [See Table 2]

Again, however, a majority of our older children predicted small outcome differences as a function of age, intelligence, etc. This was also true of a majority of two subsamples that might have been expected to show particularly mature contingency judgments: (1) subjects who were aged 12 and older—i.e., those who seem likely to have been at the threshold of formal operations; and (2) the subsample of 16 who had explicitly identified "luck" as the cause of their outcome. Some of these latter youngsters seemed to be trying, unsuccessfully, to come to grips with the noncontingent nature of luck. For example, one child predicted 0 wins for the "not very smart" child, but for the "smart" child predicted "1, if lucky." Another, who predicted 5 wins for the child with practice, predicted 2 wins for the child who had no practice, then added ". . . and *that* by luck only."

The findings across four tasks in a natural setting, are consistent with the Piagetian view that young children perceive noncontingent events as covarying with people's behavior, and that only with development does such illusory contingency begin to dissipate. In addition to this evidence on the *direction* of development, the findings suggest an hypothesis regarding the *nature* of developmental change. For low levels of the four personal attributes (i.e., first grade, not smart, etc.) the two age groups sampled showed similar low outcome expectancies (See Table 2). It was only when high levels of the personal attributes were specified (i.e., tenth grade, smart, etc.) that the two age groups diverged significantly. This suggests the possibility that children across a broad range of developmental levels assume that there are certain baselines for chance outcomes under conditions of low skill and effort—i.e., that no matter how low in intelligence, effort, etc., children may sink, they are still expected to win at least certain minimal amounts. Following this reasoning, the impact of developmental change would be felt primarily in judgments about children *not* covered by the

Table 2.   Predicted Winnings on Children's Paired Prediction Questions

				Characteristics of Hypothetical Child			
	Grade 10	Grade 1	Smart	Not Smart	Try	Not Try	Practice	No Practice
Children aged 6–10	3.16	1.58	3.25	1.61	3.30	1.09	3.78	1.54
Children aged 11–14	2.23	1.55	1.88	1.59	2.18	1.18	2.43	1.55

baseline assumption—i.e., children above the minimal levels in intelligence, etc. An intriguing, though speculative possibility for future consideration is that the "baseline assumption" referred to here is actually an incipient chance concept.

Despite the developmental gains in sophistication that the findings reveal, the evidence indicated that even older children and adolescents, like many adults in research by Langer (e.g., 1975) and Wortman (1975), are susceptible to a subtle form of illusory contingency, i.e. the belief that factors related to skill outcomes, such as grade level and effort, may not be totally irrelevant to noncontingent outcomes, but may instead be associated with slight outcome differences. Even children who correctly identified the outcomes as caused by "luck" fell prey to this form of the illusion. A significant implication of this finding for attribution theorists (e.g., Weiner, 1979) who construe "luck" as an uncontrollable cause, may be that children often do not.

Study 3: Chance Versus Skill Events

The prediction data of Studies 1 and 2 pose a significant problem of interpretation. Older subjects in both studies predicted smaller outcome differences as a function of age, intelligence, and the other contingency variables than did younger subjects. This was interpreted as evidence of a developmental decline in illusory contingency. An alternative interpretation is that the data reveal, not a developmental decline in illusory contingency, but a developmental increase in conservatism. As children mature, they may simply prefer predicting finer shades of difference; when an adolescent predicts smaller outcome differences than a 7 year old this may simply reflect age differences in predictive style. So the question remains, does development really lead to a decline in illusory perceived contingency?

This question can be answered more definitively than in the research I have just described. One way of doing this is to compare the predictions that people at selected age levels make about noncontingent (chance) outcomes with the predictions people at similar age levels make about contingent (skill) outcomes. If developmental effects are similar for chance and skill outcomes, then the effects could properly be regarded as evidence of predictive style differences, not differences in recognition of noncontingency. However, if the kinds of age group differences found in Studies 1 and 2 are more pronounced with chance tasks than with skill tasks, this would indicate a developmental increase in recognition of noncontingency.

We have conducted two studies involving the kind of skill-chance comparison just described. In one study, we gathered data exactly like those of Study 2, and in the same State Fair setting, but we interviewed children about skill activities that they had just completed along the midway. We then compared these data with those of Study 2, where interviews concerned purely chance activities. In another study we used a laboratory procedure involving skill and chance tasks.

The results of the two skill-chance studies were similar in pattern, but the laboratory study yielded results that were clearer in several respects than those of the state fair study. In addition, the lab study involved four age levels, ranging from kindergarten through college, whereas the state fair study involved a much narrower age range. Consequently, we will focus our attention here on the laboratory study (Weisz, Yeates, Robertson, & Beckham, 1982).

Procedure

Subjects were drawn from kindergarten, fourth grade, and eighth grade public school classes, and from introductory psychology classes at the University of North Carolina, Chapel Hill. The four age levels were selected to roughly reflect late preoperations, middle concrete operations, early formal operations, and mature formal operations, respectively. All children participated in both a chance and a skill task, with order randomly determined. The chance task involved white cards, each with either a blue or yellow circular spot on one side. This task was much like that of Study 1. The cards were shuffled. The experimenter tossed pairs of cards face down in front of the subject. The subject's job was to point to one of the two cards each time and whenever the card pointed to turned out to be blue (yellow for half the subjects), the subject was awarded a chip. There were six trials. Ostensibly the two cards on each trial always included one with a blue spot and one with a yellow. In reality, though, the two cards always had a spot of the same color. In this way the experimenter could insure that all subjects won exactly four chips.

The skill task closely resembled the chance task in format. Subjects were again shown a series of six pairs of cards with colored spots face down, then asked to point to one card in each pair. When the designated color (blue or yellow) was chosen, a chip was awarded. The skill procedure, though, was designed to make such skill factors as memory and concentration seem relevant to outcomes. The procedure began with a memorization task. The subject studied six white cards, each of which had either a yellow or blue spot at the bottom and a line drawing at the top. The drawings were adapted from Kagan's (1965) Matching Familiar Figures Test, and each was different from the other five in some small detail(s). For example, in six line drawings of a house, only one had a chimney on the right side, another had a tilted window, and so forth. Each subject was told to study the cards and to try to remember which pictures went with blue, and which with yellow. A thirty second study period was given for each set of cards. There were six sets in all. The remaining procedure was just like that of the chance task, except that when pairs of cards were tossed on the table, each card had a line drawing on the "blank" side. As in the chance task, the experimenter arranged for each pair to have either both blues or both yellows. In this way the experimenter insured that every subject won on four of the six trials. Even kindergartners seemed to understand the procedure fairly easily.

Our objective had been to construct a task in which subjects perceived that their concentration and memory played a role in outcomes, but in which absolute certainty about any particular memory would be rare. We tried to minimize certainty by requiring storage of many (36) memories, all of which hinged on small, nonsalient details of complex pictures. Subjects' behavior suggested that this condition, in general, was probably satisfied. Subjects at all age levels seemed involved in the memorization task and, during the choice task, appeared to be searching their memories for connections between colors and drawings. Moreover, none of the subjects voiced any suspicion about the procedure.

Results with the Prediction Data

As in the previous studies, subjects made predictions for fictitious other players after they had completed their own series of trials. In this case, predictions were made for the skill task just after it had been completed, and for the chance task just after it had been completed. In either case, subjects predicted the

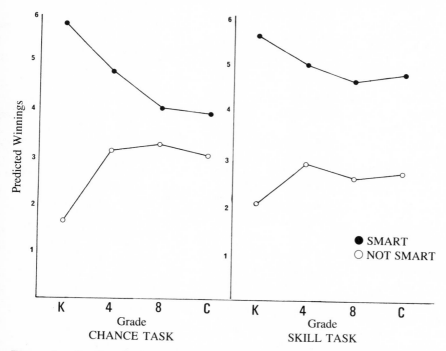

Figure 2. Predicted winnings of smart versus not–very–smart person at the chance and skill tasks of Study 3.

Source: "Perceived contingency of skill and chance events: A developmental analysis." John C. Weisz, Keith Owen Yeates, Dan Robertson, and Jean C. Beckman. *Developmental Psychology,* copyright © 1982, vol. *18,* (6), 898–905. Reprinted with permission.

number of trials out of six on which the following individuals would succeed: (1) a person one grade lower and a person one grade higher than the subject, (2) a person who was smart and a person who wasn't, (3) a person who tried hard and one who didn't, and (4) a person who ''got to practice lots of times before trying to win chips,'' and a person who had no practice. The pattern of predictions across the skill and chance tasks is best conveyed visually.

Take a look at Figure 2. It shows the results for the smart-not smart questions. The right side of the figure, labeled ''Skill Task,'' shows in a rough form the kind of developmental increase in predictive conservatism discussed earlier. With increasing age, there was a statistically significant decline in the magnitude of smart-not smart differences; but it is clear from the figures that the real age difference is between the kindergarteners and the rest of the sample. Now compare the skill side of the figure to the chance task side. This comparison shows

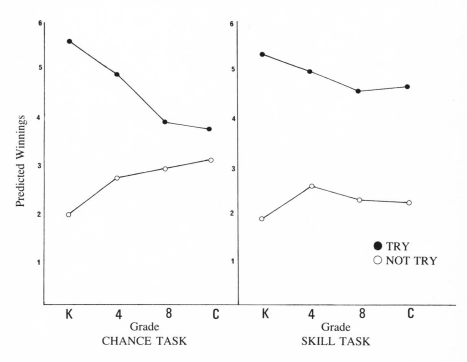

Figure 3.   Predicted winnings of a person who tries very hard versus a person who does not try very hard, at the chance and skill tasks of Study 3.

Source: ''Perceived contingency of skill and chance events: A developmental analysis.'' John C. Weisz, Keith Owen Yeates, Dan Robertson, and Jean C. Beckman. *Developmental Psychology,* copyright © 1982, vol. *18,* (6), 898–905. Reprinted with permission.

the pattern underlying a significant age group × skill vs. chance interaction. The interaction makes it clear that the developmental differences reflected more than merely a change in predictive conservatism. The relatively sharp convergence of the smart and not smart prediction lines on the chance side of the figure, contrasted with the not-so-sharp convergence on the skill side, suggest that there are real developmental gains here in awareness of noncontingency. [Note also, however, that even eighth graders and college students continue to predict that smart people would do *somewhat* better than not-so-smart people on the chance task—more evidence that illusory contingency does not completely disappear, even at an age that many would consider the peak of formal operational reasoning.]

The results for the try-not try questions and for the practice-no practice questions were very similar to what you have just seen. This can be seen in Figure 3 and 4. So far, so good . . . but Figure 5 shows the results for the older-younger

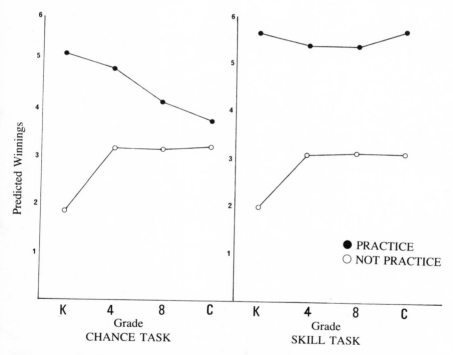

Figure 4. Predicted winnings of a practiced person versus an unpracticed person at the chance and skill tasks of Study 3.

Source: "Perceived contingency of skill and chance events: A developmental analysis." John C. Weisz, Keith Owen Yeates, Dan Robertson, and Jean C. Beckman. *Developmental Psychology,* copyright © 1982, vol. *18,* (6), 898–905. Reprinted with permission.

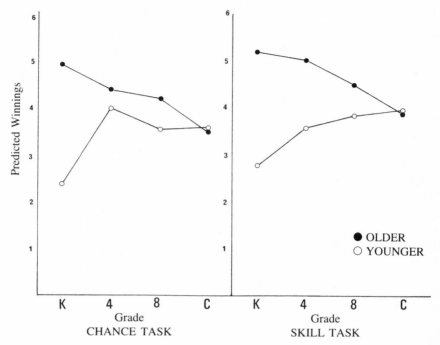

Figure 5. Predicted winnings of an older versus a younger person at the chance and skill tasks of Study 3.

Source: "Perceived contingency of skill and chance events: A developmental analysis." John C. Weisz, Keith Owen Yeates, Dan Robertson, and Jean C. Beckman. *Developmental Psychology,* copyright © 1982, vol. *18*, (6), 898–905. Reprinted with permission.

questions. Something strange is going on here. There is a complete convergence of the older-younger prediction lines for both the chance and the skill conditions. Fortunately, we had begun this experiment with a real sense of curiosity about how our subjects would perceive the distinction(s) between the contrived chance and skill tasks. With this in mind, we had included in our procedure a series of questions about why our subjects made the particular predictions they had made. What the eighth grade and college level subjects often told us about the age difference questions was that the age difference was too small to have much impact on the task outcome. And of course they were right. Even in the skill condition, the difference between a seventh and ninth grader is insignificant compared to the difference in intellectual capacity, memory, etc., between a preschooler and a first grader. In a perverse way, I find these data encouraging. They suggest that the subjects in our study were attending to the questions we asked, and thinking carefully about their answers.

In general, the prediction data shown in the preceding figures seem to reflect a mostly monotonic developmental increase in the ability to distinguish between contingent and noncontingent events. Two other lines of evidence supported this conclusion. One came from some open-ended questions we asked subjects after each task: (1) Why they think they won 4 chips out of 6 tries; (2) Why it is that in this game sometimes you get the right color and other times you get the wrong color; (3) Why they think another student who played this game once got the right color every time, and (4) Why they think another student who played once got the wrong color every time. We coded answers to all these questions as reflecting perceived contingency or noncontingency, or as not codable. Using only the codable responses, we then classified each subject's skill-chance pattern as logical (i.e., skill task contingent, chance task noncontingent) or illogical (the other three possible patterns). Table 3 shows the results. In general, all four questions showed the expected developmental trends but the age group difference was only statistically significant for questions 3 and 4; the questions about subjects' *own* outcomes did not yield significant age effects. If we combine percentages across all four questions, though, the percentage of correctly patterned judgments overall shows a pretty steady developmental increase; from kindergarten on, the mean percentages of correct pattern were 29%, 67%, 72%, and 81%.

A second line of supporting data came from some post-task comparison questions. After both chance and skill tasks had been completed, materials for the two tasks were placed side-by-side and subjects were asked to point to the one that, (a) is just a matter of luck, (b) you would get better at as you get older, (c) it helps to be smart on, (d) is just guessing, (e) it helps to remember well on, (f) it helps to try hard on, and (g) it helps to practice on. Accuracy scores on this set of questions could range from 0 to 7. Means showed a highly significant increase

Table 3. Percentage of Children Making Logical Patterns of Contingency Judgments on Unstructured Questions

Question	Group			
	Kindergarten	*4th Grade*	*8th Grade*	*College*
1. Why Subject Won 4 of 6	33	67	69	79
2. Why Subject Guessed Some Right and Some Wrong	50	82	69	73
3. Why Another Person Won No Chips	22	62	79	87
4. Why Another Person Won All 6 Chips	10	57	73	86

Note: Grade level differences were significant for question 3 and 4 (both $ps < .01$) but nonsignificant for questions 1 and 2 (both $ps > .05$).

across the four age groups. Kindergarteners averaged 3.3 (roughly the chance expectancy); means for the fourth, eighth, and college groups were 5.4, 6.8 and 7.0, respectively. So, the ability to make virtually perfect comparative judgments was apparently in place by the eighth grade.

Overview of Key Findings

In this third study we sought a broadened understanding of the development of contingency judgment. By comparing people's reasoning about chance and skill outcomes we were able to test for the existence of developmental differences in predictive style independently of differences in perceived contingency *per se*. The evidence suggests that both kinds of differences exist. As age level increased, predictive style grew more conservative; that is, older subjects expected such contingency factors as age, intelligence, effort and practice to have more modest effects than did younger subjects, for both chance and skill tasks. However, this developmental decline in the predicted effects of various contingency factors was markedly sharper for chance than for skill outcomes. The findings showed that younger subjects did not distinguish skill from chance outcomes in their predictions, but that older subjects did. So, with increasing age there was a general reduction in the perceived effects of contingency factors on both skill and chance tasks and a general sharpening of the distinction between chance and skill tasks. These results are consistent with the data from the seven questions in which skill and chance outcomes were directly compared. Both lines of evidence strongly suggest that, over and above age differences in predictive style, there are reliable age increases in the ability to recognize noncontingency.

Self-Serving Judgments

One other aspect of our findings in two of the studies should be mentioned here. As many careful lay observers and many researchers have noted, judgments about the causes of events are often made in ways that seem quite self-serving (see Bradley, 1978; Wortman, Costanzo, & Witt, 1973). One example of self-enhancing contingency judgments has been provided by Charles Schulz; it is shown in Figure 6. Other examples appeared in the data of Studies 1 and 2.

In Study 1, kindergarteners showed a pattern that might be seen as rather self-serving. When asked to predict the winnings of a child who had practiced the task and another child who had not, kindergarteners who had themselves won 4 out of 5 possible chips predicted very small (and nonsignificant) effects of practice. By contrast, kindergarteners who had themselves won only 1 out of 5 chips predicted large practice effects; they predicted that a child with practice would win an average of 3½ more chips (out of 5!) than would a child who had no practice. None of the children making the predictions had had practice at the card task before trying to win chips. For those kindergarteners with low win-

Figure 6.   Self–serving bias in attributions of noncontingency–Charlie Brown-style.

© 1952 United Feature Syndicate, Inc., reprinted with permission.

nings, one might imagine that it would be comforting to believe that lack of practice is a major handicap. In Study 2, the evidence of self-serving judgments cut across age levels. Children who had won the prize they wanted at the state fair game believed that outcomes were highly contingent on effort. They predicted that a player who tried hard would win an average of 2½ more chips (out of 5) than would a player who did not try hard. However, children who had not won the prize they wanted predicted a nonsignificant mean difference of only .77 between a player who tried hard and one who did not. Once again, one can imagine that it is gratifying to believe that effort makes a big difference *if* one has won at the game; but if one has lost, such a belief could add insult to injury.

I want to stress the limited nature of this evidence. Most of the measures in Studies 1 and 2 did *not* reveal patterns indicative of self-serving bias and in Study 1, the only measure that did show a pattern showed it only among kindergarteners. (The reader may also note that there was no self-serving bias evidence in Study 3; but recall that all subjects in that study received exactly the same outcome.) Despite its limited nature, this evidence may be showing us glimpses of the kinds of self-enhancing judgments that have long been studied among adults (see Bradley, 1978; Wortman, Costanzo, & Witt, 1973). If so, it suggests that self-protective uses of ostensibly cognitive judgments may begin considerably earlier than many of us would have thought. It also may help to reveal early modes of both self-esteem enhancement and denigration of innocent victims, two processes which often go hand-in-hand among adults. For example, to believe that effort makes a big difference in the outcome of a purely chance activity may also imply the belief that (a) I must have tried hard, and thus deserve the "achievement" that I chalked up, and (b) the individual who lost must have not tried as hard, and thus must deserve her fate. These notions are quite speculative, of course, but they deserve attention in future research.

THE DEVELOPMENTAL FINDINGS AND SOME RUMINATIONS ON THEIR MEANING

Overall, the three studies present a fairly consistent picture of developmental differences in reasoning about contingency. If we can make certain assumptions about correspondences between age levels and Piagetian stage levels, we can summarize the results in Piagetian terms. Pre-operational children (presumably most of our kindergarteners in the first and third studies) showed little evidence of an ability to distinguish contingent (skill) from noncontingent (chance) outcomes in any way. Concrete operational children (presumably most of our elementary age youngsters) were able to distinguish the two types of outcomes on at least some of the comparison questions; they also recognized that their own outcomes and those of others resulted from such noncontingent forces as "luck." In short, they seemed to recognize some gross qualitative differences between contingent and noncontingent outcomes. Yet, when asked to predict outcomes on the chance tasks, concrete operational youngsters failed to fully appreciate the quantitative implications of noncontingency, i.e., they illogically expected variations in contingency factors (e.g., intelligence, effort) to influence the noncontingent outcomes. It was only at formal operations (presumably many of our eighth grade and college students in Study 3) that we began to see substantial numbers of people correctly identifying the noncontingency of chance outcomes, correctly distinguishing contingent from noncontingent tasks on all post-task comparison questions and correctly predicting no effects of contingency factors on noncontingent outcomes.

Because cognitive developmental levels were not assessed independently in the three studies just discussed, the relation between our findings and Piagetian stages cannot be firmly established. Nonetheless, it is fair to ask how our findings seem to mesh with the views of Piaget and Inhelder (1975) on the development of chance concepts within the physical domain. Piaget and Inhelder described the preoperational child as unable to distinguish between chance and nonchance; our findings strongly agree with this view. They described the concrete operational child as distinguishing between the two domains, but as often failing to apply the distinction perfectly when predicting chance events; our findings support this view. Finally, Piaget and Inhelder argue that when reversibility combines with the formal operational capacity to reason in terms of combinations and proportions, a consolidated awareness of chance emerges, fostering logical predictions in the realm of chance. Our results generally support this view, at least with respect to *when* logical prediction begins to be observed. As for the dynamics underlying this development, our studies provide little evidence, pro or con, on the Piagetian view. Determining the degree to which reversibility and combinatorial reasoning are prerequisite to logical contingency judgment remains a task for future research. The support found here for Piaget and Inhelder is interesting given the fact that their views and their research actually dealt primarily with rules of probability and people's use of those rules in making probabilistic predictions of random physical events. The present research, by contrast, was focused specifically on people's awareness of the fact that chance events are totally noncontingent, not on people's capacities to reason probabilistically. Yet, the present findings appear to be consistent, at least in broad strokes, with the Genevan view of development.

I should stress, though, that even our oldest subjects showed a notable departure from the kind of ideal information processing one normally associates with Piagetian formal operations. More than 45% of both eighth graders and college students in Study 3 illogically predicted that at least one of the contingency factors would influence outcomes on a chance task. The persistence of such illusory contingency into young adulthood is consistent with earlier findings based on quite different research methods (e.g., Langer, 1975, Wortman, 1975).

Susceptibility to illusory contingency is difficult to explain when it occurs among adults, at least if we assume that adults define noncontingent events logically as, say, events not influenced by variations in human behavior, and that they base their predictions on such a conception. In contrast to this rather traditional view of category definitions, however, consider the perspective of Rosch (e.g., Rosch & Mervis, 1975). Building on the work of Wittgenstein (1953), Rosch has argued that people assign many events and objects to categories not by definitionally listing criterial attributes, but rather by judging the similarity of these events and objects to an abstract "prototype" of the category. To explain our findings, one might argue that many adults carry in mind an abstract prototypical "contingent event" and a contrasting prototypical "noncontingent event," and that these adults base contingency judgments and predictions on the perceived similarity of a target event to the two prototypes. If the target event bears a marked similarity to the contingent event prototype, perhaps because it contains cues typical of achievement situations, then predictions will reflect a high level of perceived contingency (e.g., substantial perceived effects of an actor's level of effort). If the target event bears only a slight resemblance to the contingent event prototype, but a strong resemblance to the noncontingent event prototype, then the adult involved may classify the target event as caused by noncontingent forces yet still predict in a way that reflects a modicum of perceived contingency (e.g., predicting that an actor's level of effort would have a very slight effect on outcomes). Even a few inadvertent achievement cues might be enough to trigger this latter process, and such cues are virtually always present in chance activities (see Langer, 1977). In our studies, for example, the very fact of being given information on effort, ability, etc., and then being asked to predict, may have suggested that such information was relevant to task outcomes; this, in turn, according to the model just presented, could have caused the chance task to resemble, however faintly, a contingent event prototype that some of our adults relied on when making predictions (for related lines of reasoning see Kahneman & Tversky, 1973, on the ''representativeness heuristic'' and the ''availability heuristic'').

The virtually complete lack of competence shown by our youngest subjects has an important characteristic that invites interpretation: their errors were not random. Instead, their responses point to a strikingly consistent belief that the chance outcomes they had experienced were contingent. These data together with the more anecdotal reports of Piaget (e.g., 1930, 1932), suggest that such a belief may be quite pervasive in early childhood and that it succumbs only slowly and haltingly to the onslaught of logical operations. Why would young children err so consistently in the direction of perceived contingency? One might argue that these errors are stimulated by a powerful motive to exert control over events (White, 1959), and the concomitant aversiveness of a perception that events are uncontrollable (see Langer, 1977). Yet this explanation alone seems ill-equipped to account for the consistency and pervasiveness of the young child's errors. As strong as children's motivation to control events may be, it is probably less powerful than, say, their motivation to eat when they are hungry. Yet, significant levels of hunger do not cause the child to regard most objects as edible. It seems unlikely, then, that the motive to exert control could alone provoke the belief that most events are inherently controllable (i.e., contingent).

It is conceivable that illusory contingency in young children may be a largely cognitive phenomenon and that it may have evolved through a process of natural selection. To picture this evolutionary process, let us assume a population of infants and young children whose cognitive limitations prevent them from accurately distinguishing between contingent and noncontingent events. All of them make frequent errors in contingency judgment. The direction of the errors each individual makes will have significant adaptive consequences. Let us imagine three subgroups who show quite different response tendencies. One subgroup tends to err randomly; its members alter their behavior in response to outcomes only in those cases where events are perceived as contingent. A second subgroup errs most often in the direction of perceived noncontingency, and consequently shows a persistent under-responsiveness to environmental contingencies. A third subgroup errs most often in the direction of perceived contingency, and consequently shows a hyper-responsiveness to environmental events. Members of the third group, despite their intellectual limitations would seem to have a greater likelihood of surviving and eventually contributing to the gene pool of their species than would members of the other two groups. Members of the third group would profit more often than the other groups from situations where contingency does prevail. In those situations they would be more likely than members of the other two groups to repeat behaviors that are followed by satisfying events and to terminate behaviors that are followed by aversive events. They would also surpass the others in exercise of basic motor skills during the years when parents could protect them from the more adverse consequences of their faulty reasoning. Of course, even the hyper-responsive group would have limited adaptive possibilities if they never developed a capacity to distinguish between contingent and noncontingent events. Their tendency to be excessively responsive to environmental events would certainly lead to wasted effort, fatigue, disappointment, and a failure to assimilate critical information about the world. Fortunately for our species, the evidence thus far shows that a capacity to make the contingent-noncontingent distinction begins to emerge by about the sixth or seventh year of life and becomes reasonably polished in adolescence.

Forces of natural selection, then, may help to explain an early bias in the direction of illusory contingency. The bias may linger because certain key cognitive developments cannot be rushed (see Piaget & Inhelder, 1975), because even mature contingency concepts are prototypic rather than definitional (see Rosch & Mervis, 1975), and/or because at least some achievement cues are associated with most noncontingent events (Langer, 1975; 1977). I would suggest, in addition, that normal socialization within western cultures may contribute to prolonged illusory contingency. Such an innocuous tradition as the tooth fairy myth, for example, involves the assumption that good behavior and virtuous suffering will be followed reliably by contingent rewards. And need we even mention Santa Claus, that jolly agent of contingency, who makes a list (and checks it twice!) of each child's naughty and nice behavior so that appropriate degrees of reward can be provided at the appropriate time.

Much of Western religious training also carries a forceful contingency message. Consider the Biblical assertion, "No one makes a fool of God. A person will reap exactly what he plants" (Galatians 6:7, *Good News Bible*). It seems that many of our Western customs and myths, like the aphorisms quoted at the beginning of this chapter, may reflect *and promote* a commitment to strong beliefs in the pervasiveness of contingency. While these beliefs may foster a certain optimism about the "fairness" of the world, they also appear to have some negative effects. Some of these lie in the achievement domain, as the following discussion will indicate.

ACHIEVEMENT BEHAVIOR, CONTINGENCY JUDGMENTS, AND PERCEIVED CONTROL

Findings like those presented here should enhance our understanding of the development of achievement behavior. As I suggested at the outset, the intensity and persistence of achievement activity may depend in part on the degree to which people perceive target outcomes as contingent. Taking a somewhat broader perspective, though, achievement behavior certainly depends to a great extent on the degree to which people expect that they will be able to exercise control. Deborah Stipek and I (Weisz & Stipek, 1982) have dealt with this issue in some detail. We have proposed that for an individual to control a class of outcomes, two conditions must exist: (1) the outcomes must be contingent on variations in people's behavior—a noncontingent outcome is of course inherently uncontrollable, and (2) the individual must be competent to produce the behavior on which the desired outcomes are contingent. Following this reasoning, I would suggest that to make an accurate judgment about the degree to which one can exercise control in a given situation, one needs to answer the following two questions accurately: (1) To what degree are outcomes in this situation contingent upon variations in people's behavior? (2) How competent am I to produce the specific behavior on which the desired outcomes are contingent?

Table 4 presents this model, simplified to include only two levels of perceived contingency and two levels of perceived competence. Faulty reasoning about control—and concomitant poor judgments about how to allocate one's achievement-related energy—may derive from inaccurate answers to either of the two key questions. The research described above strongly suggests that young children will often wrongly answer question number 1 affirmatively; moreover, the evidence from this research and other studies (e.g., Langer, 1975) suggests that even adults will sometimes do the same. Still other research (e.g., Nicholls, 1978, Stipek chapter in this volume) indicates that young children often are not very good at answering question 2 accurately. All this research, considered in the light of the model shown in Table 4, indicates that young children's cognitive limitations may make it particularly difficult for them to orient their achievement behavior to activities in an optimal way. The research and the model may help us to understand some aspects of developmental change that foster improved "targeting" of our achievement behavior.

The model and the research evidence may also help us to diagnose achievement deficits with greater precision than in the past. It seems likely that many such deficits could result either from low levels of perceived contingency or low levels of perceived competence. The deficits may look the same in both cases, but the underlying dynamics would be different in significant ways. Consider a child who responds to negative evaluative feedback from her teacher by reducing her perseverance and the quality of her work. Analysis at the relatively global level of "perceived control" may tell us that she perceives herself as lacking

Table 4. Levels of Perceived Control as a Function of Levels of Perceived
Contingency and Competence

		Perceived Competence	
		Low	*High*
Perceived Contingency	Low	Control = Low	Control = Moderate
	High	Control = Moderate	Control = High

Note: For clarity of presentation, the table deals with only two levels of perceived contingency and competence; certainly it is likely that most people construe the two dimensions as continua.

control over these achievement outcomes, but this information is too imprecise to generate either a clear understanding of her failure to persevere or a properly focused intervention. It may be that this girl believes that achievement feedback in her class is contingent on the children's actual school work and that her failures reflect a lack of competence on her part. Or she may be confident of her competence in school work, but convinced that her failure experiences are non-contingently administered by an unfair teacher. Although these different cognitive underpinnings might lead to the same manifest achievement behavior (lack of perseverance), they would have quite different implications in other respects.

Similar points have been suggested by Heider (1958), Weiner, Frieze, Kukla, Reed, Rest, and Rosenbaum (1971), and recently by Bandura (1977). For example, in elaborating his "self-efficacy theory," Bandura discusses the origins of "futility" in a way that seems to involve perceived contingency and competence, although his terminology is somewhat different:

> People can give up trying because they lack a sense of efficacy in achieving the required behavior, or they may be assured of their capabilities but give up trying because they expect their behavior to have no effect on an unresponsive environment or to be consistently punished. These two separable expectancy sources of futility have quite different antecedents and remedial implications. To alter efficacy-based futility requires development of competencies and expectations of personal effectiveness. By contrast, to change outcome-based futility necessitates changes in prevailing environmental contingencies that restore the instrumental value of the competencies that people already possess (Bandura, 1977, pp. 204–205).

A related analysis is Abramson, Seligman, and Teasdale's (1978) reformulated learned helplessness model; it distinguishes between two forms of helplessness. People experience *personal helplessness* when they perceive that some relevant persons in their situation would be able to avoid a particular aversive outcome (e.g., failure in a school subject), but that they themselves cannot avoid it. Personal helplessness is associated with achievement deficits, depressed affect, and loss of self-esteem. in *universal helplessness,* individuals perceive that neither they nor any relevant others are able to avoid the aversive outcome. Universal helplessness is associated with depressed affect and achievement deficits, but not with a loss of self-esteem. As Table 5 suggests, the reformulated helplessness model may be construed in terms of perceived contingency and perceived competence. People who believe that their failures result from noncontingency (i.e., inherent uncontrollability) of the outcome will suffer from universal helplessness. People who perceive their failures as resulting from their own incompetence with respect to a contingent outcome will suffer from personal helplessness.

How does this analysis relate to the findings presented here, and in turn to the problem of achievement deficits? The findings suggest that young children have difficulty recognizing noncontingency when they see it. If these findings can be extrapolated to the school setting, they suggest that young children will not be likely to identify classroom achievement outcomes as noncontingent. In fact, there is evidence that elementary school children fail to identify adult bias and unfairness as the cause of inequitably administered rewards, even when they are placed in experimental situations designed to make such bias very salient (Gray-Little & Teddlie, 1978; Gray-Little, 1980). Children in these studies seemed convinced that low and blatantly unfair levels of reward assigned to them were somehow the just consequences of their own performance levels. If young children do have difficulty identifying noncontingency as a cause of adverse outcomes, then the preceding analysis would suggest that they are not likely to experience universal helplessness. By contrast, our data would suggest adolescents and adults are probably relatively good candidates for universal helplessness. How do young children react to a series of adverse outcomes, if not with universal helplessness? Perhaps with personal helplessness. There is some anecdotal evidence that supports this notion with respect to such adverse outcomes as parents' divorce or the death of loved ones (see, e.g., Gardner, 1976, 1977; Lifton, 1967)—outcomes for which children sometimes illogically blame themselves.

In the area of achievement, though, young children seem remarkably resilient in the face of failure (e.g., Rholes, Blackwell, Jordan & Walters, 1980), and it is clear to me that they are not prone to indict their competence at *anything!* But on this issue I will defer to others in this volume who are actively studying the development of perceived competence (Harter, Nicholls, Stipek, etc.). I will simply suggest here that in the presumed absence of universal helplessness, young children may show an increased susceptibility to personal helplessness, or they may simply show limited susceptibility to learned helplessness generally. This is an area in which new evidence could make an important contribution, both theoretically and practically.

New evidence would also be useful with respect to the impact of noncontingent positive outcomes. The findings of Gray-Little (1980) and Gray-Little and Teddlie (1978) do indicate that young children who benefit from noncon-

Table 5. Relation of Perceived Contingency and Competence to Learned Helplessness Theory

Control Orientation	*Responses to Failure*			
	Cognitive/Interpretive	*Achievement Behavior*	*Self-esteem*	*LH Label*
Contingent Outcome, Competent Self	My failures result from insufficient effort. The controlling response is in my repertoire.	Perseverance, increased performance intensity	Minimal loss	Mastery orientation (Diener & Dweck, 1978)
Contingent Outcome, Incompetent Self	My failures result from insufficient competence. There is a controlling response that relevant others can produce, but I cannot.	Deficits in perseverance, declining performance intensity	Significant loss	Personal helplessness (Abramson et al., 1978)
Noncontingent Outcome, Personal Competence Not At Issue	My failures result from the inherent uncontrollability of the outcome. There is no controlling response that I or relevant others could produce.	Deficits in perseverance, declining performance intensity	No loss	Universal helplessness (Abramson et al., 1978)

tingently-administered rewards are prone to attribute such rewards to their own behavior, even when the evidence flatly contradicts such an attribution. This pattern might be interpreted as linked to a general tendency on the part of young children and even infrahuman species to fall prey to "superstition," as described by Skinner (1948). Skinner found that when grain was noncontingently dropped at regular intervals near hungry pigeons, the pigeons soon "learned" to emit idiosyncratic, superstitious behaviors, as if they were controlling the appearance of the grain by means of those behaviors. One pigeon, for example, hopped up and down in the middle of the cage until grain appeared. Skinner maintained that the hunger reduction afforded by the grain reinforced whatever behavior each pigeon happened to be engaged in when the grain appeared; as a result, he argued, the frequency of that behavior increased, making it more likely that the behavior would be present the next time grain was dispensed. This process, Skinner argued, led pigeons to perceive a nonexistent contingency between positive events (the appearance of grain) and their own behavior. An obvious result was that the pigeons engaged in a good deal of misdirected, essentially wasted activity.

It might be argued that young children's inclination to perceive noncontingent events as contingent on their behavior exposes them to a risk something like that faced by Skinner's pigeons. When noncontingent positive events are perceived as dependent upon one's behavior, one result in children as in pigeons, can be gratuitous behavior aimed at producing those positive events. Apparent examples of this process can be found in a collection of adults' childhood memories assembled by Piaget (1960). One of the adults quoted by Piaget recalled:

> When I particularly wanted something I often used to step on every other stone as I walked on the pavement. . . . Or I would touch the stones of a wall, tapping every third stone and if I thus succeeded in reaching the last stone of the wall, I was certain of my success" (p. 138).

Another adult recollected that as a little girl of six she used to pass by a lake where water lilies grew. Every time she passed, she threw some round, white stones in the water, believing that lilies would grow where the stones fell. She pointedly threw stones near the edge so that lilies would grow where she could reach them. Examples like these are apt to stir childhood memories in many of us—memories of our own ill-fated attempts to produce or reproduce desirable events that were essentially noncontingent. There memories suggest the possibility that even in the realm of positive, desirable events the child's tendency to perceive contingency where it does not exist may stimulate misdirected behavior and eventual disappointment.

CONCLUDING COMMENT

This chapter has been built on the assumption that effective achievement behavior requires selectivity; that each of us needs the capacity to distinguish clearly between outcomes that are amenable to human influence and outcomes that are not. This capacity evidently requires cognitive abilities that develop slowly throughout childhood, are consolidated in adolescence, but are not consistently utilized even in adulthood. Erroneous judgments about the contingency or influenceability of outcomes often mean misplaced achievement energy. The kinds of research discussed in this chapter may ultimately help us to understand one cause of such misplaced energy and one ontogenetic process that underlies the development of achievement motivation.

ACKNOWLEDGMENTS

The research reported here was supported by grants from the National Institute of Mental Health (# R03 MH34652–01) and from the University Research Council, University of North Carolina. I want to thank Jeannie Beckham, Susan Caldwell, Mary Gratch, Sharon Hollandsworth, Lisa Ney, and Gregory Ray for their help in gathering and analyzing the data for these studies.

REFERENCES

Abramson, L. Y., Seligman, M. E. P., & Teasdale, J. D. Learned helplessness in humans: Critique and reformulation. *Journal of Abnormal Psychology,* 1978, *87,* 49–74.

Bandura, A. Self-efficacy: Toward a unifying theory of behavioral change. *Psychological Review,* 1977, *84,* 191–215.

Bradley, G. W. Self-serving biases in the attribution process: A re–examination of the fact or fiction question. *Journal of Personality and Social Psychology,* 1978, *36,* 56–71.

Diener, C. I., & Dweck, C. S. An analysis of learned helplessness: Continuous changes in performance, strategy, and achievement cognitions following failure. *Journal of Personality and Social Psychology,* 1978, *36,* 451–462.

Gardner, R. A. *Psychotherapy with the children of divorce.* Garden City, N.Y.: Doubleday, 1977.

Gardner, R. A. *The parents' book about divorce.* Garden City, N.Y.: Doubleday, 1977.

Gray-Little, B. Race and inequity. *Journal of Applied Social Psychology,* 1980, *10,* 468–481.

Gray-Little, B., & Teddlie, C. B. Victims and innocent beneficiaries. *Journal of Applied Social Psychology,* 1978, *13,* 107–116.

Heider, F. *The psychology of interpersonal relations.* New York: Wiley, 1958.

Huang, I. Children's conception of physical causality: A critical summary. *Journal of Genetic Psychology,* 1943, *63,* 71–121.

Kagan, J. Impulsive and reflective children: The significance of conceptual tempo. In J. D. Krumholtz (Ed.), *Learning and the educational process.* Chicago: Rand McNally, 1965.

Kahneman, D., & Tversky, A. On the psychology of prediction. *Psychological Review,* 1973, *80,* 237–252.

Karniol, R. A conceptual analysis of immanent justice responses in children. *Child Development,* 1980, *51,* 118–130.

Langer, E. J. The illusion of control. *Journal of Personality and Social Psychology,* 1975, *32,* 311–328.

Langer, E. J. The psychology of chance. *Journal for the Theory of Social Behavior,* 1977, *7,* 185–207.

Lerner, M. The justice motive: Some hypotheses as to its origins and forms. *Journal of Personality,* 1977, *45,* 1–52.

Lifton, R. J. *Death in life: Survivors of Hiroshima.* New York: Random House, 1967.

Nicholls, J. G. The development of the concepts of effort and ability, perception of academic attainment, and the understanding that difficult tasks require more ability. *Child Development*, 1978, *49*, 800–814.

Piaget, J. *The child's conception of physical causality*. London: Routledge & Kegan Paul, 1930.

Piaget, J. *The moral judgment of the child*. New York: Harcourt, Brace, 1932.

Piaget, J. *The child's conception of the world*. Totowa, N J: Littlefield, Adams, 1960.

Piaget, J. *The origins of intelligence in children*. New York: Norton, 1963.

Piaget, J., & Inhelder, B. *The origin of the idea of chance in children*. New York: Norton, 1975.

Rholes, W. S., Blackwell, J., Jordan, C., & Walters, C. A developmental study of learned helplessness. *Developmental Psychology*, 1980, *16*, 616–624.

Rosch, E., & Mervis, C. B. Family resemblances: Studies in the internal structure of categories. *Cognitive Psychology*, 1975, *7*, 573–605.

Sedlack, A. J., & Kurtz, S. T. Review of children's use of causal inference principles. *Child Development*, 1981, *52*, 750–784.

Seligman, M. E. P. *Helplessness: On depression, development, and death*. San Francisco: Freeman, 1975.

Skinner, B. F. "Superstition" in the pigeon. *Journal of Experimental Psychology*, 1948, *38*, 168–172.

Weiner, B. A theory of motivation for some classroom experiences. *Journal of Educational Psychology*, 1979, *71*, 3–25.

Weiner, B., Frieze, I., Kukla, A., Reed, L., Rest, S., & Rosenbaum, R. M. *Perceiving the causes of success and failure*. Morristown, N J: General Learning Press, 1971.

Weisz, J. R. Transcontextual validity in developmental research. *Child Development*, 1978, *49*, 1–12.

Weisz, J. R. Developmental change in perceived control: Recognizing noncontingency in the laboratory and perceiving it in the world. *Developmental Psychology*, 1980, *16*, 385–390.

Weisz, J. R. Illusory contingency in children at the state fair. *Developmental Psychology*, 1981, *17*, 481–489.

Weisz, J. R. & Stipek, D. J. Competence, contingency, and the development of perceived control. *Human Development*, 1982, *25*, 250–281.

Weisz, J. R., Yeates, K. O., Robertson, D., & Beckham, J. C. Perceived contingency of skill and chance events: A developmental analysis. *Developmental Psychology*, 1982, *18*, 898–905.

White, R. Motivation reconsidered: The concept of competence. *Psychological Review*, 1959, *66*, 297–323.

Wittgenstein, L. *Philosophical investigations*. New York: MacMillan, 1953.

Wortman, C. B. Some determinants of perceived control. *Journal of Personality and Social Psychology*, 1975, *31*, 282–294.

Wortman, C. B., Costanzo, P. R., & Witt, T. R. Effects of anticipated performance on the attributions of causality of self and others. *Journal of Personality and Social Psychology*, 1973, *27*, 373–381.

THE DEVELOPMENT OF ACHIEVEMENT-RELATED JUDGMENT PROCESSES

Colleen F. Surber

This paper focuses on developmental changes in judgments of a number of achievement-related variables, and the possibility of representing the developmental changes in terms of mathematical models of judgment. It is hoped that the reader who is only minimally familiar with mathematical models of judgment will find the present chapter to be a useful introduction to some of the important issues in applying these models to the analysis of developmental change. The principal types of judgments considered are predictions of performance, inferences of ability, and inferences of effort. These three types of judgments have been chosen partly because there is a reasonable quantity of quality experimental literature on the development of these three types of judgments. A second reason for focusing on ability, effort and performance is that these three variables form a natural set that allows a test of the general hypothesis that causal inferences

Advances in Motivation and Achievement, vol. 3, pages 137–184
Copyright © 1984 by JAI Press Inc.
All rights of reproduction in any form reserved.
ISBN 0-89232-289-6

follow from one's assumptions about how a set of causes combine to predict some event. That is, this subset of literature allows us to address the question of how "causal schemata" for achievement concepts develop, and whether such schemata are reversible.

THE GENERAL CONCEPT OF A CAUSAL SCHEMA

The term "causal schema" is used with a number of different nuances by different authors (Kelley, 1972, 1973; Reeder & Brewer, 1979; Tversky & Kahneman, 1980). Kelley (1973) characterizes a causal schema as "an assumed pattern of data in a complete analysis of variance framework" (p. 115). According to Kelley, a causal schema can be used either to predict an event or to infer the causes of an event. That is, schemata are reversible mental structures for making both predictions and attributions. The use of the term causal schema in this chapter will be closest to Kelley's use. One goal of research on achievement judgments is to identify the nature of the assumptions or schemata used in making such judgments, and to examine developmental changes in the schemata.

One obvious way to examine a person's assumptions or schema for achievement is to present information about variables, such as ability, effort, task difficulty, past performance, etc., and to solicit a prediction of performance for each stimulus combination. The pattern of judgments of performance could be assumed to reflect the subject's schema or assumptions about how the manipulated variables influence task performance. Similar experiments can be conducted to examine the schema for other achievement concepts. Many researchers implicitly accept this view that the pattern of judgments directly reflects the subject's assumptions. An alternative is a view based on modern theoretical approaches to human judgment (Anderson, 1970; Birnbaum, 1982; Krantz, Luce, Suppes, & Tversky, 1971) that propose that the pattern of judgments reflects the composition of several separate processes. In order to understand how to use modern approaches to human judgment to explore causal schemata, we turn to some technical issues in human judgment.

An Approach to Human Judgment

Figure 1 presents an outline of the steps in the judgment process (Anderson, 1979; Birnbaum, 1982; Birnbaum, Parducci, & Gifford, 1971). On the far left of the diagram are the objective stimuli that are presented to the subject. These stimuli are evaluated subjectively and given some implicit values, termed s_i, or scale values. The function relating the objective stimuli to their subjective values is denoted by H and is analogous to the psychophysical function in perception since it relates physical stimuli to psychological values. The subjective values of the stimuli are combined according to some set of assumptions to form an integrated impression, denoted ψ_{ij}. The assumptions or rule for combining the subjective values is called the integration rule and is represented by the symbol I in Figure 1. The final step in the judgment process is to translate the impression, ψ_{ij}, into a response, R_{ij}, on the judgment scale. This final transformation is called the judgment function[1] by Birnbaum et al. (1971) or the "psychomotor" law by Anderson (1980), and is denoted by J in the figure. The function J is assumed to be a strictly monotonic function of the values of ψ_{ij}. This means that the final responses preserve the rank order relations in the subject's integrated impressions of the stimuli. The observable response, R_{ij}, is thus regarded as the result of the composition of the functions H, I, and J.

Researchers who are interested in exploring developmental changes in schemata for achievement judgments are most likely to be interested in making inferences about the integration function, I, in Figure 1, since it represents the way the subject combines the information. To this author, Kelley's concept of a causal schema as a set of assumptions about how causes combine to produce an effect is best represented by the integration function, I (see Surber, 1981b for a more complete discussion of other interpretations of the notion of a causal schema in terms of Figure 1). It should be apparent from Figure 1 that a difference in the pattern of final responses can be due to developmental differences in the way information is evaluated (the psychophysical function), the way

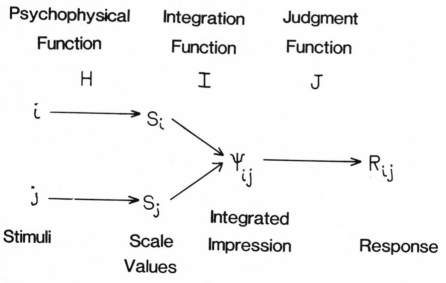

Figure 1.   Outline of judgment (after Birnbaum, 1974a). Subscripts *i* and *j* at left represent the stimuli that are presented, S_i and S_j represent the subjective values of the stimuli, ψ_{ij} represents the integrated impression based on the stimuli, and R_{ij} represents the subject's response on the rating scale.

information is combined (the integration function) or response production processes (the judgment function). Thus, separating these explanations is an important task for research on children's judgments.

This point can be best understood by means of a concrete example. Imagine an experiment in which children from three age groups are asked to predict the performance of imaginary individuals given the ability and effort of each individual. A completely hypothetical set of results is presented in Figure 2. As can be seen, the pattern of responses varies with age. The left-hand panel shows an ability by effort interaction in which the curves converge as the values of ability and effort increase, the middle panel shows an additive or statistically parallel pattern of results, and the right-hand panel shows an ability by effort interaction in which the curves diverge as the values of ability and effort increase.

If taken at face value, the results in Figure 2 would seem to provide evidence of between group differences in the causal schema for performance. The reader will be surprised to find that all three panels were generated from the same additive integration function and the same scale values. The results of the additive integration function were then transformed by applying one of two different functions: either a logarithmic or an exponential function. The dashed lines connecting the panels indicate the transformations. These transformations could represent the judgment function, J, in Figure 1.

The reader may be concerned about the likelihood of such drastically different judgment functions existing. Research with both social and nonsocial stimuli has shown that manipulation of the stimulus distribution can change the pattern of responses from a converging interaction such as shown in the left-hand panel of Figure 2, to a diverging interaction such as is shown in the right-hand panel (Birnbaum et al., 1971; Mellers & Birnbaum, 1982, 1983). Birnbaum and his

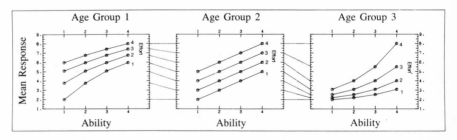

Figure 2. Hypothetical results illustrating that differences in response patterns do not necessarily imply differences in information integration. The three panels represent predictions of performance based on an additive integration function (Performance = Effort + Ability), subjected to a log transformation (left hand panel), no transformation (middle panel), and an exponential transformation (right hand panel). The rank orders of the data are identical in all three panels. Lines connecting the panels show the transformations.

colleagues concluded that the shifts in the interaction patterns caused by changes in the stimulus distribution could best be accounted for by postulating that the judgment function changes rather than that the integration function changes. Thus, such shifts in the shape of the judgment function should be a real concern to researchers using judgment methods to draw conclusions about the schema used to make various types of judgments.

An important issue raised by the distinction between I and J in Figure 1 is how any conclusions at all can be drawn about the form of the integration rule, I, if the observed response also reflects the effects of J, the judgment function. In fact, there is a long history in the field of psychophysics of controversy over whether stimulus comparisons are made by taking subjective ratios or subjective differences (Birnbaum, 1979, 1980; Marks, 1974; Rule & Curtis, 1980; Stevens & Galanter, 1957; Torgerson, 1961). A full consideration of this controversy and the approaches to resolving it is beyond the scope of this paper, and the reader is referred to Birnbaum (1982). In the present context, there are two approaches to constraining the possible forms of the integration rule, I, that could account for an observed set of responses. The first approach is to examine the rank orders of the responses and eliminate those integration rules that are not capable of reproducing the observed rank ordering of the responses. This is made possible by the assumption that the judgment function preserves the rank orders of the impressions, ψ_{ij}. A second approach is to embed the integration process in which the investigator is interested in a judgment task that requires only assumptions about the rank order properties of the responses. Birnbaum's "scale free test" is an example of the latter approach and will be discussed further below.

What is a Reversible Causal Schema?

The idea that causal schemata are reversible is central to their use in attribution theory. For example, Kelley (1972) states that, "The schema is characterized by 'reversibility' in that it permits going in various opposite implicational directions. . . The set of possible implications has the properties of organization that Piaget specifies as characteristic of an 'operational system'" (p. 153). The notion of a reversible causal schema is thus taken partly from Piaget's concept of reversible mental operations, and the study of reversible causal schemata for achievement concepts provides researchers with an opportunity to study reversible operations in social cognition.

Given that the concept of a causal schema is identified with the integration function, what does it mean for a schema to be reversible? Assume that a given individual's impressions of performance are a multiplicative function of ability and effort. That is, assume that the integration function for performance is ability times effort. A hypothetical set of impressions of performance are given in the right-hand panel of Figure 3. Reversibility of causal reasoning implies that subjective impressions of ability should be performance divided by effort (left-

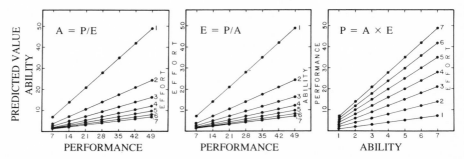

Figure 3.   Predictions of the multiplying model for impressions of ability (left
hand panel), effort (middle panel), and performance (right hand panel).

hand panel), and impressions of effort should be performance divided by ability.
That is, in order for a causal schema to be fully reversible the integration
functions should all be derivable from the same equation. Figure 3, then, represents an ideal, fully reversible causal schema.

Testing the hypothesis that a single, fully reversible schema underlies both
judgments of performance and inferences of ability and effort requires methods
of separating the integration function from the judgment function, however.
Failure to include the possibility that the judgment function can change with the
variable being judged is equivalent to requiring predictions of performance,
ability and effort to be in exact agreement. For example, imagine that predictions
of performance were plotted in a three-dimensional space with ability on the x-
axis, effort on the y-axis, and judged performance on the z-axis. Then imagine
that judged ability, given performance and effort information, were plotted in the
same three-dimensional space. The view that the judgment function cannot vary
requires that all the points should fall on the same surface in the three-dimensional space. This view of a reversible causal schema would be contradicted if the
data for the three types of judgments (performance, effort and ability) could be
best fit by separate but similarly shaped surfaces in the space. Thus, allowance
must be made for the judgment function.

Inverse Compensation as a Component of Reversibility

A causal schema could be partially reversible in the sense that the direction of
the effects of the variables is as predicted, even though the variables may not be
combined in a way that agrees exactly with a single equation. Consider again the
example of judging performance given ability and effort information. Impressions of performance are likely to be an increasing function of both ability and
effort. Impressions of ability should then be an increasing function of performance, but a decreasing function of effort. That is, the higher the given effort

value, the lower the judged value of ability should be. The decreasing effect of effort on the impressions of ability can be seen in the left hand panel of Figure 3 in that the *top* curve represents the *lowest* effort value, while the bottom curve represents the highest effort value. This negative relationship between judged ability and given effort (or vice versa) will be termed "inverse compensation" after Kun (1977). Kelley (1972, 1973) calls this same effect the discounting principle.

It is important to notice that inverse compensation is a prediction of the concept of a reversible causal schema that can be tested without concern for the form of the judgment function, J. This is so because lack of inverse compensation would drastically alter the rank orders of the responses. If two age groups differed in their use of inverse compensation, it would be necessary to attribute the differences in their data to either the integration function of the psychophysical function, rather than to the judgment function. This fact should come as a relief to developmental researchers since it allows the development of inverse compensation to be studied without concern for age shifts in the judgment function.

Overview of the Chapter

Using the approach of Figure 1, the developmental changes in judgments of achievement-related variables are examined below. The review begins by considering the issue of whether there are developmental changes in predictions of task performance. The outline in Figure 1 is employed to elucidate the possible sources of the observed developmental changes in predictions of performance (i.e., whether they are due to developmental changes in H, I, or J), and the loci of the effects of variables such as task difficulty, type of task on which performance is to be predicted, etc., that may influence the observed pattern of responses. As the reader will discover, the developmental data on predictions of performance are difficult to interpret, in part because the findings from studies with adults are complex.

Second, the review examines the implications of the literature on judgments of ability and effort for the development of reversible causal schemata. This section of the review concentrates on the development of inverse compensation in judgments of ability and effort, but also considers the issue of whether "fully" reversible causal schemata for achievement concepts exist in adults. The developmental trends in inverse compensation are also difficult to ascertain because of the complexity of the adult data. Although the findings to be reviewed are not simple, it is hoped that this chapter will not merely confuse the reader about the developmental trends in judgments of achievement-related variables, but will provide a new perspective with new hypotheses for research on developmental differences in judgments of achievement related variables.

JUDGMENTS OF TASK PERFORMANCE

This section deals with research examining how various types of information are used in making predictions of the performance of another person. The study of children's predictions of performance can be regarded as falling in the general category of the study of metacognition, and is of interest because (a) there is the possibility that fundamental developmental changes in use of causal schemata may be discovered; and (b) the development of schemata for predicting performance may be related to children's actual achievement behaviors. How an individual uses information to predict performance may have important effects on a person's actual achievement strivings, since predictions of performance are essentially expectancies, which have been shown to influence children's task persistence (Dweck & Gilliard, 1975).

Combination of Ability and Effort

Several experiments have been conducted in which children have been asked to predict another person's performance based on the person's ability and effort. One such experiment was conducted by Kun, Parsons, and Ruble (1974) with children 6, 8, and 10 years old, and with college students. Each subject was asked to imagine someone working on a set of puzzles, and each hypothetical puzzle solver was described in terms of his ability at solving puzzles (very good at puzzles, OK at puzzles, or very bad at puzzles) factorially combined with information about his effort at the puzzles (tried very hard, tried a little, didn't try at all). The subject was asked to predict the number of puzzles out of seven that would be completed by each puzzle solver. Kun et al. (1974) reasoned that if there were a developmental shift in the way children assume ability and effort combine to produce performance, then the pattern of judged performance should vary across age groups.

The results showed a significant ability by effort interaction for all age groups except the 6-year-olds, leading the authors to conclude that there is a developmental shift in the way ability and effort are combined to determine performance. On the basis of further statistical tests, Kun et al. concluded that the adults and 10-year-olds combined ability and effort multiplicatively (the data pattern resembled the right-hand panel of Figure 2). In contrast, the authors concluded that the 6-year-olds combined ability and effort in an additive fashion, while the data of the 8-year-olds, represented a transition between the additive rule used by the 6-year-olds and a multiplicative combination rule.

The multiplying combination rule for predicting performance is interesting since it is an approximation to a logical conjunctive rule (cf. Einhorn, 1970; Oden, 1977; Surber, 1981b; Wyer, 1976). That is, a multiplicative rule predicts performance to be high only when *both* ability and effort are high. This pattern of predictions is also what Kelley (1972, 1973) calls the schema for multiple necessary causes (see Surber, 1981b, for a detailed explanation). Thus, Kun et al.'s conclusion that there is a developmental shift toward use of a multiplying rule can be considered to be a conclusion that there is a developmental shift toward a belief that both ability and effort are necessary for success, or a shift toward use of the schema for multiple necessary causes. This type of developmental shift would be important since a conjunctive rule implies that there is a limit on the degree to which effort can compensate for lack of ability (and vice versa).

Response Production Explanation

The conclusions of Kun et al. (1974) about how children combine ability and effort to predict performance are based on the implicit assumption that there is no developmental shift in the way the response scale is used. That is, if it is possible that the age differences reflect changes in the judgment function, J, rather than process of combining the information (or integration function), then the conclusions of Kun et al. could be questioned. One way of ruling out the possibility that developmental changes in response production processes (the J function in Figure 1) alone account for the observed developmental differences is to examine the rank orders of the responses. If there are large differences between age groups in the rank orders of the data, then there must be differences between the age groups in either the evaluation (H in Figure 1) or combination (I in Figure 1) of the information (or possibly both).

The means from Kun et al.'s (1974) study[2] are reproduced here in Table 1 to illustrate this point. By rank ordering the means of each age group in Table 1, it is apparent that the rank orders of the four age groups are almost identical. The ranks of means of the 10-year-old and adult samples are identical. This might be expected since Kun et al. concluded that both groups combine the information in

Table 1. Mean Judged Number of Puzzles Solved and Rank Orders of the Means for Study 1 of Kun et al. (1974)

Stimulus		Age Group							
		6 years		8 years		10 years		College	
Ability	Effort	Mean	Rank	Mean	Rank	Mean	Rank	Mean	Rank
Low	Low	1.75	1	1.04	1	0.75	1	0.00	1
	Med	2.71	3	2.92	3	3.00	4	1.50	4
	High	3.29	6	3.92	6	3.79	6	3.92	6
Med	Low	2.33	2	1.38	2	1.75	2	.88	2
	Med	3.25	5	3.13	5	3.71	5	3.08	5
	High	5.38	8	5.67	8	5.17	8	5.79	8
High	Low	2.75	4	2.96	4	2.25	3	1.42	3
	Med	4.29	7	4.04	7	4.58	7	4.46	7
	High	5.88	9	6.54	9	6.71	9	6.96	9

the same way. However, the rank orders of the 6- and 8-year-olds differ from the two older age groups only in that the order of two points is reversed.

The problem, of course, is in deciding when an age difference between rank orders justifies an inference of age differences in either information valuation or information integration (H or I in Figure 1). It can be shown that the rank orders of the data of any age group presented in Table 1 can be predicted by *either* a multiplicative or additive integration rule. The slight difference in rank orders can be predicted by postulating that the integration rule for combining ability and effort is developmentally constant, but the spacing of the scale values for either ability or effort differs across ages (i.e., the valuation process, or H, is assumed to change developmentally). Thus, the rank orders of the data of Kun et al.'s Study 1 do not allow us to exclude the hypothesis of no age change in the process of combining ability and effort to predict performance. The data of Kun et al.'s Study 1 also do not rule out the possibility that effort and ability are combined in an additive (rather than a multiplicative) manner, with the interactions resulting from the judgment function. Since the multiplying and additive models cannot be distinguished by examining the rank orders of the data (Krantz & Tversky, 1971), other methods must be used.

The possibility that the judgment function might account for the ability by effort interactions has been examined empirically by Surber (1980). In this experiment, subjects from kindergarten, third grade, fifth grade and college judged the performance of hypothetical participants in a weight-lifting contest. Each hypothetical weight-lifter was described by ability (very very strong, kind of strong, kind of weak, or very very weak) and effort (tried very very hard, tried pretty hard, tried a little bit, and didn't try at all). Subjects predicted performance by selecting the size of the weight that was lifted by each hypothetical partici-pant. This much of the experiment replicates Kun et al.'s work, except that the stimuli refer to weight-lifting rather than puzzle-solving.

In a second part of the experiment, subjects judged the differences in perfor-mance between pairs of hypothetical participants, allowing application of Birnbaum's (1974a, 1978) "scale-free" method for separating the subjective rule for combining information (I in Figure 1) from the response production process (J in Figure 1). Basically, the method assumes that the judgments of differences reflect (at least ordinally) the differences between the subjective impressions of performance (ψ_{ij} in Figure 1). Thus, the scale-free method can be used to decide whether interactions in the final judgments should be attributed to the way the information is combined or the response production process. (The details of the assumptions of the scale-free method as applied to developmental change may be found in Surber, 1980 and 1984a).

The results for the judgments of weight-lifting performance replicated the results of Kun et al. reasonably closely. The adult, fifth and third grade data all showed the type of interaction between ability and effort that is predicted by a multiplicative integration process (the interaction variance was concentrated in the linear × linear component, and performance was judged to be very high only when both effort and ability were high). The kindergarten children showed a significant ability by effort interaction that was similar to that found with 8-year-olds by Kun et al., and that was interpreted as a transition between an additive and a multiplicative integration process.

The results for the judgments of the differences in performance (which allow application of the scale-free test) for the adult and fifth grade samples showed significant effects that agreed with the multiplicative rule. If the assumptions of the scale-free method are accepted, this result allows the additive combination rule to be rejected for the adults and fifth graders. For the third grade and kindergarten samples, these same comparisons were nonsignificant, but there were no effects of or interactions with age in the overall analyses of the difference judgments. Thus, the hypothesis of no age difference in the way ability and effort information are combined still cannot be discarded. Although not completely conclusive, the study illustrates the potential utility of the scale-free method in separating developmental change in response production (i.e., the judgment function) from changes in the way information is combined. Further research is needed in which the experimental designs have more statistical power and allow better tests of the assumptions on which the scale-free test is based.

Multiplicative Combination of Ability and Effort Revisited

The data of both Kun et al. (1974) and Surber (1980) are consistent with the interpretation that ability and effort are combined in a multiplicative manner by children approximately 9 years of age or older. Anderson and Butzin (1974) also concluded that college-age subjects' predictions of graduate school and college track performance were consistent with the multiplying model. However, Anderson and Butzin noted that other integration rules could produce the ability by effort interaction typical of a multiplying model. For example, an averaging process in which the weight or importance placed on a stimulus depends on its scale value can also approximate a conjunctive rule.

Averaging versus multiplying model. The averaging model was tested against the multiplying model by Surber (1980) by including trials in which only ability information or only effort information was presented.[3] The results of these trials supported the averaging integration rule over the multiplying rule. Thus, based on the findings examined so far, we might conclude that there is a developmental shift toward combining ability and effort conjunctively in predicting performance, but that the combination process can be better represented by an averaging model than a multiplicative one. The fact that a conjunctive interaction (such as shown in the left-hand panel of Figure 2) has been obtained from college-age subjects in three different laboratories (Anderson & Butzin, 1974; Kun et al., 1974; Surber, 1980) for four different types of achievement (puzzles, weight-lifting, track, and graduate school) and for difference judgments would seem to be strong support for the conjunctive combination of ability and effort as the "mature" schema for predictions of performance.

Nonconjunctive Combination of Ability and Effort by Adults

Four recent studies challenge the conclusion that a conjunctive rule for combining ability and effort is "the schema" used by mature subjects. Singh, Gupta and Dalal (1979) found no ability by effort interaction in the performance judgments of Indian engineering students. Gupta and Singh (1981) also found no ability by effort interaction in the performance judgments of either 6-to-13-year old Indian public school students or Indian college students. Surber (1978, 1981a) found a small ability by effort interaction for college students' judgments of academic performance, but the interaction was the *opposite* of that predicted by a conjunctive rule. That is, high performance was predicted when either ability or effort was high. An interesting aspect of the results reported in Surber (1978) was that in a separate experiment run concurrently with that reported by Surber (1980), the very same subjects who predicted weightlifting performance conjunctively failed to show this type of response pattern in predicting the math test performance of elementary school students (Surber, 1978, Experiment 5). These results suggest that the conjunctive rule may *not* be the universal schema for mature performance judgments (see also Surber, in press).

A researcher committed to the idea that ability and effort are combined conjunctively might object that the results of these studies may be due to the judgment function. For example, perhaps the subjects combine the information using a conjunctive rule, but the judgment function is a decelerating function. The composition of these two processes could produce an interaction of effort and ability that is in the opposite direction of that predicted by the conjunctive integration rule when the judgment function is linear. On the other hand, it could be argued that the integration process is an additive rule and that the judgment function is approximately linear. Since the data of these studies are ordinally consistent with either an additive or a conjunctive process, the findings cannot really eliminate either possibility. Again, it is important for researchers to make the distinction between I and J.

Whatever the interpretation, these results raise a number of questions about how individuals predict performance. For example, what causes the pattern of judgments to vary between studies? Should the different patterns be attributed to variation in the process of combining ability and effort (the integration function), or to variation in the process of reporting the subjective impressions of performance (the judgment function)? In either case, what variables are responsible for producing the different patterns of data? Do the same variables influence the pattern of children's performance judgments? These issues must be addressed before the developmental course of schemata for predicting performance can be fully described.

Effects of Task Difficulty Information

Task difficulty may influence performance judgments. One possible cause of different patterns of performance judgments is a difference in the implied difficulty of the task on which performance is to be predicted. Surber (1981b) examined this hypothesis and found that college subjects' performance judgments varied with the difficulty of the hypothetical task (described as a final exam in a college course). The conjunctive response pattern was obtained only for predictions of exam performance when the exam was described as extremely difficult. When the exam was described as easy, a disjunctive pattern was obtained (i.e., performance was predicted to be high when either ability or effort was high), and when the exam was described as of moderate difficulty, there was no ability by effort interaction. An additional feature of this study is that subjects were asked to answer a questionnaire designed to tap belief in conjunctive versus disjunctive rules. The results showed that subjects reported the belief that both high ability and high effort were needed for high performance on the difficult exam, while for the easy exam they reported the belief that either high ability or high effort was alone sufficient for high performance.

One conclusion from the findings of Surber (1981b) is that task difficulty influences the way college-age subjects assume ability and effort combine to determine task performance.[4] This conclusion has the potential to explain some of the apparently conflicting findings discussed earlier. For example, Anderson and Butzin (1974) concluded that college-age subjects combined ability and effort conjunctively in judging graduate school performance and college track performance. Examination of their instructions shows that these tasks (graduate school and college track) were described to the subjects as very difficult. In the study by Surber (1981a) which did not find a conjunctive pattern, the task was described as a medium difficulty comprehensive final in a college course. Singh et al. (1979), Gupta and Singh (1981) and Surber (1978, Experiments 1 and 5) did not explicitly describe task difficulty, and did not find a conjunctive pattern.

Implicit task difficulty may explain developmental changes. A new hypothesis suggested by the review above is that the developmental differences in predictions of performance might be explained in terms of the subjective difficulty of the task. Kun et al. (1974) and Surber (1980) found that 6- and 8-year-old children were less likely than older children and adults to show a conjunctive pattern of performance predictions for solving puzzles or lifting weights. If we assume that the younger children regard these tasks as easier than the older children and adults, then the observed developmental differences can be predicted. According to this hypothesis, the subject is assumed to generate task difficulty information from the description of the task, and is assumed to use this information in selecting a schema or rule for combining ability and effort to predict performance.[5] When a task is thought to be relatively easy, the conjunctive rule should be an unlikely choice for predicting performance no matter what the age of the subject. In order to test this hypothesis as an explanation of the developmental differences, an experiment with several age groups is necessary in which task difficulty, ability and effort are all manipulated. If the implicit task difficulty explanation is correct, then the pattern of judgments of performance should vary with task difficulty at all age levels in approximately the manner observed by Surber (1981b).

Developmental Differences in Understanding Task Difficulty

The above hypothesis for the developmental differences in performance predictions requires that we explain why younger children might view a given task as easier than older children or adults. Intuitively, we might suppose that younger children would regard most tasks as more difficult than older children, since they have fewer skills and are likely to perform more poorly than older children on any given task. Quite the opposite appears to be the case, however. Several sources of evidence suggest that younger children regard most tasks as easier than older children do. First, recent research on the development of metamemory shows that preschool and kindergarten children are more likely than older children to make unrealistically high predictions of the performance of either themselves or others in memory tasks (Flavell, Friedrichs, & Hoyt, 1970; Flavell & Wellman, 1977; Yussen & Levy, 1975). Second, the achievement motivation literature has produced evidence that young children are more optimistic than older children in predicting their own future performance, even when they have recently failed the task (Parsons & Ruble, 1977; Stipek, this volume).

Both of these lines of research provide only indirect evidence of age changes in the estimated difficulty of tasks, since it must be assumed that the group differences in predicted performance reflect differences in subjective difficulty. Reference to the outline of judgment in Figure 1 shows that age differences in average predicted performance could be produced by developmental differences in response production (J in Figure 1) without any developmental changes in the way the information is used in forming an impression of task performance (either H or I in Figure 1).

The issue of between group comparisons of judgments can be most easily understood by an analogy to two scales for measuring temperature: degrees celcius and degrees fahrenheit. Suppose, on a particular day a researcher in Paris asks a passerby, "What is the temperature today?" The passerby answers, "about 20 degrees." On the same day, a colleague of the researcher in New York asks a passerby the same question and receives the answer, "about 68 degrees." Suppose the researcher erroneously concludes that it was warmer in New York that day than in Paris (or perhaps that New Yorkers feel warmer than Parisians). Of course, degrees celcius is a simple linear function of degrees fahrenheit, and we know that 20°C represents the same temperature as 68°F. The two passersby transformed the subjective temperature into a response using different functions. The problem in research on human judgment is that we have no a priori knowledge of the nature of the function relating subjective impressions to overt responses (research on this topic may be found in Birnbaum, 1974b, 1982; Helson, 1964; Parducci, 1968, 1974, 1982). Given this ignorance, we cannot firmly conclude that one age group thinks a given task is more difficult than does another age group because their mean predictions differ. Similar logic applies to all between–group comparisons in judgment research.

Other research relevant to the development of the concept of task difficulty is reported by Shaklee (1976). Shaklee conducted two experiments in which preschool, kindergarten and second grade children were asked to make judgments of the difficulty of four different tasks given information about how four individuals performed on each task. There were four levels of outcome for each task: all performers succeeded, three out of four succeeded, three out of four failed, and all failed. For each level of outcome, the subject judged task difficulty on a six-point scale labelled from "very hard" to "very easy". The results of Shaklee's Experiment 1 showed that the preschoolers did not significantly vary their judgments of task difficulty with outcome level, while the other age groups did. The results of a second experiment by Shaklee, however, showed that the preschoolers did significantly vary their judgments of task difficulty with outcome when the four outcomes were summarized so that they were easier to remember.

Even if Shaklee's second experiment had resulted in an Age by Outcome interaction, it would not necessarily have provided evidence of developmental change in the use of outcome information to infer task difficulty. Age differences in the slope of judged task difficulty as a function of outcome could result fom a difference in a tendency to use extreme points of the rating scale (a developmental difference in the J function) as well as from a difference in how task difficulty is inferred from outcome. Thus, the analogy of the temperature scales applies here as well. This analysis of Shaklee's findings does not, of course, rule out the possibility that in the absence of any information about the difficulty of a task, there will be age differences in its assumed difficulty.

Note that Shaklee's experiment does not fit the outline of judgment given in Figure 1 since only a single stimulus is presented at a time. Shaklee's study can be diagrammed as: Stimulus $\rightarrow s_i \rightarrow R_i$, since there is no information integration step. In this "direct scaling" methodology there is less leverage for distinguishing the sources of developmental changes than in an experiment in which subjects combine two or more pieces of information (Birnbaum & Viet, 1974). The reason there is less leverage is that a difference in the rank orders of the responses across age groups is unlikely. As long as all age groups judge the manipulated variable to be monotonically related to the judged attribute, rank order differences between groups will not occur and the psychophysical function for the attribute cannot be separated from the judgment function. Hence, a single variable judgment experiment really lacks the power to detect developmental differences.

Effects of the Nature of the Task

As noted before, it is possible that the assumed difficulty of a task can determine the rule an individual uses in predicting performance. In the absence of explicit information about task difficulty, individuals must rely on the task description in combination with either their own experiences or culturally transmitted information about the task in drawing conclusions about task difficulty. Thus, in the absence of explicit information about task difficulty, we might expect to find differences in predictions of performance that depend on the nature of the task. Unfortunately, there has been little research attention to the nature of the task. Most studies have used a single type of task: Kun et al., (1974) used puzzles, Surber (1980) used weight-lifting, Anderson and Butzin (1974) studied predictions of performance for two types of tasks (college track and graduate school) but described both as difficult, Gupta and Singh (1981) studied predictions of elementary school performance, Singh et al. (1979) studied predictions of engineering school performance, Surber (1981a; 1981b) studied predictions of college exam performance, Shaklee (1976) studied judgments of task difficulty for four different carnival games (but her experiment was not intended to assess the effects of type of task per se), and Surber (1978) reported that college students failed to show a conjunctive pattern in predicting the performance of elementary school students on a math test, but that the same subjects did show a conjunctive pattern in predicting weight-lifting performance.

These last results raise the importance of further research on how task characteristics influence predictions of performance and perceived task difficulty. Intuitively, we might expect individuals who perform well in a given achievement domain to differ in their predictions of performance from those who perform poorly in that area. For example, if individuals who excel regard their field of excellence as an "easy" field, we would expect them to produce a disjunctive pattern of performance predictions. There may also be differences between tasks in the degree to which there are age differences in predictions of performance. For example, Surber (1978) reported no age differences (between kindergarten and college) in predictions of performance on a school math test.

Although these results are far from conclusive, they suggest that age differences in performance predictions may depend on either direct experience with, or culturally transmitted information about the task on which performance is to be predicted. Children and college students in our culture may share the same knowledge regarding how to do well on an elementary school math test, but not for performance on other types of tasks. In any event, research is needed exploring the degree to which the nature of the task, individual experience with the task, and developmental level interact in influencing one's assumptions in making predictions of performance.

Individual Differences in Weight of Ability versus Effort

Adult data. Another topic that has not been given much research attention is the weight or importance placed on ability versus effort in predicting performance. In the experiment by Surber (1981a), college students were asked to report the relative importance of ability versus effort in their judgments of performance. The results showed that there were individual differences in the reported relative importance of ability versus effort, and that the reported importances of the variables were related to the actual effects of the information on the subject's judgments of performance. For example, the judgments of those subjects who reported that ability was more important than effort showed a larger effect of ability. These results raise questions about the source of the individual differences in weighting ability versus effort. For example, do individuals who weight ability more than effort tend to attribute their own accomplishments (or failures) to ability? What experiences lead to belief that one variable is more importance than the other, and is there any relationship between these beliefs and actual behavior? These issues should be fruitful topics for future research.

Developmental data. A related question is when individual differences in weighting ability and effort first appear and when subjects first become capable of reporting the importance of cues in their judgments. There has apparently been no research directly addressing this issue. The paper by Kun et al. (1974) provides data relevant to whether there are age differences in reliance on ability versus effort in predicting performance. Kun et al. evaluated the percentage of variance accounted for by ability versus effort and found that the effect of effort increased with age. The percentage of variance controlled by the ability variable also increased with age, but the increase was not nearly as large as for effort. Another interesting aspect of Kun et al. (1974) work is that in one of their three experiments they analyzed the data of individual children and found that although a number of the subjects showed only one significant main effect (31 and 19% of the kindergarten and second graders, respectively), in all such cases of ''centration,'' the significant effect was for effort. That is, when the children based their judgments of performance on only one cue, it was the effort cue. A similar finding was reported recently by Gupta and Singh (1981) for Indian school children. Thus, the question of whether there are developmental shifts in the weighting of effort and ability remains to be answered by future research, as do the issues of when individual differences appear and when children become capable of accurately reporting weights.

Information About Past Performance

Adult Data

A variable that obviously may be of great importance in predicting performance is a person's past performance on the same or similar tasks. Singh et al., (1979) examined the effects of past performance information in combination with information about ability and effort, and concluded that these variables were combined using an averaging model. Not surprisingly, higher past performance was used to predict higher future performance. Similarly, Levin, Ims and Vilmain (1980, Experiment 1) found that two separate sources of information about the first semester performance of hypothetical college students (paper grades and test grades) were combined by college subjects in predicting second semester performance in a way that was consistent with an averaging model.

An important question in discovering how past performance information influences predicted performance is whether the sequencing of past performance information has an effect. For example, in predicting the performance of a candidate for admission to graduate school, should recent grades have more influence than earlier grades? The studies by Singh et al. (1979) and Levin et al. (1980) did not address this issue. Ryan and Levine (1981) gave college students twelve different graphs depicting the performance of hypothetical first, sixth or twelfth grade students over a 6-month period. The graphs showed five different patterns of increasing performance, five decreasing patterns of performance, and one stable high and one stable low pattern. The results were interpreted by the authors as evidence that subjects place more weight on recent information in predicting future performance, and that the weight given to the most recent score decreased as a function of the discrepancy between the person's most recent score and the score preceding it. Other studies have also found recency effects (Cooper, Lowe, & Baron, 1976; Jones, Rock, Shaver, Goethals, & Ward, 1968).

Developmental Data

Developmental studies of how past performance information influences predictions of future performance have generally presented only past performance information, rather than combining past performance information with other cues. An exception to this is a recent paper by Gupta and Singh (1981) in which children 6-13 years old judged the performance of persons described by ability, effort, and past performance. The authors concluded that judgments of performance could be represented as an equal-weighted average of the three variables. Most developmental studies have manipulated a child's performance on a task over a series of trials and have asked the child to predict his own performance on the next trial (Dweck & Gilliard, 1975; McMahan, 1973; Parsons, & Ruble, 1977). Fewer studies have asked the child to predict the future performance of a hypothetical performer (Stipek & Hoffman, 1980). Since the literature is small and the effects of outcome on one's own expectations are dealt with elsewhere in this volume (Stipek), further discussion of the effects of past performance on predicted performance is omitted.

Other Unexamined Variables

There are a number of other variables that people may use in making predictions of performance in everyday life. For example, Porac (1981) points out that there are two types of effort that may predict achievement: effort in preparing for a performance (study effort, work–outs, or practice) and effort during the performance (concentration and attempts to do one's best during an exam or a contest). Some of the studies above dealt with effort during performance (Kun et al., 1974; Surber, 1980), others dealt with effort in preparing (Gupta & Singh, 1981; Singh et al., 1979; Surber, 1978, 1981a, 1981b), while in Anderson and Butzin's (1974) study the term "motivation" seemed to imply both effort during preparation and during performance. It would be interesting to study the separate effects of these two aspects of effort on judgments of performance developmentally. Other unexamined variables that may enter into an individual's schema for performance include the reliability of the information about ability and effort (Surber, 1981a), chance factors, task difficulty during preparation (as opposed to during performance), and test or performance anxiety.

Recapitulation—Unsolved Puzzles in the Development of Predictions of Performance

It should be apparent from the review of the literature above that there are many gaps in our knowledge of children's predictions of performance. One important gap is in how (or whether) task difficulty information influences children's predictions of performance. Research on this topic has the potential to unify the developmental and adult literature on performance predictions, in addition to providing substantive information about children's understanding of the concept of task difficulty. Related to this is the issue of how one's developmental level interacts with the nature of the task. Determining the variables that control when children assume that ability and effort combine conjunctively versus disjunctively to predict performance may have applied importance. When the variables are assumed to combine conjunctively, it implies that an increase in effort has a greater impact on the performance of a person with high ability than on the performance of a person with low ability. In contrast, a disjunctive rule is a more egalitarian view of performance since it allows a person without ability to achieve high performance by working hard (cf. Gupta & Singh, 1981; Singh et al., 1979). These two different beliefs about how performance results from ability and effort obviously have different implications for one's actual motivation. The implications of these beliefs for inferences of ability and effort are considered below.

A second area in which our knowledge is very limited is in the developmental course of individual differences in weight given to ability versus effort in predicting the performance of others. Although there have been a large number of studies of individual differences in attribution of one's own past performance to ability versus effort (Crandall, Katkovsky, & Crandall, 1965; Dweck, 1975; Weiner, Frieze, Kukla, Reed, Rest, & Rosenbaum, 1971), there has apparently been no developmental study addressing the issue of individual differences in the weight of ability versus effort in predicting either one's own or others' performance. This topic, combined with research on when children's capacity to accurately report the relative importance of ability versus effort (or other types of information) in their judgments could have both theoretical and applied significance. The theoretical significance of such research is in describing the developmental course of the conscious control of judgment processes, a topic about which practically nothing is known. The applied significance of research on children's capacity to report the relative importance of variables is that if the importance can be reported, then it might be possible to change the importance of cues with instructions or other persuasive communications. Since the belief that ability is the cause of one's own failures seems to have debilitating effects on actual performance (Dweck, 1975), exploring ways of changing such beliefs may help to change the performance of such individuals.

INFERENCES OF ABILITY

Are there developmental changes in how individuals make inferences about the ability of another person, given information about that person's performance, effort, the difficulty of the task, and/or other related variables? This is an important question for a number of reasons. First, ability is (ideally) a stable, internal variable. Hence, research on inferences of ability may reveal general developmental trends in how children infer the stable internal characteristics, or traits, of others. Second, as mentioned earlier, the evaluation of one's own ability in comparison with the ability of others is an important influence on a person's achievement motivation. A third reason for studying judgments of ability is to test the idea that attributions are based on one's assumptions about how causes combine to bring about events. That is, whether schemata are reversible mental structures can be tested using both predictions of performance and inferences of ability.

Development of Inverse Compensation in Judging Ability

A few studies have examined ability judgments by giving subjects information about performance and effort (Anderson & Butzin, 1974; Karabenick & Heller, 1976; Kun, 1977; Surber, 1980, Note 1). If judgments of task performance are an increasing function of both effort and ability (and we found that they were at all ages examined), then when judgments of ability are made, ability should be judged to be inversely related to effort at fixed levels of performance. Inverse compensation in judging ability is similar to a cognitive skill called "compensation" (Brainerd, 1976; Larsen & Flavell, 1970). In both cases, there is an event of some magnitude (performance on a task, or a quantity of liquid to be transferred from one container to another), information about the level of one variable that is functionally related to the event (effort expended, or the diameter of the container into which the liquid is to be transferred), and the subject is asked to infer the level of a second variable (ability, or the height the liquid will reach in the new container). Based on the formal similarity of the two types of judgments, they might be expected to have a similar developmental course. Since compensation for judging physical quantities develops between approximately 6 and 8 years of age (Larsen & Flavell, 1970), we might expect inverse compensation for judgments of ability to develop at about the same age. The relevant research findings are reviewed in this section, and the reader will see that the developmental trends are not simple.

In one experiment by Kun (1977, Study 1), children in first, third, and fifth grades were given factorial combinations of information about the performance (1, 4, or 7 puzzles done) and effort (barely tried at all, tried a little, tried very hard) of hypothetical individuals solving puzzles. Subjects were asked to judge how "good at puzzles" each story character was, using a 9-point scale labelled from "very bad at puzzles," to "all right at puzzles," to "very good at puzzles." The results of this experiment showed no significant main effect of effort, and no age group by effort interaction. Based on these results, we might conclude that the children ignore effort information and base their inferences of ability solely on the performance information, since the main effect of performance was significant at all ages while the main effect of effort was not. (This was not Kun's conclusion.)

Findings by Surber (1980) cast doubt on this interpretation of Kun's results. Children in kindergarten, third and fifth grades, and college students judged the strength of hypothetical weightlifters on a 7-point scale, given the size of weight lifted (very very light, kind of light, kind of heavy, or very very heavy) and the effort expended (didn't try at all, tried a little bit, tried pretty hard, and tried very very hard). Initial analyses were quite similar to Kun's results: there was no main effect of effort and no age by effort interaction when the adult sample was excluded from the analyses. Cursory examination of the data of individual children, however, showed that they did not appear to be ignoring the effort cue. Instead, it appeared that some children judged ability to be directly related to effort (a pattern Kun called the "halo schema") and others judged ability to be inversely related to effort.

Formal criteria were developed to separate the children into groups based on the slope of their judgments of ability as a function of effort. The results of this classification showed that for each of the elementary school age groups, some of the children showed inverse compensation while others did not. Analyses of judgments of the differences in ability showed the same effects, even though the difference judgments were not used in classifying the subjects. This shows that the classification did not merely capitalize on chance, but reflected real individual differences. A second finding was that there was no clear relationship between the proportion of children showing inverse compensation and age group. Thus, the lack of a main effect of effort on the children's ability judgments was not due to neglect of the effort information. Almost all the children made use of the effort information, but they used it in two different ways.

Could the lack of an effect of effort in Kun's (1977) Study 1 also be due to individual differences in use of effort to judge ability? When Kun's data were categorized using criteria similar to those used by Surber (1980), the same type of individual differences were obtained. At each level of performance, the difference was taken between the subject's judgments of ability when effort was high and when effort was low. A subject was classified as showing an inconsistent slope if all three differences were zero, or if one was positive, one was negative, and the third was zero. A subject was classified as showing a negative slope if at least two out of three of the differences were negative, or if one was negative and the other two were zero. The criteria for the positive slope group were analogous to the negative slope criteria.

The results of the classification of Kun's (1977) data are presented in Table 2. A chi-square test of independence computed by combining the inconsistent group with the positive group was nonsignificant ($\chi^2(2) = 2.489, p > .10$). Inspection of Table 2 shows that there is a mild increase in the proportion of subjects showing negative slopes (or inverse compensation) with increasing grade. Since this and the results of a similar analysis of the data of Surber (1980) were not significant, the best conclusion from these two studies is that there are no age trends in use of inverse compensation to judge ability during the elementary school years. Instead, it appears that there are individual differences in use of inverse compensation.

This conclusion is also supported by Karabenick and Heller (1976). In this experiment, subjects in first, third, and fifth grades and college students made judgments of ability in two procedures: (a) serial presentation, and (b) paired comparison. In the serial presentation condition, subjects were first given information that a story character succeeded at a task (solved a puzzle) and were asked to estimate the character's ability. Then information about the character's effort was added (had to try very hard or didn't have to try at all) and the subject was

Table 2. Number of Subjects in Each Grade Level Classified as Showing Positive, Negative, and Inconsistent Slopes as a Function of Manipulated Effort.

	Slope		
Grade	Negative	Inconsistent	Positive
First	7	2	15
Third	8	4	12
Fifth	12	2	10

Source: Data are from Kun (1977) Study 1. (See text for classification criteria.)

again asked to estimate the character's ability. In the paired comparison procedure, subjects were given information about the effort of two story characters (one was described as having exerted high effort and the other low effort) who both successfully completed a puzzle. The subject was asked to choose which character was better at puzzles. This part of the procedure was repeated and so provides an estimate of consistency of use of inverse compensation in inferring ability.

Karabenick and Heller's paired comparison procedure showed that all age groups made a significantly greater proportion of total inverse compensation choices than chance (72, 72, 69 and 94% of the low effort characters were chosen by the first grade through college-age subjects, respectively). In addition, 60.4% of the children made the inverse compensation choice on both trials of the experiment. These findings also suggest no change in inverse compensation during the elementary school years. In the serial presentation condition, all age groups also showed a significant decrease in their ability judgments when high effort information was added, providing independent support for the choice data.

Karabenick and Heller's (1976) results show a larger overall proportion of elementary school age children using inverse compensation in inferring ability than the studies of Kun (1977, Study 1) and Surber (1980). Approximately 60% of Karabenick and Heller's elementary school subjects used inverse compensation, while 49% of Surber's and 38% of Kun's did. These between-study differences in use of inverse compensation remain to be explained. It is useful to note that Karabenick and Heller's procedure made the lowest memory demands of any of the studies, since performance was constant over the whole experiment (all characters succeeded). Kun's study and Surber's study were similar to each other with the exception that Surber presented line drawings representing the values of the component stimuli as memory aids on each trial. Kun also presented line drawings, but the drawings did not represent the values of the stimulus components.

This post hoc ordering of the three studies in terms of their memory demands suggests that information processing demands of the task may interfere with use of the "mature" strategy of inverse compensation in judging ability. It is also interesting that in spite of the many differences among the three studies, they are in agreement in providing evidence that there is little (or no) relationship between age and inverse compensation in judging ability between approximately 6 and 12 years, and that there are individual differences in inverse compensation at all age levels. These conclusions differ quite drastically from those of Sedlak and Kurtz (1981). In a review of children's ability judgments that was apparently prepared before the data of Surber (1980) were published, Sedlak and Kurtz concluded that ability judgments may not show systematic inverse compensation during the elementary school years. The data presented here show that inverse compensation for ability inferences definitely does exist in elementary school children but it has been masked from past reviewers by the individual differences.

Consistent Individual Differences in Inverse Compensation?

The conclusion that use of inverse compensation to judge ability varies between individuals but not with age during the elementary school years poses several questions for further research. One important question is whether individual children consistently use the same judgment strategy (inverse compensation versus the halo schema) in estimating ability across either different achievement settings (e.g., academic versus athletic) or different sessions of an experiment. Neither the data of Kun (1977) nor of Surber (1980) are capable of providing an answer to this question.

A more recent experiment provides information regarding these issues (Surber, Note 1). Children ranging from 5 to 12 years of age made inferences of both weightlifting ability and academic ability in two sessions. The academic ability judgments were obtained from a 4 x 4 factorial combination of performance on a math test and effort in studying for the test. The judgments of weightlifting ability were obtained using procedures that replicated Surber (1980). The experiment also included two measures of compensation for physical quantity which required the children to predict the height that a quantity of beans would reach when transferred from a standard container to one either wider or narrower than the standard.

The results showed an equal percentage of children using inverse compensation in judging academic and athletic ability. Nevertheless, there was no relationship between use of inverse compensation in judging academic and athletic ability, and only a weak relationship between inverse compensation for either of the ability judgments and compensation for the physical quantity judgments. These results replicate the individual differences in inverse compensation found by Surber (1980) and Kun (1977), and suggest that those individual differences are not consistent across achievement settings and are not tied to development of inverse compensation for physical quantities.

Adults Also Vary in Use of Inverse Compensation

All of the experiments discussed up to this point that included a college-age sample of subjects have reported that the college subjects almost all judge ability to be inversely related to effort. For example, Karabenick and Heller (1976) found that 91% of their college sample made the inverse compensation choice on both trials of the paired comparison choices, and Surber (1980) reported that 83% of the college sample was classified as showing inverse compensation in judging ability. An exception to this is that the college sample in Study 2 of Kun (1977) showed no significant effect of effort on their ability judgments.

A recent experiment by Surber (1984b) found that under some circumstances, college-age subjects failed to use inverse compensation in judging ability. In this experiment, college subjects judged the ability of hypothetical students described in terms of study effort and performance. Effort was described as based on one of three different-sized samples of the student's studying (one day, one week, or one month of observation), and performance was described as based on one of three different tests (a 10-item quiz, a midterm, or a comprehensive final exam). Surprisingly, there was no main effect of effort in the total sample, but subjects could be separated into two groups based on their response patterns. Approximately half the sample judged ability to increase as the given level of effort increased, while the other half of the sample judged ability to be inversely related to effort. Based on these findings, it does not seem appropriate to conclude that inverse compensation in judging ability is determined by an age-correlated variable.

Another interesting aspect of Surber (1984b) is that the effect of the reliability of the information (the size of the sample of the student's studying or the type of test taken) varied depending on the direction of the effect of effort. For subjects who judged ability to be directly related to effort, the reliability of the effort and performance information influenced the judgments in the way predicted by an averaging model in which the weights depend on reliability. These effects are shown for the positive slope group in Figures 4 and 5. Note that the slope in each panel of Figure 4 increases as the reliability of the information increases. For example, the slope of the one month study time curve is steeper than the slope of the one week and one day study time curves. This also follows intuitively since

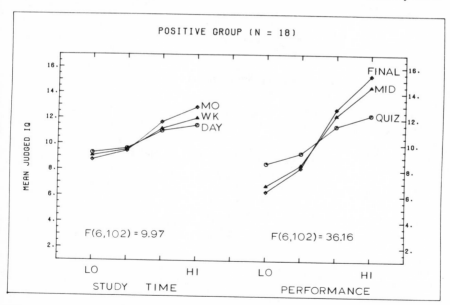

Figure 4. Mean judged IQ for positive slope group (ability judged directly related to effort) as a function of Study Time and Study Time Reliability (left panel) and Performance and Performance Reliability (right panel).

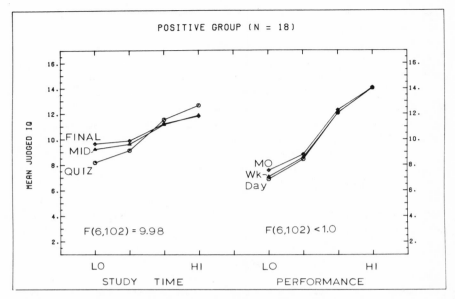

Figure 5.   Mean judged IQ for positive slope group (ability judged to be directly related to effort) as a function of Study Time and Performance Reliability (left panel) and Performance and Study Time Reliability (right panel). The effects are as predicted by an averaging model.

reliable information should have more influence on one's judgment than unreliable information.

These predictions of the averaging model can be shown formally. The increase in the effect of a variable as its reliability increases is predicted if reliability influences weight because weight multiplies the value of the information in an averaging model. An averaging model for ability judgments can be written:

$$R_A = J_A \left\{ \frac{w_E s_E + w_P s_P + w_O s_O}{w_E + w_P + w_O} \right\} \tag{1}$$

where R_A is the subject's rating of ability, J_A is a monotonic function relating the subjective impression of ability to the responses, w_E and w_P are the weights of effort and performance, s_E and s_P are the scale values of effort and performance, and $w_O s_O$ is the "initial impression" or impression of ability in the absence of any information. This model predicts that the net effect of effort is proportional to $w_E s_E / (w_E + w_P + w_O)$. Therefore, the effect of effort should increase as the value of the weight of effort, w_E, increases. If the value of w_E is changed by the reliability of the study time information, then the pattern shown in the left hand panel of Figure 4 is predicted. Analogous logic predicts the results for performance and performance reliability in the right hand panel of Figure 4 from the averaging model in Equation 1.

A second prediction of an averaging model is that as the reliability of one type of information increases, the net effect of other information decreases. For example, since the net effect of effort is $w_E s_E / (w_E + w_P + w_O)$, as the weight of performance (w_P) increases the effect of effort *decreases*. This prediction can be seen in the left hand panel of Figure 5. As the reliability of performance increases, the slope of the judgments as a function of effort decreases. An analogous prediction follows for the effects of effort reliability and performance. The actual results, shown in the right hand panel of Figure 5, are in the predicted direction but are not significant. Thus, the overall pattern supports the idea that when ability is judged to be directly related to effort, the results can be represented by an averaging model. It is also important to note than the predictions of the averaging model when information reliability influences the weight are ordinal predictions that do not depend on the exact form of the judgment function, J_A.

When ability is judged to be inversely related to effort, however, the results fail to agree with the predictions of an averaging model. Increasing the reliability of effort and performance also increases the effects of those cues, as can be seen

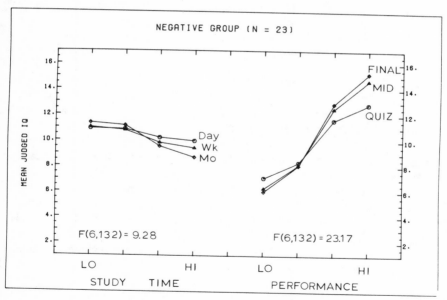

Figure 6. Mean judged IQ for negative slope group (ability judged to be inversely related to effort) as a function of Study Time and Study Time Reliability (left panel) and Performance and Performance Reliability (right panel).

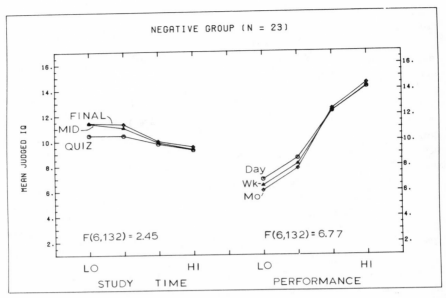

Figure 7. Mean judged IQ for negative slope group (ability judged to be inversely related to effort) as a function of Study Time and Performance Reliability (left panel) and Performance and Study Time Reliability (right panel). Effects are the *opposite* of those predicted by an averaging model.

in Figure 6. However, as shown in the left panel of Figure 7, increasing the reliability of performance *increases* the effect of effort, contrary to the averaging model. Analogously, increasing the reliability of effort increases the effect of performance, also contrary to Equation 1.

The results of Surber (1984b) show that rather different inference processes are engaged by subjects when they judge ability to be inversely versus directly related to effort. When the two variables are judged to be directly related, an averaging model provides an adequate account of the data. Thus, whatever the inference process involved in judging ability to be directly related to effort, it must map on to the averaging model. When ability and effort are judged to be inversely related, the averaging model fails, implying that the underlying inference process is different. Analogous conclusions regarding the averaging model were reported in Surber (1980).

Possible Explanations of Individual Variation in Inverse Compensation

How can the relatively high proportion of adults in Surber (1984b) who fail to show inverse compensation be explained? The answer to this question, if it were known, might help to explain the variability in use of inverse compensation found in the studies of children. One hypothesis is that the higher cognitive load required in order to use the reliability information leaves less work space for formulating impressions of ability. That is, as hypothesized by Shatz (1978), when the processing load increases, subjects may shift to using more routinized, overlearned, or ''immature'' cognitive strategies in order to distribute processing capacity over the total task. Judging any two variables to be directly related may be more routinized than judging them to be inversely related. This assumption seems plausible since studies of intuitive prediction find that negative relationships between variables are often more difficult to learn (Slovic, 1974). This hypothesis can also explain the children's data if it is assumed that the processing load was subjectively higher for those children who judged ability to be positively related to effort. What is needed in order to test this hypothesis is some way of manipulating or independently measuring the processing load of a task for an individual subject.

A second hypothesis for explaining variation in inverse compensation is to propose that the subjects are judging the influence of effort on ability. That is, they are judging how effort causes ability. Given this interpretation of the judgment task, it seems likely that ability would be judged to be positively related to effort. This hypothesis is simliar to a proposal by Dweck and Elliott (1983) that there are two ways of conceptualizing ability: as a stable trait or entity as opposed to a continuously growing set of skills. If ability is conceptualized as a growing set of skills, then effort should cause one's ability to increase. The problem with this explanation is in specifying when a subject interprets ability as a collection of skills versus as a fixed trait.

Dweck and Elliott have suggested that (a) individuals vary in the degree to which they regard their own abilities as traits versus growing collections of skills, and (b) certain situational factors (such as evaluative cues) may influence an individual to think of ability as a fixed trait instead of a growing collection of skills (see also Nicholls & Miller, this volume). These speculations provide testable hypotheses for the individual variation in inverse compensation. First, one could examine the relationship between a measure of each subject's concept of ability (trait versus growth concept) and use of inverse compensation in judging the ability of others. Second, manipulation of evaluative cues in the task on which performance was described might influence a proportion of the subjects to conceptualize ability as a fixed trait. Since Dweck and Elliott hypothesize that the trait and growth concepts of ability are both available to the child from approximately the beginning of school, the two hypotheses may ultimately help explain the individual differences in children's as well as adults' use of inverse compensation.

Is There a Fully Reversible Causal Schema?

Developmental Data

Considering the data of only those individuals who judge ability to be inversely related to effort, is there evidence for a reversible causal schema? Strictly speaking, this question requires that judgments of both performance and ability be obtained from each individual. None of the developmental studies provide this sort of within-subject data. If we are willing to assume that the individuals who judged ability in Kun (1977) and Surber (1980) would produce the same pattern of results as those who judged performance in Kun et al., (1974) and Surber (1980), then the reversibility hypothesis can be considered. If we also make the assumption that the judgment functions for both ability and performance are linear, then the pattern of performance judgments can be used to make a prediction about the pattern of ability judgments. Specifically, the multiplying rule for judgments of performance predicts that judgments of ability should show a significant effort by performance interaction such as is shown in the left-hand panel of Figure 3. This was not the case for the data of either Surber (1980) or Kun (1977). In fact, the adult data of Surber (1980) showed a significant interaction that was the *opposite* of the predicted pattern.

Within-Subject Data with Adults

Two published studies with adults provide within-subject data that can be used to examine the reversibility hypothesis (Anderson & Butzin, 1974; Surber, 1981b). In both of these studies, subjects judged performance, ability, and effort. At present, only the relationship between the performance and ability judgments will be considered, although consideration of the effort judgments leads to parallel conclusions.

Recall that Anderson and Butzin (1974) found that college students' predictions of the performance of track athletes and applicants to graduate school showed significant interactions of motivation and ability. The ability judgments in the same experiment, assuming that the judgment functions are linear, should also show significant interactions of the form described above for Kun's and Surber's studies. Instead, the results showed no significant interaction for judgments of track ability, and a small, but nonsystematic, interaction for judgments of academic ability. Anderson and Butzin concluded that "cognitive algebra is not a simple mirror of mathematical algebra" (p. 598).

In Surber (1981b), college students judged the ability of hypothetical college students, given information about each hypothetical student's grade on an exam that was either very difficult, moderately difficult, or easy, and the student's effort in studying for the exam. As mentioned in the section above, the pattern of performance judgments varied with exam difficulty. Thus, assuming that the judgment functions are linear, the reversible causal schema hypothesis predicts that the pattern of ability judgments should also vary with exam difficulty. The results contradicted this prediction. Under the assumption that the judgment functions for both performance and ability are linear, the data of both Anderson and Butzin (1974) and Surber (1981b) are contrary to the notion that inferences of ability are based on the same "schema" as predictions of performance.

Response Production Explanation

The predictions of the reversible causal schema hypothesis were evaluated above under the assumption that the judgment functions (J in Figure 1) for both judgments of performance and ability are linear (or more generally, that they have the same form). It is possible that the patterns of ability judgments do not agree with the patterns of performance judgments because the judgment functions vary. This explanation of the inconsistency across judged dimensions can rescue the hypothesis that a causal schema is an algebraically invertible integration process. For the data of Surber (1981b), one could propose that task difficulty influences the judgment function but leaves the integration process unaffected. For example, an additive integration process might be proposed for predictions of performance for all three levels of task difficulty. Similarly, for Anderson and Butzin's data the impressions of performance might be based on an additive integration process, and the impressions of ability might be based on a subtractive process. The judgment function for performance would then have to be positively accelerated, while the judgment function for ability would be assumed to be approximately linear.

Implications for the Notion of Reversible Operations

Regardless of whether the inconsistency between the pattern of performance and the pattern of ability judgments is due to the integration process or the judgment function, the results of Anderson and Butzin (1974) and Surber (1981b) have implications for the general idea of reversible operations. Based on these results, it does not appear that adult achievement judgments are based on a reversible operational system since there is no predictable relationship between predictions of performance and inferences of ability. There is a qualitative reversibility in the results of Anderson and Butzin (1974) and Surber (1980) in that inverse compensation was found for most adults. Quantitative reversibility was absent in that the patterns of judgments did not agree. Results from other task domains also support this conclusion (Wilkening, 1981).

Surber (1980, 1981b) summarized a number of possible explanations of the failure of the college students' judgments to be fully reversible. First, it is possible that subjects cannot mentally invert their intuitive rule for predicting performance. Second, it is possible that for some reason that social ecology for achievement induces the different patterns of ability and performance judgments. Both of these explanations can be tested with an experiment in which predictions and inferences are made for a hypothetical event. If the cognitive capacity to form and use a reversible operational system for intuitive judgments is present, then it ought to be evident for a hypothetical laboratory event with which the subject's experience is carefully controlled. Recent research of this sort also shows that the patterns of predictions do not necessarily agree with the patterns of inferences (Surber, Note 2). Third, it is possible that the conditions of the experiment (for example, the particular combinations of stimuli) induce the subjects to shift their pattern of judgments between the prediction and attribution sections of the experiment. A fourth possibility is that the rule for predicting performance is not invertible. These latter two explanations imply that the general idea of a causal schema for making both predictions and inferences is questionable.

Summary

Research examining the development of ability judgments has produced two important findings. First, inverse compensation for judging ability does not follow a simple age-correlated developmental course. A substantial proportion of adults, as well as children, fail to show inverse compensation under some conditions. At the present time, the variables that influence whether an individual judges ability to be inversely related to effort are unclear. More research is needed in exploring variables that may influence inverse compensation, such as the cognitive load of the judgment task, or how the subject interprets the concept of ability.

A second important finding is that judgments of ability and performance do not follow the same pattern. An implication of this latter result is that it may not be possible to represent ability and performance judgments as based on a fully reversible causal schema. Research allowing separation of conclusions about the information integration process from assumptions about the judgment function is needed before a firm conclusion can be drawn about the existence of reversible causal schemata. These two topics are important tasks for future research.

INFERENCES OF EFFORT

In many ways, the literature examining judgments of effort recapitulates the controversies and issues discussed above for ability judgments. Two central topics are the development of inverse compensation for judging effort, and whether there is a relationship between inverse compensation in judging effort and inverse compensation in judging ability. A third issue is whether effort judgments are related to judgments of performance in the way predicted by the causal schema hypothesis.

Development of Inverse Compensation in Judging Effort

The studies by Kun (1977), Karabenick and Heller (1976), and Surber (1980) described above, plus an experiment by Kassin and Gibbons (1981), provide the core findings regarding the development of inverse compensation for effort judgments. As will be seen, the findings lead to the conclusion that effort judgments may follow a slightly different developmental course from ability judgments.

Children Vary in Use of Inverse Compensation

Kun (1977, Study 1). Kun's first, third, and fifth graders were also given information about puzzle performance and ability at puzzles, and were asked to judge how hard each puzzle-solver tried. The results for the first graders showed a significant positive relationship between ability and judged effort, while the third and fifth grader's results showed significant inverse compensation. The results of the categorization of the data of individual subjects, using the criteria described above for ability, are shown in Table 3. A chi-square test of independence computed by combining the positive and inconsistent groups was significant ($\chi^2(2) = 17.47$, $p < .01$) showing that there are age differences in the proportion of children who use inverse compensation. This result is in contrast to the absence of age differences in the ability inferences in Kun's study.

Surber (1980). In this experiment, children in kindergarten, third, and fifth grades, and college students judged the effort of hypothetical weightlifters given performance and ability information. (The subjects were different individuals from those who judged ability.) The results showed inverse compensation at each age level. A chi-square test of independence based on the categorization of individual data patterns was not significant ($\chi^2(3)=2.64$, $p > .10$). Thus, the results of Surber (1980) show no developmental trend in inverse compensation for judging effort between kindergarten and college. All ages showed inverse compensation.

Karabenick and Heller (1976). The same first, third, and fifth graders, and college students whose ability judgments were described above also judged effort. Recall that Karabenick and Heller used two procedures, serial presentation and paired comparison. In the serial presentation procedure, subjects first judged effort only on the basis of information that the character successfully solved a puzzle. Information about ability was then added (very bad at puzzles, or very good at puzzles) and the judgment was repeated. The results of this

Table 3. Number of Subjects in Each Grade Level Classified as Showing Positive, Negative, and Inconsistent Slopes as a Function of Manipulated Ability.

Grade	Slope		
	Negative	Inconsistent	Positive
First	4	4	16
Third	16	4	4
Fifth	17	3	4

Source: Data are from Kun (1977) Study 1. (See text for classification criteria.)

procedure showed that when high ability information was added, a nonsignificant decrease in the effort judgments occurred for all ages except the college students, who did show a significant decrease in their effort ratings. For the paired comparison procedure, the results showed that a very high proportion of all students (86%) chose the character with low ability as the harder worker on *both* trials. There were no age differences in the proportion making the inverse compensation choice (91, 84, 81, and 88% for first through college, respectively). The overall conclusion from Karabenick and Heller's data is that inverse compensation for effort judgments is present from first grade.

Kassin and Gibbons (1981). Although not directly pertinent to achievement, this study is included because it deals with inference of effort. In this experiment children in kindergarten and second grade observed a brief animated sequence in which two triangles approached a house from different directions. One of the triangles was "carried" by a square while the other moved by itself. The children were asked (a) to choose which triangle tried harder to get to the house, (b) to explain why he or she thought that triangle was trying harder to go to the house, and (c) to judge how much each triangle tried (on a 4-point scale). It is important to note that this study examines use of inverse compensation in attributing effort when the alternative cause is external (being "carried") rather than internal (ability). The results showed significant use of inverse compensation for the choice measure (71 and 81% of the kindergarten and second graders, respectively), and for the rating measure. There were no age differences on either of the two measures. These results are similar to those of both Surber (1980) and Karabenick and Heller (1976) in showing significant use of inverse compensation for kindergarten and second graders.

The data of these four studies present a puzzling picture of the development of inverse compensation for effort judgments. Kun's study stands out from the other three in showing a developmental trend from use of the "halo schema," or a positive slope, to use of inverse compensation. The difference between Kun's results and those of the other studies might be explained by a post-hoc appeal to the memory and information-processing demands made by the experimental procedures. Since Kun's procedures appear to have made the highest demands on the subjects, we might expect her results to show the largest age effects. The other studies show that the capacity to use inverse compensation in judging effort is present by approximately age 6.

Adults Also Vary in use of Inverse Compensation

Surber (1984b) also asked college students to judge the effort of hypothetical students described by performance and ability information that varied in reliability. Surprisingly, 22% (10 out of 46) of the subjects judged effort to be directly related to ability. As in the experiment described above for ability judgments, the data of those who judged effort to be positively related to ability were qualitatively consistent with an averaging model. In contrast, the data of those subjects who judged effort to be negatively related to ability failed to agree with the averaging model predictions.

These data from a college student sample seem to raise the plausibility of the information-processing-load hypothesis as an explanation of the "halo schema" in the first grade data of Kun's (1977) study. The only study in which a sizable proportion of college students fail to show inverse compensation in judging effort is that of Surber (1984b). In this study subjects had to consider not just performance and ability information, but also the reliability of the information (type of IQ test or type of exam). If the inclusion of the reliability of information raises the processing demands, then a proportion of the subjects would be expected to use a judgment strategy that requires less processing. Judging effort to be directly related to ability may be less cognitively demanding. As mentioned earlier, an experimental test of this hypothesis requires a way of measuring the processing load of a task for an individual subject if we are to predict either which individuals or what proportion of individuals will shift from inverse compensation to judging the variables to be directly related.

Relationship Between Inverse Compensation in Judging Ability and Effort

The studies by Kun (1977) and Karabenick and Heller (1976) allow assessment of the relationship between inverse compensation in judging ability and in judging effort. In both of these studies, the same subjects judged both ability and effort for the same achievement scenario, allowing evaluation of the consistency of subjects' judgment strategies across the two tasks.

For Kun's data, a 2x2 (strategy for judging effort by strategy for judging ability) contingency table was constructed for each age group. From these tables, the number of subjects who used the same strategy for both ability and effort could be determined (the strategy classification combined the positive and inconsistent slope groups). The results are shown in the top portion of Table 4. A chi-square test of independence was not significant ($\chi^2(2)=2.22$, $p>.10$) showing no evidence of age differences in strategy consistency.

For Karabenick and Heller's (1976) data, a similar procedure was used.[6] Individuals at each grade level were classified in a 2x2 table according to their responses on the choice questions for each type of attribution (the positive and inconsistent slope groups were combined). The number of subjects at each age showing the same strategy for both ability and effort attributions, versus different strategies, is shown in the bottom portion of Table 4. As with Kun's data, a chi-squared test for age differences in consistency was nonsignificant ($\chi^2(3) = 3.50$, $p > .10$).

A second question that can be answered using Table 4 is whether subjects are more likely to maintain the same strategy across the two types of attributions than

Table 4.   Number of Subjects at Each Grade Level Who
Show the Same Versus Different Strategies in Judging
Ability and Effort.

	Kun	
	Strategy Across Tasks	
Grade	*Same*	*Different*
First	17	7
Third	12	12
Fifth	15	9
	Karabenick & Heller	
First	21	11
Third	18	14
Fifth	21	10
College	25	7

Source: Data are from Kun (1977) Study 1, and Karabenick and Heller's (1976)
choice measure. (See text for classification criteria.)

to change strategies. Binomial tests, assuming that the a priori probability of the
same versus a different strategy is .5, were significant only for the college
students in Karabenick and Heller's study ($p < .01$). For the other age groups in
either Kun's or Karabenick and Heller's study, the number of subjects using the
same versus different strategies was not significantly different from chance.
These results imply that for elementary school children there is little relationship
between inverse compensation when judging ability and when judging effort,
whereas the adults show some consistency. If use of inverse compensation during the elementary school years were determined primarily by the development
of a cognitive structure, we would expect to see some relationship between
inverse compensation for judgments of ability and judgments of effort.

Is There a Reversible Causal Schema?

Those individuals who judge effort to be positively related to ability cannot be
said to use a reversible causal schema. For those who show inverse compensation, there was no evidence that the pattern of effort judgments was systematically related to the pattern of performance judgments. As noted above in discussing ability judgments, the hypothesis that both performance and effort
judgments are based on a single invertible integration function can be saved by
postulating differences in the judgment functions. Because of this possibility, it
is important for future research to try to separate the information integration
function from the judgment function.

THE UTILITY OF MATHEMATICAL MODELS OF JUDGMENT

Other discussions of the utility of mathematical models of judgment for studying either developmental or individual differences may be found in Anderson (1980), Birnbaum and Stegner (1981), and Kaplan (1975; Note 3). From this author's point of view, the major advantage of using mathematical models of judgment in the study of children's concepts is that it has the potential to allow both qualitative description and quantitative measurement. It should be clear from the data and discussions above that judgment methods can discover and describe at least some types of structural stage-like changes. The shift from positive to negative slope in judging ability is the type of change that can be regarded as a structural shift. This slope shift can be described in terms of a mathematical model of judgment either by specifying the scale values for effort to be the reverse order of the scale values of the positive slope subjects (i.e., higher effort is assigned a lower scale value for the negative slope subjects), or by postulating a subtractive or ratio integration process for the negative slope subjects (cf. Anderson & Butzin, 1974), and an additive process for the positive slope subjects. Thus, qualitative or structural developmental changes can be described by changes in the form of the equation for the information integration process or by changes in the rank orders of the scale values.

Nonstructural, or gradual quantitative developmental changes can be described and measured by changes in the parameter values. The importance of the quantitative measurements made possible by mathematical models of judgment is illustrated by considering the experiment discussed above by Surber (1981a). This experiment showed that the importance (or weight) placed on effort versus ability varied across individuals. Such individual differences in weighting could evolve gradually, requiring a model that allows for gradual changes in parameter values. The individual differences in the importance of effort versus ability in judging performance in Surber (1981a) were described by varying the values of the weights in an averaging model. This illustrates the potential of mathematical models for describing either gradual developmental changes or individual differences.

The distinction between weight and scale value in particular has important implications for developmental psychologists since we are often interested in making inferences about age changes in the understanding of a variable versus the degree to which a variable is employed in some experimental task. The weight and scale values of a variable provide separate measurements of these types of developmental changes. Using an averaging model, whether a variable is understood by a subject can be equated with whether scale values for the different manipulated levels may be distinguished in the subject's judgments. The degree to which a variable is employed by a subject can be measured by the weight it is given in a judgment. For example, results reported by Surber (1977,

1982) show that in moral judgments, motives are understood before they are given much weight when combined with consequences. Application of methods of separating weight from scale values to achievement judgments could isolate the source of developmental differences in the effects of effort and ability on judgments of performance. In this case, mathematical models of judgment have the potential to provide more accurate measurements of developmental changes than may otherwise be possible.

Potential Disadvantages of Mathematical Models of Judgment

Mathematical Models May Not be Explanatory

A potential criticism of the use of mathematical models of judgment is that the models are not explanatory or causal theories, but merely provide descriptions of the phenomena for which there could be any of a multitude of underlying psychological causes. Although it may be true that the models are primarily descriptive, Isaac Newton's work was regarded by many of his contemporaries as merely a mathematical formula without explanatory value (Hanson, 1958) and precise description has always been an integral part of science.

A researcher should not be fully satisfied with an adequate descriptive model, of course. Krantz (1972) argues that once a simple measurement structure is established for a phenomenon, it is often possible to generate new theoretical ideas that lead to further experiments, that may further explain the model or some of its parameters. One way to shed light on the nature of the processes involved in evaluating, weighting, combining information, and reporting one's impression on a rating scale is by manipulating variables that can be shown to influence these steps of the judgment process. Thus, having observed that the theory that performance judgments are a weighted average of ability and effort information accords with the data, we may seek an explanation for the parameter values (e.g., what variables influence the weights?) or for the general form of the equation (what variables might influence whether the judgments will agree with an averaging model versus some other integration function?). In this way the parameters acquire enriched empirical meaning and the scope of the theory is extended.

Responses May Not Be Based on the Intended Variable

Another potential disadvantage is that judgments may be based on variables other than those that the experimenter intended to manipulate. In the present context, a possible example is that predictions of performance could be an increasing function of both ability and effort if the subject totally ignored the information type and used only the descriptive adjectives as a basis for the judgments. For example, judgments could increase as a function of the descriptions of effort (not at all, a little bit, etc.) without the subject having any concept of effort and its relationship to the judged variable.

This disadvantage is not inherent in judgment methods, however. In a judgment experiment, if it can be shown that two variables are used in distinctly different ways by the subjects, then at the very least the subjects can be inferred to distinguish between the concepts represented by the variables. Second, if judgments were based solely on the adjectives used to qualify the variables, then a bipolar variable would be expected to result in a pattern of judgments that decreases and then increases (or vice versa). For example, the adjectives used by Surber (1980) in describing strength (very very weak, kind of weak, kind of strong, and very very strong) begin at an extreme point, become less extreme ("kind of") and then more extreme again. If subjects did not know the difference between strong and weak, their responses would be expected to be equivalent for the corresponding weak and strong portions of the stimuli. This did not occur.

Comparison of Judgment Methods with the Structural Developmental Approach

It has been argued above that the use of mathematical models of judgment (with appropriate experimental designs) can provide measures of either qualitative structural developmental changes, or continuous quantitative changes. In the emphasis on considering the full pattern of a person's responses, the present approach can be regarded as loosely analogous to traditional Piagetian concept assessment (Elkind, 1969). In Piagetian concept assessment, the interviewer presents several variations on the same task and questions the child about each version. The child's pattern of answers is used to assess the child's concept. In the judgment methodology employed in the author's research, the child is presented with various combinations of stimuli, and the overall pattern of the child's responses is used to assess the child's concept. A key difference is that Piagetian concept assessment focuses more (though not exclusively) on the intensive content of concepts, while judgment methods focus on extensive content.

Nicholls's (1978) structural analysis of achievement concepts can be used to illustrate the way judgment methods can address issues raised by the structural approach. In Nicholls's study, children were questioned about three films showing pairs of children working at a task. Each film portrayed the efforts of the two children as unequal, and the experimenter verbally described (and visually presented) the performance of the two children as either equal or unequal. Nicholls classified the children's verbal responses into a series of four hierarchical levels. The implications for judgments of each of Nicholls's four levels of reasoning about ability and effort are discussed below. These interpretations of Nicholls's levels are also summarized in Table 5.

Level 1

Level 1 of Nicholls's theory states in part that children center on effort and do not distinguish effort from outcome (i.e., effort is not distinguished as a cause of outcome), but sometimes these children center on outcomes instead of effort. This level of reasoning, as defined by Nicholls, predicts that in an experiment in which children are asked to judge ability given effort and performance information, their judgments should show no effect of performance, but an effect of effort such that the higher the effort the higher the judged ability. A child at this level of reasoning who centers on performance would be expected to show no effect of the effort information on his judgments of ability. It is worth noting that in Surber (1980) the ability judgments of a few subjects did not vary at all with the effort information.

Level 2

Level 2 of Nicholls's approach states that effort is viewed as the prime cause of outcome; equal effort is expected to lead to equal outcomes, and that if two people obtain the same score they must have exerted equal effort. Children at this level have problems explaining a situation where one person tries harder than another but obtains a lower score, but do acknowledge that the person obtaining the lower score is less able. Two aspects of this definition of Level 2 refer to how outcome might be predicted from effort (effort is the prime cause of outcome, and equal efforts produce equal outcomes). These statements imply that in judging performance, subjects should at least place greater weight on effort than on ability, and should perhaps center on effort (since equal efforts produce equal outcomes). The mathematical models described above provide a way of measuring development within this stage, since the weight of ability in predicting performance might be expected to increase gradually.

Another aspect of this stage refers to inferences of effort (equal outcomes imply equal efforts). Nicholls intended this aspect of the definition to imply that information about unequal efforts will be denied when equal outcomes result. To test this, subjects could be asked to judge effort, given effort and performance information (cf. Kepka & Brickman, 1971). Judgments of effort at this level of reasoning should depend on performance, *not* on the given effort information. The final aspect of the definition of Level 2 implies that when the harder working of two individuals obtains the lowest score, the harder working individual will be judged lower in ability. This aspect of the definition of Level 2 reasoning does not distinguish between subjects who judge ability to increase versus decrease with changes in effort (i.e., it does not distinguish between those who show inverse compensation and those who show the halo schema). Depending on the particular values of performance and effort, the harder working individual with the lower score can be judged lower in ability whether the slope of the subject's judgments is positive or negative. This criterion does imply that performance would be given some weight in judgments of ability, an implication that would distinguish the ability judgments of those reasoning at Level 1 from those reasoning at Level 2.

Level 3

Level 3 is characterized by reasoning inconsistencies. Specific features of this level are that effort is not the only cause of outcome, when equal outcomes result from different efforts the person working less is higher in ability, but sometimes these subjects will assert that when equal effort is applied equal outcomes will result or that harder work implies higher ability. In terms of judgments, Level 3 subjects would be expected to show effects of both ability and effort if they are asked to predict performance, since they are said to believe that effort is not the only cause of outcome. When judging ability given effort and performance information, Level 3 subjects should show negative slopes (if they believe that equal outcomes resulting from different efforts imply that the lessor effort individual has more ability). The inconsistencies in the reasoning of children at this level would be expected to manifest themselves in inconsistent slopes in the ability judgments.

Level 4

Level 4 is the mature level of knowledge of ability and effort, and is characterized by the conceptualization of ability as capacity that can limit (at low ability levels) or increase (at high ability levels) the effectiveness of one's efforts. At this level, "Ability is correctly inferred from effort and outcome, and outcomes are seen as determined jointly by effort and ability" (Nicholls, 1978, p. 812). The term "correctly" here can be taken to imply that ability is consistently judged to be inversely related to effort when subjects are asked to infer ability given effort and performance information. Thus, Level 4 subjects should show consistent negative slopes in judging ability. Nicholls's description of the Level 4 concept of ability as a capacity that either limits or magnifies the effect of effort can be taken to imply that at Level 4, subjects' judgments of performance should fit the multiplying model. In the multiplying model, when ability is low, effort has little effect on one's performance but when ability is high, effort has a large effect on performance.

Table 5 summarizes the predictions derived from Nicholls's levels of reasoning for judgments of ability, effort and performance. From this translation of Nicholls's stages into predictions for judgment tasks, we can see how reasoning level should be tied to judgment, and we can also see how the structural and information processing approaches to development might benefit from interchange. For example, the mathematical models of judgment provide a more precisely formalized way of describing children's use of information in judging ability, effort and performance. The models can also describe gradual changes within each of Nicholls's four levels. On the other hand, Nicholls's structural

Table 5.   Predicted Effects in Judgment Tasks at Each Level of Reasoning as Defined by Nicholls (1978)

Nicholls's Reasoning Level	Ability (given effort and performance)	Effort (given ability and performance)	Performance (given ability and effort)
		Judgment Task	
1	Perf—no effect Effort—pos. slope or Perf—sig. effect Effort—no effect	Not specified	Not specified
2	Perf—sig. effect Effort—either positive, negative, or inconsistent slopes, but not flat	Not specified *	Effort—large effect Ability—no effect or only a small effect
3	Perf—sig. effect Effort—inconsistent slopes	Not specified	Effort—sig. effect Ability—sig. effect
4	Perf—sig. effect Effort—consistent neg. slopes	Not specified	Perf = Effort · Ability

*Level 2 should judge effort = performance when *effort* and performance information are given.

analysis of children's reasoning about ability and effort suggests relationships among judgments of ability, effort and performance that might otherwise be overlooked. For example, Level 3 predicts that as subjects begin to give more weight to ability in predicting performance, they may be showing inconsistent slopes in judging ability. This is a hypothesis worth exploring in future research.

Relationships Between Verbal Explanations and Judgments

An important difference between the judgment approach and traditional Piagetian concept assessment, of course, is that Piagetian methods rely on both verbal explanations and choice responses, while the judgment methodology relies on only the child's rating scale responses. Verbal production abilities show large developmental changes, and so assessing concepts through the use of verbal protocols is inextricably tied to developmental changes in verbal production. On the other hand, judgment researchers need to bear in mind that age changes in abilities related to the use of rating scales (such as memory for the end anchors of the scale, ability to order stimuli on a continuum, etc.) probably also change developmentally.

A second difference between the judgment methods advocated here and the Piagetian approach is that Piagetian protocols are scored into discrete categories.

Although transitional categories are often included, it is awkward for the structural approach to represent continuous developmental changes or individual differences that vary in degree. This is also true of other uses of verbal protocols in assessing cognitive states (Diener & Dweck, 1978, 1980; Ericcson & Simon, 1981). The judgment approach more readily allows representation of continuous changes than the use of verbal protocols.

The analysis of Nicholls's structural model of reasoning about ability and effort above raises the importance of research addressing the relationship between verbal explanations and judgments. Although some have argued that there is little relationship between verbal reports and other behavior (Nisbett & Wilson, 1977), others have argued that what is needed is a theory that predicts the conditions under which the conclusions based on verbal explanations will provide valid measures of the cognitive processes on which behavior is based (Dulany, 1968; Ericcson & Simon, 1981). Very little is known about the degree to which cognitive structures as indexed by children's verbal explanations correspond to structures as indexed by other methods. In the area of achievement concepts, the comparison of Nicholls's structural model with the judgment approach provides one context in which the relationship between explanations and judgments could be studied empirically.

CONCLUSIONS

This chapter is a selective review of the literature on children's judgments of achievement-related variables. The review concentrates on what mathematically stated theories of judgment can reveal about two issues: (a) the development of reversible causal schemata for making both predictions of performance and inferences of the causes of performance, and (b) the development of a strategy for judging ability and effort that is termed inverse compensation. A detailed examination of the literature reveals that inverse compensation for judging either ability or effort shows little or no relationship to chronological age during the elementary school years. Recent findings show that under some conditions college students also fail to show inverse compensation, a result that points to the need for research exploring the conditions that may control the strategy employed by an individual for judging ability or effort. This conclusion differs from the conclusions of most researchers of the development of attribution strategies who have regarded inverse compensation as an age-correlated phenomenon.

The review also shows that it is not clear whether there is a relationship between a person's judgments of ability and effort and judgments of performance. The finding of past researchers that ability and effort are combined multiplicatively by mature subjects is shown to be open to question. The pattern of performance predictions has been found to vary as a function of the described difficulty of the task and, possibly, as a function of the nature of the task (for example, academic versus physical) or the implicit difficulty of the task. Regardless of the way ability and effort are combined, there appears to be little relationship between the pattern of performance predictions and the pattern of ability or effort judgments. This finding questions the widely held assumption that how a person assumes causes combine to produce an event determines how the person makes attributions of the causes (i.e., that attributions are based on reversible causal schemata). By reinterpreting the general notion of a reversible causal schema in terms of mathematical models of judgment, it becomes clear that future research needs to distinguish between two separate processes that influence the patterns of predictions and inferences, the subjective rule for combining the information and the process of producing a response on a rating scale.

ACKNOWLEDGMENTS

Research by the author reported in this paper was supported in part by Grant BNS-7912414 from the National Science Foundation and by a grant from the Graduate School, University of Wisconsin. The author is grateful to Steven Gzesh for assistance with various aspects of the research.

NOTES

1. The reader should not confuse the "judgment function," or J in Figure 1, that represents the process of translating psychological impressions into overt responses on a rating scale, with the more general term, "judgment." The term "judgment function" is used here to maintain consistency with the terminology of Birnbaum (1974, 1978, 1982). In contrast, the term "judgment" is used, either as a synonym for the subject's rating scale response or as an omnibus term representing the overall process of judgment from stimulus input to rating scale response output.

2. The author is grateful to Anna Kun for making the data of Kun, Parsons, and Ruble (1974) and Kun (1977) available for these analyses.

3. A multiplying model really makes no predictions about how a subject should respond to a single piece of information. If it is assumed that the missing piece of information is replaced by the identity operator, however, then the multiplying model predicts that the curve for a single source of information should not cross the curves for the ability-effort combinations. The single-source curve should appear as another curve in the bilinear fan. This adaptation of the multiplying model is equivalent to dropping terms from the equation that pertain to information that is not presented. It is possible for the multiplying model to predict a greater slope for the curve for the judgments of a single type of information (e.g., if the scale values of the other source of information are less than 1.0), but the curve should not cross the other curves. The predictions of a multiplying model are ordinally the same as the predictions of an additive model. The averaging model predicts that the single–cue curve should both be steeper and cross the other curves. These predictions for both models require that the judgment function be constant over judgments of both single cues and combinations, and that the values of the parameters (scale values and weights) not vary between judgments based on single cues versus combinations. It is not required that the judgment function be linear, however.

4. An alternative interpretation of the results of this experiment is that the manipulation of task difficulty influenced only the process of translating one's impressions into responses (the judgment function, J, in Figure 1), and not the process of combining the information (I in Figure 1). This is possible since the manipulation of task difficulty involved the grade distribution on an exam, and subjects were asked to give grades as their responses. In order for this interpretation to explain the

data, however, it is necessary to assume that when the subjects report their beliefs about how ability and effort combine they report beliefs that reflect their pattern of responses, or the composition of I and J in Figure 1. An implication of this is that reported beliefs do not reflect the way a person combines information.

5. The interpretation of developmental changes as due to implicit task difficulty can also be based on the premise that task difficulty influences only the judgment function, J, and not the way information is actually combined.

6. The author is grateful to Julie Karabenick for making these data available for analysis.

REFERENCE NOTES

1. Surber, C. F. *Asynchrony in development of the discounting principle for social and nonsocial judgments.* Paper presented at the biennial meeting of the Society for Research in Child Development, Boston, MA, 1981.

2. Surber, C. F. *Effects of configural prediction rules on causal inferences.* Paper presented at the annual convention of the American Psychological Association, Los Angeles, CA, 1981.

3. Kaplan, M. *Cognitive processes in morality judgment.* Paper presented at the annual convention of the Midwestern Psychological Association, Chicago, 1979.

REFERENCES

Anderson, N. H. Functional measurement and psychophysical judgment. *Psychological Review,* 1979, *77,* 153–170.

Anderson, N. H. Algebraic rules in psychological measurement. *American Scientist,* 1979, *67,* 555–563.

Anderson, N. H. Information integration theory in developmental psychology. In F. Wilkening, J. Becker & T. Trabasso (Eds.), *Information integration by children.* Hillsdale, NJ: Erlbaum, 1980.

Anderson, N. H., & Butzin, C. A. Performance = Motivation × Ability: An integration–theoretical analysis. *Journal of Personality and Social Psychology,* 1974, *30,* 598–604.

Birnbaum, M. H. The nonadditivity of personality impressions. *Journal of Experimental Psychology,* 1974, *102,* 543–561.(a)

Birnbaum, M. H. Using contextual effects to derive psychophysical scales. *Perception & Psychophysics,* 1974, *15,* 89–96.(b)

Birnbaum, M. H. Differences and ratios in psychological measurement. In N. J. Castellan & F. Restle (Eds.), *Cognitive theory* (Vol. 3). Hillsdale, NJ: Erlbaum, 1978.

Birnbaum, M. H. Reply to Eisler: On the subtractive theory of stimulus comparison. *Perception & Psychophysics,* 1979, *25,* 150–156.

Birnbaum, M. H. Comparison of two theories of "ratio" and "difference" judgments. *Journal of Experimental Psychology: General,* 1980, *109,* 304–319.

Birnbaum, M. H. Controversies in psychological measurement. In B. Wegener (Ed.), *Social attitudes and psychophysical measurement.* Hillsdale, NJ: Erlbaum, 1982.

Birnbaum, M. H., Parducci, A., & Gifford, R. K. Contextual effects in information integration. *Journal of Experimental Psychology,* 1971, *88,* 158–170.

Birnbaum, M. H., & Stegner, S. E. Measuring the importance of cues in judgment for individuals: Subjective theories of IQ, heredity, and environment. *Journal of Experimental Social Psychology,* 1981, *17,* 159–182.

Birnbaum, M. H., & Viet, C. Scale convergence as a criterion for rescaling: Information integration with difference, ratio, and averaging tasks. *Perception & Psychophysics,* 1974, *15,* 7–15.

Brainerd, C. J. Does prior knowledge of the compensation rule increase susceptibility to conservation training? *Developmental Psychology*, 1976, *12*, 1–5.

Cooper, H. M., Lowe, C. A., & Baron, R. M. Pattern of past performance and expected future performance: A reversal of the unexpected primacy effect. *Journal of Applied Social Psychology*, 1976, *6*, 31–39.

Crandall, V. C., Katkovsky, W., & Crandall, V. J. Children's beliefs in their own control of reinforcements in intellectual-academic situations. *Child Development*, 1965, *36*, 91–109.

Diener, C. I., & Dweck, C. S. An analysis of learned helplessness: Continuous changes in performance, strategy, and achievement cognitions following failure. *Journal of Personality and Social Psychology*, 1978, *36*, 451–462.

Diener, C. I., & Dweck, C. S. An analysis of learned helplessness: II. The processing of success. *Journal of Personality and Social Psychology*, 1980, *39*, 940–952.

Dulany, D. E. Awareness, rules, and propositional control: A confrontation with S-R behavior theory. In T. Dixon & D. Horton (Eds.), *Verbal behavior and general behavior theory*. Englewood Cliffs, NJ: Prentice–Hall, 1968.

Dweck, C. S. The role of expectations and attributions in the alleviation of learned helplessness. *Journal of Personality and Social Psychology*, 1975, *31*, 674–685.

Dweck, C. S., & Elliott, E. S. Achievement motivation. In E. M Hetherington (Ed.), *Handbook of child psychology, Vol. IV* (4th edition). New York: Wiley, 1983.

Dweck, C. S., & Gilliard, D. Expectancy statements as determinants of reactions to failure: Sex differences in persistence and expectancy change. *Journal of Personality and Social Psychology*, 1975, *32*, 1077–1084.

Einhorn, H. J. The use of nonlinear, noncompensatory models in decision making. *Psychological Bulletin*, 1970, *73*, 221–230.

Elkind, D. Conservation and concept formation. In D. Elkind & J. Flavell (Eds), *Studies in cognitive development*. Oxford University Press: New York, 1969.

Ericcson, K. A., & Simon, H. A. Verbal reports as data. *Psychological Review*, 1980, *87*, 215–251.

Flavell, J. H., Friedrichs, A. G., & Hoyt, J. D. Developmental changes in memorization processes. *Cognitive Psychology*, 1970, *1*, 324–340.

Flavell, J. H., & Wellman, H. M. Metamemory. In R. V. Kail, Jr. & J. W. Hagen (Eds.), *Perspectives on the development of memory and cognition*. Hillsdale, NJ: Erlbaum, 1977.

Gupta, M., & Singh, R. An integration-theoretical analysis of cultural and developmental differences in attribution of performance. *Developmental Psychology*, 1981, *17*, 816–825.

Hanson, N. R. *Patterns of discovery*. Cambridge: Cambridge University, 1958.

Helson, H. *Adaptation–level theory*. New York: Harper & Row, 1964.

Jones, E. E., Rock, L., Shaver, K. G., Goethals, G. R., & Ward, L. M. Pattern of performance and ability attribution: An unexpected primacy effect. *Journal of Personality and Social Psychology*, 1968, *10*, 317–340.

Kaplan, M. F. Information integration in social judgment: Interaction of judge and informational components. In M. F. Kaplan & S. Schwartz (Eds.), *Human judgment and decision processes*. New York: Academic Press, 1975.

Karabenick, J. D., & Heller, K. A. A developmental study of effort and ability attributions. *Developmental Psychology*, 1976, *12*, 559–560.

Kassin, S. M., & Gibbons, F. X. Children's use of the discounting principle in their perceptions of exertion. *Child Development*, 1981, *52*, 741–744.

Kelley, H. H. *Causal schemata and the attribution process*. New York: General Learning Press, 1972.

Kelley, H. H. The processes of causal attribution. *American Psychologist*, 1973, *28*, 107–128.

Kepka, E., & Brickman, P. Consistency versus discrepancy as clues in the attribution of intelligence and motivation. *Journal of Personality and Social Psychology*, 1971, *20*, 223–229.

Krantz, D. H. Measurement structures and psychological laws. *Science,* 1972, *175,* 1427–1435.

Krantz, D. H., Luce, R. D., Suppes, P., & Tversky, A. *Foundations of measurement.* New York: Academic Press, 1971.

Krantz, D. H., & Tversky, A. Conjoint-measurement analysis of composition rules in psychology. *Psychological Review,* 1971, *78,* 151–169.

Kun, A. Development of the magnitude-covariation and compensation schemata in ability and effort attributions of performance. *Child Development,* 1977, *48,* 862–873.

Kun, A., Parsons, J., & Ruble, D. Development of integration processes using ability and effort information to predict outcome. *Developmental Psychology,* 1974, *10,* 721–732.

Larsen, G. Y., & Flavell, J. H. Verbal factors in compensation performance and the relation between conservation and compensation. *Child Development,* 1970, *41,* 965–977.

Leon, M. Coordination of intent and consequence information in children's moral judgments. In F. Wilkening, J. Becker & T. Trabasso (Eds.), *Information integration by children.* Hillsdale, NJ: Erlbaum, 1980.

Levin, I. P., Ims, J. R., & Vilmain, J. A. Information variability and reliability effects in evaluating student performance. *Journal of Educational Psychology,* 1980, *72,* 355–361.

Marks, L. E. On scales of sensation: Prolegomena to any future psychophysics that will be able to come forth as a science. *Perception & Psychophysics,* 1974, *16,* 358–376.

McMahan, I. D. Relationships between causal attributions and expectancy of success. *Journal of Personality and Social Psychology,* 1973, *28,* 108–114.

Mellers, B., & Birnbaum, M. H. Loci of contextual effects in judgment. *Journal of Experimental Psychology: Human Perception and Performance,* 1982, *8,* 582–601.

Mellers, B., & Birnbaum, M. H. Context effects in social judgment. *Journal of Experimental Social Psychology,* 1983, *19,* 157–171.

Nicholls, J. G. The development of the concepts of effort and ability, perception of academic attainment and the understanding that difficult tasks require more ability. *Child Development,* 1978, *49,* 800–814.

Nisbett, R. E., & Wilson, T. D. Telling more than we can know. Verbal reports on mental processes. *Psychological Review,* 1977, *84,* 231–259.

Oden, G. C. Integration of fuzzy logical information. *Journal of Experimental Psychology: Human Perception and Performance,* 1977, *3,* 565–575.

Parducci, A. The relativism of absolute judgment. *Scientific American,* 1968, *219,* 84–90.

Parducci, A. Context effects: A range-frequency analysis. In E. C. Carterette & M. P. Friedman (Eds.), *Handbook of perception* (Vol. II) New York: Academic Press, 1974.

Parducci, A. Category ratings: Still more contextual effects. In B. Wegener (Ed.), *Social attitudes and psychophysical measurement.* Hillsdale, N.J.: Erlbaum, 1982.

Parsons, J. E., & Ruble, D. N. The development of achievement-related expectancies. *Child Development,* 1977, *48,* 1075–1079.

Porac, J. F. Causal loops and other intercausal perceptions in attributions for exam performance. *Journal of Educational Psychology,* 1981, *73,* 587–601.

Reeder, G. D., & Brewer, M. B. A schematic model of dispositional attribution. *Psychological Review,* 1979, *86,* 61–79.

Rule, S. J., & Curtis, D. W. Ordinal properties of subjective ratios and differences: Comment on Veit. *Journal of Experimental Psychology: General,* 1980, *109,* 296–300.

Ryan, K. M., & Levine, J. M. Impact of academic performance pattern on assigned grade and predicted performance. *Journal of Educational Psychology,* 1981, *73,* 386–392.

Sedlak, A., & Kurtz, S. T. A review of children's use of causal inference principles. *Child Development,* 1981, *52,* 759–784.

Shaklee, H. Development of inferences of ability and task difficulty. *Child Development,* 1976, *47,* 1051–1057.

Shatz, M. The relationship between cognitive processes and the development of communication skills. In C. B. Keasey (Ed.), *Nebraska symposium on motivation 1977* (Vol. 25) Lincoln, NE: University of Nebraska Press, 1978.

Singh, R., Gupta, M., & Dalal, A. K. Cultural difference in attribution of performance: An integration-theoretical analysis. *Journal of Personality and Social Psychology*, 1979, *37*, 1342–1351.

Slovic, P. Hypothesis testing in the learning of positive and negative linear functions. *Organizational behavior and human performance*, 1974, *11*, 368–376.

Stevens, S. S., & Galanter, E. H. Ratio scales and category scales for a dozen perceptual continua. *Journal of Experimental Psychology*, 1957, *54*, 337–411.

Stipek, D. J., & Hoffman, J. M. Development of children's performance–related judgments. *Child Development*, 1980, *51*, 912–914.

Surber, C. F. Developmental processes in social inference: Averaging of intentions and consequences by moral judgment. *Developmental Psychology*, 1977, *13*, 654–665.

Surber, C. F. *Organization in social inference: Is there a schema for judgments of ability, effort, and task performance?* Unpublished doctoral dissertation, University of Illinois at Urbana–Champaign, 1978.

Surber, C. F. The development of reversible operations in judgments of ability, effort and performance. *Child Development*, 1980, *51*, 1018–1029.

Surber, C. F. Effects of information reliability in predicting task performance using ability and effort. *Journal of Personality and Social Psychology*, 1981, *40*, 977–989. (a)

Surber, C. F. Necessary versus sufficient causal schemata: Attributions for achievement in difficult and easy tasks. *Journal of Experimental Social Psychology*, 1981, *17*, 569–586. (b)

Surber, C.F. Separable effects of motives, consequences, and presentation order on children's moral judgments. *Developmental Psychology*, 1982, *18*, 259–266.

Surber, C. F. Issues in using quantitative rating scales in developmental research. *Psychological Bulletin*, 1984, *95*, 226–246. (a)

Surber, C. F. Inferences of ability and effort: Evidence for two different processes. *Journal of Personality and Social Psychology*, 1984, *46*, 249–268. (b)

Surber, C. F. Measuring the importance of information in judgment: Individual differences in weighing ability and effort. *Organizational Behavior and Human Performance*, in press.

Torgerson, W. S. Distances and ratios in psychological scaling. *Acta Psychologica*, 1961, *19*, 201–205.

Tversky, A., & Kahneman, D. Causal schemata in judgments under uncertainty. In M. Fishbein (Ed.), *Progress in social psychology*. Hillsdale, NJ: Erlbaum, 1980.

Weiner, B., Frieze, I., Kukla, A., Reed, L., Rest, S., & Rosenbaum, R. Perceiving the causes of success and failure. In E. E. Jones et al. (Eds.), *Attribution: Perceiving the causes of behavior*. Morristown, NJ: General Learning Press, 1971.

Wilkening, F. Integrating velocity, time, and distance information: A developmental study. *Cognitive Psychology*, 1981, *13*, 231–247.

Wyer, R. S. An investigation of relations among probability estimates. *Organizational Behavior and Human Performance*, 1976, *15*, 1–18.

Yussen, S. R., & Levy, V. M., Jr. Developmental changes in predicting one's own span of short-term memory. *Journal of Experimental Child Psychology*, 1975, *19*, 502–508.

DEVELOPMENT AND ITS DISCONTENTS:
THE DIFFERENTIATION OF THE CONCEPT OF ABILITY

John G. Nicholls and Arden T. Miller

Reviewing earlier work on the development of achievement motivation, Atkinson (1969) asked "Why don't the researchers now studying children profit from the hard-won gains in conceptual analysis of the determinants of achievement-oriented behavior? Why do they dart in and out of the conceptual scheme evolved studying older subjects but never seem to make full and systematic use of it in their analysis of their problems?" (p. 201–202). We sought to make the fullest possible use of the various schemes worked out with adults. However, our attempt to describe the development of achievement motivation highlighted certain deficiencies of these schemes. These deficiencies in general achievement motivation theory made if difficult to formulate a coherent and internally consistent analysis of the development of achievement motivation. Ironically, the

Advances in Motivation and Achievement, vol. 3, pages 185–218
Copyright © 1984 by JAI Press Inc.
All rights of reproduction in any form reserved.
ISBN 0-89232-289-6

developmental research we describe here provided a key to a new perspective on adult achievement behavior. This research highlighted certain features of achievement motivation that appear unique to adults and others that appear common to adults and children. The achievement behavior of most adults can, at times, resemble that of children. At other times it has features not found in children. This insight led to a framework that enables prediction of situations where mature individuals act in uniquely adult-like versus child-like ways. Thus, our developmental research provided insights on adult achievement motivation.

The research we discuss here also highlights an irony of a different kind. White (1959) has suggested that intellectual development is fostered by compe-tence motivation: An intrinsic tendency to master or to gain knowledge. The development of knowledge of one's causal role in events and of the nature of ability is presumably also fostered by competence motivation. Ironically, a more mature understanding of ability can have unfortunate consequences for compe-tence motivation and, thereby, for continued intellectual development. Develop-ment has its discontents. These discontents stem not only from the imposition of civilization's imperatives on growing children (Freud, 1931), but also from the "natural" process of cognitive and affective development.

THE GENERAL FRAMEWORK

Our initial assumption was that individuals' perceptions of their competence or ability play a central role in achievement behavior (Kukla, 1972, 1978; Nicholls 1983, in press). This position is supported by evidence that feelings of accom-plishment appear to be maximized by perception that one has demonstrated ability (e.g., Covington & Omelich, 1979; Nicholls, 1976); that expectancies of future success and failure are a function of attribution of past outcomes to ability (e.g., Weiner, Nierenberg & Goldstein, 1976)[1]; and that attribution of failure to lack of ability mediates maladaptive achievement behavior (e.g., Dweck & Goetz, 1978).

The claim that conceptions of ability are central to achievement behavior is, however, as much a matter of definition as a matter of evidence. Achievement behavior is best defined as behavior on skill tasks or, at least, on tasks where individuals believe or feel that their competence affects outcomes. Achievement behavior is distinguished from other forms of behavior by its purpose: the goal of achievement behavior is to be or to feel competent rather than incompetent (Maehr & Nicholls, 1980; Nicholls, in press).

Whether one starts with the definition or with the related evidence, one comes to the same conclusion. Namely, the development of the concept of ability is central to the development of achievement motivation. Here, the development of the concept of ability is conceived as a process of differentiation. Following Heider (1958), attribution theorists (Weiner, Frieze, Kukla, Reed, Rest, & Rosenbaum, 1971) hold that adults explain success and failure on skill tasks in terms of ability, effort, luck, and task difficulty among other factors. This implies that these factors are clearly differentiated from one another. For example, we assume than an individual who responds to success with, "I could do it because it was easy," means something quite different from the individual who says "I could do it because I'm smart." In young children such meanings are imperfectly differentiated from one another.

When mature individuals say "This is too hard," they usually imply that it is too hard for most people and that failure will not show they lack ability. However, when the concepts of ability and difficulty are imperfectly differentiated, the statement "This is too hard" can imply a lack of ability. That is, ability and related concepts have different meanings at different levels of development. The inference that one has high or low ability has, therefore, different affective and behavioral implications at different levels of development. The conclusion that one has low ability can, for example, hurt adults more and hurt them differently from the way it hurts young children.

Stated another way, our concern was with the intensive content of achievement-related concepts. That is, with the type of content that might be assessed by asking for verbal definitions—by asking "What does it mean to say that someone has high ability?" (Elkind, 1969). But, simply asking children to define or explain concepts is, as Piaget found, a rather poor method of establishing the intensive content of children's concepts. Accordingly, we based our work on Piaget's method of critical exploration (Inhelder, Sinclair, & Bovet, 1974) wherein children are presented carefully designed stimuli and questioned about these in a flexible but systematic, hypothesis-testing fashion.

The extensive content (Elkind, 1969) of children's ability-related concepts refers to the decision rules children use to infer ability or probabilities of demonstrating ability. Such decision rules were also of interest and were seen as an expression of the intensive content—what we call the meaning of ability, difficulty, and so on. Young children's less differentiated conceptions of ability, for example, mean that they use different criteria to judge whether they have demonstrated or developed ability. Similarly, they use different criteria to judge their chances of demonstrating or developing ability. Accordingly they will, at times, differ from adults in the way they respond to task characteristics (e.g., difficulty cues), performance outcomes (e.g., scoring higher than others), and social feedback (e.g., teacher anger after a child's failure). Young children differ from adults in the way they interpret the implications of such information for their ability. Consequently, they also differ in their related affective and overt behavioral responses to such information.

To provide an overview, we present a comparison of the intensive and extensive content of the conception of ability at about twelve years of age with that of children of about five years of age. The more differentiated conception of most twelve years olds is embodied in standard ability testing procedures (Nicholls, 1978b). First, an individual's level of ability is defined with reference to the performance of others. A raw ability test score is not very informative. It must be compared with the performance of a suitable reference group if one is to make an adequate inference of ability. Second, a valid ability inference demands evidence that optimum effort was employed. It is assumed that ability will not be revealed if effort is low. On the other hand, it is assumed that effort will increase performance, but only up to the limit of one's capacity. That is, ability is conceived as capacity—an underlying trait that is not observed directly but is inferred from both effort and performance in a context of social comparison. When mature individuals believe their ability is low, they believe they lack capacity. This is not the case for young children.

For young children, high ability is implied by learning or by success at tasks they are uncertain of being able to complete. They do not judge ability with reference to performance norms or social comparisons. They can be induced to adopt another's performance as a standard, but normally they make self-referenced rather than norm-referenced judgments of ability: high ability means higher performance than before. Ability does not, in this case, imply an inferred trait. For young children, more effort implies more learning (or is more learning) which is more ability. Effort can have quite different implications for adults and young children. Both realize that more effort produces more learning. For adults, however, higher effort implies lower ability if others require less effort for the same performance. For young children, more effort means more learning or a larger accomplishment which means more ability.

The younger child's perspective could be termed subjective. For them, the subjective experience of gaining insight or mastery through effort is the experience of competence or ability. For adults, a gain in mastery can also lead to feelings of competence. However, for them, a gain in mastery could lead to a feeling of incompetence if, on adopting the more objective viewpoint which the young child lacks, they observe that their peers master more with equivalent effort or achieve the same with less effort. Adults can employ both more and less differentiated conceptions. However, we will leave this issue aside for the moment and focus on the development of the capacity to use increasingly differentiated conceptions.

This preliminary comparison of more and less differentiated conceptions of ability overlooks a number of intermediate transitions. The differentiation of the concept of ability involves three levels of increasing differentiation of difficulty and ability and four levels of differentiation of effort and ability in a context of social comparison. The major transitions have been found to be accompanied by theoretically meaningful changes in both achievement affect and overt behavior. These findings provide validation of our measures of level of differentiation of the concept of ability and of the related theory that gives perceptions of ability a central role in achievement motivation. First, we will examine the evidence on the development of the concept of ability. Then we will consider affective and behavioral development.

THE DIFFERENTIATION OF DIFFICULTY AND ABILITY

We have distinguished three levels of differentiation of the concepts of difficulty and ability. These have been termed ego-centric, objective, and normative conceptions of difficulty. Rather than take readers over the tortuous route we took to reach this position, we present it in its present form (Nicholls & Miller, 1983). This differs somewhat from earlier positions (Nicholls, 1978b, 1980b).

The Normative Conception of Difficulty

At the most complex of the three levels, the concepts of ability and difficulty are clearly differentiated from one another. This differentiation depends on understanding of the implications of performance norms or social comparison for ability and task difficulty. Tasks are judged more difficult if fewer members of a reference group can do them. Correspondingly, higher ability is inferred when individuals succeed on tasks than fewer others can do. If performance norms are not used in this way, it is not possible to tell whether a given success reflects high ability or task ease or whether a given failure reflects high difficulty or low ability. In other words, the normative conception of difficulty embodies a clear differentiation of the concepts of difficulty and ability.

Attainment of the normative conception is indicated when children recognize that more ability is required for success on unseen tasks on which few others are said to succeed (Nicholls, 1978b, 1980b; Nicholls & Miller, 1983). This conception is achieved at about seven years with the stimuli we have used and slightly earlier with Shaklee's (1976) method. In one study, Ruble, Boggiano, Feldman, and Loebl (1980) found that second but not first graders used normative performance feedback to infer task difficulty and their own ability. In a second study, they found ability inferences and expectancies of winning affected by social comparison feedback at fourth but not second grade.

Young children's lack of understanding of normative difficulty in our studies cannot be attributed to a failure on their part to understand our question, "Which puzzle would you have to be very smart to do?" Most first graders who do not respond to this question by choosing unseen tasks that fewest others are said to succeed on do, nevertheless, recognize that the most complex of an array of jigsaw puzzles demands most ability (Nicholls & Miller 1983). Thus, it appears that they encounter "problems" with the normative cues rather than the question.[2]

There is more involved in the development of the normative conception of difficulty, however, than a change in the way normatives cues are processed. If children are presented unseen tasks described as "easy," "moderate," and "hard," results are similar to those obtained with performance norms. In this case, children do not have to infer task difficulty because difficulty is stated. Yet, recognition that difficult tasks demand more ability occurs at about the same age for direct statements of difficulty and for normative cues (Nicholls, 1980b). This implies that the attainment of the normative conception involves a change in the intensive content of children's conceptions of difficulty. It involves a change in the meaning of terms like ''hard'' and ''easy'' as well as a change in interpretation of performance norms.

Most children over the age of seven have attained the normative conception. For them, a ''hard'' task is one that few others can do. Thus, task difficulty can be understood independently of one's own actual or expected performance. Regardless of one's own expectancies of success it can be seen that more difficult tasks—those that few can do—demand more ability. At the earlier levels, the concept of difficulty is less clearly distinguished from the concept of ability and from one's own expectations of success.

The Objective Conception of Difficulty

At the second level, performance norms are not employed to establish task difficulty or ability. At this level, individuals understand a continuum of difficulty levels based on observed objective task properties such as complexity or size, e.g., complexity of jig-saw puzzles or distances from a ring-toss target.

From the perspective of the normative conception of difficulty, the implication of any given outcome for one's ability is obscure at the objective level. Failure, for example, could be said to occur ''Because the task is hard.'' But this cannot be distinguished from ''It is too hard for me,'' or ''I'm not smart enough for it.'' Norms are necessary to judge task difficulty and ability independently of the subjective experience or expectation of difficulty in doing a task. If performance norms are not understood or are unavailable, no performance outcome provides a precise basis for inferring high or low ability. Thus, at the objective level, difficulty and ability are imperfectly differentiated despite a recognition that more objectively difficult tasks require more ability.

The existence of the objective conception of difficulty was initially suggested by evidence that children below six years of age (who would not understand normative difficulty) engage in calculated goal-setting when concrete difficulty cues are available (Heckhausen, 1967). That is, if given repeated opportunities to perform tasks, they select objective difficulty levels where they have moderate probabilities of success. This suggests that these children recognize, at some level, variations in objective task difficulty and realize that more objectively difficult tasks demand more ability.

Mastery of the objective conception of difficulty was directly established by asking children which of an array of jigsaw puzzles varying in complexity would require most ability (Nicholls & Miller, 1983). Most first and second grade children, including those who did not understand normative difficulty, had mastered objective difficulty. They claimed that more complex puzzles demanded more ability and explained this with reference to the greater number of pieces in these puzzles.

The Ego-Centric Conception of Difficulty

A still less differentiated conception of difficulty and ability, termed ego-centric difficulty, was proposed and evidence consistent with its existence obtained (Nicholls & Miller, 1983). It seemed that younger children might discriminate tasks on the basis of their own subjective certainty of being able to complete them. At this level, a task could be judged hard if one was certain of failure on it and easy if success appeared certain. At the objective level, a continuum of objective difficulty levels is perceived independently of the individual's subjective probabilities of success. At the ego-centric level, however, objective difficulty is imperfectly differentiated from one's subjective probability of success.

The ego-centric conception of difficulty could, like the objective conception, mediate calculated goal setting when concrete difficulty cues are available. Children, like adults, appear to prefer tasks they are uncertain of being able to complete to those they are certain they either can or cannot complete (Schneider, this volume). If children at the ego-centric level discern task difficulty in terms of their own uncertainty of being able to complete tasks, they could display calculated goal-setting even though they may not perceive correlated continuua of ability and difficulty.

The presence of the ego-centric level was indicated by evidence of calculated goal setting in children who did not understand objective difficulty. Though they did not consciously recognize that objectively more difficult jigsaw puzzles demanded more ability, they displayed consistent individual differences in the level of difficulty they preferred to attempt (Nicholls & Miller, 1983). A small proportion of first graders and fewer second graders were found to be at this level.

The different meanings of difficulty could account for age differences in children's explanations for liking or disliking of school subjects. Blumenfeld and Pintrich (Note 1) found second graders were more likely to mention difficulty of subjects than were sixth graders who more often cited personal reasons like being good or bad at subjects. On face value, it might look as if younger children are less concerned about their ability and more concerned about task difficulty. As we will see, there may be some truth to this. However, for children with the objective and ego-centric conceptions of difficulty, the statement "It is too hard" can be close in meaning to an older child's statement that "I'm no good at it."

The Question of Sequence

The likelihood that the above three levels would form a sequence was suggested by the fact that the more complex levels subsume the simpler ones. At all levels, individuals' subjective probabilities of success are lower when tasks are perceived as more difficult. But, at the ego-centric level, difficulty is not understood independently of subjective probabilities of success. At the objective level, variations in objective difficulty are recognized independently of one's own expectancies of success. Yet, this level does not permit a precise distinction between the contributions of task difficulty and ability to outcomes. This is only achieved at the normative level. Thus, mastery of later levels implies mastery of the earlier levels.

Because the normative and objective conceptions of difficulty were assessed independently (understanding of norms or of jig-saw puzzles respectively) we were able to use both cross-sectional and longitudinal methods to assess sequence of attainment or usage of these two levels. The cross-sectional data strongly supported the hypothesis that normative difficulty implies mastery of objective difficulty (Nicholls & Miller, 1983). If we consider one point in time, understanding of normative difficulty appears to demand prior understanding of objective difficulty. Over a one-year time span, there were significant progressive trends from ego-centric to objective and from objective to normative difficulty levels. However, there were more violations of sequence in the longitudinal data. These data indicate that a neat stepwise pattern of longitudinal development may not follow even when later levels subsume earlier ones. Other data on cognitive development (e.g., Damon, 1981) show similar patterns. There is some temporal instability when maturity is assessed close to a transition point, but progressive trends are still evident. Thus, longitudinal and cross-sectional data both support the proposed developmental sequence.

Accuracy of Social Comparison

The normative conception of ability implies a realization that social comparison is necessary for adequate ability inferences. It does not follow, however, that attainment of this conception will immediately be accompanied by accurate social comparisons of performance or ability. In fact, comparisons of self and others increase in accuracy up to about 12 years of age. This is revealed when children are asked to rank their own academic attainment relative to that of their classmates. Young children rank themselves at or close to the top of their class. It gets lonelier at the top as they get older. Older children's self-perceptions are also more highly correlated with attainment (Nicholls, 1978b, 1979a, 1980a). Five-and six-year-olds' self-rankings are not significantly associated with attainment whereas 12-year-olds' self-rankings correlate up to .80 with teacher rankings. This increase in accuracy may not merely be a function of the greater number of opportunities older children have had to compare themselves with others. There is some indication that more mature conceptions of ability are associated with more accurate self-rankings when age is partialled out (Nicholls, 1978b).

These age trends in accuracy of perception of academic attainment relative to those of others are paralleled by similar trends in perception of sociometric status (Ausubel, Schiff, & Gasser, 1952), social characteristics (Phillips, 1963), physical strength (Goss, 1968) and toughness (Freedman, 1975). Similar age-trends are also evident in expectations of performance where social comparison cues are not available (Stipek, this volume).

Cognitive maturity and number of opportunities for social comparison are doubtless involved in these age differences. Young children's tendency to overestimate their attainment and competence can also reflect a self-serving tendency (Stipek, this volume). For our purposes, however, the important point is that the full behavioral and affective consequences of attainment of the normative conception of difficulty will not always be fully apparent on attainment of that conception. Since comparisons can remain inaccurate and somewhat self-serving for some time after this conception is attained, many younger children whose performance is low relative to that of others may not perceive their ability as low. They will be less likely than older children with similar levels of performance to perceive their ability as low.

THE DIFFERENTIATION OF EFFORT AND ABILITY

Four Levels of Differentiation

In intelligence testing, it is normally assumed that ability will only be revealed when effort is optimum (Heider, 1958). If two people perform equally well, the one who uses less effort is judged more able because their score does not reflect capacity as fully as does the score of the other individual. Ability and effort are, in this view, interdependent concepts (Nicholls, 1978b); One concept cannot be defined without defining the other. This conception of ability as capacity implies that the effect of effort is limited by ability. Conversely, the trait ability is only fully evident when effort is high. Also, these concepts make sense only in a context of social comparison. A lone individual's ability to do any specific task with high or low effort does not enable a valid inference of ability. High ability means higher ability than that of others. Thus we have a conception of ability as capacity: an inferred trait which is judged relative to the effort and performance of others rather than in terms of an individual's ability to do specific tasks with any level of effort.

The stimuli used to study the development of the above conceptions of ability and effort employed the simplest possible constellation of relevant cues presented in a realistic manner. Children were shown films or videotapes of two children who simultaneously performed identical tasks with different amounts of effort. In one stimulus situation (Nicholls, 1978b; Nicholls & Miller Note 2), the two children achieved the same score. In another (Nicholls, 1978b), the harder worker achieved a lower score.

These situations do not depend on children's understanding of effort and ability-related statements. Also, they are a simplified form of the situations children are likely to observe in school and on playing fields. Ability is not observed directly in the real world, but is inferred from comparisons of performance and effort. This, however, is not merely a characteristic of the external world. It is a characteristic of the concept of ability. Let anyone who doubts this try to make a film that "shows" ability in the direct way that effort and performance can be shown. They will find themselves making a film in which effort, performance, or other cues such as age or physical size, imply rather than show ability.

From this perspective, studies that elicit children's reasoning about verbal description of ability and other factors (e.g., Kun, 1977, Study 1) are seen as studies of the inferences children make about these words and as implying that these words are understood in the same way by children of different ages and by the experimenter. Other studies (e.g., Kun, 1977, Study 2) employ such verbal terms in combination with visual representations of ability (e.g, physical size). Because ability in the sense of capacity cannot be represented directly, such studies appear to confound inferences about ability-related visual cues with inferences about ability-related verbal terms. These different methods appear to differ in more than details of method. They differ also in the conceptions of knowledge they imply (Elkind, 1969).

Our method was adapted to age differences by developing, in pilot work, a set of questions that elicited the fullest possible interpretations of the filmed situations from both younger and older children. Questions and stimuli differed in their usefulness for generating clearly interpretable responses at different ages, but a standard set of both was used at all ages (Nicholls, 1978b). Also in keeping with Piaget's method of critical exploration, supplementary questions were used with the aim of ensuring that the child's knowledge was fully revealed without distorting it to reflect experimenter preconceptions. A structural-developmental analysis of responses to the films and the associated questions produced the following four levels of differentiation of effort and ability:

Level 1: Effort or Outcome is Ability

Effort and outcome are not distinguished as cause and effect. Explanations are tautological, and ability, effort, and outcome are not distinguished as separate dimensions. Children center on effort (people who try harder are seen as smarter even if they get a lower score) or, less commonly, on outcome (people who get a higher score are said to work harder—even if they do not—and are seen as smarter).

Level 2: Effort is the Cause of Performance Outcomes

Effort and outcome are distinguished as cause and effect. Effort is the prime cause of outcomes: Equal effort is expected to lead to equal outcomes. Ability, in the sense of capacity which can increase or limit the effectiveness of effort, is not conceived as a cause.

When people get the same score but differ in effort, this is seen as due to compensatory effort by the student who tried less (e.g., she/he worked really hard for a while, worked at the end, might have started earlier, or must have been thinking while fiddling) or as due to misapplied effort by the person who tried harder (e.g., she/he tried too hard or went too quickly and made mistakes).

Limits to the effectiveness of effort are tacitly acknowledged, however, when one person tries harder than another but gets a lower score. Though the concept of ability as capacity is not used, the reality of this situation is acknowledged: people are correctly classified and ordered in terms of effort and outcome and the higher score implies higher ability.

Level 3: Effort and Ability Partially Differentiated

The concept of ability is partially differentiated from effort. Effort is not the only cause of outcomes. Explanations of equal outcomes following different effort involve suggestions such as: The person trying less is faster, brighter, has a better understanding, or is naturally good at the activity. These explanations imply the conception of ability as capacity; they imply that high ability can compensate for lack of effort and that low ability limits the effect of effort. These implications are not, however, systematically followed through. Despite such explanations, children may assert that students gaining equal scores after unequal effort are as smart as each other or that harder workers are smarter and that students would get the same scores if they worked as hard as each other. Occasionally, explanations are of the level 2 type, but children expect that students who try less will improve more if both try hard.

Level 4: Ability is Capacity

Ability is conceived as capacity which, if low, may limit or, if high, may increase the effect of effort on performance. Ability is correctly inferred from both effort and outcomes; when performances are equal, lower effort implies higher ability. Effort and ability are seen as interdependent causes of outcomes; higher ability means that less effort is needed to achieve a given outcome.

The following interview transcript illustrates Level 4 reasoning. In this case the subject applied more effort on spatial reasoning problems than a videotaped other he observed. He was told they both scored the same. Initially this boy's reasoning suggests Level 1 or 2. However, the third question elicits a Level 4 response and this level is sustained. As noted below (see also Nicholls & Miller, Note 2), initial responses often fail to reveal a child's capacity.

> Did one of you work harder or did you work the same?
> I worked more.
> Is one of you smarter at these puzzles or are you the same?

I'm smarter.

How can you tell?

'Cause he goofed off and I worked harder.

How come you both got the same score when you worked hard and he didn't?

I guess he is smarter 'cause normally when someone works harder they are smarter, but if you goof off and can do well then you must be smarter.

Does it often happen that someone who doesn't work hard gets high scores?

Usually if you goof off you get bad grades. The smart people work hard to get their good grades.[3]

What would happen if you both worked really hard? Would one of you get more or would you both get the same?

He'd get a better score.

How can you tell?

He goofed off and I didn't and we got the same. So, if we were both serious, then he would get higher.

So do you think one of you is smarter or are you the same?

He's smarter.

A structural-developmental analysis implies that knowledge can be described as an invariant sequence of qualitatively different forms of reasoning, each of which involves an organization uniting a variety of superficially different responses. Also, the levels should be hierachical integrations. Higher levels should include lower ones as components reintegrated at a higher level (Kohlberg 1969; Piaget 1960). Each level described above can be seen as a differentiation and qualitatively more advanced restructuring of the previous one. Effort, ability, and outcome are not systematically distinguished from one another at level 1. At the second level, effort as a cause is differentiated from outcomes, but the particular conception of ability that is necessary to explain how equal scores can result in spite of unequal effort is not established. Level 3 does not have the internal consistency of the other levels. It represents an advance on level 2 in that ability is distinguished from effort. However, ability is not consistently understood as capacity. Thus, this level might best be seen as a transitional state rather than a level with its own distinctive logic. Only at Level 4 is ability as capacity clearly differentiated from effort, and ability and effort seen as interdependent causes of outcomes. These levels appear to satisfy the criteria of a sequence of qualitatively different, hierarchically integrated, levels of reasoning. Though we have no longitudinal data on order of attainment or usage, age trends (Figure 1) are consistent with the sequence.

A significant association between the Level 2 conception of effort and ability and the normative conception of difficulty (Nicholls, 1978b) suggests that these develop at about the same time. This suggests that the changes in the concept of ability occurring at about the time when concrete operations emerge are considerable. It also indicates how far the child has to go after attaining the normative conception of difficulty before ability means what it means to an adult. Children at level 2 recognize that being smart means being more able than others. At level

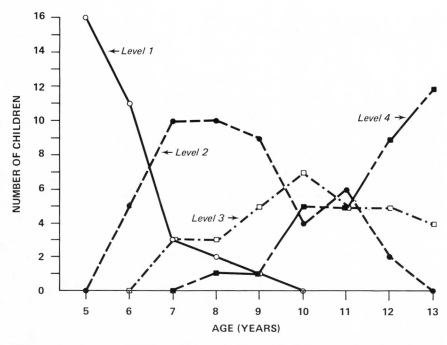

Figure 1. Levels of differentiation of effort and ability as a function of age.

2, however, being able is not clearly distinguished from trying harder or scoring higher than others. For children at level 2, effort is the prime cause of performance outcomes. It seems that ability, being imperfectly differentiated from effort, is limited primarily by effort. At this point effort is not merely virtuous in the sense that it is socially desirable: effort will make you smarter and there is no danger that trying harder might indicate lower ability. At level 4, the possibility that higher effort will imply lower ability is recognized. Level 4 children understand that if one has to work harder to do as well as others, one has less ability than they do. Harari and Covington (1981) also found that such inferences were made by older more than by younger children.

If the above picture of the development of the conception of ability as capacity is correct, as age increases, ability should be seen as increasingly necessary for high achievement. In other words, the qualitative changes in the concepts of effort and ability should be accompanied by changes in perception of the relative importance of effort and ability for performance. This prediction was confirmed by a comparison of 11- and 15-year-olds (Kessell, 1979). Fifteen-year-olds rated ability as more important, relative to effort, for outstanding performance in school than did 11-year-olds. Thus, the development of the concept of ability involves not only changes in the meaning of effort and ability and in the way children use effort and performance information to infer ability, it also involves changes in perception of the relative importance of effort and ability.

Reasoning About Own Ability and Effort

Our primary concern was with children's inferences about their own ability. For this reason, and because adequate judgment of ability depends on comparison of the effort and performance of self and others, we went on to compare reasoning about own ability and effort with reasoning about the ability and effort of others. The concept of difficulty was studied by asking children questions about tasks they were about to attempt. Thus, the applicability of those results to children's own behavior is not in question. In the case of effort and ability, however, it was necessary to establish whether children are able and inclined to apply to themselves the reasoning they apply to others.

To do this, we retained the procedures of the first study of effort and ability (Nicholls, 1978b) and added conditions where children themselves applied either higher or lower effort and gained the same score as another child (Nicholls & Miller, Note 2). In this study, responses to individual questions as well as to the interview as a whole were analyzed. The whole interview is necessary to make a sound judgment of level of reasoning because the individual questions each deal with different aspects of the concepts of ability and effort. Nevertheless, objective responses to individual questions were of interest. These varied across self and other and high and low effort conditions. Children tended to be reluctant to acknowledge their own lack of effort and were, in some cases, less likely to make mature ability judgments when they were involved. Judgments of ability were also significantly less mature at the beginning than at the end of the interview. This might explain why methods employing only initial objective responses (Harari & Covington, 1981; Nicholls, 1978a) reveal less mature ability inferences than does our method (Nicholls & Miller, Note 2). However, no condition effects were found for the structural analysis of responses to the whole interview. That is, children employ the same conceptions of effort and ability when reasoning about the self and when reasoning about others. The situational variability of objective responses is of interest in its own right (see also Surber, this volume). However, the absence of condition effects on conceptions of ability as revealed by structural analysis suggests that this index tells us something substantial about the way children think about themselves.

Further evidence that the changes in the concepts of ability and effort revealed by our index manifest themselves in children's inferences about themselves comes from an experimental study of attributions of effort and ability after success and failure (Rholes, Blackwell, Jordan, & Walters, 1980). Fifth grader's effort and ability attributions were negatively related: higher perceived effort was associated with lower perceived ability at an experimental task. Perceptions of effort and ability tended to be positively associated in younger children. This is as expected. An inverse relationship between perceptions of effort and ability should depend on the conception of ability as capacity that begins to emerge at about fifth grade. Similar results were obtained by Miller (1982) in a comparisons of second and sixth graders. Miller also found a significant difference between correlations of self-ratings of effort and ability for sixth graders who had partially or completely attained the conception of ability as capacity (levels 3 and 4) and those who had not. These correlations were negative for level 3 and 4 children and positive for less mature children.

The above experiments did not deal with children's reasoning about naturally occurring successes and failures. However, convergent results were obtained in a study where children were asked to select the causes of their academic successes and failures (Nicholls, 1979a). The findings of relevance to the present theme are the correlations between these causal attributions and children's actual and perceived attainment. The correlations between attributions of success and perceived attainment are shown in Table 1. Correlations involving grades were slightly lower but showed the same age-trends.

The positive correlation between perceived attainment and attributions of success to high effort for 6-year-old boys is consistent with younger children's tendency to see effort as the prime cause of success. More salient, however, is

Table 1. Correlations of Perception of Own Reading Attainment With Grades in Reading and Causal Attributions for Success in Reading

Age & Sex	n	Grades	Attribution of Success to			
			Ability	Effort	Difficulty	Luck
6 years						
F	63	.07	.09	.01	−.12	.02
M	84	.19	.03	.24*	−.03	−.26*
8 years						
F	54	.30*	.19	−.16	.10	−.15
M	71	.44***	.28**	−.12	−.09	−.08
10 years						
F	58	.37**	.17	.10	−.07	−.16
M	76	.55***	.40***	−.35**	−.04	−.07
12 years						
F	57	.76***	.59***	−.28*	−.12	−.49***
M	77	.67***	.57***	−.37**	−.05	−.49***

Note: A positive correlation indicates perception of high attainment associated with high grades or perception of cause as important.

*p < .05.
**p < .01.
***p < .001.

"Reprinted with permission," from the *Journal of Educational Psychology*, Copyright © 1979, *71*, p. 76.

the consistent age increase in associations of ability and effort attributions with perceived attainment. The correlations appear to reflect the progressive differentiation of these concepts up to 12 years. When ability is conceived as underlying capacity (level 4), children who believe they frequently perform well would be expected to be more inclined than those with low perceived attainment to attribute their successes to high ability rather than to effort or luck. When ability is seen as equivalent to or as a function of effort (levels 1 and 2), such a selective use of ability and effort attributions would not be expected. These results are, therefore, consistent with the above evidence of age differences in the differentiation of the concepts of ability and effort. They also suggest that the age trends observed in experimental studies occur in the real world of achievement behavior.

The developments described in this section can be summarized by restating the changes in the role of effort in inferences of ability and the changes in the meaning of both effort and ability. First, in young children, high effort implies or is virtually equivalent to high ability. For younger and older children, effort may increase performance or learning, but for older children, when other things are equal, higher effort implies lower ability. So the implications of effort for perceived ability change dramatically. Second, for younger children, having high or low ability does not mean having high or low capacity. It means something closer to what a mature individual would understand as trying or not trying hard or completing or not completing a task. Ability does mean capacity for older children. For them, ability, compared to effort, is seen as more critical for high performance than it is for younger children. Conversely, lack of ability is seen as more crippling by older than younger children. That is, the meaning of ability as well as the method of inferring it changes with age. These conclusions indicate that the implications of perceptions of effort and ability for children's competence-related emotions should also undergo developmental change.

AFFECTIVE AND EVALUATIVE RESPONSES

Before the role of the development of the concept of ability in achievement-related affect and evaluations can be considered, we need a general conception of the nature of achievement affect. We start with White's (1959) position that higher organisms that are not under physiological or psychological stress find the experience of increasing one's mastery or competence satisfying. That is, the experience of ability in the less differentiated sense is satisfying. White argued that this satisfaction cannot and need not be explained with reference to other incentives. Many others have concurred with this view and, like White, have pointed out the evolutionary value of this tendency (e.g., Deci, 1975; Flavell, 1977).

Our argument is that as the criteria whereby individuals judge competence change, so will the situations that occasion feelings of competence change. The differentiation of the concept of ability also implies that there will be qualitative changes in the emotions associated with perceptions of ability and the factors that become differentiated from it—most notably, effort. That is, as achievement-cognitions become more differentiated with age, so do achievement-related emotions. Similar views of the development of moral and altruistic emotions have been presented (Dienstbier, Hillman, Lenhoff, Hillman, & Valkenaar, 1975; Hoffman, 1975).

Difficulty and Ability

As noted above, the development of the normative conception of difficulty is accompanied by corresponding changes in the understanding of the terms "hard" and "easy." It is also accompanied by changes in perception of teacher evaluations of success on tasks described as "hard" or "easy" (Nicholls, 1980b) and on tasks where difficulty is communicated by norms alone (Nicholls, 1978b, 1980b). The expectation that teachers would be more pleased by success on difficult tasks was associated with the normative conception of difficulty (where hard means hard for most children and ability is judged relative to the performance of others). Few children who had not yet attained the normative conception of difficulty expected a teacher to be most pleased by success on the most difficult task. (See also Heckhausen, this volume.) In other words, the attainment of the normative conception of difficulty is accompanied by increased awareness of the evaluative significance of outperforming others and of doing well on tasks labeled as hard.

This conclusion is also supported by evidence of increases, from kindergarten to second grade, in the number of times children compare their performance with that of peers in an experimental situation (Ruble, Feldman, & Boggiano, 1976). Similarly, in a naturalistic study of classroom interaction, Ruble and Frey (Note 3) found age increases in requests for information about peer progress on academic tasks. First graders made more such requests than kindergarten children and fewer than second or fourth graders. This trend probably reflects children's increasing recognition that to be smart means to be smarter than others. These findings also indicate that the age trends found in experimental studies also apply in the "real world."

Effort and Ability

The above studies (Nicholls, 1978b, 1980b) had the advantage that maturity of the concept of ability and of evaluative interpretations was measured with the same children. Except in one instance (Nicholls, 1978b), this condition was not met in the studies discussed in this section. Variations across studies in the cognitive demands of tasks and in the nature of populations preclude the establishment of precise empirical linkages between cognitive and affective or evaluative measures. (Meyer et al., 1979, for example, found considerable age differences in two studies with the same stimuli.) However, convergence of age trends across different populations and stimuli is encouragingly high.

A number of studies have examined evaluative responses to descriptions of children who have succeeded or failed due to different combinations of high and low effort and ability. These are studies of evaluative reactions to ability and effort-related terms rather than studies of evaluative reactions to effort and ability. Our interpretation of these studies depends on the assumption that at different ages children have different conceptions of effort and ability. Consequently, statements about effort, ability, and performance are presumed to be understood differently by researchers and by children of different ages: effort and ability-related terms are postulated to be assimilated to different conceptions or schemes at different ages. These different conceptions are postulated to be the cognitive bases of different evaluative reactions or different affective meanings.

In the first group of studies considered below, children were either asked how teachers would react to these different children or were instructed to reward or punish the children. In the second group, children were asked how much they would like to be the described children. Important differences emerge from these different methods. The first strategy appears to elicit perceptions of socially approved characteristics or perceptions of virtue. The second appears to elicit more personal preferences (Nicholls, 1976).

When asked to predict a teacher's reaction to children who were said to succeed with high effort and low ability versus low effort and high ability, children at levels 1 and 2 of the concepts of effort and ability expected teachers to give close to maximum possible approval in each case. Less approval was predicted in the low effort, high ability case by level 3 and still less by level 4 children. Like the less mature children, level 3 and 4 children predicted close to maximum approval for success with high effort and low ability (Nicholls, 1978b). The expectation of high approval for effort (on the part of all subjects) corresponds to adult responses to similar stimuli (e.g. Weiner & Kukla, 1970). However, level 1 and 2 children's expectation of reward for ability does not conform to the adult pattern. These children do not clearly distinguish effort from ability. Therefore, for them, the description of someone as high in ability presumably implies something resembling what a statement that a person tries hard and does well implies for an adult. Only when effort is distinguished from ability (partially at level 3 and completely at 4) would the statement that someone does well with high ability and low effort clearly imply low effort and, thereby, lack of virtuous intent.

Other studies have manipulated all possible combinations of descriptions of high and low ability, effort, and outcome (Harari & Covington, 1981; Salili, Maehr & Gillmore, 1976; Weiner & Peter 1973). These studies show age increases in child reward or expected teacher reward for described effort from four up to about 13 years. The initial increase in reward for effort, occurring at about seven years (Weiner & Peter, 1973), is likely to reflect the differentiation of effort—as a cause—from outcomes (level 2). Only when effort is distinguished from outcomes would a description of a child as high in effort clearly imply virtuous intent as distinct from high outcomes. An increase in reward for effort through middle childhood (Harari & Covington, 1981; Nicholls, 1978a; Salili et al. 1976; Weiner & Peter, 1973) may reflect the continuing differentiation of effort from ability (levels 3 and 4).

The pattern changes significantly when children are asked how much they would like to be similar to the described students. Nicholls (1978b) found that children at all levels of maturity indicated close to maximum desire to be like both individuals described as succeeding with high effort and low ability and with low effort and high ability. The latter result contrasts with the decline at levels 3 and 4 in expected teacher approval of individuals succeeding with low effort and high ability. A similar contrast was reported by Harari & Covington (1981). Up to about 13 years, both high effort and ability were valued. After 13, only ability was highly valued. As do adults (Covington & Omelich, 1979; Nicholls, 1976; Sohn, 1977), older students prefer ability more than effort. Presumably, when ability and effort are undifferentiated, the labels "effort" and "ability" are both valued as indicators of learning or competence. When effort and ability become clearly differentiated, ability would be valued because it implies capacity to do well. On the other hand, because effort no longer implies competence or capacity to succeed, its value for the individual is diminished.

Interpretation of Evaluative Feedback

Just as evaluative feedback is mediated by perceptions of effort, ability, and other causal factors, evaluative feedback can itself provide cues for inferences of ability and effort. Adults and older children, for example, approve more strongly when they believe that success reflects effort rather than ability (Weiner & Kukla, 1970, and studies cited in previous section). Thus, they might infer that a teacher who gives more approval to one of two children who perform equally would see that child as less able and harder working. When the concepts of effort and ability are undifferentiated, however, more praise would imply both higher ability and effort.

Meyer et al. (1979) confirmed these predictions for inferences of ability. (Effort was not examined.) They presented subjects with vignettes where a teacher responded to students who had succeeded on the same task with ". . . that's correct" to one student and "You have done very fine; I'm very pleased" to another. Most third and fourth graders thought the teacher perceived the praised student as the more able of the pair. Only at about 12 years and older did most children believe that the teacher perceived the unpraised student as more able. It appears that when effort and ability are undifferentiated, praise will generally imply high ability. The differentiation of ability from effort appears necessary for the inference of lower ability from higher praise. This implies that, with development, it becomes increasingly difficult for teachers to use praise to raise perceived ability.

Weiner (1980a, 1980b; Weiner, Russell, & Lerman, 1978) has shown that different emotions, not merely different amounts of approval or disapproval, can be elicited by perceptions of ability, effort, and other causal factors. Adults, for example, react with anger to perceived lack of effort and with sympathy or pity to lack of ability. One would expect less differentiated emotional responses in children for whom the concepts of effort and ability are undifferentiated (Weiner, Kun, Benesh-Weiner, 1980). Specifically one would expect adults, more than young children, to use evidence of teacher anger and pity to make differential inferences of teacher perception of lack of effort versus lack of ability.

Results in accord with this prediction were obtained by Weiner, Graham, Stern, and Lawson (1982). More seven-year-olds than five-year-olds inferred perception of lack of effort from teacher anger. This parallels the differentiation of effort as a cause from outcomes (level 2). Inferences of perception of lack of ability from pity emerged later as would be expected from the later differentiation of the concept of ability from effort and performance (levels 3 and 4).

All in all, there are many parallels between the differentiation of the concept of ability and evaluative reactions to descriptions of effort and ability and in interpretations of evaluative reactions. The major age trends are: (1) An increased value for performance that compares favorably with that of others. This is associated with the development of the normative conception of difficulty; (2) An increased tendency to reward and expect reward for effort. This appears associated with the differentiation of the concept of effort as a cause; (3) A decline in personal preference for effort while valuation of ability remains high. This appears associated with the differentiation of the concept of ability as capacity; and (4) More differentiated use of evaluative feedback to infer ability. Finally, the fact that our measures of differentiation of ability, effort, and difficulty predict age related changes in evaluative responses helps establish the validity of the cognitive measures.

ACHIEVEMENT BEHAVIOR

Prediction of overt achievement behavior requires consideration of both the level of differentiation of the concept of ability and the level of ability individuals expect to be able to demonstrate. The latter is held to be a function of perceived ability (Kukla, 1972, 1978; Nicholls, in press). That is, individuals with higher perceived ability generally have higher expectations of demonstrating high ability. At different levels of differentiation of ability, the cues and processes used to infer one's ability and one's chances of demonstrating or developing ability differ. Thus, the same cues or feedback can produce different ability inferences and different behavior at different levels of maturity. Further, at any specific level of differentiation of ability, perceptions of high versus low ability will have different behavioral consequences. The expectation that one is unable to demonstrate high ability is, at all levels of differentiation, likely to lead to less effective performance. However, because the affective and informational significance of ability changes with age, there will also be changes in the behavioral implications of perceptions of any given degree of low or high ability. Even when children at different levels of maturity infer similar levels of ability, these perceptions of ability can have different meanings and, therefore, different behavioral consequences.

Changes in the impact of achievement-related cues on inferences of ability and, thereby, on behavior can best be illustrated with reference to the differentiation of the concepts of difficulty and ability. Changes in the implications of perceptions of similar levels of ability are better illustrated with reference to the differentiation of the concepts of ability and effort.

Difficulty and Ability

The development of the normative conception of difficulty is accompanied by an increase in the affective value of performing well compared to others. We would, therefore, expect stronger attempts to perform well compared to others in those children with the normative conception of difficulty than in those at the objective and ego-centric levels.

This hypothesis is supported by evidence that children who have attained the normative conception of difficulty are more likely than less mature children to attempt normatively difficult or moderate tasks (Nicholls, 1978b; 1980b; Nicholls & Miller, 1983). Those at the less differentiated levels choose normatively easy tasks—presumably because they have higher expectancies of success on these tasks and do not realize the evaluative significance of success on the normatively more difficult tasks.

This systematic preference for the easiest of an array of tasks was not found in children at any level of differentiation of difficulty and ability when the tasks had directly observable concrete difficulty cues (jig-saw puzzles). With such cues, children at all levels showed consistent individual differences in difficulty level preferences (Nicholls & Miller, 1983). However, significant correlations between difficulty level preferences with objective and normative difficulty cues were found only for those at the level of normative difficulty. This was predicted because only when normative difficulty is mastered would each type of difficulty cue have similar evaluative significance: success on more normatively and more objectively difficult tasks would appear more attractive because more difficult tasks of both types are understood to require more ability. Accordingly, among children with the normative conception, those with higher perceived ability chose harder tasks in both cases—presumably their choices reflected the desire to demonstrate their highest possible level of ability and their judgment of the task that would enable them to demonstrate this level. At the objective and ego-centric levels, on the other hand only objective difficulty preferences reflected individual differences in perceived ability. Normative difficulty level preferences of these less mature children (preponderantly for the easiest task) presumably did not reflect perceived ability. Rather these choices reflected the failure of the less mature children to realize that success on more normatively difficult tasks implies more ability.

The attainment of the normative conception of ability should produce changes in the impact of social comparison feedback on perceived ability and, thereby, on achievement behavior. Understanding of the implications of norms for ability presumably mediated 9- to 11-year-olds' higher preference for tasks when they were informed that they had performed better than others than when told their performance was worse than others' (Boggiano & Ruble, 1979). Those perceiving themselves as having done better than others presumably perceived their ability as higher, had greater expectations of demonstrating ability on similar tasks, and therefore were more inclined to attempt such tasks (Kukla, 1978; Nicholls, in press). The fact that 3- to 5-year-olds did not exhibit such effects (Boggiano & Ruble, 1979) can be explained by their lack of understanding of the implications of normative feedback for ability.

Though the development of the normative conception leads to changed behavior in response to social comparison feedback or normative difficulty cues, the ego-centric and objective conceptions are often sufficient to maintain behavior that is similar to that of older children and adults. Most notably, when concrete difficulty cues are available, these conceptions can mediate selection of tasks children are uncertain of mastering. As mastery and certainty of mastery increases, these conceptions would mediate selection of increasingly difficult tasks. This phenomenon of rising aspirations has often been noted in young children (e.g., Elkind, 1971; White, 1959).

A paradox remains, however, in the data on the effects of social comparison on behavior. Informal observation—of sibling rivalry for example—suggests that children well below the age when normative difficulty is mastered can become concerned about performing better than another individual. Formal observation (Mosatche & Bragonier, 1981) and experimental evidence supports such observations. For example, if, in a competitive context, another completes a task before they do, young children will do such things as make up excuses or cheat (Heckhausen, this volume, 1982; Ruble, in press). It might seem that such behavior must be mediated by the normative conception of difficulty and ability. This, however, might not be so.

At the objective and ego-centric levels, high and low ability and difficulty are imperfectly distinguished from one's own expectancies of success. At these levels, low ability would be implied by failure to do something one expected to be able to do. At the normative level, such a failure would only imply low ability if others performed more effectively. If others also failed, one's own failure could be attributed to task difficulty. For children at the objective and ego-centric levels, however, the performance of another could establish an expectancy of being able to do as well as the other and a belief that one must do so to demonstrate high ability. Failure to do so would violate this expectancy and imply low ability. Young children's defensive responses to performing worse than another may be reactions to or attempts to avoid such inferences of low ability. As Ruble (in press) and Suls and Sanders (in press) note, competitive behavior of this type may be a precursor of more mature social comparison behavior. It does not, however, appear to demand the normative conception of difficulty and ability.

Perhaps as important as the specific conclusions about the development of the concept of difficulty and its behavioral accompaniments are the general features of the present approach to the analysis of behavioral development. In particular the capacity to define developmental maturity (in this case, maturity of the concept of difficulty) independently of overt behavior (choice of difficulty level or response to social comparison feedback) offers a number of advantages.

When changes in overt behavior alone are used as evidence of personality or motivational development (e.g., Veroff, 1969), the meaning of apparently immature behavior in older children can be obscure. As noted here and elsewhere (Veroff, 1969), when difficulty levels are not concrete and observable, young children almost invariably choose easy tasks. But, so do an appreciable proportion of older children. Should these older children be described as immature? The present approach suggests not and provides a basis for distinguishing immature from mature reasons for choice of easy tasks. If children are aware that normatively difficult tasks require more ability, choice of normatively easy tasks will reflect low perceived ability. If they do not understand this, choice of easy tasks will *not* reflect low perceived ability. That is, overt behavior may reflect individual differences in perceived ability at a given level of cognitive and affective development or it may reflect the general characteristics of a given level of maturity. Only when maturity is conceived independently of overt behavior can such distinctions be made.

Take, for example, the finding of greater preference for normatively easy tasks in blacks than whites in a combined first and fourth grade sample (Ruhland & Feld, 1977). It is not possible to be certain whether fewer black children in this sample understand normative difficulty or whether they have lower perceived ability. Both explanations for black's lower aspirations are plausible, but their implications are quite different. On the other hand, Harter and Zigler's (1974) finding that retarded children choose easier tasks than do normal children of the same mental age (seven) appears to indicate that the retarded children have lower perceived ability. Because difficulty cues in this study were concrete and observable, it is likely that all children realized that the difficult tasks would demand more ability. If so, their choices would reflect their perceived ability.

As Wohlwill (1973) observed, "By and large, the study of developmental change has remained divorced from the study of individual differences in behav-

ior'' (p. 45). Stage theories of personality and social development generally fail
to deal with individual differences within a given level of maturity (e.g,
Kohlberg, 1969). In the language of cognitive-developmental theory (Kohlberg,
1969; Kuhn, 1979), maturity refers to the level of structure of the cognitions
mediating behavior or giving that behavior meaning for the individual. Structure
is distinguished from content. In the present instance the crucial components of
content are the individual's perceived level of ability and perceived task difficulty. Structure, on the other hand, is the level of understanding of difficulty and
ability. At any given level of structure, individuals can have different content.
Most importantly, they may have high or low perceived ability. Individuals can
also differ in structure of the mediational process—the concepts of difficulty and
ability. As we have argued, adequate explanation and prediction of overt behavior demands consideration of both structure and content. This approach makes it
possible to coordinate the analysis of individual differences and developmental
change within one conceptual framework.

Effort and Ability

The development of the concept of ability as capacity should mean that perception of low ability will "feel" worse and make future failure seem more
inevitable. Lack of capacity reflects on the person and on their chances of
success in a more serious manner than does a lack of ability when ability is
imperfectly differentiated from effort. Low perceived ability should, therefore,
lead to more severe performance impairment in more mature children.

This prediction is supported by Rholes et al. (1980) in a study of the effects of
induced success versus failure on performance in kindergarten through fifth
grade children. They found significant performance impairment and less persistence after failure relative to success treatments only in fifth graders. Particularly significant for our thesis is the fact that ability attributions of failing students were very similar for first, third, and fifth graders. This means that fifth
graders' performance impairment cannot be explained in terms of lower perceived ability. There were no grade effects for perceived ability. It can, however,
be explained in terms of the more serious implications of low perceived ability
when ability is conceived as capacity (level 3 and, more clearly, level 4).

This interpretation is supported by the Rholes et al. evidence that only at fifth
grade were perceptions of effort and ability negatively correlated. This indicates
the conception of ability as capacity where higher perceived effort leads to
inferences of lower ability. Rholes et al. also found ability attributions positively
correlated with performance only in fifth graders. This is consistent with the
present thesis that older children are more likely than younger children to see
ability as indispensable for adequate performance. The age differences in the
effect of failure on performance described by Rholes et al. cannot be readily
explained in terms of developmental changes in level of perceived ability, at-

tributional capacities, or in the way ability is inferred. Nor can the changes in relations between perceived ability and effort and between perceived ability and performance be explained in these terms. These phenomena can, however, be explained in terms of the development of the conception of ability as capacity.

The role of the development of the concept of capacity in this age-increase in performance impairment after repeated failure was directly established by Miller (1982). He found impairment of performance after a series of failures in sixth graders but not second graders. He also found that, among sixth graders, performance was significantly impaired only in those who had partially or completely mastered the concept of ability as capacity (levels 3 and 4). (This result was obtained with a simplified measure of conception of ability employing photographs rather than film or videotape of two other children.)

Miller's study also helped support the role of perceived ability, as opposed to a mere perception that outcomes are not contingent on one's behavior (Abramson, Seligman, & Teasdale, 1978), in the impaired performance of more mature children. Rholes et al. described the impaired performance they found in fifth graders as learned helplessness. However, they did not establish the mechanism involved. The impairment could, as the term helplessness suggests, reflect a belief that it is hopeless to apply effort (Abramson et al.) or it could be a consequence of interferring effects of anxiety. When ability is construed as capacity, perception that one is likely to demonstrate low ability would be more likely to produce performance-impairing anxiety. Alternatively, children with the conception of ability as capacity could recognize that low ability will be less strongly implied if they reduce their effort. This third possible mechanism, termed egotism (Frankel & Snyder, 1978; Snyder, Smoller, Strenta, & Frankel, 1981), would only be available to children who conceive ability as capacity. Miller's (1982) data were more consistent with the latter two possibilities than the first. After a series of failures designed to induce an expectation of failure, performance impairment of level 3 and 4 students on a subsequent task was not found when the subsequent task was described as very normatively difficult. This condition would induce an expectation that effort would not lead to success but, because the subsequent task was seen as normatively difficult, would not face children with the likelihood of demonstrating low ability. Performance impairment was found only when the subsequent task was described as moderately difficult. In this case, further failure—though less likely—would imply low ability. Thus, Miller's data support the view that the greater propensity to "helplessness" on the part of older children is best understood as a consequence of expectancy of demonstrating low ability rather than of noncontingency per se and that it is mediated by the conception of ability as capacity.

In summary, we have evidence that age-related changes in the concept of ability are accompanied by theoretically meaningful changes in overt achievement behavior. These data not only strengthen the validity of our theoretical framework which gives perceptions of ability a major role in achievement behavior, they also help validate our measures of the differentiation of the concept of ability.

SUMMARY: DEVELOPMENT AND ITS DISCONTENTS

In general, the development of social cognition is rightly considered desirable. More mature moral reasoning, for example, is more ethically adequate than less mature reasoning (Kohlberg & Mayer, 1972) and is indispensible for ethically justifiable action (Blasi, 1980). Similarly, mature social cognition appears to mediate more adequate altruistic behavior (Hoffman, 1975). As well as being inherently desirable, social cognitive development may play an important role in the development of nonsocial cognition (Damon, 1981). We would not go so far as to advocate retardation of development of the achievement-related cognitions we have discussed. However, one can hardly overlook the possibility that the differentiation of the concept of ability may have a variety of negative consequences for mental health and for the continuing intellectual development of individuals.

As ability becomes increasingly differentiated from other factors, high ability is increasingly seen as something that everyone cannot have. When ability and difficulty are undifferentiated, high ability is, for the most part, indicated by learning or by improved performance. As most of us can improve, most of us can have high ability in this less differentiated sense. Attainment of the normative conception of difficulty increases the likelihood that at least some members of any group will perceive their ability as low; someone has to be below average. The full impact of this is not observed immediately upon attainment of the normative conception of difficulty. It becomes increasingly marked up to about twelve years of age by which time children make very accurate judgments of their achievement levels compared to those of others.

Over the same period, children become increasingly "logical" in interpretations of their performance. Most notably, those with low relative attainment, more than those with higher attainment, attribute their failures more reliably to low ability. Concurrently, with age, perception of low ability increasingly means lack of capacity and has more negative affective consequences and more debilitating effects on learning and performance. Also, effort may not merely appear fruitless to older children with low perceived ability. They may also see lowered effort as a means of salvaging some pride when failure appears inevitable. This, however, will further reduce their chances of learning. Furthermore, they now find their tendency to value ability over effort in conflict with teachers' tendency to reward high effort.

These developments also present teachers with new dilemmas. When children realize that ability is judged relative to that of others and become competent at making such comparisons, it will be more difficult to make all children feel competent. Feedback implying competence in one child is, for example, likely to imply incompetence in others (Miller, Brickman, & Bolen, 1975). The development of the conception of ability as capacity also makes it harder for teachers to give praise for success on normatively easy tasks or for high effort without thereby implying low ability.

Life appears less beset with such dilemmas when high effort and any consequent gain in performance implies high ability. Motivation to learn and, thereby, continuing intellectual development also appear more assured when the concept of ability is less differentiated. In short, development of the concept of ability has its discontents.

Fortunately, the picture is not always this grim for mature individuals. For the sake of simplicity we have, up to this point, assumed that individuals always employ their most differentiated conception of ability when judging their competence or their chances of developing or demonstrating competence. This is not so. Adults can employ either more or less differentiated conceptions of ability. This is the key to improved understanding and prediction of adult achievement behavior and may be the key to minimizing the problems consequent on the differentiation of the concept of ability.

IMPLICATIONS FOR A GENERAL THEORY OF ACHIEVEMENT MOTIVATION: AN OUTLINE

Established theories of achievement motivation have not acknowledged the fact that adults and older children can employ more or less differentiated conceptions of ability in achievement situations. Consider, for example, the conceptions of difficulty and ability implied in the theories of Atkinson and Kukla.

According to Atkinson's theory (1957), "degree of difficulty can be inferred from the subjective probability of success" (p. 362). This position implies that a task is hard if an individual expects to fail at it. This view is not consistent with evidence (Atkinson, 1957, 1969) that high and low resultant achievement motive individuals differ in subjective probability of success when difficulty is controlled. Atkinson's use of the concept of difficulty resembles the ego-centric conception. Like children with the ego-centric conception, Atkinson's theory fails to make the distinction between task difficulty and subjective probability of success that the normative and objective conceptions permit. Kukla's (1978) theory of task choice embodies the objective conception of difficulty. Although Kukla acknowledges the importance of norms for adequate ability inference, his formal theoretical statement refers only to continua of objective difficulty and individual differences in expectancy of success at points on these continua. Kukla's (1972) theory of performance, on the other hand, embodies the ego-centric conception of difficulty.

There is evidence that adults can employ either more or less differentiated conceptions of ability. We can also predict when they will employ the different conceptions (Nicholls, in press). If situational factors such as presence of an audience, competition, or other evaluative cues induce individuals to focus on their personal competence, a more differentiated conception of ability will serve more adequately than less differentiated conceptions. Only the normative conception enables one to distinguish the contributions of task difficulty and ability to performance. The less differentiated conceptions do not permit an adequate evaluation of the role of personal competence, as opposed to task difficulty, in performance. The conception of ability as capacity is also necessary if one is to distinguish the more basic personal trait of capacity from effort—which anyone, or almost anyone, can have. We would, therefore, expect the most differentiated conception of ability to be employed when attention is focused on the individual's competence. If, however, the individual's concern is simply to learn or to improve, the most differentiated conception provides surplus information and the ego-centric or objective conceptions provide all that is necessary: they enable one to judge whether one's level of mastery has improved. If individuals process only that information that is relevant to their goals, they should employ the differentiated conception only when actively concerned with evaluating their personal competence.

This hypothesis is supported by Diener and Srull's (1979) evidence that college students evaluate their performance in terms of peer performance norms when self-awareness is induced. When nonself-aware, however, they self-reinforce primarily on the basis of their own previous performance—even if norms are readily available. That is, they act like children with the ego-centric or objective conceptions. Scheier and Carver (Note 4) also found higher interest in social comparison feedback associated with heightened self-awareness.

The more and less differentiated conceptions of effort and ability are also both accessible to adults. Jagacinski and Nicholls (in press), found that students expected more effort to lead to greater gains in competence. However, a competitive situation produced perceptions of higher ability when effort was low. In this situation, students employed the differentiated conception where the "fact" that effort improves competence coexists with the "fact" that higher effort implies lower capacity. In a noncompetitive, learning for learning's sake situation, the less differentiated conception—where higher effort does not imply lower capacity—was employed.

This and other evidence (Nicholls, in press) indicates that more and less differentiated conceptions of ability are accessible to adults and that differentiated conceptions displace less differentiated conceptions when situational factors focus attention on the individual's competence. This state is, therefore, termed ego-involvement. The state when the less differentiated conception is employed and where more attention is focused on the task and methods of improving mastery is termed task-involvement.

Further derivations (Nicholls, in press) indicate that in task-involvement, learning will be experienced as an end in itself. In Kruglanski's (1975) terms, learning will be more endogenously attributed. In ego-involvement, on the other hand, learning is predicted to be experienced more as a means to the end of developing or demonstrating higher ability than that of others: learning is exogenously attributed. There is evidence (Nicholls in press) in support of these further predictions. Task-involvement is characterized by greater focus of attention on the task and by endogenous attribution for action. Ego-involvement is distinguished by greater focus of attention on the self and by more exogenous attribution for action.

Task choice and performance are also predicted and found to be different in task- and ego-involvement (Nicholls, in press). Most important from an educational point of view is the evidence that maladaptive task choices and performance impairment are not found in task-involvement. In ego-involvement, on the other hand, individuals with low perceived ability choose unrealistically easy or difficult tasks—tasks that provide little opportunity for the development of competence. Their performance is also impaired when they are ego-involved. This impairment may result from the interfering effects of attention to the self and self-derogatory affect, egotism, or from a sense of hopelessness and task avoidance.

The theory of adult achievement motivation stimulated by the developmental research outlined here implies that establishment and maintenance of task-involvement should be a major goal of educators (Nicholls, 1979b, 1983). Attribution theory has led to suggestions that training children to attribute failure to lack of effort rather than ability will alleviate much maladaptive motivation. By way of contrast, our position is that we should maintain an environment that induces children to focus on tasks and strategies for mastering them. Instead of encouraging children to favor one rather than another type of explanation of their own role in performance outcomes, we should encourage them to become task-involved. As Heckhausen (Note 5) suggests, we should stop rather than change causal attributions. Regrettably, our schools generally do not do this. Eccles, Midgley, and Adler (this volume) show that as children progress through school, schools adopt an increasing number of practices that are likely to induce ego-involvement. Thus, rather than minimizing the potential negative consequences of the differentiation of the concept of ability, schools may amplify them.

It is probably because most theories of motivation have not distinguished conceptions of ability or task- and ego-involvement that there is not as much research on methods of maintaining task-involvement as one might hope for. Nevertheless, there are approaches (Covington & Beery, 1976; Maehr, 1983; Nicholls, 1983; Nicholls & Burton, 1982; Eccles et al., this volume) that might help alleviate the discontents that follow from the differentiation of the concept of ability.

ACKNOWLEDGMENTS

Preparation of this chapter was supported in part by NSF Grant BNS 7914252, University of Illinois and Harvard University subcontracts. We are grateful for comments by Virginia Crandall, Martin Maehr, Diane Ruble, and Marjorie Steinkamp on a draft.

NOTES

1. There is other evidence that expectancies and feelings of accomplishment are associated with perceptions of effort. If one assumes that the meaning of ability is fixed and clearly differentiated from effort, this evidence would raise doubts about the claim that affect and expectancies depend largely on perceptions of ability. However, as noted at the conclusion of this paper, effort is not always clearly differentiated from ability and there are circumstances when effort implies ability. This may explain these apparently "troublesome" findings (Nicholls, in press).

2. A very small proportion of children did "misinterpret" normative difficulty cues in the sense that they incorrectly identified the easiest task as the hardest and thought it would require most ability. When this misinterpretation was taken into account, these children's task preferences were the same as choices of those who fully understood normative difficulty. This was not the case for those at the less differentiated levels.

3. As this observation indicates, Level 4 children as well as less mature children and many researchers (Bloom, 1976) recognize that effort improves performance and that more able students usually try harder. However, the perception that more able students usually try harder tells us nothing about the nature or intensive content of children's concepts of ability and effort. The level 4 conception does not embody a general view of the ways that effort and ability might be correlated in the real world. According to the level 4 conception, people who have to try less for a given level of attainment are more able. This does not mean that more able people generally apply less effort.

REFERENCE NOTES

1. Blumenfeld, P. G., & Pintrich, P. R. Children's perceptions of school and schoolwork: Age, sex, social class, individual, and classroom differences. In J. E. Parsons (Chair), *Defining the meaning of success and achievement.* Symposium presented at the meeting of the American Educational Research Association, New York, March 1982.

2. Nicholls, J. G., & Miller, A. T. *Reasoning about the ability of self and others: A developmental study.* Unpublished manuscript, Purdue University, 1983.

3. Ruble, D. N., & Frey, K. S. Self-evaluation and social comparison in the classroom: A naturalistic study of peer interaction. In S. Nelson-LeGall (Chair), *Social comparison: Implications for education.* Symposium presented at the meeting of the American Educational Research Association, New York, March 1982.

4. Scheier, M. F., & Carver, C. S. *Self-directed attention and the comparison of self with standards.* Unpublished manuscript, Carnegie-Mellon University, 1980.

5. Heckhausen, H. Attributional analysis of achievement motivation: Some unresolved problems. In W. U. Meyer and B. Weiner (Chairpersons), *Attributional approaches to human motivation.* Symposium presented at the Center for Interdisciplinary Research, University of Bielefeld, West Germany, August 1980.

REFERENCES

Abramson, L. Y., Seligman, M. E. P., & Teasdale, J. D. Learned helplessness in humans: Critique and reformulation. *Journal of Abnormal Psychology,* 1978, *87,* 49–74.

Atkinson, J. W. Motivational determinants of risk-taking behavior. *Psychological Review,* 1957, *64,* 359–372.

Atkinson, J. W. Comments on papers by Crandall and Veroff. In C. P. Smith (Ed.), *Achievement-related motives in children.* New York: Russell Sage, 1969.

Ausubel, D. P., Schiff, H. M., & Gasser, E. B. A preliminary study of developmental trends in socioempathy: Accuracy of perception of own and others sociometric status. *Child Development,* 1952, *23,* 111–128.

Blasi, A. Bridging moral cognition and moral action: A critical review of the literature. *Psychological Bulletin,* 1980, *88,* 1–45.

Bloom, B. S. *Human characteristics and school learning.* New York: McGraw-Hill, 1976.

Boggiano, A. K., & Ruble, D. N. Competence and the overjustification effect. *Journal of Personality and Social Psychology,* 1979, *37,* 1462–1468.

Covington, M. V., & Beery, R. G. *Self-worth and school learning.* New York: Holt, Rinehart, Winston, 1976.

Covington, M. V., & Omelich, C. L. Effort: The double-edged sword in school achievement. *Journal of Educational Psychology,* 1979, *71,* 169–182.

Damon, W. Patterns of change in children's social reasoning: A two-year longitudinal study. *Child Development,* 1980, *51,* 1010–1017.

Damon, W. Exploring children's social cognition on two fronts. In J. H. Flavell & L. Ross (Eds.), *Social cognitive development: Frontiers and possible futures.* New York: Cambridge University Press, 1981.

Deci, E. L. *Intrinsic Motivation.* New York: Plenum, 1975.

Diener, E., & Srull, T. K. Self-awareness, psychological perspective, and self–reinforcement in relation to personal and social standards. *Journal of Personality and Social Psychology,* 1979, *37,* 413–423.

Dienstbier, R. A., Hillman, D., Lenhoff, J., Hillman, J., & Valkenaar, M. C. *Psychological Review,* 1975, *82,* 299–315.

Dweck, C. S., & Goetz, T. E. Attributions and learned helplessness. In J. H. Harvey, W. Ickes & R. F. Kidd (Eds.), *New directions in attribution research* (Vol. 2). Hillsdale, N.J.: Erlbaum, 1978.

Elkind, D. Conservation and concept formation. In D. Elkind & J. H. Flavell (Eds.), *Studies in cognitive development: Essays in honor of Jean Piaget.* New York: Oxford University Press, 1969.

Elkind, D. Cognitive growth cycles in mental development. In J. K. Cole (Ed.), *Nebraska Symposium on Motivation.* Lincoln, Nebraska: University of Nebraska Press, 1971.

Flavell, J. H. *Cognitive development.* Englewood Cliffs, NJ: Prentice-Hall, 1977.

Frankel, A., & Snyder, M. L. Poor performance following unsolvable problems: Learned helplessness or egotism? *Journal of Personality and Social Psychology,* 1978, *36,* 1415–1423.

Freedman, D. G. The development of social hierarchies. In L. Levi (Ed.), *Society, stress, and disease (Vol. 2): Childhood and adolescence.* London: Oxford University Press, 1975.

Freud, S. *Civilization and its discontents.* London: Hogarth, 1930.

Goss, A. M. Estimated versus actual physical strength in three ethnic groups. *Child Development,* 1968, *39,* 283–290.

Harari, O., & Covington, M. V. Reactions to achievement behavior from a teacher and student perspective: A developmental analysis. *American Educational Research Journal,* 1981, *18,* 15–28.

Harter, S. & Zigler, E. The assessment of effectance motivation in normal and retarded children. *Developmental Psychology,* 1974, *10,* 169–180.

Heckhausen, H. *The anatomy of achievement motivation.* New York: Academic Press, 1967.

Heckhausen, H. The development of achievement motivation. In W. W. Hartup (Ed.), *Review of Child Development Research* (Vol. 6). Chicago: University of Chicago Press, 1982.

Heider, F. *The psychology of interpersonal relations.* New York: Wiley, 1958.

Hoffman, M. L. Developmental synthesis of affect and cognition and its implications for altruistic motivation. *Developmental Psychology,* 1975, *11,* 607–622.

Inhelder, B., Sinclair, H., & Bovet, M. *Learning and the development of cognition* (Susan Wedgwood, trans.) Cambridge, Mass.: Harvard University Press, 1974.

Jagacinski, C. M., & Nicholls, J. G. Conceptions of ability and related affects in task-involvement and ego-involvement. *Journal of Educational Psychology,* in press.

Kessell, L. J. *Age and sex differences in causal attributions for mathematics and English achievement in adolescence.* Unpublished Ph.D. dissertation, University of Illinois at Urbana–Champaign, 1979.

Kohlberg, L. Stage and sequence: The cognitive–developmental approach to socialization. In D. A. Goslin (Ed.), *Handbook of socialization theory and research.* Chicago: Rand McNally, 1969.

Kohlberg, L., & Mayer, R. Development as the aim of education. *Harvard Educational Review,* 1972, *42,* 449–496.

Kruglanski, A. W. The endogenous-exogenous partition in attribution theory. *Psychological Review,* 1975, *82,* 387–406.

Kuhn, D. Mechanisms of cognitive and social development: One psychology or two? *Human Development,* 1979, *21,* 91–118.

Kukla, A. Foundations of an attributional theory of performance. *Psychological Review,* 1972, *79,* 454–470.

Kukla, A. An attributional theory of choice. In L. Berkowitz (Ed.), *Advances in Experimental Social Psychology* (Vol. 11). New York: Academic Press, 1978.

Kun, A. Development of the magnitude-covariation and compensation schemata in ability and effort attributions of performance. *Child Development,* 1977, *48,* 862–873.

Maehr, M. L. On doing well in science: Why Johnny no longer excells; Why Sarah never did. In S. G. Paris, G. M. Olson, & H. W. Stevenson (Eds.), *Learning and motivation in the classroom.* Hillsdale, NJ: Erlbaum, 1983.

Maehr, M. L., & Nicholls, J. G. Culture and achievement motivation: A second look. In N. Warren (Eds), *Studies in cross–cultural psychology* (Vol.2). New York: Academic Press, 1980.

Meyer, W. U., Bachmann, M., Biermann, U., Hempelmann, M., Ploger, F. O., & Spiller, H. The informational value of evaluative behavior: Influences of praise and blame on perceptions of ability. *Journal of Educational Psychology,* 1979, *71,* 259–268.

Miller, A. T. *Self–recognitory schemes and achievement behavior: A developmental study.* Ph.D. dissertation, Purdue University, 1982.

Miller, R. L., Brickman, P., & Bolen, D. Attribution versus persuasion as a means for modifying behavior. *Journal of Personality and Social Psychology,* 1975, *31,* 430–441.

Mosatche, H. S., & Bragonier, P. An observational study of social comparison in preschoolers. *Child Development,* 1981, *52,* 376–378.

Nicholls, J. G. Effort is virtuous, but it's better to have ability: Evaluative responses to perceptions of effort and ability. *Journal of Research in Personality,* 1976, *10,* 306–315.

Nicholls, J. G. The development of causal attributions and evaluative responses to success and failure in Maori and Pakeha children. *Developmental Psychology,* 1978, *14,* 687–688. (a)

Nicholls, J. G. The development of the concepts of effort and ability, perception of own attainment, and the understanding that difficult tasks require more ability. *Child Development,* 1978, *49,* 800–814. (b)

Nicholls, J. G. Development of perception of own attainment and causal attributions for success and failure in reading. *Journal of Educational Psychology,* 1979, *71,* 94–99. (a)

Nicholls, J. G. Quality and equality in intellectual development: The role of motivation in education. *American Psychologist,* 1979, *34,* 1071–1084. (b)

Nicholls, J. G. A re–examination of boys' and girls' causal attributions for success and failure based on New Zealand data. In L. J. Fyans (Ed.), *Recent trends in achievement motivation theory and research.* New York: Plenum, 1980. (a)

Nicholls, J. G. The development of the concept of difficulty. *Merrill-Palmer Quarterly,* 1980, *26,* 271–281. (b)

Nicholls, J. G. Conceptions of ability and achievement motivation: A theory and its implications for education. In S. G. Paris, G. M. Olson & H. W. Stevenson (Eds.), *Learning and motivation in the classroom.* Hillsdale, NJ: Erlbaum, 1983.

Nicholls, J. G. Achievement motivation: Conceptions of ability, subjective experience, task choice, and performance. *Psychological Review,* in press.

Nicholls, J. G., & Burton, J. T. Motivation and equality. *Elementary School Journal*, 1982, *82*, 367–378.

Nicholls, J. G., & Miller, A. T. The differentiation of the concepts of difficulty and ability. *Child Development*, 1983, *54*, 951–959.

Phillips, B. N. Age changes in accuracy of self-perceptions. *Child Development*, 1963, *34*, 1041–1046.

Piaget, J. The general problems of the psychobiological development of the child. In J. M. Tanner & B. Inhelder (Eds.), *Discussions on child development* (Vol. 4). London: Tavistock, 1960.

Rholes, W. S., Blackwell, J., Jordan, C., & Walters, C. A developmental study of learned helplessness. *Developmental Psychology*, 1980, *16*, 616–624.

Ruble, D. N. The development of social comparison processes and their role in achievement–related self–socialization. In E. T. Higgins, D. N. Ruble, & W. W. Hartup (Eds.), *Social cognition and social development: A socio-cultural perspective*, New York: Cambridge University Press, in press.

Ruble, D. N., Boggiano, A. K., Feldman, N. S., & Loebl, J. H. Developmental analysis of the role of social comparison in self-evaluation. *Developmental Psychology*, 1980, *16*, 105–115.

Ruble, D. N., Feldman, N. S., & Boggiano, A. K. Social comparison between young children in achievement situations. *Developmental Psychology*, 1976, *12*, 192–197.

Ruhland, D., & Feld, S. The development of achievement motivation in black and white children. *Child Development*, 1977, *48*, 1362–1368.

Salili, F., Maehr, M. L., & Gillmore, G. Achievement and morality: A cross-cultural analysis of causal attribution and evaluation. *Journal of Personality and Social Psychology*, 1976, *33*, 327–337.

Shaklee, H. Development in inferences of ability and task difficulty. *Child Development*, 1976, *47*, 1051–1057.

Snyder, M. L., Smoller, B., Strenta, A., & Frankel, A. A comparison of egotism, negativity, and learned helplessness as explanations for poor performance after unsolvable problems. *Journal of Personality and Social Psychology*, 1981, *40*, 24–30.

Sohn, D. Affect-generating powers of effort and ability—self attributions of academic success and failure. *Journal of Educational Psychology*, 1977, *69*, 500–505.

Suls, J. & Sanders, G. S. Self–evaluation via social comparison: A developmental analysis. In L. Wheeler (Ed.), *Review of Personality and Social Psychology* (Vol. 3), in press.

Veroff, J. Social comparison and the development of achievement motivation. In C. P. Smith (Ed.), *Achievement–related motives in children*. New York: Russell Sage, 1969.

Weiner, B. A cognitive (attributional)–emotion–action model of motivated behavior: An analysis of judgments of help–giving. *Journal of Personality and Social Psychology*, 1980, *39*, 186–200. (a)

Weiner, B. "May I borrow your class notes?": An attributional analysis of help-giving in an achievement-related context. *Journal of Educational Psychology*, 1980, *27*, 676–681. (b)

Weiner, B., Frieze, I. H., Kukla, A., Reed, L., Rest, S., & Rosenbaum, R. M. *Perceiving the causes of success and failure*. Morristown, NJ: General Learning Press, 1971.

Weiner, B., Graham, S., Stern, P., & Lawson, M. E. Using affective cues to infer causal thoughts. *Developmental Psychology*, 1982, *18*, 278–286.

Weiner, B., & Kukla, A. An attributional analysis of achievement motivation. *Journal of Personality and Social Psychology*, 1970, *15*, 1–20.

Weiner, B., Kun, A., & Benesh-Weiner, M. The development of mastery, emotions, and morality. *Minnesota Symposium on Child Development*, 1980, *13*.

Weiner, B., Nierenberg, R., & Goldstein, M. Social learning (locus of control) versus attributional (causal stability) interpretations of expectancy of success. *Journal of Personality*, 1976, *44*, 52–68.

Weiner, B., & Peter, N. A cognitive-developmental analysis of achievement and moral judgments. *Developmental Psychology*, 1973, *9*, 290–309.

Weiner, B., Russell, D., & Lerman, D. Affective consequences of causal ascriptions. In J. H. Harvey, W. J. Ickes, & R. F. Kidd (Eds.), *New directions in attribution research* (Vol. 2). Hillsdale, NJ: Erlbaum, 1978.

White, R. W. Motivation reconsidered: The concept of competence. *Psychological Review,* 1959, *66,* 297–333.

Wohlwill, J. F. *The study of behavioral development.* New York: Academic Press, 1973.

A MODEL OF CHILDREN'S ACHIEVEMENT AND RELATED SELF-PERCEPTIONS OF COMPETENCE, CONTROL, AND MOTIVATIONAL ORIENTATION

Susan Harter and James P. Connell

The construct of intrinsic motivation has intrigued many over the last two decades, and our own research group can be counted among such enthusiasts. Our interest was initially stimulated by the theorizing of Robert White (1959, 1960). In his challenge to traditional drive theory, White urged that behaviors such as exploration, mastery attempts, play, and curiosity be viewed as an expression of an intrinsic need to deal effectively with one's environment. Within the field of child psychology, in particular, the concept of effectance or competence motivation has had widespread appeal.

Advances in Motivation and Achievement, vol. 3, pages 219–250
Copyright © 1984 by JAI Press Inc.
All rights of reproduction in any form reserved.
ISBN 0-89232-289-6

Although the concept of a motive which impels the organism toward competence has considerable appeal, it is less than satisfactory to the rigorous at heart. The very globalness of the effectance motive construct has precluded any precise operational definition. Thus, our initial efforts were directed toward specifying what we felt might be measurable components of intrinsic mastery motivation, particularly as they applied to the domain of classroom learning. The first such components or dimensions we identified were: preference for challenge (is the child intrinsically motivated to seek challenging material to learn or master?), curiosity (is the child intrinsically motivated to learn new things, is he/she inquisitive?), and independent mastery (is the child motivated to figure things out on his/her own?)

White's major emphasis was on the intrinsic properties of the effectance motive system. However, in considering the child within the classroom context, it seemed critical to identify what might be *extrinsic* motivational factors as well. For example, to what extent is the child motivated to perform in the classroom in order to obtain external approval from the teacher or good grades? This framework allowed us to consider the relative strength of a child's intrinsic versus extrinsic motivational orientation, as an individual difference variable. Moreover, we sought to determine how these orientations might change with the developmental level of the child.

The original model (see Harter, 1978, 1981a) sought to identify both antecedents as well as correlates of a child's motivational orientation. The present chapter focuses only on the correlates which were postulated. Two psychological constructs or self-perceptions were identified as critical correlates: perceived competence and perceived control. In addition, we sought to examine the relationship of motivational orientation, perceived competence, and perceived control, not only to each other, but to scholastic achievement. Critical to our model was the assumption that the perceived competence and perceived control constructs be viewed as domain-specific, rather than as global or trait-like constructs such as self-concept or locus of control. Thus, within our chosen domain of school learning, our focus was on cognitive or scholastic competence and on the child's perceptions of who controls or is responsible for his/her academic successes and failures.

The model, then, postulates relationships between motivational orientation in the classroom, perceived cognitive competence, perceived control over academic events, and actual scholastic achievement. Specifically, we hypothesized that the child who is intrinsically motivated within a given mastery domain would also perceive himself/herself to be relatively competent in that domain, and to feel in control of his/her successes and failures. Conversely, the more extrinsically motivated child was expected to have lower feelings of competence and feel less responsible for successes and failures within a given mastery domain. Finally, it was our expectation that the child's motivational orientation and related self-perceptions should predict his/her actual achievement, objectively assessed.

Thus, an intrinsic motivational orientation, coupled with positive feelings of competence and perceptions of personal control over outcomes, should be associated with higher levels of actual achievement. Lower levels of achievement would be expected from the child whose motivational orientation was more extrinsic, whose perceptions of competence were relatively low and whose perceptions of control were relatively external.

Within the psychological and educational literature, each of these variables has been of interest. However, for the most part, studies have focused on the relationship between given pairs of constructs rather than the pattern of relationships within this network of constructs. For example, there is a vast literature attempting to establish the relationship between self-concept and achievement (see Harter, 1983; Wylie, 1979). However, these studies have typically examined the relationship between very global measures of self-concept or self-esteem and academic achievement, reporting correlations which range between .10 and .50, with most falling within the .30s and low .40s. As has been pointed out (Harter, 1983; Wylie, 1979), measures such as the Coopersmith Self Inventory (1967) and the Piers-Harris self concept scale (Piers & Harris 1969) yield a single score based on self-perceptions across a wide variety of characteristics and attributes. Thus, it is not surprising that when such global measures of self-concept are related to specific behaviors such as scholastic achievement, only low to moderate correlations are obtained.

The locus of control construct, which has received widespread attention in the adult literature, has recently become very popular in studies with children. Most investigators, following in the conceptual footsteps of Rotter (1966), have viewed locus of control as a relatively global, unidimensional trait along a continuum of internal to external. The locus of control scale for children devised by Nowicki and Strickland (1973) is based upon such a model, and samples perceptions of control over a wide range of behavioral demains. In contrast, the Intellectual Achievement Responsibility Questionnaire (Crandall, Katkovsky, & Crandall, 1965) focuses on the academic domain and allows for a separate assessment of one's sense of control over successes and failures. It is not surprising, therefore, that the latter measure has been found to relate more highly to achievement than the Nowicki and Strickland scale.

Other studies have sought to examine the relationship between locus of control and self-esteem or self-concept (reviewed in Harter, 1983). Typically, global measures of locus of control are related to global measures of self-concept. These moderate correlations do not, however, illuminate the underlying self-evaluative processes involved.

There are virtually no studies which have examined the relationship between motivational orientation, as it is defined in our model, and constructs involving perceptions of competence and control. Nor has motivational orientation been related to academic achievement. While motivation to achieve has been examined, it is important to distinguish between achievement motivation, as it has typically been defined in the literature (cf. Atkinson, 1964) and mastery motivation, as it is being used in the present study. Achievement motivation typically refers to the *level* of one's motivation to engage in achievement behaviors, based on the interaction of such parameters as need for achievement, expectancy of success, and the incentive value of success.

Our construct of motivational orientation refers to the *type* of motivational stance which the child adopts toward classroom learning. Thus, one may engage in scholastic endeavors for intrinsic reasons, because the work is challenging, enjoyable, and piques one's curiosity, or alternatively, one may engage in schoolwork for extrinsic reasons, either to obtain external approval or because the educational system requires it. How type of motivational orientation relates to level of achievement motivation is an interesting issue to pursue, both theoretically as well as empirically. However, in the present study, the focus is restricted to how motivational orientation relates to perceived competence, perceived control, and achievement, all within the scholastic domain.

A CAUSAL MODELING APPROACH

The specific purpose of this chapter is to go beyond correlational analyses, and to examine the relationship among these variables employing path-analytic techniques which rely on structural equation procedures. Through such causal modeling techniques, we can begin to make more precise statements about the direction of influence of a given variable upon others in the network. This type of approach has received some attention in the educational literature, with regard to two variables in our nomological network, self-concept and achievement. The question of cause has been of primary concern to educators, given the implications for remediation. Prior to the 1960s, the prevalent view emphasized the influence of academic success on enhanced self-esteem. During the 1960s, however, a contrasting viewpoint emerged, highlighting the impact of self-esteem enhancement on one's academic performance. As Calsyn and Kenny (1977) note, however, ''. . . the debate between self-enhancement and skill development theorists has been largely rhetorical for both conceptual and methodological reasons'' (p.136). In part, the ambiguity of the findings on this issue is due to the use of global self-esteem measures, rather than self-evaluative indices which are more specific to the domain of academic achievement (see Harter, 1981a, 1982).

In the present study, two model-testing strategies were initially considered. We could have restricted our analyses to an empirical search for the model which best fit the data, followed by an attempt to replicate the fit in a separate, comparable, sample. Alternatively, we could test several possible models derived from various theoretical perspectives, in order to determine which best fit the data, and then attempt to replicate these findings. We chose the latter strategy, comparing four different models, each of which plausibly emerged from a particular literature or point of view. Moreover, we sought to examine causal pathways separately for elementary school and junior high school pupils, to explore possible developmental differences. A general developmental framework, emphasizing increasing differentiation and integration, would lead to the expectation that in junior high, the pattern of relationships might be more complex. Moreover, we wanted to explore the possibility that particular constructs in the network might have more of an impact at one developmental level than another, particularly if we could replicate such an influence in a second sample. The distinction between elementary school pupils and junior high pupils seemed to represent a plausible beginning point, since these groups correspond to the developmental periods of middle-childhood (concrete operations) and early adolescence (the beginning of formal operations).

A major limitation of much of the existing research in this area has been the use of global self-evaluative measures which have been employed to predict very specific behaviors such as achievement in reading or math. The lack of measuring instruments to measure domain- or situation-specific self-perceptions has hindered our search for meaningful relationships within particular domains. Since such measures did not exist, we set out to devise a battery of instruments which would meet our needs.

The psychometric saga of our measurement construction efforts has been chronicled in detail elsewhere (Harter, 1981a). From these efforts, three self-report instruments have now been devised: The Perceived Competence Scale for Children (Harter, 1982), A Multi–dimensional Measure of Children's Perceptions of Control (Connell, 1980), and A Scale of Intrinsic versus Extrinsic Orientation in the Classroom (Harter, 1981b). Both the perceived competence and perceived control measures tap self-perceptions in three mastery domains: cognitive or scholastic competence, social competence vis-à-vis one's peers, and physical or athletic competence. The measure of intrinsic versus extrinsic orientation is specific to the cognitive/scholastic domain.

In the course of our measurement construction efforts, each of the constructs took on a new look, becoming more differentiated than they appeared in our original theorizing. Thus, before describing the four models to be compared, we will first provide a description of each measure and the constructs which have emerged. The more differentiated network which has resulted from these efforts has permitted a much richer picture of the potential relationships among the variables of interest, allowing for the comparison of more complex causal models.

NETWORK OF VARIABLES

Table 1 presents the network of variables which we examined. The major constructs are listed on the left: actual competence, perceived competence, perceived control, and intrinsic versus extrinsic orientation. Each of these will be described in that order.

Table 1.   A Causal Model of the Relationships Among Intrinsic vs. Extrinsic
Orientation, Perceived Control, Perceived Competence, Actual Competence
For the Cognitive Domain: Network of Variables.

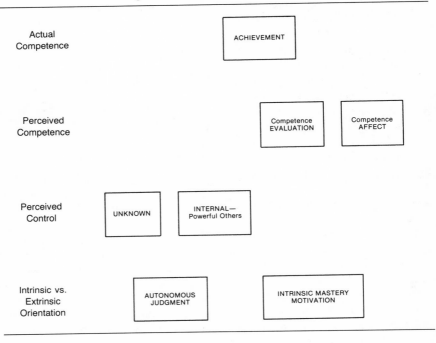

Actual Competence

The IOWA Test of Basic Skills, a group-administered achievement test given
by the school system each year, was the measure of actual scholastic competence. Three scores were available: reading, math, and language. Each of these
three subscales scores was converted to a percentile score for each subject,
standardized according to grade level. Given that the correlations among the
three indices were all greater than .80, a single composite for achievement was
derived by taking the average of these three percentile scores for each subject.

Perceived Competence

Perceived cognitive competence was assessed with the Perceived Competence
Scale for Children (Harter, 1982). The construction of this measure was based on
the assumption that children can make meaningful distinctions about their competence in different domains of their life. Thus, the scale structure reflects three
competence domains: (a) cognitive competence, with an emphasis on academic

performance; (b) social competence in one's peer relationships, and (c) physical competence which primarily taps athletic ability. In addition to these specific competence domains, a fourth subscale taps the child's general sense of self-worth, independent of a particular skill domain. Factor analytic procedures indicate that children clearly make distinctions among these domains, a finding which has been replicated in numerous samples (Harter, 1982).

In constructing this scale, considerable energy was devoted toward devising a question format which would offset the child's tendency to give socially desirable responses. This tendency has proved to be a problem with the typical true-false or like me—unlike me formats utilized on existing self-concept scales for children, e.g., Coopersmith's Self-Esteem Inventory (1967). Items on the perceived competence scale are presented in a "structured alternative format." The child is given a statement such as: "Some kids often forget what they learn but other kids remember things easily." They are first asked to decide which kind of kids they are most like, the ones who forget or the ones who remember things easily. After making this judgment, they then decide whether they are just "sort of like" these kids or "really like" them. Each item is scored on a four point ordinal scale where a score of 4 indicates high perceived competence and 1 indicates the lowest perceived competence. (A discussion of the reasons underlying the effectiveness of this format can be found in Harter, 1982.)

Only the cognitive items were utilized, given that our first structural modeling efforts have been restricted to the domain of scholastic achievement. However, upon closer scrutiny of these cognitive items, it appeared that they were tapping two dimensions of one's self-perceptions of cognitive competence. Approximately half of the items seemed to tap an evaluation of one's competence based on relatively objective criteria such as the speed of doing one's work, the ease of remembering, and getting good grades. However, a separate subset were couched in more *affective* language making reference to feeling good or badly about one's work, worrying about completing schoolwork, etc. On the basis of these clusters, therefore, two scores were calculated, the first of which was labelled competence *evaluation*, whereas the second was designated as competence *affect* (see Table 1). It was anticipated that these two variables might bear somewhat different relationships to other constructs in the model.

Perceived Control

This construct was assessed through the administration of the Multidimensional Measure of Children's Perceptions of Control (Connell, 1980). This 96-item self-report measure assesses the reasons children give for their successes and failures. It was designed, in part, to assess domain-specific judgments of perceived control. As such, it was viewed as an alternative to other more trait-like measures of children's locus of control assessed along a general internal-external dimension (Bialer, 1961; Nowicki & Strickland, 1973). The domains assessed are the same as those included on the perceived competence scale just described, i.e., cognitive, social, and physical competence. A fourth general subscale is also included. Following Crandall, Katkovsky, and Crandall's (1965) work, control over both successes and failures is assessed separately.

Three sources of control can be tapped independently. The first two sources, *Internal* control, and *External* control in the form of powerful others, have been employed on previous scales (e.g., Levenson, 1972). The third source of control, *Unknown,* emerged in the construction of this particular scale. Initially, the measure included a chance or luck subscale, based on the model of certain locus of control scales for adults (e.g., Levenson, 1972). However, the findings from this earlier version revealed that children do not make systematic attributions based on luck or chance. Subsequent revisions, though, revealed that children *will* indicate that they simply *don't know* who or what is responsible for their successes and/or failures. Moreover, this "unknown" dimension has emerged as a very powerful predictor of other variables in the network.

The items themselves are presented in the form of statements such as "When I get a bad grade in school, it's usually because I didn't try hard enough." The children are then asked to indicate whether this statement is "very true," "sort of true," "not very true," or "not at all true." These responses are scored 4, 3, 2, 1, respectively. This item represents internal source of control over a failure outcome within the cognitive domain. A sample external—powerful others item would be: "If I do well in school, its because the teacher likes me."

Unknown control items were worded in the direction of *not* knowing who or what is in control, e.g., "If I get a good grade in school, I usually don't understand why." Thus, the *higher* the unknown score, the *less* the child claims to understand or know about the reasons for successes or failures. A *low* score on the unknown scale implies that the child *does* understand the reasons for such outcomes. That is, the child is denying that he/she doesn't know. The precise reasons for either endorsement or denial of these "don't know" statements will require further investigation. At first glance, the unknown subscale appears to bear some resemblance to Seligman's (1975) learned helplessness construct. However, they are not synonymous. Seligman's construct is construed as the product of experiences in which behaviors and outcomes are viewed as non-contingent, ultimately leading the perceiver to feel not only helpless but depressed. However, the unknown score, if high, may not necessarily reflect this type of non-contingent experience but rather *lack* of experience or knowledge concerning the particular cause of an outcome. Developmentally, one might then expect that younger children, with lack of experience in a particular domain, would have higher unknown scores, a finding which Connell (1981) has documented. Precisely what types of affects might accompany high unknown scores at different developmental levels is a further question of empirical interest.

Only the items pertaining to scholastic (cognitive) successes and failures were used in this study. Twelve items from this scale were included in the study—four items tapping the child's perceptions of internal control over successes and failures in school, four items tapping powerful others' control over these same outcomes and four items tapping unknown perceptions of control. For the purpose of this study, success and failure scores were combined within each source of control, for two reasons. First, the reliabilities of the four items combined were considerably higher than the separate two-item composites of success and of failure. Secondly, we had no a priori predictions at this point concerning how perceptions of control over success versus failure might differentially relate to the other constructs in the network. This issue will be the topic of further research.

Two control scores were calculated for use in this particular structural modeling endeavor (see Table 1). The first, labelled Unknown, represents the average of the child's responses to items on the Unknown subscale. The second score represents a contrast between the two possible sources of known control, calculated as Internal control minus Powerful Others. This score can be interpreted as "relative internality," i.e., of what the child *does* know, how internal are these perceptions?

Intrinsic versus Extrinsic Orientation

The instrument designed to tap this construct was the Scale of Intrinsic versus Extrinsic Orientation in the Classroom (Harter, 1981b). As a starting point, we restricted this scale to the academic or cognitive domain. The following general question guided our scale construction efforts: To what degree is a child's motivation for classroom learning determined by an intrinsic interest in learning and mastery, curiosity, preference for challenge, versus a more extrinsic orientation in which teacher approval and grades are the motivation and the child is very dependent on the teacher for guidance? We then set out to determine whether we could identify components of classroom learning that could be defined by both an intrinsic and extrinsic motivational pole. Our efforts have now revealed that children make clear distinctions between five different aspects of classroom learning, as substantiated by a replicable five-factor solution. Each of these components constitutes a separate subscale, which we have defined as follows:

1. *Preference for challenge versus preference for easy work assigned.* Is the child intrinsically motivated to perform hard, challenging work or does the child prefer to do the easier work assigned by the teacher?

2. *Incentive to work to satisfy one's own interest and curiosity versus working to please the teacher and obtain good grades.* Here, as the title indicates, we were interested in the relative strength of the child's intrinsic interest and curiosity compared to a more extrinsic orientation to obtain teacher approval and grades.

3. *Independent mastery attempts versus dependence on the teacher.* This subscale taps the degree to which a child prefers to figure out problems on his or

her own in contrast to a dependence on the teacher for help and guidance, particularly when it comes to figuring out problems and assignments.

4. *Independent judgment versus reliance on teacher's judgment.* This subscale assesses whether the child feels that he or she is capable of making certain judgments about what to do in the classroom in contrast to a dependence on the teacher's opinion or judgment about what to do.

5. *Internal criteria for success/failure versus external criteria for success/failure.* Does the child have some internal sense of whether he/she has succeeded or done poorly on a test or on a school assignment or is the child dependent on external sources of evaluation such as teacher feedback, grades, and marks?

In constructing the actual scale, we utilized the forced-choice format that we designed for the perceived competence scale. Thus, the child is given a statement such as the following: "Some kids like to learn things on their own that interest them but other kids think it's better to do things that the teacher thinks they should be learning." The child first decides which kids he/she is most like, and then indicates whether this is just sort of true for him/her or really true. Items are scored on a four-point ordinal scale in which 4 is the maximum intrinsic orientation and 1 represents the other extreme in terms of an extrinsic orientation.

Correlational and factor analyses of the data from this scale revealed two clusters of subscales. One was defined by the first three subscales described, preference for challenge versus preference for easy work assigned, incentive to work to satisfy one's own interest and curiosity versus working to please the teacher and obtain good grades, and independent mastery attempts versus dependence on the teacher. The second cluster was defined by the remaining two subscales, independent judgment versus reliance on teacher's judgment, and internal criteria for success/failure versus external criteria for success/failure.

In attempting to interpret these data, it struck us that the subscales in the first cluster—challenge, curiosity, and mastery—each had a distinct *motivational* flavor in that they tapped issues involving what the child *wants* to do, *likes* to do, *prefers.* In contrast, the independent judgment and internal criteria subscales seemed to tap more *cognitive-informational* structures: What does the child *know?* On what basis does he or she make decisions? How much has the child learned about the rules of the game called "school?"

These findings caused a refinement in our thinking since they indicated that our scale did not simply tap motivational parameters, but what we have now labelled as cognitive-informational or knowledge parameters, as well. Based on the magnitude of the correlations of the subscales within each of these two clusters, we created two scores for the purposes of the present analyses. A given child's scores from the two *cognitive-informational* subscales (Independent Judgment vs. Reliance on the Teacher's Judgment and Internal vs. External Criteria for Success/Failure) were combined into a single variable which we have labelled as Autonomous Judgment in Table 1. The three *motivational* subscales (Preference for Challenge vs. Preference for Easy Work Assigned, Curiosity/Interest vs. Pleasing the Teacher and Getting Grades, and Independent Mastery Attempts vs. Dependence on the Teacher) were combined into a single variable which is labelled Intrinsic Mastery Motivation. Bear in mind that while these two variables are labelled in terms of the intrinsic pole, represented by high scores, a low score on these variables designates an extrinsic orientation.

Developmental differences. Some of the most interesting findings to emerge from this scale have involved striking developmental trends across grades three through nine. While not predicted, these trends appear to be interpretable, and have caused us to alter our conceptions of the underlying constructs being tapped. The cognitive-informational cluster—independent judgment versus reliance on teacher's judgment and internal criteria versus external criteria—shows dramatic linear trends across the third to ninth grades. Scores for third graders are relatively extrinsic, crossing the midpoint in the later elementary school grades into the intrinsic range for the junior high pupils. The opposite linear trend is found for the motivational cluster defined by preference for challenge versus preference for easy work, curiosity/interest versus teacher approval/grades, and independent mastery versus dependence on the teacher. For each of these dimensions, children begin with relatively intrinsic scores in the younger grades and shift towards a more extrinsic orientation. (See Harter, 1981b, where these data are presented.)

In interpreting these trends, it seemed plausible that with increasing grade level, children become more knowledgeable, more capable of making their own judgments, and more able to determine whether or not they are successful. The converse developmental shift from intrinsic to extrinsic, on the three *motivational* subscales, requires a different interpretation. The findings suggest that over the grade levels sampled, children's intrinsic interest in learning wanes or is stifled, particularly with regard to preference for challenge, curiosity, and desire to independently master material. It may also reflect the tendency for children to adapt to the demands of a school culture which reinforces a relatively extrinsic orientation. These hypotheses warrant further examination. Moreover, the developmental differences obtained in the levels of these two clusters suggests the fruitfulness of determining whether the motivational and cognitive-informational constructs bear different relationships to the other constructs in the network, at different developmental levels.

THE FOUR ALTERNATIVE MODELS TESTED

Our next task was to specify four different, seemingly plausible models which could account for the relationships among the seven variables in this network: academic achievement and the six self-related perceptions assessed through our measures. Each of these models specifies a pattern of functional relationships or paths, implying the direction of influence of certain variables upon others in the network. The four models postulated are in no way meant to be exhaustive, given the large number of possible models which could be generated from the relationships among seven variables. These four models were chosen as plausible alternative conceptualizations which logically follow from existing formulations in the literature.

The four models are presented schematically in Figure 1. Each model contains an identical number of paths (six), an initial constraint which was necessary for the purposes of statistical comparison. In each model, one variable is surrounded by a box. This variable represents the hypothesized causal construct at the beginning of the predictive chain, the "prime mover" as it were. The arrowheads indicate the predicted direction of influence of a given variable upon another. The minus signs (−) indicate that the relationship between those two variables is negative, e.g., a high unknown control score is associated with a low level of achievement.

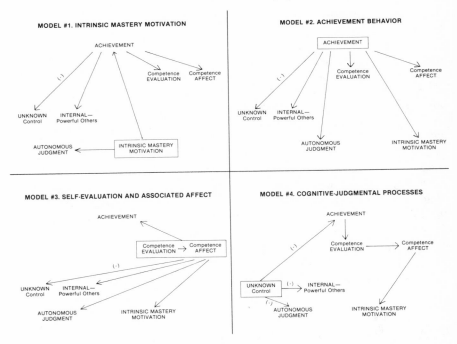

Figure 1. The four alternative models tested.

Model Number 1

The first model places major emphasis on the role of one's motivational orientation, and as such is consistent with those positions (Harter, 1978; White, 1959) which highlight the importance of intrinsic mastery motivation. Thus, intrinsic motivation gives the ''push'' to one's achievement efforts leading to relatively high levels of achievement. Conversely, this path represents the fact that an extrinsic orientation would lead to relatively low levels of achievement. Achievement, in turn, is postulated to affect both components of perceived competence. High levels of achievement lead to a positive evaluation of one's competence as well as to positive affects or feelings about one's competence. Conversely, a low level of achievement would lead to a negative competence evaluation and negative affective reaction toward one's competence. In this model, achievement is also postulated to exert an influence on the perceived control variables. High achievement should result in relatively low unknown perceptions of control, as well as a more internal orientation, relative to powerful others. Low achievement levels lead to unknown perceptions of control, as well as the perception that powerful others are responsible for one's intrinsic mastery motivation and one's ability to make autonomous judgments, i.e., both the motivational and cognitive-informational functions of one's intrinsic-extrinsic orientation are related.

Model Number 2

In this model, which enjoys the support of many traditional educators, achievement behavior is conceptualized as the prime mover, impacting each of the other variables in the network. This model was derived from the position of those proponents of skill development who emphasize how increases in one's actual skill level will lead to enhanced self-esteem or a more positive self-concept (see Calsyn & Kenny, 1977; Purkey, 1970). Thus, achievement behavior is predicted to influence both competence evaluation and competence affect. Moreover, this model assumes that high levels of achievement will lead to a relatively intrinsic motivational orientation (in contrast to the directionality specified in Model No. 1 which predicts that one's motivational orientation will influence one's achievement level). Model No. 2 also gives causal primacy to achievement with regard to its effect on the two perceived control variables in that high levels of achievement will lead to low unknown scores as well as a relatively internal perception of control. Achievement is also predicted to influence autonomous judgment in that the higher a child's achievement level, the more able that child is in making independent judgments in the classroom.

Model Number 3

This model was tested to give a fair hearing to those who have emphasized the impact of a child's self-evaluation of his/her competence upon achievement behaviors and classroom motivation, in particular. Such a model reflects the view of those within the educational field who have proposed that efforts to enhance a child's sense of self-esteem and competence will in turn lead to improvements in their actual performance. Models 2 and 3 can be contrasted in light of the controversy concerning whether achievement best predicts self-concept (Model No. 2) or whether self-concept best predicts achievement (Model No. 3). See Purkey (1970) as well as Harter, (1983) for a further discussion of these issues.

In Model No. 3, therefore, the influential link between competence evaluation with its associated affect and achievement is a particularly critical path. This model also predicts that self-evaluative appraisals will have an impact on the child's perceptions of control and his/her ability to make autonomous judgments. The more positive one's feelings of competence, the more likely one is to be relatively internal, to have low unknown control scores, and to be able to make independent judgments in the classroom.

Model Number 4

In light of the increasing emphasis on cognitive-attributional variables as determinants and mediators of behavior, the fourth model places perceived control at the beginning of the predictive chain. Moreover, recent sequential models (see Bandura, 1978; Kanfer, 1980; Wicklund, 1978) also emphasize how one's self-evaluative reactions to one's performance produce self-affects which in turn impact one's tendency to engage in a given behavior. Thus, in Model No. 4, Unknown Control, in particular, is identified as the most critical cognitive-attributional variable in the network in that it directly influences achievement, in addition to one's relative internality and one's ability to make autonomous judgments. The path to achievement reflects the expectation that the lower one's unknown score (the less one says one doesn't understand the reason for one's successes and failures) the higher one's achievement level. Achievement, in turn, leads to one's competence evaluation. The higher one's actual achievement level, the more likely one is to perceive oneself as competent in that domain. This competence evaluation leads, in turn, to one's affective reaction to one's competence, and it is this affective component which influences one's motivational orientation. That is, the more positive the affective reactions, the more likely one is to be intrinsically motivated. Conversely, negative evaluative judgments leading to negative competence affect will result in an extrinsic motivational orientation.

PROCEDURAL CONSIDERATIONS

Sampling and Administration

Seven grade levels were sampled in this cross-sectional study representing grades three through nine. There were a total of 784 subjects, with approximately

100 pupils at each grade level. Subjects were from the Ventura School System in California, drawing from primarily lower-middle, middle-middle, and upper-middle class families. In this sample, 85% were Caucasian, 12% were Mexican-American, and the remaining 3% were from other ethnic backgrounds. Both elementary and junior high schools could be characterized as relatively traditional in terms of classroom structure and curriculum. Elementary school pupils were drawn from schools containing grades one through six. The junior high school contained grades seven, eight, and nine. It was a relatively large school, with four homeroom classes of approximately 25 pupils at each grade level, and followed a model in which different subjects were taught by different teachers, in different locations of the school complex.

The three self-report scales assessing perceived competence, perceptions of control, and intrinsic vs. extrinsic orientation were administered to pupils in their classroom, in groups of approximately 25. Three 35-minute testing sessions were conducted over three consecutive days. The order in which measures were administered within and between testing sessions was counterbalanced.

After the data were collected, a random subsampling procedure was employed in order to obtain one sample which would be employed for exploratory analytic purposes and one which could be utilized for purposes of confirming or replicating the initial effects obtained. Thus, half of the males and half of the females within each grade level were randomly selected as the exploratory sample (Total $N = 386$) and the remaining pupils were designated as the confirmatory sample (Total $N = 398$).

Analytic Strategy and Model Comparisons

The goals of the model-testing were fourfold: (a) to test the relative goodness of fit of the four alternative models separately for elementary and junior high pupils, employing the exploratory subsamples; (b) to modify the best-fitting of these models in order to achieve an acceptable statistical fit using multiple criteria for goodness of fit; (c) to determine whether the best fitting model for each group could be replicated using the confirmatory sample; and (d) to test for model differences between elementary and junior high school pupils.

The data-analytic technique employed was structural equation modeling (Joreskog 1973). This technique allows for two or more models to be compared in terms of overall goodness of fit to the same set of correlational data. The technique also allows for particular parameters (relationships) within a given model to be evaluated for statistical significance—individually, and in terms of their contribution to the overall fit of the model. Finally, the technique allows the researcher to assess statistically the comparability of models in different groups of subjects; these models may include some parameters which are restricted to be the same between groups and others which are allowed to be different. Thus, the technique offers much greater flexibility than traditional path analytic procedures.

Indices of Relative Goodness-of-Fit

A complete discussion of the criteria employed to test the relative adequacy of each of the four models can be found in Connell (1981), including many of the precautions involved in such model-testing. As noted earlier, each of the four models was designed in order to equalize the number of structural relationships or paths postulated to account for the same correlational matrix upon which these procedures operate. A key component of structural equation modeling is the evaluation of a model's goodness of fit. In this study, two primary sources of information were used to make this evaluation. First, the overall chi-square indicates the degree to which the model fits (or doesn't fit) the observed data. The larger the chi-square statistic, the *less* likely that the observed data (the pattern of correlations) emerged from the specified model. A second index of goodness of fit is the size of the residual correlations associated with each of the models. The residual correlations represent the degree to which the correlations "predicted" by a particular model differ from the observed correlations which the model is seeking to explain. The larger the residual correlations, the worse the fit of the model.

CORRELATIONS AMONG THE SEVEN VARIABLES IN THE NETWORK

The correlations for the elementary school and junior high school exploratory samples are presented in Tables 2 and 3, respectively. It is this pattern of correlations that each of the four major alternative models described above will be attempting, in effect, to explain. For the *elementary* school pupils, the highest correlations are between Competence Evaluation and Competence Affect ($r = .52$) and between these two perceived competence constructs and Mastery Motivation (r's $= .58$ and $.47$, respectively). The next highest relationships are between the two control constructs, Unknown Control and Relative Internality (Internal-Powerful Others), namely $r = -.38$ and between Unknown Control and Achievement ($r = -.41$). Lower values were obtained between the two control constructs and other variables in the network, particularly for relative internality. While Achievement correlates most highly with Unknown Control (indicating that high achievement is associated with low Unknown Control), Achievement also bears a moderate and significant relationship to each of the other five variables assessed.

For the *junior high school* pupils, there are similarities in the pattern of correlations as well as differences. As in the elementary sample, the highest correlations are between competence evaluation and competence affect ($r = .60$) and between these two perceived competence constructs and mastery motivation (r's $= .56$ and $.60$, respectively). Unknown Control correlates highly with Achievement ($r = .45$) as it did for the elementary sample. Achievement also bears moderate and significant relationships to all other variables. However, unlike the elementary group, Unknown Control for the junior high school pupils also bears significant relationships to each of the other variables in the network. Competence affect is also more strongly related to other variables than in the elementary grades, e.g., to Mastery Motivation ($r = .60$) and to Unknown Control ($r = -.47$). Thus, the differences in the pattern of correlations for the two age groups suggest the fruitfulness of keeping these two groups separate in the subsequent analyses designed to test the goodness of fit for each of the four models.

BEST-FITTING MODEL FOR ELEMENTARY AND JUNIOR HIGH SCHOOL PUPILS

For both elementary school and junior high school pupils, Model No. 4, emphasizing cognitive-judgmental processes as a primary predictor, best fits the data. Moreover, this fit was replicated in the confirmatory sample. That is, both exploratory and confirmatory analyses indicate that the overall chi-square index of goodness of fit associated with Model No. 4 is lower (better) than the other three models in both age groups. Similarly, the residual correlations associated with Model No. 4 are lower than the other three models in both age groups. However, for both elementary school and junior high school groups, additional paths were needed to improve the fit. Thus, the best-fitting modifications of Model No. 4 are presented in Figure 2. (See Connell, 1981, for a detailed account of the model-fitting procedure.)

Elementary School Pupils

As can be seen in Figure 2, the level of a child's understanding of the reasons for his/her successes and failures, as reflected in the Unknown Control score, is a critical variable in this sequential representation of how the child processes and reacts affectively to his/her school performance. The fact that the path between unknown control and achievement is *negative* reflects the manner in which the unknown items are scored. *High* Unknown scores, denoting the child's admission that he/she doesn't understand the causes of successes and failures, are associated with *low* Achievement. Conversely, it is the child who is "in the know," as it were, (whose Unknown score is low) who is the achiever. This path is one of the strongest in the model. Achievement level in turn influences judgments about his/her performance. Thus, if the child is objectively achieving at high levels, his/her evaluation of competence is also high. Competence Evaluation, in turn, influences the child's affective reaction. Feelings of competence breed positive feelings about schoolwork. Competence Evaluation also has a major impact on motivational orientation. If one judges that one is competent, one is more likely to be intrinsically motivated. Conversely, if one thinks one is

Table 2. Correlations Among Self-Related Constructs and Achievement: Exploratory Elementary Subsample.

	Achievement	Mastery Motivation	Autonomous Judgment	Competence Affect	Competence Evaluation	Relative Internality
Mastery Motivation	.31					
Autonomous Judgment	.26	.20				
Competence Affect	.25	.47	.30			
Competence Evaluation	.33	.58	.16	.52		
Relative Internality	.21	.22	(.00)	(.02)	(.05)	
Unknown Control	-.41	-.23	-.28	-.19	-.21	-.38

Average *N* for each correlation equals 210. Correlations in parentheses are nonsignificant.

Table 3. Correlations Among Self-Related Constructs and Achievement: Exploratory Junior High School Subsample.

	Achievement	Mastery Motivation	Autonomous Judgment	Competence Affect	Competence Evaluation	Relative Internality
Mastery Motivation	.34					
Autonomous Judgment	.33	.46				
Competence Affect	.36	.60	.47			
Competence Evaluation	.33	.56	.50	.60		
Relative Internality	(.07)	.20	(.15)	(.16)	(.17)	
Unknown Control	-.45	-.32	-.36	-.47	-.42	-.26

Average N for each correlation equals 133. Correlations in parentheses are nonsignificant.

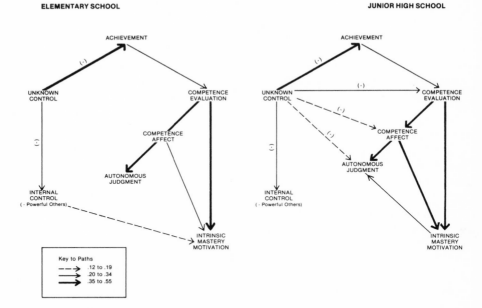

Figure 2.   The best-fitting models for elementary and junior high school
  pupils.

not very competent, one is more likely to prefer easy assignments, and merely
work to please the teacher and obtain the necessary grades.

For the elementary school pupils, Competence *Affect* also influences one's
motivational orientation, although the magnitude of this influence is not as great
as the impact of Competence Evaluation on motivation. An empirical link which
was not included in the original Model No. 4 involves the path from Competence
Affect to Autonomous Judgment. This path indicates that if one feels good about
one's performance in school, one prefers to make independent judgments about
one's schoolwork. Conversely, if a child feels badly about his/her competence,
he/she is more likely to seek guidance from the teacher.

The major chain for elementary school pupils seems to involve the impact of
the child's knowledge about the factors controlling his/her successes and failures
on achievement; achievement, in turn, influences competence evaluation, which
then impacts one's motivational orientation. The level of a child's knowledge, as
reflected in the Unknown Control score, also influences the degree to which
he/she feels personally responsible for outcomes. The less one says one doesn't
know who or what is in control, the more likely one is to be internal. Conversely,
the more a child claims that he/she doesn't know what is responsible for outcomes, the more likely it is that the child will see powerful others in control.

One final path from Internal Control to Intrinsic Mastery Motivation emerged in the empirical modification of Model No. 4. Though it is modest in magnitude, it was found to improve the overall fit. This path suggests that the more a child feels in control of his/her successes and failures in the classroom, the more he/she will be intrinsically motivated in the pursuit of learning. Conversely, the child who sees powerful others in control is more likely to be extrinsically motivated to engage in schoolwork.

Junior High School Pupils

The best-fitting modification of Model No. 4 for junior high school pupils is presented on the right-hand side of Figure 2. As this figure illustrates, the same basic chain is obtained in that Unknown Control influences one's actual Achievement which in turn feeds into one's Competence Evaluation. Competence Evaluation, then, influences both Competence Affect and one's motivational orientation.

A major difference between the junior high school and elementary school models is the greater number of paths required at the junior high school level to account for the observed relationships among these variables. Eleven paths were needed in the junior high school model, compared to eight for the elementary school pupils. Competence Affect also plays a somewhat greater role at the junior high school level in that it has as big an impact on one's motivational orientation as does one's evaluation of one's competence.

The additional paths required in the junior high school model suggest that the adolescent is a thinker, as well. The adolescent's cognitions about control, as reflected in the magnitude of the Unknown Control score, not only influence achievement level, but also have an impact on perceived competence and on sense of autonomous judgment. The path from Unknown Control to Competence Evaluation suggests that a lack of understanding about who or what is responsible for successes and failures in the scholastic domain makes one feel relatively stupid. Moreover, if lacking this knowledge, one also has a negative affective reaction to lack of cognitive competence. Finally, this portrait suggests that if the adolescent doesn't know who or what is responsible, he/she is more inclined to feel that it's best to simply let the teacher make judgments about what to do. These additional paths from Unknown Control suggest, conversely, that the child who *is* in the know thinks he/she is competent, feels good about this competence, and is inclined to make independent judgments in the classroom.

There is also a path from Intrinsic Mastery Motivation to Autonomous Judgment in the junior high school model, a path which was not necessary to account for the observed relationships at the elementary school level. It is the intrinsically motivated adolescent who feels capable of making autonomous judgments about schoolwork, or who desires to do so. The extrinsically motivated student, on the other hand, prefers to rely on the teachers' judgments.

INTERPRETATION OF THE BEST-FITTING MODELS

An initial purpose of our research was to test the hypothesis that there were two important correlates of a child's motivational orientation: perceived competence and perceived control. While this assumption has clearly received support in our findings, our modeling efforts have represented an attempt to go further, in order to specify the directions of influence among these variables, as well as how they relate to the child's achievement level within the academic domain. In testing four plausible models of the concurrent influences among these variables, the findings revealed that the model emphasizing the primacy of a child's perceived level of knowledge concerning the events controlling his academic successes and failures best fit the data for both elementary and junior high school pupils, although there were important differences between these two groups as well.

For both age groups, it was Unknown perceived control which appeared at the beginning of the chain, not the Internal minus Powerful Others variable. That is, the extent to which a child feels that he/she knows or doesn't know the causes of academic outcomes is most directly related to academic achievement, a premise objectively defined through test performance.

The failure of the Internal minus Powerful Other contrast score to directly impact achievement can be plausibly interpreted, if one considers the classroom context in which these effects were examined. That is, either an internal or an external orientation could reasonably lead to academic success, and different children may opt for different routes. A child who achieves success may attribute this to hard work and personal effort. Alternatively, a child may opt for a strategy of pleasing the powerful others in charge, a perfectly reasonable stance to take in a relatively traditional school setting where the teachers, as authority figures, place numerous external demands upon the pupils. In both cases, each child claims to have knowledge of who or what controls successes, but merely pursues a different course, depending upon whether the attributions are internal or focus on powerful others. Thus, the internal-powerful others construct would not be expected to have a major impact on achievement per se, although the perceived level of knowledge of control, as reflected in the unknown score, does have a direct impact.

Other investigators, e.g., Covington and Omelich (1979), have argued that causal attributions do not play a large role in achievement behavior. However, in their analysis, tested with college students, attributions refer primarily to the internal attributions specified in Weiner's model, i.e., effort (unstable) versus ability (stable) attributions (see Weiner, Russell, & Lerman, 1978). In the Covington and Omelich analysis, there is nothing analogous to the unknown-known dimension which has been revealed in our own work. Moreover, as the previous discussion suggested, an internal attribution per se may not necessarily be related to achievement level, given other attributional stances which may also lead to success.

How is the role of the knowledge of control construct best interpreted within our causal model? As suggested earlier, this construct appears to bear some conceptual similarity to Seligman's (1975) learned helplessness construct. Learned helplessness, however, is a more specific construct referring to the person's observation that his/her behaviors do not appear to be contingently related to outcomes, i.e., there is nothing one can do that will lead to success. Ultimately, according to Seligman's analysis, this pattern leads to lack of motivation to engage in those behaviors, and to eventual depression.

While a high unknown score may, in some children, reflect such a history, it may also reflect a normative developmental level in which the child, due to *lack* of maturity or length of experience (rather than a high frequency of non-contingent experiences), has simply not yet acquired the knowledge necessary to make appropriate causal inferences. Support for this latter interpretation comes from the finding of a significant relationship between grade level and the unknown score (Connell, 1981). Within both the elementary and the junior high grade groups, the higher the grade level, the lower the unknown score, i.e., the less the children indicate that they don't understand the reasons for their successes and failures.

Within any given grade, however, there are also marked individual differences in the amount of knowledge children claim concerning the reasons for their successes and failures. Thus, further research needs to examine the particular factors responsible for the level of a child's perceived knowledge of control, e.g., amount of experience in that domain, degree of noncontingent behavior-outcome experience, *willingness* to *admit* that one doesn't know or understand, to name a few possible determinants. In addition, it would be interesting to examine the particular affects which are associated with the different determinants of a high unknown score, for example. While frustration and depression may accompany a perception of non-contingency, anxiety or perhaps perplexity may be more characteristic of the child who has not yet had sufficient experience to understand the causes of his/her academic success and failures.

For both the elementary school and junior high samples, a basic chain, common to both, was identified. At each age level, an understanding of what makes one succeed or fail directly impacts one's level of understanding of the academic subject material tapped by standardized achievements tests. One implication of this evidence is that by improving the child's understanding of why he/she succeeds or fails, his/her level of academic improvement might be improved. For both age groups, level of actual achievement also had a direct impact on the child's perceived competence. Thus, behavioral achievement influences one's self-judgments concerning one's abilities in this domain, rather than the converse (as tested in an alternative model). That is, no support was found for the view that self-judgments directly affect achievement.

Of particular interest at both age levels was the discovery that the two components of competence-judgment process, competence evaluation and competence affect, represent links in this chain. An evaluation of one's competence has a direct impact on one's feelings about that competence. Both self-perceptions, in turn, influence the type of motivational orientation which one manifests in the classroom. Thus, if a child thinks he/she is doing well, and feels good about his/her competence, it is more likely that such a child will be intrinsically motivated to engage in challenging tasks, be curious, and independently attempt to master material. The child who thinks poorly of his/her academic competence and feels badly about it will avoid challenging mastery situations, preferring easier assignments in which he/she can enlist the teacher's aid.

Interestingly, competence *affect* also has an influence on a child's orientation toward making judgments in the classroom. The child who feels good about his/her competence appears to feel confident about his/her ability to make independent judgments in the classroom. Conversely, the child who feels badly about his/her competence is much more likely to rely on the teacher's judgment and feedback, presumably because such a child may not trust his/her own ability to make independent judgments.

The role of affect in this process is consistent with recent models in which emotion is viewed as an important mediating link between one's cognitions and one's behavior. Historically, it was both James (1898) and Cooley (1902) who alerted us to the fact that most self-evaluations carry with them self-affects, e.g., pride, self-confidence, shame, guilt, etc. Recently, in the sequential models of Wicklund (1975) and Bandura (1978), it is the affective reaction (positive or negative) to a self-evaluative judgment which mediates or determines the resulting behavior in the chain, e.g., subsequent approach or avoidance. Weiner's recent work (see Weiner, Kun, & Benesh-Weiner, 1980) on the particular emotions associated with different types of causal attribution is another good example of the renewed interest in affect. From differing perspectives, therefore, affect is being resurrected, not only as a legitimate construct in its own right but an important mediating link between one's cognitions and behavior.

DEVELOPMENTAL DIFFERENCES IN THE BEST-FITTING MODELS

While there are commonalities between the models describing the elementary and junior high groups, there are also significant differences. The model for the junior high pupils includes more paths; certain constructs are more multiply-determined, e.g., competence evaluation, competence affect, and autonomous judgment; and affect plays a stronger role as a determinant of one's motivational orientation at the junior high school level.

The differences between the best-fitting models for junior high school pupils and the elementary school children can be interpreted in terms of some major developmental shifts between middle childhood and adolescence. One such shift involves the adolescent's ability to think in terms of abstractions and to focus on the inner world of thoughts and feelings. In the junior high school model, support for this transition is suggested by the fact that the constructs are more multiply-determined and, at the same time, more integrated into a single abstract system of cognitions and affects about the self and school performance.

Consider, for example, the impact of unknown control. In the elementary school children the influence of unknown control on competence evaluation, affect, and autonomous judgment was largely mediated through achievement; however, at the junior high school level, unknown control directly influences these three self-perceptions. Thus, an adolescent who claims not to understand the factors controlling academic successes and failures also judges himself/herself to be less competent about his/her cognitive abilities, and experiences negative affect as a result of this lack of understanding as well. Autonomous judgment is also adversely affected by lack of understanding of causes of performance, because the unknowing adolescent decides that it is better to let the teacher decide. Thus, the pattern for the adolescent is more psychologically complex, with more self-perceptions intimately affecting others within this network.

The autonomous judgment construct is particularly interesting, at the junior high level, as an example of a variable that is multiply-determined at this age but not for the elementary school child. The adolescent's belief in his/her ability to make independent judgments is affected by certain *cognitions,* namely knowledge of control, by *affect,* in the form of feelings about competence, and by *motivational* orientation. Thus, if one understands why one succeeds or fails, feels good about one's competence, and is intrinsically motivated, one feels capable of making independent judgments. If one doesn't understand the causes of personal successes and failures, feels badly about one's competence, and is extrinsically motivated to do easy assignments and meet teacher demands, one opts to let the teacher make decisions in the classroom. Thus, one can see that for the junior high pupils, cognitions, affects, motivation, and behavioral orientation in the classroom are all intimately intertwined; to attempt to understand the adolescent in piecemeal fashion by treating these systems separately, would, therefore, lead to an inadequate if not distorted picture of this developmental level.

The link between intrinsic mastery motivation and autonomous judgment, which occurs in the junior high school model, is absent at the elementary level. Thus, while motivational orientation affects the adolescent's view of his/her ability to make independent judgments in the classroom, this influence is not found for younger pupils. That is, the two clusters, motivational and cognitive-informational, are related at the junior high school level but not at the elementary school level. The absence of this link for younger pupils may reflect the fact that in the earlier grades, a child may be very motivated to perform for intrinsic reasons, but may not yet have had sufficient experience to master the "rules of the game called school" which would enable him/her to make autonomous judgments. Thus, it would behoove such an intrinsically motivated young child to depend, in part, on guidance and feedback from the teacher.

The final interesting difference between the two age groups involves the finding that affect becomes a more potent predictor of one's motivational orientation during the junior high school years. This finding is consistent with our portrait of adolescence as an emotional and particularly turbulent transitional period of development. Thus, not only do emotions run high during this period, but they would appear to have more of a direct impact on one's behavior than during the elementary years. We are currently conducting an interview study which may have some bearing on this interpretation. Children and adolescents are being asked to describe the ways in which they have control over their emotions, as well as the ways in which emotions seem to control their behavior.

One way to characterize the general differences between the two age groups is that the elementary school model represents more of a *chain*, whereas the junior high model depicts a more integrated network of constructs. At the elementary level, cognitions concerning control directly impact achievement evaluation. Competence evaluation directly influences one's motivational orientation. While competence affect also influences motivation, the impact is not as strong as it is for the adolescent. The picture for the elementary school child, then, is consistent with our view of the child in the period of concrete operations who is attempting to organize his/her world around a reality which is very concrete. One's actual performance, therefore, represented by achievement in our model, should have a powerful mediating impact on one's thoughts and self-perceptions. For the adolescent, on the other hand, inner thoughts, attitudes and perceptions of control can also directly influence others' thoughts and attitudes about the self.

STRUCTURAL MODELING AND THE CASE FOR CAUSE

The path-analytic procedures employed here are referred to by many as causal modeling techniques. As the language of our own description of the data reveals, we have postulated a sequence of events, a process model, in which particular variables influence others in the network. However, it should be emphasized that the data are "static" in the sense that they were collected at only one point in time. Thus, we have not *directly* tested the temporal or causal claims of the model. At best, then, the model represents a hypothesized chain of influences which must ultimately be tested using longitudinal procedures over an actual time course.

The best-fitting models for both elementary and junior high school pupils give considerable weight to cognitive attributions involving the children's perceptions of control. The model implies that these are causally prior to other constructs in the network. This inference, in turn, carries with it certain educational implications. It suggests, for example, that efforts to improve a child's understanding of the events that control his or her successes may enhance achievement level which in turn will enhance perceived competence and stimulate an intrinsic motivational orientation. This may or may not be the case, since we have yet to demonstrate that efforts to improve a child's knowledge of control at time 1 causally influences achievement and other related constructs at time 2. Moreover, the temporal interval between time 1 and time 2 must also be taken into account. That is, the direct impact of one variable upon another may have a different time course, depending upon the particular variables in question. For example, increasing a child's competence evaluation may have a rather sudden impact on his/her competence affect. However, the effect of an increase in competence evaluation on intrinsic mastery motivation may require a longer time course. The model, therefore, raises any number of intriguing hypotheses which ultimately must be tested longitudinally in order to demonstrate true causal primacy.

The Addition of Other Variables to the Network

It should also be noted that the best-fitting models presented can only maximize the functional relationships among the particular variables included. The inclusion of a new variable may alter the pattern of relationships. For example, in our future modeling efforts we plan to include a new variable, anxiety, assessed through a domain-specific anxiety scale recently devised by Buhrmester (1980). We would anticipate that this measure would be highly related to what we are now terming competence affect, and would influence other variables in this network in much the same way. However, this remains to be seen. We would also like to introduce general self-worth into the network, since we have these scores available from the perceived competence scale. Other variables which we may consider are the importance of academic success as well as the enjoyment of schoolwork. How the existing pattern of relationships might change as a function of these additions will be an interesting empirical question, with theoretical implications as well.

MODELING ATTEMPTS IN OTHER DOMAINS AND WITH OTHER POPULATIONS

We should also emphasize that the relationships defined by the best fitting models presented are specific to the cognitive domain of scholastic achievement. We cannot necessarily extrapolate this pattern to other domains, e.g., the domain of athletic competence or social skills. It is our intent, therefore, to test these relationships directly in different domains. The measures we have constructed also tap each of the constructs in the model with regard to the domains of physical (athletic) competence as well as social acceptance. Thus, in collaboration with Bob Engstrom, whose focus is the athletic domain, and with Bob

Thompson, whose interest is the social domain, we will be extending these efforts to determine what type of models best characterize the relationships among constructs in these other areas of competence.

Until very recently, we have restricted our modeling to data from normative samples, testing all children in a given grade or classroom. We are now beginning to look at special groups and subgroups of children, in order to determine whether the relationships among our major constructs of interest might be different. In one study, a dissertation by Beth Ann Bierer, the focus was initially on the accuracy with which children judge their competence within the cognitive domain.

The purpose of Bierer's (1982) study was to identify three groups of children which emerge when one compares pupil and teacher ratings in the cognitive domain. There are those children who *accurately* rate their competence, in that their perceived competence closely parallels the teacher's judgments, then there are those who *underrate* their competence, relative to the teacher's ratings, and those who *overrate* their competence, in comparison to the teacher's judgment.

When one examines the pattern of relationships among constructs for these three groups, the findings suggest that we may need somewhat different models for each type of child. Among accurate raters, actual achievement, as measured by achievement test scores, predicts their perceived competence, which in turn predicts their preference for challenge. Moreover, the accurate rater's network of achievement-related self-perceptions is well integrated in that perceived competence is negatively correlated with anxiety over schoolwork as well as with unknown control. Thus, the accurate rater who feels competent reports less anxiety and less of a sense that he/she doesn't understand why. Conversely, the accurate rater who does not feel competent reports a relatively high level of anxiety over schoolwork and purports to not understand the reasons for his/her successes and failures. This pattern is consistent with the relevant portions of the best-fitting model presented earlier.

For the *underraters,* actual achievement is negatively related to perceived competence. Thus, those pupils who score relatively high on standardized tests have low perceived competence, whereas low achievers report high competence. Thus, the positive link documented for accurate raters does not exist in the predictive chain for this subgroup, nor does perceived competence correlate significantly with scholastic anxiety. The perceived competence of underraters also appropriately predicts preference for challenge. Thus, the underraters' self–perceptions do mediate their motivational orientation. For the overraters, there are far fewer links in the network of variables. Achievement scores do predict perceptions of competence. However, there are virtually no relationships among the overraters' achievement–related self–perceptions. Perceived competence bears a negligible relationship to anxiety as well as to unknown control. Perceived competence *does* predict self-reported preference for challenge; although when this group is put in a behavioral situation, they select easy items to perform, suggesting that at some level they are aware of their lack of competence.

These different patterns are interesting, in and of themselves, in that they suggest that both underraters' and overraters' perceptions of their competence are unrealistic. However, these two groups also differ from each other in that while the underraters' inaccurate perceptions of low competence do mediate their motivational orientation and behavior, this is not the case for those pupils who overrate their competence. These findings suggest that we may need different models to account for the relationships among our constructs for different groups of pupils.

TYPOLOGIES ACROSS MEASURES

The modeling attempts reported go a long way in helping us understand the general pattern of relationships among the major constructs of interest, perceived control, perceived competence, motivational orientation, as well as anxiety (which will be included in our next analyses). However, such general models do not capture many of the individual differences we are finding when we examine profiles across measures. Thus, we have begun to look for subject types which represent various combinations of scores across these four major constructs. As a first step, we have been examining profiles drawn from normative samples of elementary school pupils. As with the modeling efforts, we have restricted this first look to the cognitive domain. In collaboration with Mari Jo Renick, we have identified two types of children who exist with relatively high frequency. One type, a kind of academic super-star whom teachers adore, can be described in terms of the following constellation: high perceived competence, low anxiety, high intrinsic motivation, and high internal responsibility for success accompanied by a low Unknown Control score. Thus, these children feel good about their scholastic ability, worry very little about their school performance, are intrinsically interested in learning, and feel that they are primarily responsible for their successes in the classroom.

A second type might be called the bright-anxious child. Such a child scores as follows: high perceived competence, high anxiety, high intrinsic motivation, and high internal responsibility for both successes and failures. Thus, while this type of child feels relatively competent about his/her schoolwork, and is intrinsically motivated to perform, he or she worries about it a great deal. Moreover, this child is extremely internal with regard to his/her perceptions of control, taking personal responsibility for successes as well as failures.

Two other types emerge in much smaller numbers. There is the child whose perceptions of competence are low, who is extremely anxious about his/her scholastic performance, and whose motivational orientation is extremely extrinsic. A fourth type also has perceptions of low competence coupled with high anxiety, however this type is relatively intrinsic with regard to classroom motivation. (For these latter two types, the control dimensions do not seem to be consistently related to the other constructs.)

There are many other patterns which individual children manifest. As a first step, however, we have been searching for some of the more common profiles across measures. We have also been attempting to devise a statistical procedure for identifying these types systematically. It is our expectation that such topologies may be even more sensitive predictors of behavior than either a single score taken from a given measure or scores representing an additive combination of variables derived from a linear regression model. Although such models can take into account several variables simultaneously, the typical procedure for combining variables does not allow for the kind of meaningful interaction among variables which are embodied in the subject types we have begun to identify in our typological analysis.

SUMMARY

Our interest in a typological approach has not dampened our enthusiasm for the more general modeling endeavors which have been the primary focus of this chapter. There is considerable value, we feel, in examining the degree to which different theoretical models can account for patterns of relationships among the constructs in question. Moreover, they suggest process models of the influence of particular variables upon others in the network—models which can be put to a more causal test through the use of longitudinal designs.

The findings presented in this chapter point to developmental differences as well as commonalities in the relationships among the constructs selected. For both elementary and junior high school pupils, perceived control, defined as the amount of knowledge children claim to know about who or what is responsible for their academic successes and failures, was the critical variable at the beginning of the predictive chain. Perceived control directly influenced achievement, which in turn had a direct impact on the child's evaluation of his/her competence. Perceived competence, in turn, influenced competence affect, as well as motivational orientation. Competence affect *also* had an impact on the child's motivational orientation, as well as his/her autonomous judgment in the classroom.

The elementary school model can best be characterized as a chain, representing the influences just described. The junior high school model, however, was more complex. Additional paths were required, and many of the constructs were more multiply-determined. In addition, affect had a more powerful impact on motivational orientation than it did at the elementary school level. The findings were discussed as they relate to major developmental changes during middle childhood and adolescence. Thus, the modeling approach allows us to describe the major paths of influence, compare alternative models, as well as determine which model best characterizes a given age group.

These efforts represent one avenue for capturing a tremendous range of the individual differences which exist for constructs such as perceived competence, perceived control, motivational orientation, and anxiety. The typological approach represents another such avenue, one which ultimately may prove most useful in predicting the behavior of the individual child. Both are exciting avenues to pursue, and we hope to continue our journey forward.

ACKNOWLEDGMENT

The research presented in this chapter was supported by Research Grant HD-09613 from the National Institute of Child Health and Human Development, U.S.P.H.S.

REFERENCES

Atkinson, J. W. *An introduction to motivation*. Princeton, N.J.: Van Nostrand, 1964.

Bandura, A. The self system in reciprocal determinism. *American Psychologist,* 1978, *33,* 344–358.

Bialer, I. Conceptualization of success and failure in mentally retarded and normal children. *Journal of Personality,* 1961, *29,* 303–320.

Bierer, B. *Motivational and behavioral correlates of children's accuracy in judging their cognitive competence*. Unpublished doctoral dissertation, University of Denver, 1982.

Buhrmester, D. *Assessing elementary-aged children's anxieties: Rationale, development, and correlates of the school concerns scale*. Unpublished master thesis, University of Denver, 1980.

Calsyn, R. J., & Kenny, D. A. Self-concept of ability and perceived evaluation of others: Cause or effect of academic achievement? *Journal of Educational Psychology,* 1977, *69,* 136–145.

Connell, J. P. *A multidimensional measure of children's perceptions of control*. Unpublished Master's thesis, University of Denver, 1980.

Connell, J. P. *A model of the relationships among children's self-related cognitions, affects, and academic achievement*. Unpublished Doctoral dissertation, University of Denver, 1981.

Cooley, C. H. *Human nature and the social order*. New York: Charles Scribner's Sons, 1902.

Coopersmith, S. *The antecedents of self-esteem*. San Francisco: Freeman, 1967.

Covington, M. V., & Omelich, C. L. Are causal attributions causal? A path analysis of the cognitive model of achievement motivation. *Journal of Personality and Social Psychology,* 1979, *37,* 1487–1504.

Crandall, V. C., Katkovsky, W., & Crandall, V. J. Children's beliefs in their own control of reinforcement in intellectual academic achievement situations. *Child Development,* 1965, *36,* 91–109.

Harter, S. Effectance motivation reconsidered: Toward a developmental model. *Human Development,* 1978, *1,* 34–64.

Harter, S. A model of intrinsic mastery motivation in children: Individual differences and developmental change. In A. Collins (Ed.), *Minnesota Symposium on Child Psychology* (Vol. 14). Hillsdale, NJ: Erlbaum, 1981.(a)

Harter, S. A new self-report scale of intrinsic versus extrinsic orientation in the classroom: Motivational and informational components. *Developmental Psychology,* 1981(b), *17,* 300–312.

Harter, S. The perceived competence scale for children. *Child Development,* 1982, *53,* 87–97.

Harter, S. Developmental perspectives on the self-system. In P. Mussen (Ed.), *Carmichael's manual on child psychology* [Volume on social development, M. Hetherington (Ed.)]. New York: Wiley, 1983.

James, W. *Psychology*. New York: Fawcett, 1963. (Originally published, 1892.)

Joreskog, K. G. A general method for estimating a linear structural equation system. In A. S. Goldberger & O. D. Duncan (Eds.), *Structural equation models in the social sciences.* New York: Seminar Press, 1973.

Kanfer, F. H. Self-management methods. In F. H. Kanfer & A. P. Goldstein (Eds.), *Helping people change: A textbook of methods* (2nd edition). New York: Pergamon Press, 1980.

Levenson, H. *Distinctions within the concept of internal-external control.* Paper presented at the American Psychological Association Convention, Washington, DC, 1972.

Nowicki, S., & Strickland, B. A locus of control scale for children. *Journal of Consulting and Clinical Psychology,* 1973, *40,* 148–154.

Piers, E., & Harris, D. *The Piers-Harris Children's Self-Concept Scale.* Nashville, Tenn.: Counselor Recordings and Tests, 1969.

Purkey, W. W. *Self-concept and school achievement.* Englewood Cliffs, NJ: Prentice-Hall, 1970.

Seligman, M. E. P. *Helplessness: On depression, development, and death.* San Francisco: Freeman, 1975.

Weiner, B., Russell, D. & Lerman, D. Affective consequences of causal ascriptions: In J. H. Harvey, W. J. Ickes, & R. F. Kidd (Eds.), *New directions in attributional research* (Vol. 2). Hillsdale, NJ: Earlbaum, 1978.

Weiner, B., Kun, A., & Benesh-Weiner, M. The development of mastery, emotions and morality from an attributional perspective. In W. A. Collins (Ed.), *Development of Cognition, Affect, and Social Relations.* [*The Minnesota Symposium on Child Psychology* (Vol. 13).] Hillsdale, NJ: Erlbaum, 1980.

White, R. W. Motivation reconsidered: The concept of competence. *Psychological Review,* 1959, *66,* 297–333.

White, R. W. Competence and the psychosexual stages of development. *Nebraska symposium on motivation.* Lincoln: University of Nebraska Press, 1960.

Wicklund, R. A. Three years later. In L. Berkowitz (Ed.), *Cognitive theories in social psychology.* New York: Academic Press, 1978.

Wicklund, R. A. Objective self-awareness. In L. Berkowitz (Ed.), *Advances in experimental social psychology* (Vol. 8). New York: Academic Press, 1975.

Wylie, R. [The self-concept (Volume 2).] In *Theory and research on selected topics.* Lincoln: University of Nebraska Press, 1979.

ACHIEVEMENT MOTIVATION IN CHILDREN'S SPORT

Glyn C. Roberts

It is generally believed that games and sport play an important role in socialization because children are brought into contact with social order (Mead, 1934), prevailing social values (Roberts & Sutton-Smith, 1962), and are provided a structure within which to act and develop skills in the interest of reciprocity and social order (Kleiber & Roberts, 1981; Kleiber, Note 1). Thus, games and sport are viewed as anticipatory models of society.

The possibility that involvement in sport can contribute to personality development has long been a coveted ideal for the proponents of sport. There is good reason—if not a great deal of evidence—for the view that sport provides a forum for the teaching of responsibility, conformity, subordination of self to the greater good, and the shaping of achievement behavior by encouraging effort, persistence, delay of gratification, and the like. But even to the extent that such attributes are the consequences of sport participation, the generalization that "sport builds character" does not sit well with many who view the consequences of sport participation as mostly negative.

Advances in Motivation and Achievement, vol. 3, pages 251–281
Copyright © 1984 by JAI Press Inc.
All rights of reproduction in any form reserved.
ISBN 0-89232-289-6

Critics of organized children's sports generally focus upon the cost in human relations attributable to an excessive emphasis on winning (e.g., Orlick & Botterill, 1975; Tutko & Bruns, 1976; Coakley, Note 2), the increase in aggression as a consequence of competition (e.g., Sherif & Sherif, 1961; Berkowitz, 1972), and the stigma attached to being rejected for participation in children's sports (e.g., Orlick & Botterill, 1975; Roberts, 1980). The supportive evidence for these views is largely anecdotal and the impact of the sport experience upon such social attributes remains to be effectively determined.

THE DOMAIN OF SPORT

One of my colleagues has a print of Peter Bruegel's famous painting entitled "Children's Games" on his wall. This shows approximately 250 children playing 35 to 40 games in a sixteenth century neighborhood in Holland. The scene is rich in that boys and girls, both together and separately, are engrossed in playing a multitude of games. But the really noticeable feature my colleague is fond of pointing out is that there are only one or two adults present and they are only minimally involved in any one game. The children are clearly involved in their own game culture and are responsible for the design and maintenance of the game in which they are participating. A realistic portrayal of contemporary childhood recreation would depict a stronger emphasis upon adult-organized sport activities. In Norman Rockwell's paintings, for example, we see specialized playing fields, uniforms, and supervising adults.

Although there are conceptual similarities between sport and the games modern children play, they can be distinguished in one important respect—the degree to which participants have control over the design and maintenance of the activity (Kleiber, Note 1). Games generally involve playful competition where the outcome is determined by physical skill, strategy, or chance—either singly or in combination (Loy, 1969; Roberts & Sutton-Smith, 1962). Games have strong elements of play (see Huizinga, 1955) and some social comparison in that two or more opponents usually vie with each other in order to achieve an outcome. But a game is essentially an "occurrence" (Weiss, 1969) with the design and maintenance of the game (the process) being the major concern of the participants (Avedon & Sutton-Smith, 1971).

Sport, on the other hand, is the institutionalization of a game with established rules, national regulations, and a governing administrative superstructure (see Loy, 1969). Although sport may have game-like qualities, in that children (or adults) may engage in the activity in a playful manner, and be totally absorbed in the activity with little thought of the outcome or of any extrinsic rewards associated with the outcome; the essential feature of sport is that its organizational structure provides for the maintenance and direction of the activity through rules interpreted by officials. The concern of participants is with performance and the outcome (the product) rather than with the design and maintenance of the activity (the process) which is more characteristic of games.

Although games and sport are conceptually different, there are obvious similarities between the modern day recreational games of children and organized sport activities. Whether it is the influence of television, the increased mobility of individuals, or any of a number of other causes, children appear more and more likely to participate in childlike versions of recognized adult sport activities in their recreational time. Further, if children are observed participating in non-sport-related playful behavior, there is a tendency for older children to use the word "just" (e.g., just playing catch) to qualify such behavior (Eifermann, 1971). There is a tendency for children as they become older to increase their engagement in games which reflect sport activities. Whether or not this is a measure of the increased sophistication of children, it is a fact that children's games and organized sport are closely interrelated in modern times.

There is another reason to suspect that organized sport and games are interrelated. Inversely proportional to the rapid expansion of organized children's sport is the decline in both the quantity and variety of child-directed games (Devereux, 1976; Kleiber & Roberts, 1981; Sutton-Smith & Rosenberg, 1971; Kleiber, Note 1). For example, in 1956, Skubic found that 81% of children who were involved in Little League baseball spent over half their recreational time for that purpose.

Whether the reason is an elevated concern for the personal security of children, or a belief in the value of sport in the socialization of children, it is certainly true that organized sports for children have expanded dramatically in the last few decades. Although one tends to think of Little League baseball as the archetype of organized children's sport, competitive sport organizations have developed for many sports including hockey, football, baseball, tennis, soccer, wrestling, and swimming. Estimates of the number of children participating in sport programs in the USA run upwards of 20 million.

For example, a brief and selective telephone survey in April of 1982 revealed the following figures: Little League Baseball (9 to 12 years of age) has 2.5 million participants; The American Youth Soccer Organization (5 to 18 years of age) has over a quarter of a million participants in 28 states; Pop Warner Junior League Football (7 to 15 years of age) has almost a quarter of a million participants. This involvement, of course, is in addition to any extracurricular school sport involvement or local recreational and park district sport leagues. To the large number of child participants must be added the involvement and investment in time and money of a multitude of adults—parents, coaches, officials, and administrators. Taken all together, it is quite likely that organized sport for children has a significant impact on the individuals involved and on the larger society of which it is a part.

Despite the increased number of participants in children's sport, the growing encroachment of sport on children's recreational time, and the potential impact upon social and moral development (e.g., Kleiber, Note 1), little research is conducted in this domain. One of the hoped for consequences of this chapter is increased interest and research on this topic. Although recognizing that the organized sport experience has potential impact upon many psychological constructs, I will focus upon achievement motivation. Before discussing motivation, however, it is important to discuss the achievement domain of sport in order to set the frame of reference of the rest of the chapter.

Sport as an Achievement Domain

There are many reasons why competitive sport is an appropriate context in which to study achievement motivation. First, sport competition is a classic achievement-oriented context. It conforms to most definitions of achievement-oriented contexts in the extant literature (e.g., Atkinson, 1957; Atkinson & Raynor, 1974; Maehr, 1974). The individual or team is striving to achieve a goal (usually beating another opponent) or standard of excellence and can thus be evaluated in terms of success or failure. The individual, or team, is in most cases responsible for the outcome and a sense of uncertainty prevails so that some level of challenge is perceived. Further, the process is evaluative in that present others—teammates, opponents, coaches, parents, spectators—evaluate the performance of the individual or team as favorable or unfavorable in terms of reaching the goal or standard of excellence.

Second, being competent at physical skills is very important to children, boys in particular (Roberts, 1978, 1980; Scanlan, 1978). Indeed, Veroff (1969) suggests that sporting activities may be *the* domain in which young boys utilize social comparison processes in order to determine their standing among their peers and, by implication, determine their self-worth. In our society, it is difficult to underestimate the importance for boys of competence in physical activity settings. Duda (1981) has evidence to support this analysis.

Duda (1981) assessed the perceptions of high school boys and girls relative to their preferred domains of achievement. Duda separated both classroom and playing field achievement contexts into four general categories—group or individual achievement contexts, and ego-involved (competitive) or task-oriented (noncompetitive) achievement contexts. Thus, Duda considered group ego-involved; individual ego-involved; individual task-involved; and group task-involved contexts. When students were asked whether they would prefer to succeed or fail in these achievement contexts in either classroom or playing field contexts, interesting findings emerged. Across all four achievement categories, boys preferred to succeed in sport contexts more than in classroom contexts. This confirms previous evidence of the importance of competence in sports for boys (Coleman, 1961; Roberts, 1978, 1980; Scanlan, 1978; Veroff, 1969). Significantly, Duda found that, with the exception of the individual ego-involved achievement context, girls also preferred to succeed in sport rather than classroom contexts. Although the data for the individual, ego-involved achievement context supports previous research which has found that girls prefer to avoid direct, competitive, individual conflict with other girls (see Helmreich & Spence, 1977; Kleiber & Hemmer, 1981), it is revealing that girls consider other sport contexts (team sports in particular) entirely appropriate contexts in which to succeed against other girls.

Failure preferences were revealing also. Boys indicated that failure in academic environments was less aversive than failure in sport environments. For boys, failure in sport is very much an outcome to be avoided. The opposite was found for girls. Girls reported failure in sports was less aversive than academic failure. The findings of Duda (1981) clearly illustrate that sport contexts are salient and important achievement contexts for both boys and girls.

Finally, sport contexts offer advantages to investigators of achievement behavior because they are relatively free-choice activities. Even though peer and parental pressures affect children's participation in sport; sport, unlike school, is not mandatory. Children do elect to participate, or not to participate, in sport. Consequently, very important achievement motivation indices are at our disposal. In particular, persistence, or the lack of it, can be studied in ways that are less accessible to students of academic motivation. The "dropout" rate from children's sport programs, for example, is a particularly relevant variable.

According to coaches, dropping out is the most serious problem in children's sport. An overemphasis upon winning is the usual explanation given by sports psychologists to account for this occurrence, and the reasons given by players are often "it wasn't fun any more" or "the pressure was too much" (Orlick & Botterill, 1975). The most distressing dropout for coaches is the player who excells, then suddenly decides that he/she doesn't want to play any more. This athlete is often termed to be a "psychological burn-out" victim. But, for whatever reason, dropping out of competitive sport is a phenomenon of very real concern to the organizers of children's sport programs. A brief look at the statistics gives an indication of the magnitude of this phenomenon.

According to the best available statistics, 80% of all children drop out of organized sport programs between the ages of 12 and 17 years of age (Seefeldt, Gilliam, Blievernicht, & Bruce, 1978). This phenomenon is not peculiar to the United States. In Canada, the Canadian Amateur Hockey Association has statistics which show that only 10% of players involved in hockey leagues register to continue playing after age 15 (Orlick & Botterill, 1975). In Australia, while conducting a study using children in the soccer leagues in Brisbane, Queensland, I obtained figures supporting the dropout phenomenon. The age of greatest participation in Brisbane was the under-9 age group which had 50 teams and over 720 registered players. The numbers of children involved stayed fairly constant through the under-12 age group (40 teams and over 600 registered players), but after this age group the figures dropped off dramatically. The under-13 age group had 26 teams and 390 registered players, the under-14 age group had 24 teams and 360 registered players, and the under-15 age group had only 16 teams with approximately 240 registered players. The age groups from 15 to 18 were collapsed into one age group (termed Junior Colts) because so few players continued to engage in soccer after age 15. The American Youth Soccer Organization in the United States confirmed these trends, but were unable to give specific numbers in the various age groups (Note 3).

Similar trends exist in all organized sports (Seefeldt et al. 1978; Orlick, 1974) and this is true for girls as well as boys. For example, 1982 statistics for the Amateur Softball Association of America show that 35,200 girls participated in the under-18 age group, but 128,560 girls participated in the under-15 age category. Thus, dropping out of organized children's sports appears to be a general phenomenon for both boys and girls.

Clearly, a paradox exists. When asked, children indicate that they prefer to be successful in sport than in any other achievement context. This is particularly true of boys but it is also true of girls (Duda, 1981). Nevertheless, children drop out of competitive sport programs at dramatic rates, particularly after age 12. Although this is clearly an important topic, research on dropouts in both educational and sport contexts is disappointing and inconclusive (see Ewing, 1981; Tinto, 1975).

Tinto (1975) argues that research on dropouts suffers from two major weaknesses: a lack of an adequate definition of a dropout, and a lack of a conceptual model with which to investigate dropping out. For example, Tinto argues that researchers must distinguish between individuals who are eliminated, or ''cut'' from the competitive sport experience by coaches or withdrawn by parents for one reason or another and those who drop out of the experience of their own volition. These forms of exiting are clearly different. But conceptual models of dropouts have not always taken the different forms of exiting the achievement context into account.

Most of the research on sport dropouts has been descriptive in nature with investigators criticizing the structure of the sport experience as the primary villain causing dropping out (Deverux, 1976; Orlick, 1974; Orlick & Botterill, 1975). For example, when interviewing sport dropouts ranging in age from 7 to 19 years of age, Orlick found that at least 50% reported they dropped out due to the emphasis of the program (too serious, too concerned with winning, etc.). Further, the coach was considered to push players too hard, not give enough playing time, and other reasons showing that there was an emphasis upon achieving within the context. Most of the players indicated they went into the experience because they thought they would enjoy the activity, but, for most, enjoyment was reported to be the first victim of involvement in adult–organized sport.

Although structural factors (Orlick, 1974; Orlick & Botterill, 1975; Deverux, 1976), appear implicated, they may not provide a full explanation for dropping out. As Tinto (1975) and Ewing (1981) point out, one of the problems of much of the previous research is that it is not grounded in theory. For this reason, alternative explanations of data such as that of Orlick are plausible but have not been considered. For example, it may be argued that many of the dropouts interviewed by Orlick gave perception of low ability as a reason for dropping out (e.g., "the coach only lets better players play," "I always strike out," etc.). While Orlick concluded that when children did not enjoy the experience they dropped out, it may be argued that these children failed to enjoy it and dropped out because they perceived their own level of ability as too low. Indicating that they did not enjoy the experience or that it wasn't fun any more, are plausible reasons for children to give for dropping out, but blaming the structure of the competitive sport experience in that an overemphasis upon winning robbed the experience of its enjoyment factor may not be the real reason for the child's dropping out. These children may have been expressing through affective responses the fact that the competitive sport experience was not enabling them to meet their achievement goal—instead of making them feel competent, it made them feel incompetent (Ewing, 1981).

The foregoing illustrates the problems of an inadequate conceptual model with which to investigate achievement behaviors such as persistence, or the lack of it, in the achievement context of sport. In summary, I have suggested that the achievement context of sport is an important achievement domain for children, both boys and girls. Consequently, it is an ideal achievement context in which to investigate achievement motivation. Further, because unlike school learning, sport is a relatively free choice activity, an important dependent variable of the sport achievement context is persistence. Dropping in or out of sport is an especially interesting index of achievement motivation. But research on sport dropouts has been primarily descriptive in nature and little of it meaningfully contributes to a better understanding of motivation and, more specifically, of why children drop out. Thus, in this chapter I attempt to present conceptual models by which we may better investigate achievement behaviors such as dropping in or out of sport. Further, I discuss data which support the models and present some suggestions for changes in the practice of adult organizers of children's sport programs in order to enhance persistence and prevent dropouts.

Achievement Motivation Theory Applied to Sport

Before elaborating upon the conceptual orientation of this chapter, it is appropriate to briefly note the most popular research paradigms which have been used in sport settings. The goal of most sport psychologists is to gain an understanding of motivation in order to develop strategies to enhance the motivation and, thereby, the performance of athletes. Generally, three theoretical approaches have been adopted in attempts to meet this goal.

The most popular research paradigm has been the use of achievement motivation measures to identify "athletes" from "nonathletes." The paradigm is part of the general paradigm in sport psychology where investigators have sought to identify personality variables which are related to athletic performance, (see Carron, 1980; Kroll, 1970; Martens, 1975; Morgan, 1980). The issue has been controversial with a "credulous" camp and "skeptical" camp. The research investigating the specific question whether athletes have higher levels of achievement motivation than nonathletes (e.g., Bethe, 1968; Birrel, 1978; Teevan & Yalof, 1980; Usher, 1975) has been generally unsuccessful in demonstrating reliable differences. This research paradigm has also been criticized for use of achievement motivation measures without theory-based hypotheses about likely relationships, the inference of cause and effect from correlational data, a lack of uniform definition of athletes, and a failure to recognize the situation specificity of achievement motivation (see Kroll, 1970; Maehr, 1974; Roberts, 1982; Sherif & Rattray, 1976; Stevenson, 1975). Given the above, it is easy to see why this paradigm has fallen into disuse.

The second approach utilizes McClelland/Atkinson theorizing (McClelland, 1951; Atkinson & Feather, 1966; Atkinson & Raynor, 1974) to investigate the effect of being high or low in achievement motivation on risk taking in motor skill tasks (e.g., Roberts, 1974; Stadulis, 1977) and on motor performance (e.g., Healey and Landers, 1973; Roberts, 1972). Generally, the research investigating the taking of risk and performance of high achievement motivation individuals has supported the hypotheses coming from achievement motivation theory. But this research does not always support the prediction that low achievement motivation individuals avoid intermediate risk and have low performance (Weiner, 1972). Despite its relative popularity in motor performance settings, the achievement motivation approach of McClelland/Atkinson has attracted much criticism. The inadequacies in predicting risk taking have been noted. In addition, the approach has been criticized because of the weight it places upon personality as a crucial variable (Maehr, 1974; 1979; Maehr & Nicholls, 1980; Weiner, 1972), the ethnocentric bias of the approach in that it fails to take into account sex and cross cultural differences (Deaux, 1976; Duda, 1980; Ewing, 1981; Harris, 1978; Horner, 1968; Maehr, 1974; Maehr & Nicholls, 1980), and a failure to account for heightened performance of low achievement motivation individuals in certain achievement situations (Maehr, 1974; Weiner, 1972).

The third approach is the one which utilizes attribution theory in sport settings (see Roberts, 1982). It is assumed that causal attributions mediate overt behavior through their effect on affect and expectancies (Weiner, 1972, 1974, 1979). The attributional approach has been extensively used in sport settings. As would be expected, attributions for winning and losing have been a major focus of this research. Attributions have been studied in experimental (e.g., Gill & Martens, 1977; Iso-Ahola, 1978; Roberts, 1978; Weinberg & Jackson, 1979) and natural settings (e.g., Bird & Brame, 1978; Forsyth & Schlenker, 1977; Harter, 1978; Spink & Roberts, 1980). In addition, individuals have been asked to imagine themselves, or someone else, winning or losing in a sport environment (e.g., Roberts & Pascuzzi, 1979).

Generally, this research shows that winners attribute the internal elements of ability and effort to themselves while losers often attribute the external elements of task difficulty and, sometimes, luck (see Roberts, 1982). But the research in sport has been criticized because it fails to adequately deal with the self-serving versus information-processing approaches to determining causal attributions (Roberts, 1978), it assumes winning and losing are synonymous with success and failure (Spink & Roberts, 1980), places an overreliance upon the "traditional" causal attributions of ability, effort, luck, and task difficulty rather than determining the relevant causal attributions for the specific sport environment (see Weiner, 1979; Roberts & Pascuzzi, 1979), and fails to distinguish between trait, or general attributions (e.g., How high is your ability?), and causal attributions (e.g., Did you win because of high ability?) (see Duda & Roberts, 1980; Scanlan & Passer, 1979). In addition, although it provides an excellent model to investigate the social psychology of perception of sport outcomes and has given us powerful insights into the motivation process as it occurs in sport, the attributional approach of Weiner (1972, 1979) does not provide us with a clear conceptual basis for intervention so that fewer children drop out and that motor performance is enhanced.

CONTEMPORARY COGNITIVE APPROACHES

Two other conceptual models, which incorporate many insights from attribution theory, have been proposed which have the potential to help us better understand the psychology of motivation. The first is the approach advocated by Maehr and associates (e.g., Maehr, 1974; Maehr & Nicholls, 1980) which focuses upon the function and relevance of behavior to the individual. The second approach focuses upon the concept of perceived ability (e.g., Bandura, 1979; Harter, 1978; Kukla, 1978; Nicholls, 1978; Note 4; Nicholls & Miller, this volume) which, we will find, is particularly applicable to understanding achievement motivation in sport. We shall discuss these approaches in turn.

The Achievement Goals of Athletes

Long dissatisfied with the mechanistic approaches of McClelland and Atkinson, Maehr (1976) urges that we redefine achievement motivation and rethink the nature of achievement behavior. Maehr argues that to fully understand achievement motivation and behavior in all its forms, the function and meaning of behavior to the individual must be taken into account and the goals of action identified. Maehr and Nicholls (1980) state that it is necessary to understand the subjective meaning of achievement for an individual before we can truly understand achievement behavior.

Maehr and Nicholls (1980) suggest that the first step to understanding achievement behavior is to examine perceptions of success and failure for each individual. They argue that success and failure are best understood if they are considered to be psychological states which are based upon the individual's interpretation of outcomes. Maehr and Nicholls argue that if the outcome is seen as reflecting desirable qualities about the self, such as that they are competent, courageous, virtuous, etc., then the outcome (win or loss) is experienced as a success. If the outcome is seen as reflecting undesirable qualities about the self, then the outcome is experienced as a failure. Clearly, the essential element of this conceptualization is the achievement goal of the individual. Success and failure, and by definition achievement behavior, are only recognized when we know the individual's behavioral goals. Once the goals of behavior have been identified, then the behavior of individuals in attempting to obtain the goals becomes understandable.

Maehr and Nicholls (1980) propose that three forms of achievement behavior exist and the achievement goal of behavior determines the form of achievement behavior. The first is an ability oriented achievement behavior in which the goal is to maximize the subjective probability of attributing high ability to oneself and minimize the subjective probability of attributing low ability to oneself. Thus, a player enters into an activity believing he/she may demonstrate ability. In this way, expectations of demonstrating ability lead the player to approach the activity and success and failure are judged as to whether ability was demonstrated. Maehr and Nicholls suggest that causal attributions, especially to ability, play a central role as cognitive mediators of this form of achievement behavior. Research by Duda (1981), Ewing (1981), and Nicholls (1975, 1976) support this orientation.

Maehr and Nicholls (1980) state that some people, however, have outstanding performances even though they are not concerned with ability per se. Rather, these people focus upon performance and the goal of this behavior is to perform as well as possible regardless of the outcome. This type of achievement behavior is termed task-oriented achievement behavior. The demonstration of ability as this is normally understood by adults is not necessary in this form of achievement behavior; rather the player's goal is mastery of the activity. Research by Duda (1981), Ewing (1981), Diener and Dweck (1978) and Nicholls (1978) support the existence of this orientation.

The third form of achievement behavior proposed by Maehr and Nicholls (1980) is termed social approval behavior. Maehr and Nicholls argue that sometimes people will perform well and exhibit motivation because they seek approval from significant others. Usually, this form of achievement behavior involves effort. The goal of the player is to have significant others, coaches, parents, spectators, and teammates, attribute effort and virtuous intent to him/her rather than superior ability. Duda (1981), Ewing (1981) and Kukla (1978) have supported the social-approval function of effort.

Recognizing multiple forms of achievement behavior and multiple forms of achievement motivation is a useful approach. By adopting the concepts of Maehr and Nicholls (1980), we may investigate sport behaviors such as persistence, remaining in or dropping out of sport activities, and performance intensity in relation to the individual's stated behavioral goals. For example, an individual may play soccer for the enjoyment of playing soccer (task-orientation) but play volleyball to demonstrate ability (ability-orientation). In both situations it is important to achieve, but the goals for behavior differ and the achievement behaviors of the individual may be vastly different in each setting. Thus, a knowledge of the achievement orientation of the player is crucial to understanding the achievement behaviors of the player.

Based upon this approach, specific identifiable behaviors of importance are studied and achievement motivation is inferred from the individual's behavior and his/her stated goals for this behavior. This approach contrasts sharply with earlier approaches which measure an individual's achievement motivation prior to investigating the meaning of behavior in specific achievement contexts. If there are multiple, situationally variable achievement orientations, then it is easy to see why this earlier research was so disappointing. If there are multiple forms of achievement behavior, then it is necessary to determine how each form of achievement motivation affects behavior.

Multiple Achievement Orientations in Sport

As I suggested earlier, an achievement behavior of particular relevance is persistence in the form of continuing participation in sport. Utilizing the conceptual orientation of Maehr and Nicholls (1980), a plausible hypothesis for dropping out of sport is that the activity does not enable children to meet their achievement goals. Consequently, children select other activities more consistent with their goals.

One of my students, Martha Ewing (1981), studied this question directly. Utilizing primarily freshman and sophomore high school children (mean age 15.2 years for males and 14.9 years for females), Ewing identified children who had dropped out of sports, were nonparticipants, or were athletes who maintained participation. Nonparticipants were children who had not been involved in junior high school athletics and had not tried out for, or been a member of, any high school team. Athletes were children who had been members of junior high school or high school athletic teams.

Ewing defined a sport dropout as follows: first, a child should voluntarily approach the sport context and not be pressured into it by significant others (parents, siblings, teachers, etc.). To be pressured into sports against one's wishes would lead one to expect the child not to exhibit effort and exit the environment as soon as possible. However, to voluntarily enter the sport context implies that the person expects some positive affect from the experience. Second, the child should voluntarily withdraw from the sport. This implies that the experience is not meeting the expected goals in some way. Being "cut" by the coach, or withdrawn by a parent for any reason, means that one's withdrawal was beyond one's control. Third, a volunteer who "samples" achievement contexts and withdraws promptly was not defined as a dropout. As Ewing points out, a child must show some commitment to the activity before they can be defined as a dropout when they do, indeed, exit the environment.

According to Maehr and Nicholls (1980), the child remains within the achievement context for as long as he/she perceives that he/she is meeting an achievement goal. If a desirable personal attribute is being demonstrated then the child should remain within the context, but as soon as the context is perceived to fail to meet the achievement goal then the child should seek to withdraw.

Evidence to support the contention that individuals choose tasks which reflect their achievement goals does exist, albeit much of it indirect (Fyans & Maehr, 1979; Roberts, Kleiber, & Duda, 1981; Ogilvie & Tutko, 1971; Duda, 1981). For example, Fyans and Maehr argue that individuals who attribute achievement to effort or luck are more likely to choose tasks which reflect those attributes. After assessing the causal attributions of success of children, Fyans and Maehr asked children to select one of three identical tasks to complete. Each task differed only in that the children were informed that a task required either being lucky, knowing what to do, or trying hard to succeed. The results show that children preferred tasks which reflected their perceptions of attributes needed for success.

The major objective of Ewing's (1981) study was to determine more directly whether achievement orientations interacted with the sport experience to affect participation and persistence. If the achievement orientation of the child interacted with the competitive sport environment so that conflict between the orientation and participation existed, then the person could be expected to drop out of sport to avoid the conflict. To use an obvious example: If a child enters the sport experience to demonstrate his/her physical competence at the activity (ability orientation) and finds him/herself sitting on the bench and only playing when the outcome of the game is a foregone conclusion, then a conflict exists and the child may be expected to withdraw and look for other opportunities to exhibit competence.

Ewing (1981) developed a questionnaire specifically to investigate the achievement orientations of athletes. The athletes were asked to describe success and failure experiences in sport. Attribution statements assessing why the athletes perceived the experiences as successes or failures also were given.

Ewing (1981) used factor analysis procedures and revealed that multiple achievement orientations existed for athletes. This was strong support for the arguments of Maehr and Nicholls (1980). In particular, the ability and social approval orientations emerged as strong orientations of athletes. The task-orientation proved more elusive and Ewing suggested that task orientation may be subdivided into two factors—a task-orientation and what Ewing defines as an intrinsic-orientation. When factor analysis of other experiences was conducted, the important finding was that both ability and social-approval orientation remained consistently strong across success and failure situations. However, the intrinsic and task-orientation factors varied in strength from experience to experience.

To investigate the orientations further, Ewing (1981) analyzed the attributional responses associated with the different orientations. Utilizing regression procedures, she confirmed that the ability orientation was associated with more ability attributions. Both boys and girls confirmed the Maehr and Nicholls (1980) notion that ability oriented athletes attribute success and failure to ability. Maehr and Nicholls argue that attributions to effort would best represent the social-approval orientation. Ewing, however, found that perceived effort was the best predictor of social approval, but for *boys* only. Girls used the attribution "special skills" to explain the achieving of social approval.

The major finding of Ewing (1981) is that dropping out of sport is related to particular achievement orientations. But the specific hypothesis, drawn from previous literature (e.g., Roberts & Pascuzzi, 1979) that ability oriented children would persist longer was not supported. Ewing found that social-approval oriented children persisted longer in the sport context. Ewing argues that it could well be that the sport structure gives the relevant others (coaches, parents, spectators, and teammates) ample opportunity to socially support children and, thus, it is the children who are social-approval oriented who remain within the experience. In other words, the sport structure serves the achievement goal of social-approval oriented children to a greater extent than it serves the goals of those with the other orientations.

To support this reasoning, Ewing (1981) found that boys who were nonparticipants were more ability-oriented than athletes. Also, ability oriented players dropped out at a higher rate than social-approval players. For ability oriented players, participation certainly exposes one's limitations very quickly in unambiguous terms, but another reason why ability oriented boys drop out at a higher rate is that they may perceive that they do not get as much playing time as they deserve. They wish to demonstrate high ability, and avoid demonstrating low ability, and when they sit on the bench, as most players do from time to time, they may perceive this as an indication of low ability. Sitting on the bench is not likely to be particularly distressing for a social-approval oriented player who is praised for being a loyal team member and thereby gains satisfaction. But, for an ability oriented player, this would not fulfill his/her achievement goal.

The research by Ewing (1981) is provocative. It supports Maehr and Nicholls' (1980) claim that multiple achievement orientations exist. Further, Ewing found a relationship between achievement orientations and dropping out of sport. In particular, ability oriented children dropped out of sport at a higher rate than social-approval oriented children. What Ewing's research was not designed to do was to investigate what ability oriented children turned to in order to fulfill their achievement goals. These children may be the ones who are more likely to initiate "pick-up" games in the neighborhoods and meet their achievement goals that way. It could well be that these children turned to other competitive environments (not necessarily sport) in order to demonstrate ability. But, what is more likely, these children probably recognize that they cannot achieve their goal of demonstrating ability in sport and drop out when they judge that their competence is not sufficient for them to meet their achievement goal. If their perceived level of competence is low, they drop out as the likelihood of demonstrating a satisfying level of ability is low. If perceived competence is high, they may be more likely to continue.

The finding that the ability orientation may be linked to dropping out suggests that approaches to achievement motivation that focus on the role of perceived ability may further help explain dropping out. Such approaches are the focus of the next section.

Achievement Behavior and Perceived Ability

A persistent aspect of the research reported above is the emergence of perceived ability as an important construct in the understanding of sport motivation. This is consistent with a growing body of evidence which suggests that the perception of ability held by an individual is the central mediating construct of achievement behaviors (Bukowski & Moore, 1980; Covington & Omelich, 1979; Diener & Dweck, 1978; Dweck, 1980; Dweck & Goetz, 1978; Dweck & Reppuci, 1973; Nicholls, 1976, 1978, 1979, Note 4; Roberts, 1975; Roberts, Kleiber & Duda, 1981; Spink & Roberts, 1980). Several investigators have argued that ability attributions, and the self concept of ability, play a central role in mediating motivation (Bandura, 1977; Harter, 1978, 1981; Kukla, 1978; Nicholls, Note 4). Various terms have been used to describe this construct (such as self-efficacy, self concept of ability, perceived ability, perceived competence), but for the purpose of this review, the term perceived ability is used.

The conceptualization adopted in this chapter as being particularly relevant to achievement motivation in sport is the one by Nicholls (Nicholls & Miller, this volume, Note 4). Derived from Nicholls (1979) and Maehr and Nicholls (1980), the theory specifies achievement incentives and the most economical behaviors required to attain these. Nicholls' conceptualization assumes that individuals are intentional goal-directed organisms who operate in a rational manner. As such, Nicholls focuses upon specification of the goals of behavior and posits that the achievement goal of individuals is to demonstrate and/or develop high ability and to avoid demonstrating low ability. Nicholls (Note 4) argues that two conceptions of ability exist. The first type is exemplified when the individual's actions are aimed at achieving mastery, improving, or perfecting a skill or task. The individual is merely attempting to produce a higher level of perceived mastery. This is termed a task-involved criterion of ability. The second type is based upon social comparison processes where the individual judges their capacity relative to that of other people. The focus of attention is more on the self and this is termed ego-involved ability assessment. Social conditions, such as competition, that focus attention on the adequacy of the self tend to lead individuals to use the latter conception of ability to evaluate their competence. Each of these two conceptions of ability will be discussed, but we shall discuss the latter first.

Ego-involved Ability Assessments

An essential cognitive component of ego-involved ability is the individual's perception of his/her capacity in relation to others. The focus of attention of ego-involved individuals is on the self and one judges one's own effort and level of performance and the effort and level of performance of others in order to assess one's own ability. If own perceived ability is higher than the perceived ability of similar others, then the individual expects to demonstrate high ability, a desirable outcome. The theory assumes that individuals assess the probability that their participation will lead to demonstration of high versus low ability and that this assessment influences their subsequent behavior.

Ego-involved ability assessments are complex. In most ego-involved ability environments in sport, at least three evaluations must be made. One is an assessment of the ability of the opponent in relation to all other opponents: Is the opponent a weak or a strong team or player? Second, how does my own ability compare to the opponent's ability? Did I win or lose this game? Third, how much effort was applied by myself and/or opponent?

The assessment of opponents' and own competence in sport contexts involves social comparison processes as we shall discuss in more detail later. But the assessment of effort, an important construct in Nicholls' (Note 4) conceptualization, is crucial to consider in sport. It is the one aspect coaches, spectators, and teammates constantly emphasize. It is a variable coaches believe they have some control over and thus they constantly extoll players to "hustle." But for players, constantly applying effort has other implications. For low perceived ability players, high effort leading to failure clearly exposes one's lack of capacity. Being low in perceived ability, these players expect to demonstrate low ability. Therefore, a reasonable course for them to follow is to apply little effort: Why try hard if it only serves to expose a lack of ability?

These players have two strategies available to them. One is to drop out, which many do. This may explain why Ewing (1981) found so many children whose achievement goal was to demonstrate ability were dropouts. These children probably perceived that the sport experience did not allow them to demonstrate high ability. Then dropping out would be a reasonable alternative. Another strategy for these players is to play against other low perceived ability players so that some success is possible and they may avoid appearing incompetent. But, in organized sport, this avenue is often unavailable. Opponents are arranged for them.

Nicholls (Note 4) also considers low perceived ability individuals who retain some hope of demonstrating high ability. Because of the instability of specific abilities within sport (see Roberts & Pascuzzi, 1979), this individual would be one who has not yet given up hope of demonstrating ability and still tries hard. These individuals may, however, exhibit anxiety which reduces their effectiveness. But repeated failures would lead such low perceived ability athletes to conclude that they indeed lack capacity and to avoid such achievement contexts in the future. If constrained to remain within the sport context, by parents or peers, these players may become the "bad attitude" athletes who don't try. Coaches use the derogatory term "quitter" to describe these players.

For high perceived ability players, failure violates their perception of ability and they exert immediate and greater effort. Success, on the other hand, confirms their perceptions of high ability and they may begin to exert less effort because success with little effort implies even higher ability. Coaches often get angry with these players because while they clearly have ability, they often "hot dog" or begin to utilize risky strategies, and frequently allow inferior players to get back into contention in sport contests.

In general, high perceived ability individuals would be expected to try harder and persist longer in sport contexts when confronted by athletes who are perceived to be as good or better in ability or if the outcome is in doubt as the game unfolds. They may also "show off" within the game context if they perceive a win is likely or they perceive that they are superior to their opponent. Low perceived ability individuals are more likely to drop out, or if constrained to remain within the context, are likely to exert little effort.

There is evidence, in sport situations, to support the contentions of Nicholls (Note 4) concerning ego-involved states, albeit much of it indirect. First, the very structure of sport induces ego-involvement in that sport is inherently competitive. Inevitably, in order to determine how well or poorly one performed, one must compare oneself with a relevant other: Am I better than, equal to, or worse than my opponent? Indeed, since the difficulty of the task is most often determined by the ability of the opponent, ego-involved comparisons are usually the only means to obtain the relevant success or failure information. Beating the opponent becomes the criterion by which we judge success or failure.

Second, because of the social comparison processes involved, the outcome is generally salient and unambiguous. In academic environments, it is often difficult for children to judge how well they did: Is 8 out of 10 correct solutions to problems good or poor? If the child does not compare his/her number of correct solutions to other children, then the child does not have unambiguous ability information. Also, because it is often difficult for the child to compare with all children in the class, he/she may compare to friends who may or may not be representative of the class. Further, the number of correct solutions is often not announced publicly. In sports, however, there is often only one relevant comparison other—the opponent—and all participants and observers can readily observe who won and who lost. Consequently, there is an ultimate, salient, and very public success/failure criterion understood and recognized by all.

Third, in sport competition the outcome is often seen as *the* criterion of success and failure. The importance of the outcome is often exacerbated by the coach. Coaches are very outcome oriented and coaching folklore is replete with sayings such as: "Winning isn't everything, it's the only thing;" "If you are not playing to win, why bother to play?" and, "Coming in second is like kissing your sister." The prevailing belief appears to be that it is not how you play the game, it is whether you win or lose that is important. Adult intervention into children's sport may have the effect of formalizing the success and failure experiences of children. The coach becomes concerned with short range goals (winning this game, having a winning season) which certainly exacerbates the perception, on the part of children, that the outcome is the most important criterion of success and failure.

This outcome orientation is unfortunate because when we create leagues, playoffs, and championships, only one team can be the top of the league, win the playoffs, be the champion. Hence, we create many failure outcomes by recognizing only the "best" teams. The implication of this is that the social comparison processes utilized by players lead them to determine that they failed: they lost the game, this means that they are not as good as the other team; therefore, they failed! These characteristics of organized sport seem calculated to induce the ego–involved ability orientation referred to above. Independent evidence confirms that American children do use outcomes as an important criterion for evaluating performance (Salili, Maehr, & Gillmore, 1976). Given this orientation, many able players are virtually bound to deduce that they are not very competent in sports because they did not make it to the league championships or playoffs. This may explain why so many children, particularly ability-oriented children, drop out of the competitive sport experience (Ewing, 1981).

It is important to note here that we are addressing perceived competence, not actual competence. Consequently, when we emphasize outcomes as being an important criterion in judging success and failure, we force children to perceive that they are not competent in this experience regardless of their actual ability. It is reasonable for them to drop out when they perceive that they are not meeting their goal of demonstrating ability.

Fourth, a considerable body of research utilizing the attributional approach in sport has shown that ability and effort are the most utilized attributes in sport contexts (Bukowski & Moore, 1980; Lau & Russell, 1980; Rejeski & Lowe, 1980; Roberts & Pascuzzi, 1979). For example, Roberts and Pascuzzi found that attributions to ability consisted of 57% of all responses for winners and 36% of all responses for losers. Winners attributed the outcome to effort 17% of the time and losers attributed the outcome to *lack* of effort 11% of the time. Thus, taken together, effort and ability accounted for 60% of all attributions made. The important aspect of this study was that ability was the most frequently invoked attribution which is in contrast to Freize's (1975) research in primarily academic settings where she found that effort was the most invoked attribute. In sport, attributions to ability are exacerbated. Fifth, research exists which suggests that perceived ability is an important mediator of persistence in sport contexts. Let us discuss this latter research in a little more detail.

Sport team members are high in perceived ability. Roberts, Kleiber, and Duda (1981) investigated the relationship of sport participation to perceived ability for 4th and 5th grade boys and girls. Roberts et al. gave Harter's (1979) Perceived Competence Scale for Children to 73 boys and 70 girls. The children were also interviewed by trained graduate assistants who asked the children whether they participated in organized children's sport, their years of participation if they did, and their perception of their relative competence. Participants in organized sport were found to be higher in perceived physical competence, more persistent in sport contexts, and had higher expectations of future success than nonparticipants. Hence, children who were high in perceived ability were more likely to be on organized sport teams. The low, nonsignificant correlations between physical competence and years of participation seemed to suggest that perceived ability did not have a significant impact upon duration of involvement, at least with the subjects in this study. However, dropping out is not high in this age range. It may be then, in support of Nicholls (Note 4), that sport initially attracts those who perceive themselves as more able to begin with.

Dropouts lack sufficient perceived ability. Recently, Feltz, Gould, Horn and Perlichkoff (Note 5) replicated and extended the Roberts et al. (1981) study. Using competitive youth swimmers and competitive youth swimming dropouts aged between 8 and 19 years of age, Feltz and her colleagues found that participants in competitive swimming were higher in perceived ability than were the dropouts. Interview data on the dropouts indicated that "having other things to do" was the primary reason given for dropping out. This may, of course, have been a defensive response. In any event, "not having their skills improve" and "not being as good as they wanted to be" were also frequently used reasons. Feltz et al. report that 47.8% of their subjects considered not having their skills improve and 52.1% thought that not being as good as they wished were important reasons for their dropping out. Clearly, a large percentage of dropouts considered themselves to lack the ability to continue involvement in their sports. This data further supports Nicholls (Note 4) and the findings of Roberts et al.

These findings shed new light on the dropout phenomenon in sport. The pervasive belief in the popular sport literature, supported to some extent by the scientific literature (Gould, Feltz, Horn & Weiss, Note 6, Orlick, 1974; Orlick & Botterill, 1975), is that children drop out because they do not enjoy the competitive sport experience. Orlick and associates have indicated that children join the competitive sport experience for fun, but that aspect had been lost to many of them due to an overemphasis upon winning. Indeed, of the children who dropped out, 67% gave this as the reason for dropping out. Orlick concluded that the competitive structure of the sport experience is the primary reason why children drop out. The competitive structure, and the emphasis upon outcomes alluded to earlier, leads to a lowering of enjoyment on the part of children. This is supported by others (Devereux 1976; Kleiber, Note 1).

A reanalysis of the interview data of Orlick (1974; Orlick & Botterill, 1975), conducted for the purpose of this chapter, shows that although children who dropped out gave many reasons for dropping out, the most prevalent explanation referred to ability. For example, many children state that they didn't enjoy the experience because "the coach only lets better players play," "to get the coaches' attention you have to be good," "I always strike out," or "I never get to the puck." The list of sport ability reasons goes on. Although Orlick argues that children drop put because enjoyment is missing, it is a reasonable rival hypothesis that these children do not enjoy the experience because they believe that their skills are low. Certainly, the inference one can make from the comments of the dropouts Orlick interviewed is that they perceived their abilities as being insufficient. Consequently, it can be argued that when children perceive that their abilities do not meet the situational demands, then the context does not allow them to demonstrate ability and they drop out.

Two lines of research converge to give indirect support to the above speculation. First, the evidence already reported on dropout rates in sport show that child athletes drop out of sports at dramatic rates after age 12. Second, evidence exists which show that children become more accurate in their perception of own competence up to about age 12 (see Nicholls, 1978; Nicholls & Miller, this volume; Stipek, this volume). For example, their evidence shows that young children (under 10 years of age) are often unable, or unwilling, to accurately assess ability cues in the achievement context. Rather, these children often focus on other cues, such as amount of effort expended or the outcome itself, to evaluate achievement behavior.

Accuracy of perceived ability changes over time. In a recent study, Nicholls, (1978) looked at the reasoning capabilities of children 5 to 13 years of age. Nicholls was particularly concerned with reasoning about effort and ability and found that children go through four stages of understanding the concepts of ability and effort. The details of these stages of understanding are given in Nicholls and Miller (this volume). Briefly, level 1 is typical of young children (5 to 6 years of age) and is where they believe effort or outcome is ability. Level 2, typical of children 7 to 9 years of age, is where effort is the cause of performance outcomes. Level 3, typical of children 7 to 11 years of age, is the first level at which ability and effort are partially differentiated. It is only when children are 12 to 13 years of age do they achieve level 4 and are able to distinguish between ability and effort in the cause of outcomes and realize that ability is capacity.

Thus, children are approximately 12 years of age before they are able to fully differentiate between effort and ability and are able accurately to assess their own capacity to perform within the activity. This may help explain why so many children (and especially ability oriented children) drop out of sport after age 12. Children younger than this age appear less likely to recognize that they may be demonstrating lack of capacity as they may confuse effort and ability (Nicholls, 1978; Nicholls & Miller, this volume). Only when children are able to differentiate the causes of outcomes are they able to judge their own capacity at the task. Thus, when they perceive that participation in sport is showing or likely to establish that they lack valued physical capacities, they drop out.

Thus, the ego-involved concept of ability proposed by Nicholls (Note 4), appears very pertinent to sport motivation. As noted, the very structure of sport involves competition and social comparison processes and ego-involved ability assessments. Further, children clearly wish to succeed in sport contexts (Duda, 1981) which makes the experience an important achievement domain for them. Consequently, the belief that one has low ability (especially after age 12) should be a source of much concern to them (Orlick, 1974; Orlick & Botterill, 1975; Kleiber, Note 1). It is little wonder than many choose to exit the competitive sport environment and, perhaps, seek other arenas in which to demonstrate ability.

Implications of Ego-Involved Ability Assessments

Let us look at the implications for sport motivation of the above cognitive process of ego-involved ability assessments. Extrapolating the arguments of Nicholls (1979; Note 4) to the competitive sport experience, it is clear that children's motivation in sport and the effort they apply should be closely related to their perceived attainment in sport. In particular, as discussed above, game outcome is a frequently used criterion to infer ability: children who win perceive they are able. It is hypothesized that when the achievement goal of individuals is to demonstrate ability and avoid demonstrating low ability (Nicholls & Miller, this volume; Note 4), children who believe themselves able in sport should be more achievement oriented than children who believe themselves low in ability. But, because children who win infer high ability and children who lose infer low ability, the differences in sport attainment must be maintained or increased. This is an unfortunate aspect of children's competitive sport experiences. The amount of effort children apply becomes increasingly dependent upon their perceived attainment relative to others and whether they perceive they are demonstrating high ability.

As we have stated earlier, children drop out of the competitive sport experience at a rapid rate after age 12, the age at which their conceptualization of the contribution of effort and ability matures so that they can recognize the relative contribution of their own effort and ability to the outcome. For those children who begin to recognize, for the first time probably, that their perceived ability is not as high as they once thought, they begin to ponder their continued involvement. Children (boys in particular) regard failure in sport to be very distressing (Duda, 1981; Ewing, 1981). Consequently, for those children who perceive low ability in a valued achievement activity, the perception is distressing and dropping out is one means available to them to avoid continuation of an embarrassing experience.

It is little wonder that so many children drop out of the competitive sport experience. For those children who perceive favorable ability assessments, motivation to continue is enhanced. Consequently, the emphasis upon winning and recognizing only the "best" teams leads most children to perceive low ability and they drop out to seek other achievement domains in which to demonstrate ability. It is speculated here that it is a perceived lack of ability that leads to the lack of enjoyment (Orlick, 1974; Orlick & Botterill, 1975) or a shift in interest in having "other things to do" (Gould, Feltz, Horn, & Perlichkoff, Note 6) and is, therefore, a major reason children drop out of competitive sports.

If we believe that the sport experience is a valuable one for children and are committed to the fullest possible development of all children, then we must attempt to maintain the motivation of all child athletes, not just those who are apparent high achievers. Something is amiss if we systematically encourage some at the expense of others (Nicholls, 1979). Yet, this inequality of motivation appears inevitable in a competitive system of organized sport which focuses upon outcomes as the major criterion of success or failure. As suggested above, this exacerbates ego-involved ability assessments. This is particularly unfortunate in children's sport where ability feedback to each child is often a function of the physiological maturity and experience of the child (Roberts, 1980). The physiologically mature and experienced children are more likely to make the most favorable ability assessments in competitive sports. These children are, therefore, more motivated to remain in sports. But these children are not necessarily going to be the best athletes eventually.

There is some evidence, albeit mostly anecdotal, that children who are the superstars of junior leagues are not necessarily the superstars of major leagues. For example, many of the top stars of the major baseball leagues did not play Little League or, if they did, were not athletic standouts. There is a prevalent myth that tomorrow's superstar must be discovered early and developed carefully. But that is not always the case. Logic, and knowledge of the motor development of children (e.g., Corbin, 1973), suggest that the physiologically immature and inexperienced children of today may develop into the superstars of tomorrow. It is in the best interest of coaches at all levels of the sport experience for children, even of those whose only concern is with the "stars," to maintain the motivation and interest of all children, not just the ones who are presently excelling.

Task-Involved Ability Assessments

Nicholls' theory (Note 4) provides a conceptual framework that suggests how the teacher or coach can enhance motivation and achievement striving. In order to alleviate the social comparison processes that sport competition fosters, Nicholls argues that a second conception of ability be recognized. This conception of ability is evident as a personal goal when a person's actions are aimed at achieving mastery, improving, or perfecting a skill or task rather than demonstrating higher capacity than that of others. In this sense, high versus low ability is judged in comparison to the individual's previous level of skill. When individuals are striving to develop or demonstrate ability in this sense, they are described as task-involved or intrinsically motivated (Lepper, Greene, & Nisbett, 1973). Extreme states of task involvement are often characterized by a marked sense of personal control and an equally marked loss of ego. In Csikszentimihalyi's (1977) terms, one becomes totally absorbed in the task to the extent that all concept of time is lost and one is described as being in "flow." A sense of comparative competence is not salient; rather, the individual is completely absorbed in the task for its own sake.

Task-involved ability is less complex than ego-involved ability. The player does not have to assess competencies of others in order to reach judgments of the possibility of demonstrating ability. Rather, the players process the information provided by the task or situation simply to establish whether they are improving or performing optimally. Again effort is important in this conceptualization of ability, but in this case, effort is seen to lead to greater learning, mastery, or ability. Higher effort does not indicate lower ability as it can in ego-involvement. Individuals who are task-involved cannot display low ability. If they face an easy task, then ability may not be demonstrated, but low ability is not a probability either.

It is this type of involvement that elite athletes sometimes reflect upon when describing "peak experiences." For example, Devinatz (Note 7) describes the experiences of ultra–marathoners when they are monitoring their own body functions as they race. These racers often describe a "flow" experience (Czikszentimihalyi, 1977) in that action and awareness appear to merge rendering them unaware of irrelevant aspects of their surroundings. They also describe experiences such as "letting their minds go" or "kicking their minds out of gear." Athletes at all levels may experience this "flow," but it is apparently more common among elite athletes who are relatively secure in their own ability assessments. They appear sufficiently confident that they are outstanding that they can forget themselves and become totally absorbed in their performance.

Elements of task-involvement in sport.   There is no evidence with children to support the above, but some indirect evidence with college age adults does exist. Recently, Spink and Roberts (1980) investigated the relations between perceptions of success and failure and causal attributions. The subjects were competing in a racquetball "round robin" class tournament. Questionnaires were given to the subjects following a game. The criterion of success and failure adopted was satisfaction with own performance. Of relevance here is the fact that Spink and Roberts found that the adults in their study did not use perceived ability (capacity) as the only criterion of success or failure as would be expected if ego-involved ability evaluations were being made. Perceptions of trying hard also appeared to enhance feelings of satisfaction. This indicates some degree of task-involvement as higher effort implies lower ability in ego-involvement.

Spink and Roberts (1980) asked players to assess their own playing ability and the ability of their opponent. The data revealed that winners who felt satisfied were the ones who perceived their opponent was competent. These players felt that beating a worthy opponent was satisfying—a successful experience. Winners who were dissatisfied, on the other hand, considered that they had beaten an inferior opponent and attributed the win to the *lack* of ability of the opponent. These players did not perceive beating an inferior opponent as satisfying and the experience was not regarded as a success.

Losers made similar assessments. Those who lost to a competent opponent, and who felt that they were able themselves, felt satisfied with their performance; the opponent was just that much better. This loss was not interpreted as a failure. Rather, the players had exhibited a high level of ability for *themselves* and the experience was a relative success. Losers who were dissatisfied, on the other hand, considered that they lost to an opponent who was generally low in ability. A loss to an opponent who is perceived low in ability most clearly implies one's ability is low and occasions the clearest perception of failure.

These results indicate players used a social comparison framework to evaluate their performance. That is, they appeared to be making ego-involved ability evaluations. On the other hand, the fact that a loss to a high ability player did not produce feelings of failure suggests some degree of task-involvement—that is, self-referenced ability evaluation.

The thesis that there was a mix of task-and ego-involvement was supported by the causal attributions of these players. Satisfied winners attributed their wins to their own high ability and effort. Dissatisfied losers attributed their loss to their own lack of ability and effort. Conversely, dissatisfied winners and satisfied losers utilized external attributional elements. If a clear state of ego-involvement had existed, higher effort would have implied lower ability and, consequently, less satisfaction. The fact that attribution of winning to effort (and ability) was linked with satisfaction and attribution of losing to lack of effort (and ability) with dissatisfaction suggests some degree of task-involvement. Perhaps we have a state mid-way between task-and ego-involvement.

In a follow-up study in the same recreational context with college age adults, Roberts, Devinatz and Duda (Note 8) obtained convergent results. They attempted to focus more specifically upon satisfaction with own performance. Using regression procedures, Roberts et al. found that the variable which accounted for the most variance was perceived ability. This indicates ego-involvement. Other variables including outcome added little to the accountable variance. On the other hand, subjects were also asked to give reasons for signing up for the class and participating in the class tournament. Of the 97 subjects in the study, 93 gave task-involved reasons (e.g., I want to improve my racquetball skills) for participating. Again we appear to have a mix of task-and ego-involvement.

It is unrealistic to expect to eliminate ego-involved self-evaluations in sport. However, these studies suggest that improvement, performing well relative to one's usual level, and overcoming difficulties through effort can also be satisfying for players. In other words, some elements of task involvement can exist in competitive sport.

Implications for coaching. The distinction between task-and ego-involvement (Nicholls, Note 4) has important implications for those of us who are concerned with children in adult organized competitive sport. The foregoing indicates that coaches, parents, and teachers might do well to attempt to emphasize the task-involvement form of ability assessments in order to keep as many children as possible involved in sport. When children focus upon the task demands and their progress rather than their capacity relative to others they have the potential of maintaining their motivation at a high level. Coaches need to deemphasize the *product,* or outcome, of achievement behavior in sport, and emphasize the *process,* or performance, of the athlete within the game setting. In this way, we reduce the liklihood of athletes making ego-deflating ability assessments.

In sport contexts, however, it has been argued earlier that social comparison processes are almost unavoidable. Often the only means athletes have to assess clearly success and failure is to assess an opponent's ability and compare it to one's own ability. There are few objective criteria to assess one's own ability. Consequently, sport contests elevate the use of social comparison processes, even at very young ages (Pascuzzi, 1981), and ego-involved ability assessments are not entirely avoidable.

The last resort left to the coach is to minimize the use of ego-involving ability assessments. To do this, Roberts (Note 9), suggests that the coach recognize that social comparison has two functions in sport contests. The first is the ego-involved function discussed above. The athletes ask questions such as: "Am I better than, equal to, or worse than my opponent at this task?" The second function is a more task-involved, or informative orientation. The athletes asks questions such as: "Do I need to change, develop, or maintain my task or game strategy?" To reduce the deleterious effects of unfavorable, ego-involved social comparisons, coaches should emphasize the informative task-involving aspect of social comparisons. Athletes should be encouraged to interpret social comparison information in terms of their own need to modify or maintain strategies and achievement behaviors.

Roberts and Pascuzzi (1979) also noted that players in sport have two perceptions of sport ability. One is a general, global athletic ability. Coaches often describe players as being "natural athletes" meaning that the player has an overall high level of capacity. These are the athletes who often have the necessary competencies to excel at many sports. The second sport ability refers to more specific skills within the game context. For example, some players may be able to throw well from the outfield but not be very good with the bat, or vice versa. This suggests another possible avenue for coaches to maintain the level of interest and motivation of children. Coaches should emphasize the specific abilities within the game rather than refer to general level of ability. For example, the base running of the child may be excellent despite the dropping of two fly balls in the outfield. To do this, coaches must focus on the children and their performance within the game rather than using the team outcome as the basis of post game comments. We have evidence (e.g., Roberts, 1978) that children do distinguish between team performance and self performance in their attributions. Coaches could take advantage of this fact.

Roberts and Pascuzzi (1979) also found that athletes consider that various sport abilities are unstable in character. Many of the athletes in their study considered that they had performed well or poorly *today*. Thus, another avenue for the coach to maintain motivation presents itself. Coaches could constantly remind young children that abilities are somewhat unstable in sport contexts. For example, inform small children that they will grow and become stronger. When they have grown and are as old, or have as much experience, as superstar Joan or John, then they too will play well. Consequently, the coach should be sensitive to the instability of many of the specific abilities of children. In my own limited coaching career (soccer), I noticed that boys who were able soccer players as young children often lost a portion of their skills during the adolescent growth spurt. With the increase in their limb lengths, and the usual delay in the increase in muscle strength to cope with the biomechanical changes, the boys recognized that they were not as able relative to their peers as they had been, and sometimes dropped out because of these temporary low ability assessments.

Emphasizing task-involvement where possible, interpreting social comparison in terms of information about achievement strategy, focusing in on specific rather than general ability assessments, and recognizing that sport abilities can be unstable, may have the effect of defusing the negative impact of unfavorable ego-involved ability assessments. For those athletes who would consider giving up because they perceive their ability relative to others as low, emphasizing the above variables may lead to heightened motivation and increased achievement striving. In practical terms, the coach should attempt to have athletes move away from asking questions such as "Can we win?" or "Are we good enough?" and move toward asking questions such as "How do we improve?" "What do we have to do to win?" or "What must we improve on this or that skill?" The latter are more task-involving, skill-developing, and information seeking questions.

CONCLUSION

Clearly, we must attempt to minimize the concern of child athletes about how their capacity compares with others. We must do our best to utilize procedures which shift concern away from the outcome and ego-involved ability assessments and toward task-involvement. If we can do this, we have the potential to optimize the motivation of all athletes, not just those with high perceived ego-involved ability.

It must be noted, however, that the recommendations proferred here are only applicable to those children who make ego-involved ability assessments. Evidence indicates that children are approximately 12 years of age before the capacity to make ego-involved ability assessments is fully established. Thus, the recommendations above are most pertinent to junior and senior high school children. It is at these levels of competition that winning becomes particularly salient as the criterion of success. This major developmental shift in the concept of ability on the part of children appears to have dramatic repercussions. For those children who infer that they have low ability, a rational course of action is to drop out, as many do regardless of their own actual ability. Those children who infer high ability seek more competition and more "newspaper glory." Though the evidence is anecdotal, most coaches do confirm that the survivors of the sport experience do become more competitive and extremely outcome oriented.

By emphasizing task-involvement, coaches have the opportunity of maintaining and enhancing the motivation of all children engaged in the sport experience. But this series of recommendations does assume that the coaches of children's sport programs are able to perceive the motivational needs of all children and not just the game winning superstars. It means that coaches have to subjugate their own ego-involved ability assessments to the needs of the children. Unfortunately, the pressure to win, from parents in particular, often forces coaches to focus upon outcomes in the form of winning percentages, and so on. To the extent that coaches cede to these very real pressures, their potential to foster the motivation of all athletes is lowered. No coach who focuses purely upon outcomes can meet the motivational needs of the low perceived ability player, regardless of the actual ability of the player.

This chapter implies that we sport psychologists must attend to the needs of athletes by sensitizing adults, especially coaches, to the psychological processes inherent in the achievement domain of sport (Roberts, 1980). By "coaching" coaches on the perceptions and achievement goals of athletes and the behavioral implications thereof, we make the domain of sport more sensitive to the motivational needs of all athletes, not just those who figure prominently in newspaper reports of children's games. It is sound coaching practice to maintain the pool of available athletes at all levels, especially at the more senior level. To achieve this goal we must attempt to shift the concerns of athletes toward task-involvement and away from ego-involvement.

ACKNOWLEDGMENT

I would like to acknowledge the innumerable conversations and discussions with Doug Kleiber pertaining to the topic of this chapter. His insight into children's games and sport activities has contributed greatly to my own thoughts.

REFERENCE NOTES

1. Kleiber, D. A. *Games and sport in personality and social development.* Unpublished manuscript, University of Illinois, 1978.

2. Coakley, J. J. *Play, games and sport.* Paper presented at the AAHPERD Conference, New Orleans, 1978.

3. Personal conversation, American Youth Soccer Organization, April 1982.

4. Nicholls, J. G. Striving to demonstrate and develop ability: A theory of achievement motivation. Paper presented in a symposium, *Attributional Approaches to Human Motivation,* Center for Interdisciplinary Research, University of Bielefeld, West Germany, July 1980.

5. Feltz, D. L., Gould, D., Horn, T. S., & Perlichkoff, L. *Perceived competence among youth sport participants and dropouts.* Paper presented to the NASPSPA Annual Conference, Maryland, 1982.

6. Gould, D., Feltz, D., Horn, T. S., & Weiss, M. *Reasons for attrition in competitive youth swimming.* Paper presented to the NASPSPA Annual Conference, Maryland, 1982.

7. Devinatz, V. *The state of mind of ultra–marathoners.* Unpublished manuscript, University of Illinois, 1981.

8. Roberts, G. C., Devinatz, V., & Duda, J. L. *"Gone with the win": Losers can be winners too.* Paper presented to the NASPSPA Annual Conference, Maryland, 1982.

9. Roberts, G. C. The role of motivation in sport. Paper presented at AERA Symposium, *Quality and equality in education,* Boston, MA, 1980.

REFERENCES

Atkinson, J. W. Motivational determinants of risk-taking behavior. *Psychological Review,* 1957, *64,* 359–372.

Atkinson, J. W., & Feather, N. T. (Eds.), *A theory of achievement motivation.* New York: Wiley, 1966.

Atkinson, J. W., & Raynor, J. O. *Motivation and achievement.* New York: Wiley, 1974.

Avedon, E., & Sutton-Smith, B. *The study of games.* New York: Wiley, 1971.

Bandura, A. Self-efficacy: Toward a unifying theory of personality change. *Psychological Review,* 1977, *84,* 191–215.

Berkowitz, L. Sports, competition and aggression. In I. Williams and L. Wendel (Eds.), *Fourth Canadian Symposium on Psychology of Motor Learning and Sport,* Ottawa, Canada, 1972.

Bethe, D. R. *Success in beginning handball as a function of the theory of achievement motivation.* Ph.D. Dissertation, Ohio State University, 1968.

Bird, A. M., & Brame, J. N. Self versus team attributions: A test of the "I'm ok, but the team's so-so" phenomenon. *Research Quarterly,* 1978, *49,* 260–268.

Bukowski, W. M., & Moore, D. Winners' and losers' attributions for success and failure in a series of athletic events. *Journal of Sport Psychology,* 1980, *2,* 195–210.

Carron, A. V. *Social psychology of sport.* Ithaca, NJ: Mouvement Publications, 1980.

Coleman, J. S. Athletics in high school. *The Annals of the American Academy of Political and Social Science,* November 1961, pp. 338–343.

Corbin, C. B. *A textbook of motor development.* Dubuque, Iowa: William C. Brown, 1973.

Covington, M. V., & Omelich, C. L. It's best to be able and virtuous too: Student and teacher evaluative response to successful effort. *Journal of Educational Psychology,* 1979, *71,* 688–700.

Csikszentimihalyi, M. *Beyond boredom and anxiety.* San Francisco: Josey-Bass, 1977.

Deaux, K. *The behavior of women and men.* California: Brooks & Cole, 1976.

Devereux, E. C. Backyard versus Little League baseball: The impoverishment of children's games. In D. M. Landers (Ed.), *Social problems in athletics: Essays in the sociology of sport.* Urbana: University of Illinois Press, 1976.

Diener, C., & Dweck, C. An analysis of learned helplessness: Continuous changes in performance, strategy, and achievement cognitions following failure. *Journal of Personality and Social Psychology,* 1978, *36,* 451–462.

Duda, J. L. Achievement motivation among Navaho Indians: A conceptual analysis with preliminary data. *Ethos,* 1980, *8* (4), 316–331.

Duda, J. L. *A cross-cultural analysis of achievement motivation in sport and the classroom.* Unpublished Ph.D. Dissertation, University of Illinois, 1981.

Duda, J. L., & Roberts, G. C. Sex biases in general and causal attributions of outcome in co-ed sport competitions. In C. H. Nadeau, W. R. Halliewell, K. M. Newell and G. C. Roberts (Eds.), *Psychology of motor behavior and sport—1979.* Champaign, IL: Human Kinetics, 1980.

Dweck, C. S. Learned helplessness in sport. In C. H. Nadeau, W. R. Halliewell, K. M. Newell and G. C. Roberts (Eds.), *Psychology of motor behavior and sport—1979.* Champaign, IL: Human Kinetics, 1980.

Dweck, C. S. & Goetz, T. E. Attributions and learned helplessness. In J. Harvey, W. Ickes and R. Kidd (Eds.), *New directions in attribution research* (Vol. 2). Hillsdale, NJ: Erlbaum, 1978.

Dweck, C. S., & Reppuci, N. D. Learned helplessness and reinforcement responsibility in children. *Journal of Personality and Social Psychology,* 1973, *25,* 109–116.

Eiferman, R. R. Social play in childhood. In R. Herron and B. Sutton–Smith (Eds.), *Child's play.* New York: Wiley, 1971.

Ewing, M. E. *Achievement orientations and sport behavior of males and females.* Ph.D. Dissertation, University of Illinois, 1981.

Forsyth, D. R., & Schlenker, B. R. Attributional egocentrism following performance of a competitive task. *Journal of Social Psychology,* 1977, *102,* 215–222.

Frieze, I. H. Causal attributions and information seeking to explain success and failure. *Journal of Research Personality,* 1976, *10,* 293–305.

Fyans, L. S., & Maehr, M. L. Attributional style, task selection and achievement. *Journal of Educational Psychology,* 1979, *71,* 499–507.

Gill, D. L. & Martens, R. The role of task type and success-failure in group competition. *International Journal of Sport Psychology,* 1977, *8,* 160–177.

Harris, D. V. Assessment of motivation in sport and physical education. In W. F. Straub (Ed.), *Sport psychology: An analysis of athlete behavior.* Ithaca, NJ: Mouvement Publications, 1978.

Harter, S. Effectance motivation reconsidered: Toward a developmental model. *Human Development,* 1978, *21,* 34–64.

Healey, T. R., & Landers, D. L. Effect of need achievement and task difficulty on competitive and noncompetitive motor performance. *Journal of Motor Behavior,* 1973, *5,* 121–128.

Helmreich, R. L., & Spence, J. T. The secret of success. *Discovery: Research: Scholarship,* December 1977, *11*(2), 4–7.

Huizinga, J. *Homo ludens: A study of the play element in culture.* Boston, MA: Beacon Press, 1955.

Horner, M. *Sex differences in achievement motivation and performance in competitive and noncompetitive situations.* Unpublished Doctoral Dissertation, University of Michigan, 1968.

Iso-Ahola, S. E. Perceiving the causes of objective and subjective outcomes following motor performance. *Research Quarterly,* 1978, *49,* 62–70.

Kleiber, D. A., & Hemmer, J. Sex differences in the relationship of locus of control and recreational sport participation. *Sex Roles,* 1981, *7,* 801–810.

Kleiber, D. A., & Roberts, G. C. The effects of sport experience in the development of social character: An exploratory investigation. *Journal of Sport Psychology,* 1981, *3,* 114–122.

Kroll, W. Current strategies and problems in personality assessments of athletes. In L. E. Smith (Ed.), *Psychology of motor learning.* Chicago: Athletic Institute, 1970.

Kukla, A. An attribution theory of choice. In L. Berkowitz (Ed.), *Advances in experimental social psychology* (Vol. 2). New York: Academic Press, 1978.

Lau, R. R., & Russell, D. Attributions in the sport pages. *Journal of Personality and Social Psychology*, 1980, *39*, 29–38.

Lepper, M. R., Greene, D., & Nisbett, R. G. Undermining children's interest with extrinsic rewards: A test of the "overjustification hypothesis." *Journal of Personality and Social Psychology*, 1973, *28*, 29–37.

Loy, J. W., Jr. The nature of sport: A definitional effort. In J. Loy & G. Kenyon (Eds.), *Sport, culture and society*. New York: MacMillan, 1969.

Maehr, M. L. Toward a framework for the cross–cultural study of achievement motivation: McClelland reconsidered and redirected. In M. G. Wade & R. Martens (Eds.), *Psychology of motor behavior and sport*. Champaign, Il: Human Kinetics, 1974.

Maehr, M. L. Continuing motivation: An analysis of a seldom considered educational outcome. *Review of Educational Research*, 1976, *46*, 443–462.

Maehr, M. L. Social culture origins of achievement motivation. In D. Bar-Tal & L. Saxe (Eds.), *Social psychology of education: Theory and research*. New York: Hemisphere Corporation, 1979.

Maehr, M. L. & Nicholls, J. G. Culture and achievement motivation: A second look. In N. Warren (Ed.), *Studies in cross-cultural psychology*. New York: Academic Press, 1980.

Martens, R. *Social psychology in physical activity*. New York: Harper & Row, 1975.

McClelland, D. C. *Personality*. New York: Dryden, 1951.

Mead, G. H. *Mind, self and society*. Chicago: University of Chicago Press, 1934.

Morgan, W. P. The trait psychology controversy. *Research Quarterly for Exercise and Sport*, 1980, *51*, 50–76.

Nicholls, J. G. Causal attribution and other achievement-related cognitions: Effects of task outcome, attainment value, and sex. *Journal of Personality and Social Psychology*, 1975, *31*, 379–389.

Nicholls, J. G. Effort is virtuous, but it's better to have ability: Evaluative responses to perceptions of effort and ability. *Journal of Research in Personality*, 1976, *10*, 306–315.

Nicholls, J. G. The development of the concepts of effort and ability, perception of own attainment, and the understanding that difficult tasks require more ability. *Child Development*, 1978, *49*, 800–814.

Nicholls, J. G. Quality and equality in intellectual development: The role of motivation in education. *American Psychologist*, 1979, *34*, 1071–1084.

Ogilvie, B. C., & Tutko, T. A. Sport: If you want to build character try something else. *Psychology Today*, 1971, *5*, 61–63.

Orlick, T. C. The athletic dropout—a high price for inefficiency. *CAPHER Journal*, 1974, *40*, 12–14.

Orlick, T. C., & Botterill, C. Every kid can win. Chicago: Nelson Hall, 1975.

Pascuzzi, D. *Young children's perceptions of success and failure*. Unpublished Ph.D. Dissertation, University of Illinois, 1981.

Rejeski, W. J., & Lowe, C. A. The role of ability and effort in attributions for sport achievement. *Journal of Personality*, 1980, *48*(2), 233–244.

Roberts, G. C. Effect of achievement motivation and social environment on performance of a motor task. *Journal of Motor Behavior*, 1972, *4*, 37–46.

Roberts, G. C. Effect of achievement motivation and social environment on risk taking. *Research Quarterly*, 1974, *45*, 42–55.

Roberts, G. C. Sex and achievement motivation effects upon risk taking and motor performance. *Research Quarterly*, 1975, *46*, 58–70.

Roberts, G. C. Win-loss causal attributions of Little League players. *Mouvement*, 1975, *7*, 315–322.

Roberts, G. C. Children in competition: Assignment of responsibility for winning and losing. In L. E. Gedvilas and M. E. Kneer (Eds.), *Proceedings of the NCPEAM/NAPECW Conference*, 1977. Chicago: Office of Publications services, University of Illinois at Chicago Circle, 1977.

Roberts, G. C. Children's assignment of responsibility for winning and losing. In F. Smoll and R. Smith (Eds.), *Psychological perspecitives in youth sports*. Washington, D. C.: Hemisphere, 1978.

Roberts, G. C. Children in competition: A theoretical perspective and recommendations for practice. *Motor Skills: Theory Into Practice*, 1980, *4*(1), 37–50.

Roberts, G. C., Kleiber, D. A., & Duda, J. L. An analysis of motivation in children's sport: The role of perceived competence in participation. *Journal of Sport Psychology*, 1981, *3*, 206–216.

Roberts, G. C. & Pascuzzi, D. L. Causal attributions in sport: Some theoretical implications. *Journal of Sport Psychology*, 1979, *1*, 203–211.

Roberts, G. C. Achievement motivation in sport. In R. Terjung (Ed.), *Exercise and Sport Science Reviews* (Vol. 10). Philadelphia: Franklin Institute Press, 1982.

Roberts, J. M., & Sutton-Smith, B. Child training and game involvement. *Ethnology*, 1962, *1*, 166–185.

Salili, T., Maehr, M. L., & Gillmore, G. Achievement and morality: A cross-cultural analysis of causal attribution and evaluation. *Journal of Personality and Social Psychology*, 1976, *33*, 327–337.

Scanlan, T. K. Children in competition: Examination of state anxiety and social comparison response in the laboratory and in the field. In L. I. Gedvilas and M. E. Kneer (Eds.), *Proceedings of the NCPEAM/NAPECW Conference*, 1977. Chicago: Office of Publications Services, University of Illinois at Chicago Circle, 1977.

Scanlan, T. K. Antecedents of competitiveness. In R. Magill, M. Ash, & T. Smoll (Eds.), *Children in sport: A contemporary anthology*. Champaign: Human Kinetics Publishers, 1978.

Scanlan, T. K., & Passer, M. W. Self-serving biases in the competitive sport setting: An attributional dilemma. *Journal of Sport Psychology*, 1980, *2*, 124–136.

Seefeldt, V., Blievernicht, D., Bruce, R., & Gilliam, T. *Joint Legislative Study on Youth Sport Programs, Phase II: Agency Sponsored Sports*. State of Michigan, 1978.

Sherif, C. W., & Rattray, G. D. Socio-social deviance and activity in middle-childhood (5–12 years). In J. Albinson and G. Andrews (Eds.), *The child in sport and physical activity*. Baltimore: University Press, 1976.

Sherif, C. W., & Sherif, M. *The Robber's cave experiments*. Norman: University of Oklahoma Press, 1961.

Spink, K. S., & Roberts, G. C. Ambiguity of outcome and causal attributions. *Journal of Sport Psychology*, 1980, *23*, 237–244.

Stadulis, R. E. Need achievement, competitive preference, and evaluation seeking. In D. M. Landers & R. W. Christina (Eds.), *Psychology of motor behavior and sport—1976*. Champaign, IL: Human Kinetics, 1977.

Stevenson, C. L. Socialization effects of participation in sport. *Research Quarterly*, 1975, *46*, 287–301.

Sutton-Smith, B., & Rosenberg, B. G. Sixty-years of historical changes in game preferences of American Children. In R. Herron & B. Sutton-Smith (Eds.), *Child's play*. New York: Wiley, 1971.

Teevan, R., & Yalof, J. Need for achievement in "starting" and in "non-starting" varsity athletes. *Perceptual and Motor Skills*, 1980, *50*, 402.

Tinto, V. Dropout from higher education: A theoretical synthesis of recent research. *Review of Educational Research*, 1975, *45*, 89–125.

Tutko, T., & Bruns, W. *Winning is everything and other American myths*. New York: MacMillan, 1976.

Usher, D. M. Achievement motivation and levels of sport performance. *Mouvement*, 1975, *7*, 249–353.

Veroff, J. Social comparison and the development of achievement motivation. In C. P. Smith (Ed.), *Achievement-related motives in children*. New York: Russell Sage Foundation, 1969.

Weinberg, R. S., & Jackson, A. Competition and extrinsic rewards: Effects on intrinsic motivation and attribution. *Research Quarterly,* 1979, *50*(3), 494–502.

Weiner, B. *Theories of motivation: From mechanism to cognition.* Chicago: Rand McNally, 1972.

Weiner, B. *Achievement motivation and attribution theory.* Morristown, N. J.: General Learning Press, 1974.

Weiner, B. A theory of motivation for some classroom experiences. *Journal of Educational Psychology,* 1979, *71,* 3–25.

Weiss, P. *Sport: A philosophic inquiry.* Carbondale, IL: Southern Illinois University Press, 1969.

GRADE-RELATED CHANGES IN THE SCHOOL ENVIRONMENT:
EFFECTS ON ACHIEVEMENT MOTIVATION

Jacquelynne Eccles (Parsons), Carol Midgley and Terry F. Adler

The link between motivation and school achievement has generated consistent interest over the years among both developmental and educational psychologists. One major concern has been the determinants of variation in achievement motivation. This concern has been expressed in two types of research: (a) the impact of classroom processes on student motivation, and (b) age-related changes in motivational orientations and understanding of achievement experiences. In this chapter we explore the link between these two bodies of research. We address three basic questions: (a) Are there systematic changes in children's academic achievement motivation as they grow older? (b) Are there systematic changes in the experiences children have at school as they move through the grades? (c) Are

Advances in Motivation and Achievement, vol. 3, pages 283–331
Copyright © 1984 by JAI Press Inc.
All rights of reproduction in any form reserved.
ISBN 0-89232-289-6

these changes in school experience causally related to changes in children's academic motivation?

In answering these questions we have had to straddle the domains of developmental and educational psychology. The organization of our chapter reflects this schism. Initially we review the developmental changes in children's academic achievement motivation and conclude that children's achievement orientation declines with age and that the decline is especially marked when children first enter school and again when they enter middle or junior high school. In the second section we outline our theoretical orientation to understanding the ontogeny of age-related changes in these achievement beliefs and attitudes. We argue that systematic changes in the social experience of children can influence the cognitive processes children use in interpreting their experiences. Consequently, we suggest that systematic changes in the school environment might underlie the age-related decline in children's achievement-related attitudes. In the third section we review the literature on grade-related changes in the school environment and conclude that there are systematic changes coinciding with the decline in children's achievement attitudes. In the final section we review the general impact of school structures and environments on children's academic achievement motivation and conclude that educational environments do affect both students' attitudes toward achievement and their achievement motivation. We argue that two school environmental variables are especially important for our understanding of the decline in achievement attitudes: (a) practices which focus students' attention on ability assessment and social comparison rather than task involvement, and (b) practices which lead to teacher rather than student control of the learning environment. We propose that the grade-related changes in these school environment variables are responsible, in part, for the decline in children's academic achievement motivation, and discuss the importance of a thorough understanding of changes in children's cultural/social environments for the understanding of children's development across the school years.

DEVELOPMENTAL SHIFTS IN SELF-EVALUATIVE BELIEFS AND ACHIEVEMENT-MOTIVATION CONSTRUCTS

Many psychologists are interested in the development of children's achievement-related motivations, beliefs, attitudes, and behaviors. Most of their research has focused on two basic issues. The first issue—characterized, for example, by the work of Boggiano and Ruble (1979); Kun, Parsons, and Ruble (1974); Nicholls (1978, 1980a); Parsons (1982); Parsons and Ruble (1977); Ruble, Parsons, and Ross (1976); and Shaklee and Tucker (1979)—concerns developmental changes in the cognitive processes assumed to mediate achievement behavior; that is, changes in the structure of children's processing of achievement-related cues.

Generally, studies in this tradition find that as children get older, they process and integrate achievement-related information in a more "logical" fashion.[1] For example, older children process ability and effort information in a qualitatively different manner than younger children when asked to predict the number of puzzles a student could complete (Kun et al., 1974). Although these studies occasionally allude to the importance of social influences and of individual differences, they focus primarily on age-related changes in information processing strategies. Since several chapters in this book reflect this tradition, we will not review this literature.

The second body of research—characterized, for example, by the work of Ames (in press), Covington and Omelich (1979), Crandall (1969), Diener and Dweck (1978), Dweck (1975), Entwistle and Hayduk (1978), Harter (1981), Hill (1980), Maehr and Nicholls (1980), Nicholls (1979, 1980b), Stipek and Hoffman (1980) and the recent work of Parsons and her colleagues (Parsons, Adler, & Meece, 1982; Parsons, Kaczala, & Meece, 1982; Parsons, Meece, Adler, & Kaczala, 1982; Eccles, Adler, Futterman, Goff, Kaczala, Meece, & Midgley, 1983)—concerns the contextual, social, and psychological factors that influence the link of achievement experiences to both self-evaluation and subsequent achievement behaviors. Though some of this work has assessed age-related changes in self-evaluation, motivational constructs, and response to achievement-related feedback, it does not focus on the cognitive processes underlying age-related changes. Instead, the bulk of the work focuses on the determinants and consequences of individual differences in achievement motivational constructs. Some of the work has also assessed social/environmental influences on children's reactions to achievement experiences. The work we review in this chapter fits into this tradition.

Psychologists whose work falls into this second category have looked at many variables conceptually linked to both self-evaluation and achievement motivation. These include global self-esteem, specific self-esteem, confidence in one's specific academic abilities, confidence in one's general intellectual abilities, expectations for success on both novel and familiar tasks, learned helplessness, mastery orientation, intrinsic motivation, task choice, preference for challenging tasks, test anxiety, self-efficacy, continuing motivation, locus of control, attributional patterns, future goal orientation, subjective attainment value, and focus of attention on ability appraisal, task analysis, or social approval. Only a few of these variables have been studied developmentally. A representative sample of these developmental studies is summarized in Table 1. Three developmental patterns characterize the results of these studies. First, students' orientation to achievement gets more negative with increasing age. Second, the decline is especially marked between kindergarten and grade one, and again at about grades six, seven, and eight. Third, the magnitude of the decline varies across domains and subject areas. Each of these patterns is discussed later.

Table 1. Summary of Results of Representative Studies

Authors	Measure	Subjects	Developmental Pattern
Brush (1980)	Attitudes toward math and English (including confidence in one's ability and subjective value of subject matter)	(cross-sectional; longitudinal) 6–12: grades	Drop in attitudes toward math but not English.
Crandall, Katkovsky & Crandall (1965)	Intellectual achievement responsibility (locus of control)	3–12: grades (cross-sectional)	Increase in internality for failure (girls only).
deCharms (1980)	Origin versus pawn orientation	5–11: grades (longitudinal)	Decline; drop begins between grades 6 and 7.
Dusek & Flaherty (1981)	Global self-concept scales (semantic differential format)	11–18: years 5–12: grades (cross-sectional; longitudinal)	No consistent pattern.
Eccles, Adler, Futterman, Goff, Kaczala, Meece & Midgley (1983)	Ability self-concepts for math and English, perceptions of task difficulty for math and English, and perceived value of math and English	5–12: grades (cross-sectional)	Decline in attitudes toward math; marked drop from grade 6–7. No drop for English.
Entwistle & Hayduk (1978)	Predicted grade in math and English	1–2: grades (longitudinal)	No consistent pattern.
Epstein & McPartland (1976)	Attitudes toward school in general, commitment to schoolwork, and attitudes toward teachers.	6–12: grades (cross-sectional)	Decline in commitment to schoolwork.
Gottfried (1981)	Academic intrinsic motivation for reading, math, social studies, and science	4–7: grades (cross-sectional)	Decline in intrinsic motivation at 7th grade for all subjects, but especially for reading and science.
Haladyna & Thomas (1979)	Attitudes toward school in general and toward seven primary subject areas	1–8: grades (cross-sectional)	Decline in attitudes toward school and toward math, physical education, art, music, and science. Drop most marked from grades 6–7 for subjects and from grades 4–5 for school in general.

Study	Construct/Measure	Design	Findings
Connell (1978)	Perceptions of control	3–9: grades (cross-sectional)	Increase in known vs. unknown source of control until grade 6; dramatic decrease at grade 7; subsequent increase.
Harter (1980)	Classroom motivational orientation (intrinsic–extrinsic)	3–9: grades (cross-sectional)	Decline; two of three measures show marked drop from grades 6–7.
Harter (1982)	Perceived Competence Scale (Four scales: cognitive, social, physical, and general); achievement test scores	3–9: grades (cross-sectional)	No shift in absolute levels. Decline in relation between perceived cognitive competence and achievement test scores at grade 7.
Hill (1980)	Test anxiety and test performance	4–11: grades (cross-sectional)	Increase in both test anxiety and negative relation of test anxiety to test performance. Shift is especially marked in minority populations.
Neale & Proshek (1967)	Evaluative attitudes toward people, self, aspects of school, and behavioral standards. (semantic differential format)	4–6: grades (cross-sectional)	Decline in evaluation of teacher, classroom, self, schoolbooks, following rules, doing math, talking in front of class, and having to keep quiet.
Nicholls (1978)	Self-concept of attainment in reading	5–13: years (cross-sectional)	General decline; most extreme between ages 6 and 7 and between ages 8 and 9.
O'Connor (1978)	Perceptions of self, ideal self, and teachers' feelings	4–6: grades (6th grade in middle school) (cross-sectional)	6th graders had largest self–ideal discrepancy and perceived teachers as being most negative about them.
Parsons (1982) Parsons & Ruble (1977)	Expectancies for success following failure on lab task	3–12: years (cross-sectional)	Marked drop between ages 6 and 7 followed by gradual decline.
Piers & Harris (1964)	General self-concept	3, 6, 10: grades (cross-sectional)	Children in grade 6 have lower self-concept than children in grades 3 and 10.
Prawat, Grissom & Parish (1979)	Locus of control, achievement motivation, global self-esteem	3–12: grades (cross-sectional)	Drop in achievement motivation only during middle school years.

(continued)

Table 1. (Continued)

Authors	Measure	Subjects	Developmental Pattern
Rholes, Blackwell, Jordan & Walters (1980)	Behavioral measure of learned helplessness; assessments of one's ability and effort	K, 1, 3, 5: grades (cross–sectional)	Decline in ability and effort ratings in failure condition; learned helplessness response seen only at grade 5.
Simmons, Blyth & Carlton-Ford (1982)	Specific and global self–esteem, perceptions of opinions of others, and self-consciousness.	6–10: grades (longitudinal)	Decline in self–esteem at 7th grade among females in junior high school as compared to K–8 grouping.
Simmons, Rosenberg & Rosenberg (1973)	Specific and global self–esteem scales, perceptions of opinions of others, and self–consciousness	8–18: years (cross–sectional)	Decline; marked drop between grades 6 and 7.
Yamamoto, Thomas & Karns (1969)	Evaluative attitudes toward teacher, self, parents, and peers; attitudes toward social studies, language, science, and math (semantic differential format)	6–9: grades (cross–sectional)	Decline in attitudes toward teacher and parent and in confidence for science and math. Boys also decline for language. Most marked declines occur in either in grades 6–7 or grades 7–8.
Yarborough & Johnson (1978)	I.Q. and achievement tests; attitudes toward school, subject matter, home, self, others (semantic differential format); measure of self–reliance, adjustment, locus of control, and several components of the self-concept	7 (fall and spring); grades (experimental group—nongraded elementary; control group—graded elementary) (cross–sectional; longitudinal)	Cognitive measures equal for both groups: lower I.Q. children in experimental and higher I.Q. children in control groups experienced higher affective benefits. In grade 7, general decline in attitudes and affect measures in both groups.

Increasing Pessimism and Negativism

In most of the studies surveyed, children's attitudes toward school and toward their own academic competence decline with age, until the late high school years. For example, Neale and Proshek (1967), in a study of 350 fourth to sixth graders found that students' evaluation of both themselves and their school decreases with increasing grade level. Yamamoto, Thomas, and Karns (1969) assessed 800 students' attitudes toward four school subjects (social studies, language, science, and mathematics) and toward four sets of people (classmates, parents, teachers, and themselves). There was a decline from grade six to nine in the students' attitudes toward each of these except on the rating of their teacher. Teachers received a consistently low rating across all of the grades. Finally, Haladyna and Thomas (1979) found a sharp decline in students' attitudes toward school in general and toward specific subjects between grades six and seven.

Evidence suggests that the decline in students' self-evaluation begins as early as 6 years of age. (See Stipek, this volume, for a complete review of the early developmental changes in children's expectations for future achievement success.) For example, Parsons and Ruble (1972, 1977) have clearly demonstrated the decline in children's achievement expectancies on experimental tasks beginning at age 6. A similar decline in expectations beginning at age 6 was found by Stipek and Hoffman (1980) and by Parsons (1982). In each of these experimental studies, the age effects were most marked among children experiencing failure, suggesting that the decline in expectations results from an age-related increase in children's tendency to incorporate the implications of failure, when it occurs, into their self-image.

The data regarding age-related changes during the early elementary school years are less consistent than the data for either the 5-to-7-year-olds or the older elementary school and junior high school students. Although some studies suggest that children's self-evaluations remain fairly stable over the early years of elementary school, other studies suggest that students' self-evaluations continue to decline during this period. For example, Entwistle and Hayduk (1978) did not find any evidence of a consistent decline in children's achievement expectancies over the first two years of elementary school. In contrast, both Nicholls (1978) and Parsons and Ruble (1977) found a steady decline in students' self-evaluations and expectancies across the early and middle elementary school years. All of the studies, however, find that children's achievement expectations get more accurate over these early school years. Thus, whereas the extent of the decline in self-evaluations in grades one to three is not clear, it is clear that children fine tune their self-evaluative systems during the early elementary school years. As a consequence, by the time children are 9, they make fairly logical use of success and failure feedback in adjusting their future expectations. In addition, by third grade the children's assessments of their levels of ability are fairly consistent with their teachers' estimates.

Behavioral responses to feedback reflect a similar developmental pattern. Both Parsons (1982) and Ruble and Frey (1982) found that preschoolers and kinder-garten children do not modify their performance strategies in response to achievement feedback. It is as if they lack the metacognitive skills necessary to either change their behaviors or to seek help in solving intellectual problems. In contrast, first and second graders exhibit a quite different response; they both modify their performance strategy and seek help if they are having difficulty.

Even though early elementary school age children adjust their behavior in the face of negative feedback, they still maintain a positive attitude toward school and do not appear to over-react to failure experiences. It is not until the fourth or fifth grade that we begin to see consistent evidence of debilitating reactions to negative feedback (such as learned helplessness) in some children (Rholes, Blackwell, Jordan, & Walters, 1980). It is also in these late elementary school grades that we begin to see evidence of a second period of decline in both children's self-evaluations and their attitudes toward school and an increase in their level of anxiety regarding their school performance (Blumenfeld & Pintrich, 1982; Harter, 1980; Hill, 1977, 1980). For example, in a series of studies using a variety of self-concept/self-esteem measures, Simmons and her colleagues have found consistent evidence of a decline in academic self-esteem (Rosenberg, 1979; Simmons, Blyth, Van Cleave, & Bush, 1979; Simmons, Rosenberg, & Rosenberg, 1973). This decline was especially marked among seventh graders, particularly for females. Furthermore, for some of the measures the decline was remarkably strong; e.g., among students who valued being smart, the percent rating themselves favorably dropped from 26% among 8-11 year olds to 9% among the 12-14 year olds and to 5% among the 15-18-year-olds. Similarly, in studies of children ranging from fifth to twelfth grades, both Brush (1980) and Eccles et al. (1983) found a marked decline in students' estimates of their math ability in the early secondary school years. The decline found by Eccles et al. (1983) was especially marked between grades six and seven (see Figure 1). Finally, Piers and Harris (1964) found that sixth graders have lower general self-concepts than either third or tenth graders.

O'Connor (1978) studied the relationship between children's self-concept and ideal self-concept in grades four, five, and six. Fourth and fifth grade children had very similar discrepancy score means. Sixth graders, who had just moved to the middle school environment, had the highest discrepancy scores and also perceived their teachers as having more negative feelings toward them.

Children's increasing negativism is also apparent on their responses to questions regarding what motivates them. Harter (1980) developed three scales to tap children's intrinsic versus extrinsic orientation toward school work. She found a shift on all three scales toward an increasingly external orientation from grades three to nine. Once again the shifts were most marked between grades six and seven. Similarly, Gottfried (1981) found a sharp drop in intrinsic motivation toward several academic subjects from grade six to seven. deCharms (1980) reported a similar shift toward an external (pawn) orientation toward achievement as children move into junior high school.

Looking at indices of negative motivation, a similar pattern emerges for children in grades three to twelve. Both the levels of test anxiety and the debilitating effects of test anxiety on performance increase with age (Hill, 1980). Perception of the difficulty of academic subjects increases with age (Eccles et al., 1983). Learned helpless responses to failure increase with age (Rholes et al., 1980). Finally dropout rates, absenteeism, and general school alienation increase with age, especially as students move into junior high school (Rosenbaum, 1976).

All of these changes are well illustrated by the results of a study we have been conducting over the last several years involving over 1,200 students in grades 5 to 12, their parents, and their teachers (see Eccles et al., 1983). In order to investigate changes in children's attitudes toward math and English, we developed measures to assess (a) students' self-concept of their math and English abilities, (b) perceptions of the effort necessary to do well in each subject, (c) perceptions of the importance or value of math and English, and (d) a variety of other attitudes toward math including perceptions of their parents' and teachers' beliefs, and how much they liked their math teacher.

The developmental results were rather striking. (See Figure 1 for the results associated with measures a, b, and c). Grade effects were both more numerous and, in general, stronger than sex effects. Children became more pessimistic and negative about math from fifth to tenth grade with the low point occurring during the junior high school years. Some positive recovery, however, was evident in the last two years of high school. The older children had lower expectancies for both their current and future math performance, rated both their math ability and math performance lower, saw both their present and future math courses as more difficult, thought their parents shared these pessimistic views of their ability and performance potential, were less interested in math activities in general, liked their math teachers less, and rated the utility of advanced math courses lower than did the younger children. For most of these variables, there was a consistent downward trend as a function of grade with the girls preceding the boys.

These results are especially interesting given the nature of our sample. Since poorer math students do not take as much high school math as the better math students, our older sample included an over-representation of better students enrolled in advanced level, elective math courses. Thus, the general increase in negativism toward academic achievement summarized thus far is even characteristic of the better students in junior and senior high school.

Magnitude of the Decline

It is clear from the studies reviewed thus far that children's achievement and school-related attitudes decline with age at least until the last two years of high school. In addition, several studies suggest that the magnitude of this decline varies across grade level. The decline appears to be most marked when children first enter school and again as they move into junior high school. In a series of large scale population studies, Simmons, Rosenberg, and their colleagues have focused on this second transition (Rosenberg, 1979; Simmons et al., 1973, 1979; Simmons & Rosenberg, 1975). By comparing the effects of different school organizations on children of equivalent age, they have investigated the relative contribution of age and maturation versus transition into junior high school to the grade-related decline in the children's self-evaluations. The results of their studies, involving more than 1,000 children, suggest that the transition to junior high school is the primary cause of the decline in self-concept among early adolescents. They argue that major transitions, such as the movement into junior high school, can precipitate a reappraisal of oneself. When this transition coincides with another major transition, such as puberty, then the likelihood of reappraisal is increased. While they do discuss briefly the fact that the junior high school environment is different than the elementary school environment, they are not specific about these differences and they do not suggest that the nature of the junior high school environment is a critical variable. Instead, they attribute the decline in students' attitudes at age 12 to the fact that society forces the average 12-year-old to make two major transitions simultaneously. While in basic agreement with their suggestion that the timing of the transition is important, we also think that there are specific classroom processes characteristic of the typical junior high school environment that exacerbate the problem. We explore this possibility more fully below.

Domain Specificity

Figure 1 illustrates the third general pattern apparent in the results of the studies summarized in Table 1; namely, that the decline varies across domains. The few researchers who have actually measured attitudes across domains have found the decline in attitudes more characteristic of the academic achievement domain than other domains. For example, Epstein and McPartland (1976) constructed a self-report measure (the Quality of School Life Scale) to assess three aspects of student reactions to school. The Satisfaction subscale measures general reactions to school as a social environment; the Commitment subscale measures level of interest in assignments and academic work, and long range achievement-related life plans; and the Reactions to Teachers subscale measures students' reactions to their teachers. Based on a longitudinal study of over 4,000 students in grades 4, 5, 6, 8, and 11 (year 1) and 5, 6, 7, 9, and 12 (year 2) they concluded that the decline in attitudes was most marked on the Commitment subscale. Furthermore, their longitudinal analyses showed a consistent pattern of decreasing satisfaction with school work over time. In contrast, the students' reactions to school as a social environment remained fairly stable across these grades.

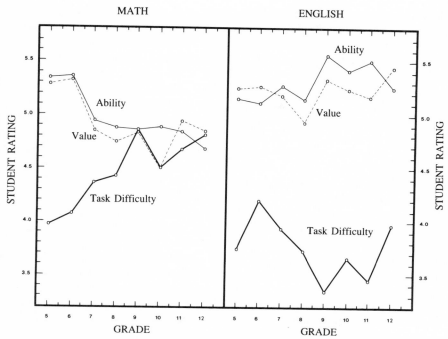

Figure 1. Grade level differences in student achievement attitudes.

Comparable results have been reported in other studies. For example, Prawat, Grissom, and Parish (1979) measured need achievement, locus of control, and global self-esteem. Only the need-achievement scores declined with age. Similarly, although Simmons et al. (1973) found the decline on most of their attitudinal measures, when they analyzed their results in more detail they found no major decline in children's estimates of their skill at either sports or making jokes and no decline in global esteem. The declines were the most extreme for academic achievement beliefs and socially prescribed behavior (such as being well-behaved and helpful). Finally, in a study of upper elementary school and early secondary school students' anxiety and concerns over performance, Buhrmester (1980) found the highest levels of anxiety associated with cognitive and school-related tasks. The children expressed much less anxiety over athletic and social competence. Thus, studies which have measured students' motivational orientations in different domains suggest that the decline in attitudes and beliefs is most marked for the academic domain.

Several studies, including our own, have found that even within the academic achievement domain the decline in beliefs and motivation varies across subject area. As is clear in Figure 1, we found the decline to be characteristic only of students' beliefs regarding mathematics and not of their beliefs regarding English. Similarly, Brush (1980) found that students' confidence in their math abilities dropped significantly more than their confidence in their language arts abilities. Gottfried (1981) found that the decline in intrinsic motivation also varied across subject areas. However, she found the biggest declines in reading and science. Though attitudes toward math did decline, they declined less than did the attitudes toward reading and science. It is unclear, however, how she defined reading; therefore direct comparison of results across these three studies is difficult.

What is clear from these studies is that the decline in students' attitudes varies across subject areas and, in some studies, across the social and achievement domains. This fact, coupled with the grade level variations discussed earlier, suggests that the decline in students' achievement beliefs and attitudes does not reflect a general cognitive maturational process but rather is the result of changes in social experience (Higgins & Parsons, 1983). In support of this interpretation, Brush (1980) found students to be quite vocal about why they liked their current math classes less than their previous math classes. They indicated they did not like the use of public drill, frequent testing, grading on a curve, competition, and the emphasis on being right or wrong rather than on exploring the processes associated with math. Furthermore, they felt that these teaching practices were used more frequently in junior and senior high school math courses than in earlier grades.

In contrast, they reported that these practices had decreased in frequency in their English classes. Their English teachers emphasized group discussion and exploration of the meaning of the readings; the English teachers encouraged students to give their opinions and did not compare the students' opinions in terms of correctness. The essence of these teaching style differences has been linked to variation in student motivation. For example, Nicholls (1979) has argued that achievement environments which focus attention on the assessment of one's ability rather than on the task itself have a debilitating effect on most children's motivation. According to his hypothesis, practices such as competitive grading and drill with public evaluative feedback should undermine and change the quality of many students' motivation. This issue is discussed in more detail in later sections. Before leaving this discussion of age-related changes in achievement motivation, we would like to clarify our theoretical position. This issue is discussed in the next section.

ONTOGENY OF AGE-RELATED CHANGE IN MOTIVATION

Developmental psychologists have long debated the ontogeny of age-related changes. Typically, the debate pits maturational against experiential processes. We, like many others, find both of these extremes inadequate. While we stress the impact of changes in experiences in this chapter, we do not believe that developmental changes in the nature of cognitive mediational processes are unimportant in the development of self-evaluation and other aspects of achievement motivation. In fact, as cognitive developmentalists, we believe that cognitive maturity sets the limits on what children can and cannot understand about the achievement domain. But we also believe that changes in the social environment influence the development of cognitive processes and, consequently, influence the nature of the cognitive processes that the child will use at any given age. As Piaget has argued repeatedly, whether a particular cognitive heuristic develops depends on the child's experiences. Furthermore, as Flavell (1974) has pointed out, even if the heuristic develops, its use also depends on experience. The fact that a child understands a particular cognitive heuristic does not necessarily mean the child will make use of that heuristic in everyday, real-life judgments. Whether a particular cognitive heuristic is used in making judgments will depend on the child's assessment of its relevance. The relevance of a particular heuristic may change with systematic changes in the child's social environment. It is this interface between systematic changes in the social environment and age-related changes in children's understanding of achievement experiences that is of primary interest to us in this chapter.

Let us illustrate our perspective with an example. Cognitive achievement theorists make certain assumptions regarding the cognitive constructs that are central to achievement beliefs and motivation. They also make certain assumptions regarding the relations among these constructs and the heuristics that people use in processing information relevant to these constructs. For example, it is generally assumed (implicitly, if not always explicitly) that (a) ability is a stable construct, (b) that individuals are motivated to assess their ability level, and (c) that individuals use social comparison information in evaluating their ability level. These assumptions have been tested in the laboratory; the evidence indicates that children understand the stable nature of ability or intellectual capacity by about sixth grade and can use social comparison information in inferring ability by about the second grade (see Nicholls & Miller, this volume). But, the extent to which children use these heuristics in assessing their own or other children's academic abilities in natural settings is not clear. As Blumenfeld, Pintrich, Meece, and Wessels (1982) have pointed out, the nature of achievement tasks, performance feedback, and other achievement-related information is quite different in laboratory and classroom settings. Outcome feedback is more ambiguous in the classroom and is often delayed. Children may work on different tasks making social comparisons of both the amount of effort and the actual level of achievement difficult. Also, tasks are often so complex that the basis of evaluation is not very clear. All of these variations should affect the degree to which children actually use a stable conception of ability in evaluating their competence.

But even more importantly, the social environment may also determine whether the child even asks the ability question in the first place. Nicholls (1979) has argued that some classroom environments focus children's attention on the question "How smart am I?" Other environments focus children's attention instead on the question "How do I solve the problem?" Still other environments may focus children's attention on "What do I need to do to satisfy my teacher?" Each of these questions has different implications for children's motivation in the classroom. Since "How smart am I?" often elicits a social comparative judgement, classrooms that focus children's attention on "How smart am I?" may have a particularly negative impact on the motivation of all but the most able children, especially if the children assume that ability is stable. Environments that focus attention on the latter two questions or that lead children to feel competent if they work hard and improve should be more conducive to continued positive motivation.

Perhaps then the developmental decline in achievement attitudes that occurs at about grades six, seven, and eight reflects, in part, an increase in the degree to which schools focus children's attention on the first of these three motivational questions. Based on their review of a wide range of naturalistic studies of classroom motivation, Blumenfeld, Pintrich et al. (1982) concluded that children in the elementary school grades do not appear to be asking themselves the question "How smart am I?" very often. These same studies of classroom motivation in the elementary school years also suggest that there is not much evidence of task-involved, intrinsic motivation in the later elementary school grades either. For example, Blumenfeld and Pintrich (1982) asked second and sixth grade children why they worked hard in school. The children, especially the older children, gave extrinsic reasons most frequently.

In summarizing classroom studies, Brophy (1983) has argued that the elementary school classroom is best characterized as a work place rather than as a setting that fosters intrinsically motivated, creative learning. These descriptions suggest that elementary schools dispose children to ask the third question, namely, "What do I need to do to satisfy my teacher?" Doyle (1979) refers to this orientation as the grade performance exchange mode of student-teacher interaction. While it does not foster intrinsic motivation, it does provide the students with some control of their reinforcements. As long as they can exchange effort or incremental learning for an acceptable grade, then their attitudes toward achievement and their motivation to continue learning can remain high.

But what happens when children enter junior high school? The decline in achievement attitudes suggests that the students are focusing more on the ability question. Virtually no studies have tested this hypothesis directly. There are, however, a sprinkling of laboratory studies from quite different research traditions which lend support to the suggestion. For example, in the domain of person perception, Montemayor & Eisen (1977) asked children from 9 to 18 years of age to describe themselves. The 14-year-olds were more likely to describe themselves in terms of relative ability and interpersonal traits than were the 10 and 12-year-olds.

Using a very different format, Parsons (1974) asked students in grades kindergarten to 9 to evaluate a set of stimulus children who varied in both the amount of effort they exerted and their actual performance level on a series of achievement and non-achievement tasks. She found a developmental shift in the use of both of these cues at the seventh grade for the achievement tasks. In particular, the importance of outcome increased while the importance of effort decreased. Interestingly, Weiner and Peter (1973) found a similar shift at the seventh grade in the weighing of outcome and effort variations in children's evaluative judgements of others. Since outcome is a joint function of ability and effort and since the importance of effort in students' evaluative schema declines, these two sets of results suggest that ability variations in the achievement domain become more salient in the junior high school. (See also Nicholls & Miller, this volume.) In the domain of test anxiety, Hill and his colleagues (see Hill, 1977, 1980) have found that the relation between test anxiety and performance increases as children enter junior high school. In addition, Buhrmester (1980) reported an increase in anxiety over academic achievement at this age level. Finally, the evidence reported by Brush (1980) clearly indicates that students feel that they are being evaluated more publicly in junior high school than they were in elementary school.

In conclusion, then, there is some evidence to support the suggestion that junior high school students may be more focused on the motivational question of "How smart am I?" than elementary school students. Furthermore when younger and older children ask themselves this question, they appear to use different heuristics in reaching their answer. That is, they appear to have different schema or concepts of intellectual ability. We believe that the environments characterizing junior and senior high schools encourage, if not force, students to ask themselves "How smart am I?" This is especially unfortunate given the fact that the older children are more likely to judge their smartness as a capacity relative to the smartness of others rather than as an incremental capacity that is growing with increased education. These age-related shifts in orientation to the question "How smart am I?" we believe account, in part, for the decline in students' attitudes toward both their own academic competence and schooling in general. In the remainder of this chapter we will explore the grade-related changes in school environment that might be contributing to this shift in orientation. We will also explore the impact of grade-related changes on other variables, such as student control and self-focus, that might mediate the decline in students' attitudes.

CHANGES IN THE CLASSROOM ENVIRONMENT WITH GRADE LEVEL

All of us have spent many hours of our lives in classrooms. Most of us would agree that there are systematic changes in the nature of the classroom environment as students proceed through the grades from preschool or kindergarten to twelfth grade. However, few studies have attempted to catalogue systematically the nature of these changes. Therefore we will begin this section with anecdotal and descriptive material based on sources such as Brim (1966); Campbell (1969); Clausen (1968); Gardner, (1963); Gronlund, (1974); Higgins and Parsons (1983); Minuchin and Shapiro, (1983); Rutter, Maughan, Mortimore, and Ouston (1979); and Parsons (1974), as well as on our own personal experiences as students and educational researchers. We will describe "typical" schools, and will highlight those changes which are likely to impact on (a) children's focus of attention on self versus the task, (b) children's perceptions of their academic abilities, (c) children's perceptions of the importance of academic performance, and (d) children's sense of autonomy and control. Our aim is to help you recall your school experiences and to stimulate your thinking about grade-related changes in the classroom environment. In the second half of this section we will present the rather limited research evidence of changes in the classroom environment with grade level.

Anecdotal and Descriptive Material

The transition from the home to the "school" environment is occurring earlier than it did a decade ago and may take a variety of forms. The definitions of a day care center, a play group, a play school, or a preschool are not firm and it is becoming more difficult to make generalizations about environmental changes as children move from home to school. But movement into the elementary school does introduce some important changes in the child's social environment. During the preschool years, children acquire so many physical skills so rapidly that they have frequent experience with failure followed by subsequent and often dramatic improvement. Consequently, their own experiences provide them with little reason to conclude that past failures are predictive of future outcomes. Other aspects of the social environment of preschool children also support a belief in the instability of both outcomes and ability. First, because parents of preschoolers are well aware of the rapid changes in the physical capacity of their children, they encourage their children to continue to try despite failure. Second, since the home environment is not age stratified, children have the opportunity to compare their performance with both older and younger people and see that there are striking shifts in both performance and ability level as one gets older. These social environmental factors should predispose preschool children to perceive abilities as unstable and more like skills to be learned than as stable entities which are enduring characteristics of the individual.

Entrance into elementary school alters several aspects of the child's social experience. First, classes are age stratified. Consequently, 6-year-olds are exposed to a dramatic increase in information regarding individual differences and individual consistency across time in relative performance. Second, since the children's maturation rate slows considerably, the experience of dramatic changes in one's own performance level decreases in frequency. Third, it is very probable that parents' attitudes regarding the stability of performance also undergo a shift at about this time. Parents may begin to look for evidence of their children's intellectual abilities and may convey this concern to their children, especially if their children are having difficulty with school work (see Higgins & Parsons, 1983, for discussion). Finally, entry into school confronts the child with all of the dynamics of student-teacher interaction, such as evaluative feedback of one's performance relative to other children.

Elementary schools tend to be neighborhood schools which encourage family involvement. Typically, elementary students are taught by a single teacher, usually female, with 20 to 30 same-aged peers in a self-contained classroom. Tasks frequently are assigned by the teacher to be completed within a specified time frame. Age segregation allows for regimentation of tasks and for comparison judgements of speed or level of mastery. Students sometimes receive descriptive evaluations or behavioral objective checklists indicating component mastery rather than letter grade report cards (Gronlund, 1974). Within class grouping by ability, particularly in reading, is common and teachers may communicate the ability differences between groups to children (Weinstein, 1976). Teachers not only instruct students in basic academic skills, but socialize children to the student role (Blumenfeld, Hamilton, Bossert, Wessels, & Meece, 1982; Brophy & Evertson, 1978).

In the upper elementary grades there are fewer "open" or "informal" classrooms than in the preschool or early elementary grades (Arlin, 1976). Within classroom ability grouping is frequently extended to include mathematics as well as reading. Social comparison in the achievement domain as well as in social and athletic domains intensifies as teachers increase the use of letter grades (Gronlund, 1974). In the last year of elementary school, most frequently the sixth grade, teachers often emphasize the importance of getting ready for junior high school and "learning how to work." In some cases this means more homework, testing, and competition among students.

A dramatic change in the school environment occurs at the transition from elementary school to junior high school. Before the advent of the junior high school, the most common grade arrangement consisted of an eight year elementary school and a four year high school. The junior high school was created to meet what were perceived to be the unique needs and characteristics of the early adolescent. In practice, however, this goal was never implemented widely. "From its inception, at the beginning of the twentieth century, the reason for the junior high school has been to intervene in the educative process between childhood and adolescence and serve the special intellectual, social, physical and emotional needs of pre-adolescent and early adolescent pupils. In recent years, however, controversy has arisen germane to the alleged failure of junior high schools to achieve aims and functions proposed for them" (Gatewood, 1971, p.264). As a result, the middle school has replaced the junior high school in many school districts. The middle school is essentially a phenomenon of the

1960s. "The middle school is a philosophy and belief about children, their unique needs, who they are, and how they grow and learn" (DeVita, Pumerantz, & Wilklow, 1970, p.25). Unfortunately the data indicate that middle schools and junior high schools are more alike than different. In many cases middle schools have produced a reorganization of grade levels and little more. While most middle schools are composed of grades five through eight, rather than grades seven through nine, they are often much like traditional junior high schools. Unfortunately, "virtually anyone who has visited a cross section of middle schools is forced to conclude that innovation is largely confined to organizational change and rhetoric; there has been little *substantive* reform" (Arnold, 1982, p.453).

Junior high schools (and middle schools) are typically larger than elementary schools, going beyond the neighborhood, and serving a more diverse student body. Unless there is a small house program, anchor teacher concept, or some similar grouping of students, classroom composition changes across the school day and students are no longer a part of a stable peer group. Students generally have a different teacher for each subject matter area which may mean as many as six or seven different teachers over the course of a school day. Additionally, the increased size of the school and the increase in the number of school personnel who interact with the students tends to reduce the amount and quality of school-home interaction (Thompson, 1982). This decrease in the close contact with significant adults in the school environment comes at a stage when parents are also becoming less dominant in the life of the early adolescent and extraparental adults are assuming new importance. Adolescent psychiatrist Derek Miller (1970, 1974) feels that the availability of extraparental relationships is crucial to the healthy development of the early adolescent and suggests that teachers may be the only non-parental adults available in modern society. He urges the development of junior high school systems which allow adolescents to remain with the same adults for a significant portion of the day, over a period of several years.

The beginning of junior high school frequently marks the student's first introduction to a counselor. But since the student/counselor ratio is generally very high, students meet with their counselors primarily for advice about course selection and for discipline. Seventh graders usually have some choice regarding course selection but often choices are quite limited until ninth grade. For example, a school district may have "required electives" at the seventh grade level to insure that all students are exposed to basic courses in art, music, etc.

Grading practices often change at the beginning of junior high school (Gronlund, 1974). In contrast to the elementary school, grades usually reflect more an assessment of ability and less an assessment of effort. Students are graded by a variety of teachers, usually receive letter grades, and may be graded on a curve. Consequently the salience of social comparison information is increased. While individualized assignments are fairly common during the elementary school years, instruction in junior high school is more often characterized by a whole class format. As a result of this teaching style, students tend to be graded in terms of their relative performance on class tests and class assignments rather than on their individual progress (Rosenholtz & Rosenholtz, 1981). The amount of homework typically increases, with many teachers expecting students to finish assignments outside of class.

At the beginning of junior high school, students may be assigned to classes on the basis of ability for the first time. Ability level may be determined by test scores, teacher recommendations, or both. Ability grouping in mathematics in the seventh grade appears to be the rule rather than the exception. In a survey of forty school districts in southeastern Michigan, we found only three districts which did not practice homogeneous ability grouping in mathematics at the seventh grade level. In classes grouped by ability the range of ability within the class is narrowed, and the available social comparison information changes. In addition, the quality of teaching may vary across groups. Teachers in the lower tracks, especially in math and science, may act as though their students have low ability and little learning potential. Consequently, the quality of teaching in these classes may be quite poor with teachers acting more as custodians than as educators (Oakes, 1981; Prawat, Lanier, & Byers, undated; Stallings, 1979). The students, aware of their teacher's attitude, may appear to give up and "turn off" to school, awaiting the time when they can escape the situation (Rosenbaum, 1976). Evidence supporting this hypothesis will be presented in the next section.

Ability grouping in one subject area may have an indirect effect on course availability in other subject areas and on extracurricular options. Special courses and extracurricular activities tend to be available only during a select number of periods. For example, if French and low track math are given during the same period, then ability grouping can interfere with a student's choice to study French.

The ninth grade, which is either the last grade in the junior high school or the first grade in the senior high school, usually marks the beginning of specific requirements for graduation and the formal tallying of grades for assessing cumulative grade point averages and class standing. Students may be made aware that grades and relative class standing are very important for admission either into college or into the adult world of employment. College placement tests such as the PSAT and SAT emphasize the link between high school and post high school education.

The senior high school is typically even larger than the junior high school, drawing students from more diverse neighborhoods and offering a wider range of curriculum choices and extracurricular activities. Students interact with a greater variety of teachers and peers. School may become more formal and impersonal. The contact between school and home may become even less frequent with parent/teacher conferences virtually disappearing. Mathematics, English, Science, and other subject matter classes are typically grouped according to ability either formally or informally. Accelerated courses and advanced placement courses may be offered. Curriculum tracking is more common in the senior high school with students being counseled formally or informally into college preparatory, vocational, business, or general curriculum areas. Once assigned to these curriculum tracks, it is usually difficult for students to alter their course selection (Rosenbaum, 1976).

A wide variety of extracurricular activities are usually offered at the senior high level and may involve a substantial amount of student time. Participation in student government and other opportunities to engage in decision-making and to define rights and privileges may increase in the senior high school. For some, the extracurricular opportunities provide a welcomed release from the academic environment, making their overall school experience more positive. For others, who have been relatively successful in their academic courses, the extracurricular opportunities may distract them from academic pursuits, reducing their academic motivation and increasing their social, athletic, or affiliative motivation. During the senior high school years, students reach the age when they can legally drop out of school. Thus for the first time students can decide to leave the social system.

This descriptive account of environmental changes indicates that in most classrooms, the environment becomes more impersonal, formal, competitive, and evaluative or ability-centered as students pass through the grades. These changes in environment, in concert with the developmental changes the maturing students are experiencing, undoubtedly have an impact on achievement motivation. The nature of that impact will be discussed in the last section of this chapter. But first, we turn to more formal research evidence of changes in the classroom environment with grade level.

Research Evidence

Most attempts to assess the school environment have included only one grade level and have related differences in the environment to student outcomes, particularly scores on achievement tests. Little research has focused on the systematic changes which occur in the classroom environment from kindergarten to twelfth grade. In fact, in some cases researchers have been interested in contrasting classrooms on some other dimension (such as urban versus rural location) and have added a grade variable almost as an afterthought. Most of the studies that have looked at more than one grade level have focused on the elementary school or the junior high school or the senior high school and not on the transition from one school environment to another.

A variety of classroom measures have been used, making comparisons of the data at different grade levels difficult. The most common ways of assessing the school environment are observational systems and self-report questionnaires. Observational systems may involve detailed counting, categorizing, and rating of teacher verbalizations, student-teacher interactions, and other classroom activities or may entail checklists of more global classroom characteristics. Self-report questionnaires have been used with teachers, students, parents, and observers. Both low inference and high inference observational measures have been used. Low inference measures are those which depend on directly observable phenomena such as the number of times a teacher interacts with males and females or whether letter grades are used on report cards. High inference measures elicit subjective appraisals of the environment made after some specified period of observation or participation. Students may be asked, for example, if their teacher enjoys teaching math or an observer may be asked whether a classroom is autocratic or democratic.

Researchers sometimes combine low and high inference measures in studies of classroom environments. Some researchers believe that observing and categorizing teacher/student behavior is a more reliable measure of the classroom environment than eliciting participant perceptions. In contrast, Moos and others make a case for the importance of the perceptions of people in the classroom.

> Rather than relying on the ratings of outside observers, we defined the classroom environment in terms of the shared perceptions of the people in that environment. This has the dual advantage of characterizing the class through the eyes of the actual participants, and of soliciting information about its long standing attributes in a manner more parsimonious than observational methods. A phenomenological approach provides important data that the 'objective' observer who counts cues or behaviors may miss (Walberg, 1976). For example, students often ignore frequently occurring stimuli and modify their actions in light of how they expect the teacher to behave. Teachers may be inconsistent in their day-to-day behavior, but they usually still project a consistent image and develop a coherent classroom environment. Furthermore, the 'same' behaviors or stimuli used in different settings may lead students to different perceptions, attitudes, or behaviors (Moos, 1980, p.240).

Brophy and Evertson and their colleagues in Texas have conducted several large scale investigations of classrooms using both low and high inference classroom observation measures. Based on these studies Brophy and Evertson (1978) concluded that there are major differences in the classroom environment across grade levels. They identified four general stages (Brophy & Evertson, 1978, p.312-313):

> 1. (roughly grades one through three). Students typically have a single teacher who concentrates both on teaching the three R's and on socializing to the role of the pupil. The latter task involves frequent behavior–related interactions, many more per unit time than occur later. However, the students are young and generally oriented toward adult authority, so that these interactions are mostly reminders to egocentric youngsters, rather than clashes with defiant students. In many ways, the teacher is a parent substitute in the early grades, and teacher-student interaction reflects this.

> 2. (grades four through six). Students still typically have only one teacher (at least in self-contained classrooms), but teacher–student relationships are much less personalized and more focused on teaching and learning. The students now have been socialized to the pupil role, and for the most part, they play this role industriously and conscientiously. Teachers have less

need to correct misbehavior, and students who formerly initiated interactions about personal matters begin to confine interactions to those caused by difficulties in work. They seldom come to the teacher to tattle, to show completed work, to try to get teacher approval or to request permission.

3. (grades seven through nine). In these grades, students undergo adolescence and shift identification to the peer group. Also, even though the need for supervision increases because of this, the adequacy of it is reduced because students typically have a different teacher each period. The result, notable generally but exaggerated at large junior high schools, is a severe reduction in teaching time and a parallel increase in time devoted to maintaining order. In many ways, junior high teachers are authority figures or classroom managers first, and teachers second.

4. (from tenth grade on). As students become more serious about schooling, teacher-student interaction once again focuses on teaching and learning, as in grades four through six. Students have a different teacher for each class, but otherwise, the similarities between the second and fourth stages are high: teacher-student interaction is relatively impersonal and focused on curriculum content; instruction is seldom interrupted for disciplinary activity; most instruction is conducted with the entire class; and students manage much of their own learning by reading and by working on individualized projects or other assignments intended to promote generalization or application. Classroom management concerns recede in favor of instructional concerns.

In addition, they noted that use of group discussion increases and use of overt praise and criticism decrease over the school years. Other researchers have also noted a decline in frequency of overt praise and criticism of students with increasing grade level (Blumenfeld & Hamilton, 1981, Blumenfeld, Hamilton, et al., 1982; Parsons, Kaczala et al., 1982.).

The findings by Brophy and Evertson that junior high school classrooms are often characterized by an increase in teacher control and authority are supported by other studies. For example, Hoy (1969), Willower (1975), and their colleagues have conducted a number of studies of educators' pupil control views using the Pupil Control Ideology Form for teacher responses and the Pupil Control Behavior Form for student responses. Elementary school educators consistently emerged as less control oriented than secondary school educators. Similar results emerged in a study by Nielsen and Gerber (1979). They interviewed 33 truants in grades 6 through 8. They found a strong association between entry into junior high school and the onset and intensification of truancy. The majority of the truants said their most negative experiences at school were difficulties they encountered with school adults. They reported arguments with teachers which often centered on the students' challenge to the teacher's authority and to school rules which were viewed as unreasonable.

The work of Moos and his colleagues also documents the prevalence of a control orientation in the secondary schools, especially in junior high schools. For many years they have used the Classroom Environment Scale (Trickett & Moos, 1973) to assess large national samples of junior and senior high school classrooms. They have identified six types of classrooms: control oriented, innovation oriented, structured relationship oriented, supportive task oriented, supportive competition oriented, and unstructured competition oriented. In general, junior high school classes are more likely than senior high school classrooms to be either control or structured relationship oriented. In contrast, senior high school classes are more likely than junior high school classes to be either innovation or supportive task oriented. Despite this apparent improvement in class structure at the senior high school level, as many as 23% of the junior and senior high school classrooms studied were almost exclusively oriented toward teacher control of student behavior.

> Strict rules for student behavior and teacher determination of those rules are the most salient characteristics of these classes. . . . Students complained of a lack of teacher-student and student-student interaction, and perceived little emphasis on task orientation or classroom organization (Moos, 1979, p.86).

Using a modified version of the Learning Environment Inventory (LEI) Welch (1979) studied over 1,000 classrooms selected at random from secondary schools in fifteen states. The LEI, developed by Anderson and Walberg (Anderson, 1973), measures student perceptions of both the interpersonal relationships and the structural characteristics of classrooms. Welch was interested in investigating whether changes in student perceptions of the learning environment occurred over time (1972 to 1976), whether students perceived a different learning environment in science versus mathematics, and whether the learning environment of the junior high school was perceived differently from that of the senior high school. The grade level differences were greater than either the time or subject matter differences. Senior high school students perceived their classes as more democratic, satisfying, and difficult. Junior high school students characterized their classrooms as more disorganized, diverse, and formal with higher levels of friction, cliquishness, and favoritism.

In a study contrasting rural and urban learning environments Randhawa and Michayluk (1975) collected data from students in 96 eighth and eleventh grade classrooms using the LEI. Grade level again yielded more significant effects than did locale. Contrary to the findings reported by Welch (1979), the scores on the LEI were generally lower at the eleventh grade level than at the eighth grade level. However, like Welch, Randhawa and Michayluk found that grade eight classrooms were rated as more formal, with more friction, favoritism, and cliquishness than grade eleven classrooms.

Lee (1979) interviewed 154 elementary school children and 47 teachers in grades two, four, and six regarding perceived constraints and prerogatives in school and those they thought students *ought* to have. Children saw much less congruence between the actual school environment and their assessment of what should be than did the teachers; the children saw themselves as much more *constrained* than teachers thought they were. Children's perceptions of their status changed significantly over grade level but teacher perceptions showed little variation with grade. The older children expressed a desire for more pre-rogatives. Lee suggests that as children move through the grades they do not have exposure to teachers who adjust to their emerging sense of competence.

Walberg, House, and Steele (1973) conducted a cross-sectional study of 121 sixth through twelfth grade classrooms using the Class Activity Questionnaire (CAQ). Students were asked to assess whether certain activities characterized their class. These activities were based on either Bloom's six levels of cognitive educational objectives or on affective conditions stressed in the class. By identifying general categories of activities emphasized in a particular class, inferences were drawn regarding the level of the cognitive processes stressed in that class. Higher level processes included application, comprehension, finding consequences, and discovering solutions. Lower level cognitive processes included memorizing and knowing the best answer. Significant grade level effects emerged. The data suggest a pattern of *decreasing* emphasis on higher level cognitive processes, involvement, and independence and an *increasing* emphasis on lower level cognitive processes from grades six through nine. Walberg et al. (1973) suggest that these results provide evidence of a mismatch between educational practices and student needs and abilities in secondary school.

Rounds and Osaki (1982) compared activity structures in 13 sixth grade classrooms and 11 seventh grade (junior high school) classrooms. They found that students experienced more complex and diverse activity structures and had more opportunities to make choices and take responsibility in the sixth grade. In the seventh grade whole group instruction was the norm, and although students still exercised some control over pacing, teachers gave few responsibilities to students.

> Junior high school teachers created an educational environment that placed repetitious structural demands on students, required a limited number of social responses, and restricted the required repertoire of cognitive skills to those of least complexity: memorization, recall, and recognition. Compared with the requirements of the sixth-grade activity structures, these students went backward when they entered junior high school (Rounds & Osaki, p.22).

Summary

Both the anecdotal material and the objective evidence support the conclusion that classroom environments change significantly across grade levels. Some schools appear to allow more student initiative in the most senior grades. However, the general trend, through at least grade 10, toward a less personal, more formal, more controlled, competitive, ability-centered environment speaks to the issue of declining achievement motivation with age. Although virtually no researchers have assessed the causal link between these coincidental shifts, the nature of the changes suggests that they are related. The changes in the school environment over time should produce an increased focus on ability assessments, increased salience of a stable conceptualization of ability, increased anxiety over one's relative ability and performance levels, and a decreased sense of control and intellectual challenge. Each of these consequences, in turn, should produce a decline in academic motivation especially in students who are not highly able or who do not perceive themselves as highly able. In order to provide support for these hypotheses, in the next section we will present evidence of a link between the environmental variables and the achievement motivation indices which discriminate among grade levels. Specifically, we will look at the effects on achievement motivation of student versus teacher control of the learning environment; grading practices; competitive, cooperative, and individualistic goal structures; and between class grouping by ability.

CLASSROOM ENVIRONMENTS AND ACHIEVEMENT ATTITUDES AND MOTIVATION

Several authors have argued that school experiences may be responsible for the decline in students' achievement attitudes, especially the drop that coincides with entry into junior high school (e.g., Harter, 1980; Higgins & Parsons, 1983; Parsons, 1974; Simmons et al., 1973). A review of the literature on classroom environments suggests that there are important grade-related changes in the school social environment that might precipitate the decline in children's attitudes. Two characteristics of the school environment seem especially important (a) teacher control versus student self-management and (b) salience of social comparison and competition in the evaluation of ability. Research in the domain of worker and student satisfaction clearly indicates that people express greater satisfaction and exhibit greater intrinsic motivation in situations which provide them with greater control over their behaviors (Arlin & Whitley, 1978; Lawler & Hackman, 1969; Stipek & Weisz, 1981; Thomas, 1980). Work within the achievement domain also suggests that environmental settings which focus individuals' attention on themselves rather than on the task at hand have debilitating effects on both motivation and achievement for all but the most competent and confident individuals (Brophy, 1983; Doyle, 1979). In general, environmental settings which emphasize evaluation, social comparison, and competition appear to increase self-focus or an ego-involved orientation (see Ames, in press; Nicholls, 1980b).

Each of these bodies of research suggest that most students will prefer and will have the most positive attitudes in an environment in which the students themselves have some choice over their academic activities and in which social comparison processes are less salient. Unfortunately, the above review of the classroom environment literature suggests that the passage through school is marked by a decrease in student choice and control in the academic area and an increase in the salience of social comparison information. As we noted, in early elementary school children spend most of the school day with the same teacher and the same group of children. Thus the students and the teachers get to know each other well and the teacher can respond to individual children's needs more easily. There is a wide range of ability within the classroom. Evaluation is relatively relaxed; many schools do not give letter grades in the early elementary grades. Open or informal classrooms are more common in the early elementary grades.

Several of these characteristics are less common in the upper elementary school grades. Furthermore, in junior high school many of these processes change abruptly. Children have a different teacher for each subject, and spend only an hour a day with each teacher, which means the student-teacher relationship is more formal, and based more on student academic performance. Evaluation becomes more rigorous as use of letter grades and competitive grading increases. In many junior high schools, between class ability grouping or "tracking" is introduced so that the ability range in classes is restricted and the value of having high ability is made salient. These kinds of changes should, as we have argued, increase the social comparative and competitive aspects of learning, and the emphasis on demonstrating ability.

Evidence relevant to this prediction is discussed in this section. In particular we will discuss those processes which show evidence of change across grade levels and which relate to social comparison such as ability grouping and competition, and to student autonomy and control over the learning environment. If variations in these classroom processes coincide with variations in student attitudes and motivation, our case for the importance of these processes is strengthened.

Student Autonomy and Control

In some classrooms the teacher makes the major decisions regarding use and organization of time. The teacher tells students what to do, when to do it, and how long to take. In addition, the teacher serves as evaluator and dispenser of rewards and punishments. In other classrooms, students work independently, select tasks and determine when to complete them, consult with teachers in evaluating their own performance, and are relatively free from external rewards and punishments. Most classrooms are somewhere on a continuum between these two extremes.

Kurt Lewin and his associates have conducted a number of studies dating back to 1939 which assess the impact of control and choice on children's motivation (e.g., Lewin, Lippitt, & White, 1939). In their classic study, ten-year-old boys were equally productive under autocratic and democratic leaders and less productive with a laissez faire leader. But the children in the democratic group developed more self-control and motivation to continue working in the leader's absence. In this study, the autocratic leaders made the major decisions regarding group activities and also used praise and criticism to control group members.

Democratic group members participated in decision-making and were not subjected to praise and criticism. Thus these groups differed along two dimensions: evaluation procedures and decision-making procedures.

Classrooms also vary along both of these dimensions. In this section we review the effect of decision-making opportunities. Three lines of research are discussed: studies of naturally occurring variations in classroom style, studies using field-based experimental designs, and studies evaluating the effectiveness of open versus traditional classrooms. In addition, we evaluate the possible interaction of autonomy with developmental level of the student in shaping motivation.

Naturally Occurring Variations in Teaching Style

Pascarella, Walberg, Junker, and Haertel (1981) studied the relationship between continuing motivation in science and four measures of classroom environment: class morale, utility of science content and science classes, teacher encouragement, and teacher control. Using a national sample of early and late adolescents, they found that extent of teacher control over, and structuring of, classroom activities was negatively associated with continuing motivation.

Epstein (1981) surveyed students in middle schools and high schools that varied in the extent of student participation in classroom decisions. Students given more opportunities for participation in classroom decisions reported more favorable reactions to school life and, especially, more positive reactions to their teachers. Longitudinal data indicated that the positive effects of participation on attitudes, when evident, were continuous and cumulative. Control over one's environment was also a stronger predictor of satisfaction with school than report card grades, self-esteem, or self-reliance. If satisfaction with school is related to continued motivation, then student perceptions of control could be an important determinant of achievement motivation.

Deci, Schwartz, Sheinman, and Ryan (1981) developed an instrument to assess adults' orientations toward control versus autonomy in their interactions with children. They found that children of autonomy-oriented teachers were more intrinsically motivated and had higher self-esteem than children of control-oriented teachers.

Arlin and Whitley (1978) used cross-lagged panel correlations to assess the causal relations between opportunities for self-management and perceptions of locus of control over the school year for students in grades five, six, and seven. Students came either from a school that encouraged individualized instruction and self-management or a school that placed more emphasis on teacher management of instruction. Their results suggested that opportunities for self-management produce increases in students' internal academic locus of control.

In conclusion, several studies relying on naturally occurring variations in classroom climate have demonstrated the predicted relationship between opportunities for student control and positive, intrinsically based, academic motivation. Experimental studies have yielded comparable results.

Experimental Studies of Teacher versus Student Control

The importance of the perception of personal responsibility in educational settings has been investigated extensively by Richard deCharms (1968, 1972, 1976). deCharms worked with teachers and students in an inner city school to change "pawn" perceptions to "origin" perceptions. The goal was to help teachers experience the feelings of being both a pawn and an origin, show them the effects of their own behavior, and then help them design ways to enable their students to be more like origins. An emphasis was placed on participation, choice, and freedom in the classroom. Measures of student motivation and achievement were taken at the end of each school year for three years from fifth to seventh grade. In the classrooms with teachers who had participated in the origin training, there was an increase on the student measures of goal setting, internal determination of instrumental activity, personal responsibility, self-confidence, and internal control. In addition, significantly more boys from classrooms in which the teacher had participated in the training program went on to graduate from high school five years later (deCharms, 1980).

Work by Wang and Stiles (1976) also indicates that feelings of student self-responsibility can be developed through the use of a learning-management program in the classroom. Experimental subjects were second grade students in a class using the Self-Schedule System, a program designed specifically to develop student abilities to manage and to plan for their learning in school. Under this system, students choose their learning tasks and decide when to work on them. The control classes consisted of second grade students participating in an individualized instructional program. The Self-Responsibility Interview Schedule (SRIS) was constructed to assess children's knowledge about what they do in school, and whether they perceive that they, rather than the teacher, are responsible for managing their own learning. The Self-Schedule group had significantly greater perceptions of self-responsibility and higher rates of task completion after participation in the program than did the control groups, suggesting that the Self-Schedule system was effective in developing students' abilities to take increasing responsibility for school learning, and developing their perceptions of having this self-responsibility for learning.

Frank (1980) and Richter and Tjosvold (1980) both investigated the effect of encouraging student participation in decision-making. Frank (1980) found that junior and senior high school classes which incorporated activities such as student-generated quiz questions, student involvement in the establishment of classroom rules, student self-evaluation of quizzes, student maintained personal progress sheets, and contracted work assignments displayed a greater change toward internality (as measured by the Nowicki-Strickland Locus of Control Scale) over a period of nine weeks than did control classes which employed traditional techniques. Richter and Tjosvold (1980) also found positive results associated with third through sixth grade classrooms which encouraged students to participate in selecting and planning learning activities. Students in participation classrooms developed more favorable attitudes toward school, worked more consistently without supervision, and learned more than students in classrooms where the teachers were responsible for all decisions.

In conclusion, experimental studies consistently demonstrate the positive effect of student control on student motivation and attitudes. We now turn to an examination of types of classrooms which tend to encourage student participation and choice: open versus traditional classrooms.

Open versus Traditional Classroom Research

Over the past ten years there have been many studies that purport to compare open and traditional classrooms. This research suffers from several deficiencies. Certainly a major problem is the definition of terms. What seems "open" to one person may seem "traditional" to another person. In one open classroom, evaluation may consist of letter grades on assignments, tests, and periodic report cards; in another open classroom students may contract for academic work and receive no formal evaluation. In addition, there may be discrepancies between the classification of the classroom and actual implementation of goals. Recently it has been suggested (Marshall, 1981) that current methods of assessing the implementation of openness are inadequate and that researchers should, instead, investigate the relationships between the component dimensions of classroom structure and particular outcome variables.

As a result of these problems, the research on open versus traditional classrooms is inconsistent, inconclusive, and often difficult to interpret. In spite of these shortcomings, however, evaluations of open education offer some support for the predicted relationship between students' responsibility and choice and positive motivational outcomes. For example, Horowitz (1979) using a "box score" method to evaluate the results of nearly 200 such studies, found that students in open classrooms tended to have positive attitudes toward themselves and school and were more internal on measures of locus of control. However, the percent of studies which showed no significant difference between open and traditional classrooms was greater than those which showed a significant difference.

Certainly one of the features associated with many open classrooms is greater student choice and self-management as well as a de-emphasis on external evaluation. Perhaps a review focusing only on those studies which assess level of student control and self-management would yield a more consistent picture. Such studies are reviewed below.

Epstein and McPartland (1979) collected test and questionnaire data from students in grades 5, 6, 7, and 12, representing both open and traditional settings. They distinguished between the formal organizational and informal aspects of school authority structures. They were interested in documenting the components of the school authority structure that were actually implemented in open schools and assessing which student outcomes were affected most by changes in the school authority system. Open and traditional schools differed greatly on formal organizational aspects of the authority structure but not nearly so much on the informal aspects of student-teacher authority relations. The features on which schools differed greatly were individualization of instruction, control of student conversation and movement, control of student assignments, and frequency of supervision of student assignments. However, there were *not* large between-school differences in students' perceptions of teachers' expectations and teachers' classroom decision-making styles (whether teachers reserved most of the decision-making prerogatives for themselves or extended decision-making opportunities informally to students).

> It appears that, in implementing open education, it was possible to implement successfully formal changes in the individualization of the instructional program that altered the amount of time students would be under the strict control and close supervision of their teachers, but it was not easy to change teachers' attitudes about their dominant role as the authority in informal encounters (Epstein & McPartland, 1979, p.298).

Using a variety of student outcome measures, including achievement test scores, educational aspirations, personality indexes, attitudes toward school, and school coping skills, the formal aspects of openness had a significant but small impact on certain nonacademic and attitudinal student outcomes, but not on measures of academic development. In contrast, positive effects on students from differences in informal authority relations were found for all student outcomes, especially for nonacademic outcomes.

Arlin (1976) tested the relationships between pupils' attitudes and the combinations of grade, sex, and open education. Teachers from first to eighth grade were chosen to represent excellent open and traditional teachers. Their students completed four questionnaires assessing attitudes toward learning processes, teachers, arithmetic, and language. For attitudes toward teachers, learning processes, and language, the pupils in open classrooms started the lower grades with attitudes that were less positive than those of pupils in traditional classrooms. By the upper grades the attitudes of pupils in the open classrooms caught up to or surpassed attitudes in traditional classrooms. "It would appear from this study that in the upper grades of the elementary school more attention might be given to providing an open learning situation" (Arlin, 1976, p.224).

Arlin points out that the differences between traditional and open classrooms in the lower grades may be minimal. "It is chiefly at the upper grades that the open and the traditional treatments become distinguishable on a scale sufficiently large to affect pupils' attitudes" (Arlin, 1976, p.225). Arlin also points out that most open classrooms are at the lower elementary level and suggests that educational policy might better be directed at providing open opportunities for pupils at the upper levels of the elementary school.

Autonomy and Grade Level

Arlin's conclusion suggests that the impact of classroom environments on student attitudes may vary across grade level. More specifically, his results suggest that student autonomy and control may be even more critical at the upper elementary grades and in secondary school.

Brophy and Evertson (1976) have also concluded that the nature of the learner and the nature of the teaching-learning situation are very different across grade levels. They suggest that teachers working with preoperational children and instructing students in mastery of the basic skills in reading, writing, and arithmetic should provide a different learning environment than teachers of older children who have more highly developed cognitive skills and are working with highly conceptual material. They believe that indirect teaching, opportunities for student-student and small group interaction, independent work, and faster paced instructional sequences are more appropriate at the upper grade levels. Similarly, Lee (1979) questions the prevailing belief that open education is more appropriate in the preschool and kindergarten than in the upper elementary grades.

> At the upper grades, . . . some version of openness may be the best context for children's experimenting with the interface between social factors and social norms, and coming to terms with the complex interactions among social constraint, individual prerogative, and participatory decision making (Lee, 1979. P.120).

Lee suggested that open teachers are in closer communication with older children's need to affect their social environment, their "competence push", their need to participate in decision-making.

Support for the suggestions of Brophy and Evertson (1976) and Lee (1979) is provided by a recent study by Blumenfeld, Hamilton et al. (1982). They studied the effects on students' academic attitudes of open classroom structure and teacher management in grades one and five. First graders' attitudes were unaffected by the openness of their class structure. In contrast, the students with the most positive attitudes toward school work were the fifth graders in well-managed, open classrooms.

Studying the impact of student, teacher, and learning environment variables on students' attitudes toward math, Shaughnessy, Haladyna, and Shaughnessy (1981) collected data from 2,000 students and their math teachers at grades four, seven, and nine. Their results provide additional support for the suggestion that the characteristics of educational environments which are most beneficial will vary across grade levels. In both fourth and seventh grade classrooms, they found that teacher and learning environment variables rather than student characteristics were the strongest predictors of positive student attitudes. By the ninth grade, student characteristics, primarily fatalism and self-confidence, emerged as the strong predictors of student attitudes. Fatalism, in fact, accounted for 67% of the variance in students' attitudes. Parental involvement also emerged for the first time as a significant predictor of students' attitudes. The authors report similar patterns in their studies of class attitudes toward science (Haladyna, Olsen, & Shaughnessy, 1980) and social studies (Haladyna, Shaughnessy, & Redsun, 1980).

Thus it seems quite likely that various educational structures have a differential impact on children of different ages. What is more striking, from our perspective, is the strong association between opportunities for both autonomy and decision-making and student attitudes in the junior high school. If, as our review indicates, such opportunities actually decrease as students enter junior high school, then we would expect their attitudes to decline concurrently.

Let us now turn to the second major category of classroom variables that we predicted would relate to student attitudes and motivation. Grading practices; competitive, cooperative, and individualistic goal structures; and ability grouping practices are classroom structures that may dramatically alter the type of self-information available to students. These structures affect the amount of social comparison information available to the student. Consequently, variations in these structural variables should be related to students' perceptions of their ability as well as to related affective outcomes. We will explore this hypothesis in this section. Grading practices will be discussed first since they are related to both student autonomy and self-evaluation.

Grading Practices

Maehr and others have hypothesized that evaluation practices in the classroom are closely tied to perceptions of student autonomy. Maehr and his colleagues have conducted a series of experiments which focus on the effect of student control over, or participation in, the evaluation process on indices of continuing motivation. For example, Maehr and Stallings (1972) engaged eighth grade students in "easy" and "hard" tasks under either an "external" or "internal" evaluation condition. In the internal condition, emphasis was put on performing the task for its own sake. Although students were able to determine if they had successfully completed the task, they were not told how their performance compared to others nor were they led to believe that the teacher or other students would see the results. In the external condition the task was presented like a standard classroom test which would be evaluated by others. Continuing motivation was measured by asking subjects if they would be willing to work on a similar task in the future and to indicate a time when they would be available. Subjects in the external condition preferred easy tasks to difficult tasks. Students, especially high need-achievement boys, exhibited higher continuing motivation for difficult tasks if they had worked on them under internal conditions.

Similar results have been reported by Salili, Maehr, Sorensen, and Fyans (1976) in a study of fifth grade Iranian students. They found that continuing motivation to work on the tasks was significantly and negatively affected by teacher evaluation. Subjects who perceived their results on the task to be internally caused tended to exhibit higher continuing motivation. This suggests that "it is the subject's perception of who is responsible for and in control of the situation that may be critical" (Salili et al., 1976, p.99). Comparable results have recently been reported by Pittman, Emery, and Boggiano (1982).

Based on these and comparable results, Maehr (undated) concluded that evaluation practices affect one's perceptions about the causes of one's behavior in a situation and that this sense of personal responsibility is related to continuing motivation. Studies examining the effects of extrinsic rewards upon intrinsic interest (Deci, 1975; Enzle & Ross, 1978; Lepper & Greene, 1975; Lepper, Greene, & Nisbett, 1973) lend further support to Maehr's conclusion that evaluation practices can influence children's sense of control and autonomy.

Grading practices can also affect children's motivation by focusing their attention on different aspects of learning and school work. Traditional grading systems typically reflect differential rates of mastery of a standardized core of material. Therefore low grades are indicative of either comparatively low effort or low ability, both of which are negatively valued personal characteristics. In contrast, since students in contract-graded classrooms are typically working on different assignments at different rates, their grades are not based as much on social comparative criteria. Instead their grades reflect the degree to which the student has accomplished what s/he has agreed to accomplish. This type of grading should make comparison with one's own goals and standards more salient than comparison with other people's ability or performance (Maehr & Stallings, 1972). Consequently, contractual grading systems should produce less self-focus, more task-focus, and more positive student attitudes. Unfortunately so little field research has actually been done on this issue that no conclusions can be reached at present.

The work of Hill and his colleagues has provided evidence that external ability based evaluative practices have a negative effect on motivation. Much of this work has centered on test taking situations. It is clear from their studies that practices which make external ability based evaluation salient have a major detrimental effect on the performance and affect of high test anxious children (see Hill, 1980).

There is evidence that evaluation procedures have an important effect on student motivation. Compared to traditional, externally based ability evaluation practices, alternative evaluation practices seem to produce more positive effects on students' performance, continuing motivation, and affect. This seems to be especially true for specific types of students, such as highly test anxious children. It thus seems as if this aspect of the classroom could be an important key in improving students' motivation.

Competitive, Cooperative, and Individualistic Goal Structures

Johnson and Johnson (1979) have studied the relationship between cooperative, competitive, and individualistic goal structures in the classroom and student
cognitive and affective outcomes. Within a cooperative structure, students
achieve their goals only if the other students with whom they are grouped also
achieve their goals. Within a competitive goal structure students believe that they
can achieve their goals only if students with whom they are grouped fail to
achieve their goal. An individualistic goal structure exists when one student's
achievement is unrelated to the achievements of other students.

Johnson and Ahlgren (1976) used the Minnesota School Affect Assessment
with students in grades 2 to 12 to assess the relationship between student attitudes toward cooperation and competition and attitudes toward school personnel, motivation to learn, involvement in learning, self-worth as a student, other
students, and restraints on student behavior. Cooperativeness of students was
consistently related to a broad range of positive attitudes, including being intrinsically motivated to learn, at all grade levels. It was only in high school that
competitiveness became positively related to intrinsic motivation and getting
good grades. However, there was also no evidence that competition produced
negative attitudes.

Given the positive relation between student attitudes toward cooperation and
intrinsic motivation, it makes sense that a large number of studies comparing
cooperative, competitive, and individualistic goal structures find that the most
positive results are associated with cooperative goal structures. Studies indicate
that cooperative structures foster motivation to learn (Slavin, 1978); and positive
attitudes toward self (Aronson & Bridgeman, 1979; Johnson & Johnson, 1974,
1975), toward school and school personnel (Blaney, Stephan, Rosenfield, Aronson, & Sikes, 1977; Johnson & Johnson, 1974, 1975), and toward peers (Aronson & Bridgeman, 1979; Devries & Edwards, 1973; Slavin, 1978). Ames (1981)
found that low performers benefit especially by working in cooperative groups.
Low performance children judged their ability higher, felt more deserving of
reward, and were more satisfied in cooperative versus competitive settings. The
importance of cooperative interactions in building better intergroup relations has
also been recognized (Serow & Solomon, 1979). Cooperative task structures in
desegregated classes have been related to a number of positive outcomes including enhanced academic achievement in minority and lower ability students
(Aronson, Bridgeman, & Geffner, 1978).

Although the use of cooperative goal structures in the classroom is not widespread, we have reviewed this literature because it enables us to evaluate the
impact of increasing competition as students enter the junior high school environment. This evidence indicates that the higher levels of competition found in
upper grades may be related to the decline in student attitudes.

Ability Grouping

Ability grouping is the practice of separating children into groups either within or between classrooms according to some indicator of their ability level. Ability grouping between classrooms is commonly referred to as ability-level tracking. Ability grouping is typically justified with the following rationale: students learn best when the material is adjusted to their level of understanding; the most efficient way to teach to a student's level of understanding is to group the students by ability and plan the entire group's curriculum at that level. Use of this teaching strategy is presumed to help the students' progress by avoiding a mismatch between the cognitive level of the lesson and the cognitive level of the student. In addition, the argument is made that lower ability students' attitudes will suffer in a heterogeneous classroom where they feel inferior to the brighter students.

Unfortunately, grouping, whether it is based on ability or future educational or occupational goals has two basic characteristics: (a) it functions to stratify the population it is grouping and (b) it ranks the strata it creates. It is generally accepted, for example, that college prep tracks are "better" than vocational tracks and that high ability tracks are "better" than low ability tracks. While evidence concerning the effect of placing students in a higher track is somewhat contradictory (Esposito, 1973), most studies agree that compared to heterogeneous grouping, placement in the lower tracks is related to lower levels of aspiration (Metz, 1978; Oakes, 1981), greater feelings of worthlessness and rejection (Byers, 1961), lower self-esteem (Oakes, 1981; Prawat, Lanier, & Byers, undated), lower self-concept of ability (Mann, 1960), less involvement in class activity (Metz, 1978) and greater test anxiety (Cox, 1962; Levy, Gooch, & Kellmer-Pringle, 1969). Data from Oakes' (1981) study support the view that low track students internalize their failure. Oakes found that while low track students were as satisfied as others with the classes they were in, they had the most negative attitudes about themselves, disagreeing less than others that "there were a lot of things about themselves they would change, that they were not as well liked as most people, and that at times they thought they were no good at all" (Oakes, 1981, p.194). Apparently students in the lower tracks accept the notion that they are to blame for their placement. These findings make sense. If students are told that track selection is based on ability, then those students who are in the lower tracks have good grounds for assuming that they are not very able.

This situation is even more unfortunate given the somewhat arbitrary nature of student placement in tracks. In a comprehensive study on tracking, Rosenbaum (1976) found no relation between objective data (i.e., test scores and grades) and track placement. It appeared that students were arbitrarily placed in tracks by their school counselors. Furthermore, in an experiment in which low track students were randomly displaced upward, Tuckman and Bierman (1971) found that teacher expectations for these students and the students' performance on standardized tests improved significantly. In addition, teachers recommended that most students remain in the higher track the following year. These results suggest that tracking is related to the differences in student attitudes between tracks and that placement in a track may not be based on true ability differences.

Our own data provide additional evidence of the effects of tracking on students' academic beliefs and attitudes. As part of our study of the determinants of students' attitudes toward math, we gathered data on students in both average and accelerated math classes. The students in the highest tracks had a higher self-concept of ability than students in the average tracks. Students in the average tracks also rated math as more difficult and expected to do less well in their math courses despite the fact that the course was supposedly geared to their level of understanding. Students in the accelerated tracks valued math more and had more interest in math.

A second set of our analyses is even more relevant to this discussion. One of the school districts involved in this study allowed each junior high school to decide whether to track its students in math in seventh grade. This resulted in a situation in which two junior high schools grouped their seventh grade math classes by ability and two schools grouped students heterogeneously in math. It was thus possible to make comparisons between the two methods of grouping students within a single school district. These comparisons are especially interesting because the ability grouped students in the study were from accelerated and average tracks (low track students were not included in the sample because of the original goals of the larger study) while the nontracked students represented an entire range of abilities. Given the fact that low ability students were not included in the tracked sample, one would expect most of the comparisons between the two samples to favor the tracked group. We found just the opposite. In comparison to heterogeneous grouping, grouping by ability had negative effects on both accelerated and average students. Students in nontracked classrooms had higher self-concepts of ability and expectancies for success. Students in tracked classrooms thought math was harder and thought they had to work harder to do well in math. Thus, while accelerated students fared better than their average peers, both groups suffered affectively when compared to nontracked students.

Why should a group of students which includes supposedly less able students have more positive attitudes than a group of more able peers? While many explanations exist, one possibility is to look at the dynamics taking place within each grouping practice. It is possible that tracked classrooms put more emphasis on the importance of ability and the use of social comparison information. Tracked classrooms may emphasize badges of ability even more than regular classrooms normally do. If individualism is hard to achieve in situations where there is a normal distribution of abilities, it should be even harder to achieve when one's comparison group consists of students having a very small range of abilities. It should be even harder to feel smart in such classrooms. A study by

Rosenholtz and Rosenholtz (1981) supports this view. They found that in classrooms which had students with a small range of ability, ranking of ability by students, teachers, and self were more frequently dispersed into high and low rankings while in classrooms which had students with a wide range of ability, the rankings tended to be more similar and tended to be average or above average.

Alternatively it is possible that the mere practice of ability grouping focuses children's attention on ability level rather than improvement across time. In other words, ability grouping may sensitize children to ask "How smart am I?" rather than "What do I need to do to master this task?" As Nicholls has pointed out, many children will find themselves deficient if they must evaluate their ability level on a social comparative standard. For these children, focusing their attention on the issue of how good they are may undercut their motivation, especially when they are placed in a system that leads them to believe that relative ability level is a stable capacity and that low levels of the ability in question are undesirable.

It is interesting to note, in light of this discussion, the results of a study by Schwarzer, Jerusalem, and Lange (undated) which examined the self-concepts of students in tracked schools in Germany (where different schools represent different tracks and an entire school is the same track). They found that entering a low track school after having been mainstreamed for four years resulted in an increase in self-esteem for poor students. Perhaps being in an environment in which everyone is in the same track reduces the salience of the information provided by knowing what track one is in. It may be that the way tracking is implemented is more important than whether or not it is implemented.

But whatever the mechanism of influence, it is clear that ability grouping can have a detrimental effect on children's achievement attitudes and motivation. Since the frequency of ability grouping increases as children move into secondary school, we have identified another viable social mediator of the decline in students' attitudes toward school.

Summary

It seems clear that classroom processes can have important effects on a student's motivation to learn. The degree of student autonomy and decision-making, the types of grading practices employed, the goal structure of the classroom, and the range of ability levels represented in the classroom have all been related to student outcome measures. It appears that the less common classroom structures are those that are most consistently associated with increased continuing motivation, greater positive affect, and more positive attitudes toward school. Teacher control, comparative grading practices, competitive or individualistic goal structures, and homogeneous grouping practices are the norm in today's classroom and become increasingly prevalent as students progress to higher grades. Given this grade-related trend and the relation between these classroom practices and student outcome measures, it seems highly possible that classroom process variables are important mediators of the decline in student motivation across the school years.

CONCLUSIONS

Our goal has been to explore the link between grade-related changes in school experiences and the age-related drop in achievement motivation. There is an age-related decline in children's response to measures of achievement beliefs and motivational orientation. Furthermore, there are two points in development when this decline is especially marked: one at about age 6 and a second at about 12 or 13. We have argued that each of these shifts, as well as the more general decline, could result from, or be amplified by, changes in the children's social experiences brought about by systematic changes in their school environment. The environment not only structures the information that is available to children, but also affects the salience of different types of information. Both of these influences can impact on children's achievement judgements. To the extent that there are systematic changes in the environment, the types of achievement judgements children make and the criteria they use in making these judgments will change. Consequently, their achievement beliefs, attitudes, and motivational orientations will also change. In this concluding section, we will outline what we think are the causal connections between changes in the school environment and changes in children's beliefs and attitudes. While we will focus our summary comments on the changes that occur across the elementary and secondary school years, we will also make a few comments about the transition into elementary school. However, before proceeding we will comment on three important methodological issues.

First, it should be noted that none of the studies we reviewed actually tested the causal relationship between transitions in school environments and changes in students' attitudes. One study (Simmons et al., 1979) has compared students of similar ages enrolled in different types of seventh grades. This study has yielded the strongest support for the hypothesized impact of school environment on students' attitudes. However, since this study did not measure the school environment directly, the results do not provide the necessary tests of our hypotheses. Thus, at present, our conclusions are based almost entirely on informed speculation based on converging lines of evidence rather than on ideal field studies.

Second, very few studies have covered the full range of school grade levels using comparable methodology. More importantly, even fewer studies have included grades on both sides of the major transition points. Typically, investigators have focused on either the preschool or elementary school grades or on junior and senior high school classes. Consequently, we often found ourselves comparing apples and oranges in order to piece together a picture of the changes in school environments across the major transition points.

Finally, because the scope of school variations reported is rather narrow, the generality of our knowledge of the effects of environment on motivation is limited. Except for occasional innovative programs, the research literature is based on school environments which are remarkably similar across the country (McPartland & Karweit, 1979). The classes which represent more extreme variation also typically represent experiments in innovative education and the students in these classes are often self-selected. Consequently, results gained in these samples may not generalize to the population at large. Increasing the normally occurring range of school variations both within and across grades would expand our knowledge base and could suggest school factors that might have sizeable effects especially if they persisted for an extended period of time or if they reached a critical level of intensity.

In summary, although there are changes in both school environment and student beliefs across grade levels, typically the changes are confounded with age level. Consequently causality cannot be assumed and the effects of increasing age and changing school environment cannot be disentangled. In order to have a better understanding of the relationship between changes in environment and changes in belief systems, we need longitudinal studies of large groups of children that extend through the children's school careers. These studies need to be executed in contrasting school environments that are carefully chosen so as not to introduce subject population confounds. Until we have such studies, we will not be able to assess the causal impact of educational environments on students' motivation and achievement attitudes. Instead, we have adopted a strategy of looking for converging evidence to bolster our hypotheses. In view of the consistency of the evidence we have reviewed, we believe a causal link between grade-related changes in educational environments and age-related student attitudes exists. We hope this chapter will stimulate the longitudinal research necessary to test our hypotheses more fully. We conclude with a summary and a discussion of these hypotheses.

The Shift from Home to School

Several investigators have found evidence of a shift in expectations and in children's use of failure feedback as children enter school. It has been suggested (Parsons & Ruble, 1977) that this developmental change is due to a shift in the children's cognitive capacity; namely, to an increase in the child's capacity to integrate a series of past outcomes in the formation of a stable concept of one's abilities. Basing one's predictions for future performance on past performance, however, also requires that one consider the past performance as a relevant and heuristically valuable piece of information. Consequently, the developmental shift in the use of failure feedback could reflect a shift in the perceived relevance of one's past outcomes rather than a shift in the children's cognitive capacity.

Preschoolers, because they are acquiring so many physical skills so rapidly, have frequent experience with failure followed by subsequent, and often dramatic, improvement. Consequently, their own experiences provide them with little reason to conclude that past failures are predictive of future outcomes. Other aspects of the social environment of preschool children also support a belief in the instability of both outcomes and ability. Entrance into elementary school, however, alters several aspects of the child's social experience. First, classes are age stratified. Second, the children's maturation rate slows. Finally, entry into school confronts the child with all of the dynamics of student-teacher interaction, such as evaluative feedback of one's performance relative to other children. We know very little about the impact of any of these social experiences on young children's achievement attitudes. However, since each of these shifts should increase the perceived relevance of past performance (especially failure for predictions of future performance), we believe they contribute to the early decline in children's expectations.

Shifts During Elementary and Secondary School

Students' orientation toward school achievement and their confidence in their own abilities continue to decline over the elementary and early secondary school years. Furthermore, there is some evidence of a marked dip as students enter and experience the junior high school environment. Some would argue that physiological and psychological changes which mark the entry into puberty are primarily responsible for these increasingly negative attitudes. One cannot deny that these are important influences. However, we propose that there is an interaction between physical and psychological development and environmental changes during early adolescence. We suggest that the school environment is contributing to this decline through the increase in practices which focus attention on relative ability assessments and the decrease in practices which provide the student with some sense of control and autonomy. These changes are particularly serious given the increasing ability of students to take responsibility for their own behavior and the growing refinement of their intellectual skills. There is then, a mismatch between children's increasing competency and social maturity and the characteristics of the school environment.

As children mature they become more skillful, knowledgeable, and competent; they become better able to take responsibility, make decisions, control their lives. They also feel more able to take responsibility and to make academic decisions (Harter & Connell, this volume). We have presented evidence of the link between student self-management and achievement motivation. One would hope that with increasing grade level, students would assume greater autonomy and control over their lives and learning. In addition, one would hope that schools would provide an environment that would facilitate task involvement rather than ego involvement, particularly as children enter early adolescence.

Unfortunately there is evidence that just the opposite is true. As students proceed through the grades, the classroom is characterized by a decrease in student autonomy and an increase in processes which enhance ego involvement at the expense of task involvement. For example, in practice open classrooms are more common at the preschool, kindergarten, and early elementary school levels. Most school systems tend to become more closed or formal across grade levels. Yet there is evidence that open classrooms are more appropriate as students grow older (Arlin, 1976; Brophy, 1983; Lee, 1979).

What is the impact of these environmental changes on achievement motivation? With age, students feel that they are less able academically and their attitudes toward learning and school become increasingly negative. We suggest that the changing nature of the school environment has a significant effect on these developing beliefs—a *negative* effect. We do not find the age-related decline in achievement motivation puzzling; it is quite predictable.

We are particularly concerned about the mismatch between the developmental needs and capacities of the early adolescent and the typical junior high school classroom environment. Does it make sense to introduce the early adolescent to departmentalized courses taught by different teachers, a changing peer group, letter grade report cards reflecting academic ability in various subject matter areas, between-class grouping by ability, and a more controlled, teacher-dominated environment? Educators and psychologists have long recognized the need for a more personal, student-managed, task focused environment for early adolescents. That recognition led to the establishment of the junior high school and later the middle school.

Unfortunately a majority of these "intermediate" schools reflect a change in grade organization and little more. In fact, taking fifth, sixth, seventh, and eighth graders out of the elementary school may often have resulted in a less facilitative environment than that which existed in the original eight year elementary, four year high school organization. Now there is renewed interest in the 8-4 grade arrangement. Recent research suggests that the transition into junior high school associated with the 6-3-3 grade arrangement may have a long range negative and disruptive effect on students (Simmons, Blyth, & Carleton, 1982). These authors have suggested that early adolescence is not a good time for a major transition. We suggest that it is the nature of the transition more than the timing of the transition that is associated with the negative effects. We believe that a different major transition at that stage, to an environment that is less formal, less competitive, less teacher-controlled, and less ability focused makes sense developmentally and would have a facilitative effect on achievement motivation during early adolescence.

In conclusion, we would like to make it clear that we are not proposing a deemphasis on the acquisition of basic skills. It is important to point out, however, that the "back-to-basics" movement of the last decade has affected both the content of the curriculum and the method of instruction. We are concerned that there is a conflict between some of the *methods* that have accompanied the concern for basic skills and some important determinants of achievement motivation. Thomas (1980), in a review of self-management, academic motivation, and basic skills achievement, cites evidence of a decline in curiosity, creativity, enthusiasm, and persistence as students proceed through school. He proposes that some of the methods associated with the back-to-basics movement (strict teacher control of on-task behavior, teacher-imposed structure and pacing, external reward systems) are in conflict with important determinants of achievement motivation. Thomas suggests that the issue is not the amount of control or structure that characterizes the classroom but rather the origin of that control.

> There is no incompatibility between control, structure, and effective reward system on the one hand and student achievement on the other. The conflict arises when the locus of responsibility for these factors is vested in individuals external to the student. Furthermore, . . . not only are a sense of personal effectiveness and competence of equal importance to achievement as instructional outcomes, but . . . instructional strategies designed to enhance a sense of agency tend also to enhance academically engaged time, achievement, and achievement-related behaviors (Thomas, 1980, p.216).

If the "back-to-basics" movement is to be more than another swing of the educational pendulum, it must be open to scientific scrutiny and responsive to the outcomes of such scrutiny. We do not believe fostering the acquisition of basic skills is incompatible with a developmentally appropriate classroom environment. We are calling for environmental changes based on a reasoned, systematic investigation of the causal relationship between age-related changes in achievement motivation and grade-related changes in the classroom environment.

ACKNOWLEDGMENT

Preparation of this chapter was funded, in part, by a grant from the National Institute of Mental Health and by a fellowship from the National Academy of Education funded by the Spencer Foundation. we would like to extend grateful acknowledgement to all of the people who have worked with us in developing the ideas and research reported in this chapter including Caroline Kaczala, David Reuman, and Tory Higgins.

NOTE

1. By logical we mean in accord with the predictions the experimenter assumes to reflect rational, mature information processing strategies.

REFERENCES

Ames, C. Competitive versus cooperative reward structures: The influence of individual and group performance factors in achievement attributions and affect. *American Educational Research Journal*, 1981, *18*, 273–287.

Ames, C. Motivation in competitive and non-competitive social structures. In C. Ames & R. Ames (Eds.), *Research on motivation in education: Student motivation*. Academic Press, in press.

Anderson, G. J. *The assessment of learning environments: A manual for the Learning Environment Inventory and the My Class Inventory.* Halifax, Nova Scotia: Atlantic Institute of Education, 1973.

Arlin, M. Open education and pupils' attitudes. *Elementary School Journal,* 1976, *76,* 219–228.

Arlin, M., & Whitley, T. W. Perceptions of self-managed learning opportunities and academic locus of control: A causal interpretation. *Journal of Educational Psychology,* 1978, *70,* 988–992.

Arnold, J. Rhetoric and reform in middle schools. *Phi Delta Kappan,* 1982, 453–456.

Aronson, E., & Bridgeman, D. Jigsaw groups and the desegregated classroom: In pursuit of common goals. *Personality and Social Psychology Bulletin,* 1979, *5,* 438–446.

Aronson, E., Bridgeman, D. L., and Geffner, R. The effects of a cooperative classroom structure on students' behavior and attitudes. In D. Bar-tal and L. Saxe (Eds.), *Social psychology of education: Theory and research.* Washington, DC: Hemisphere, 1978.

Blaney, N. T., Stephan, C., Rosenfield, D., Aronson, E., & Sikes, J. Interdependence in the classroom: A field study. *Journal of Educational Psychology,* 1977, *69,* 121–128.

Blumenfeld, P., & Hamilton, V. L. *Socialization into the student role.* Final report to the National Institute of Education, 1981.

Blumenfeld, P. C., Hamilton, V. I., Bossert, S. T., Wessels, K., & Meece, J. *Teacher talk and student thought: Socialization into the student role.* In J. M. Levine & M. C. Wang (Eds.), *Teacher and student perceptions: Implications for teaching.* Hillsdale, NJ: Lawrence Erlbaum Associates, 1982.

Blumenfeld, P. C., & Pintrich, P. R. *Children's perceptions of school and schoolwork: Age, sex, social class, individual and classroom differences.* Paper presented at the annual meeting of the American Educational Research Association, NY: 1982.

Blumenfeld, P. C., Pintrich, P. R., Meece, J. L., & Wessels, K. The formation and role of self perceptions of ability in elementary classrooms. *The Elementary School Journal,* 1982, *82,* 401–420.

Boggiano, A. K., & Ruble, D. N. Competence and the overjustification effect: A developmental study. *Journal of Personality and Social Psychology,* 1979, *18,* 105–115.

Brim, O. G. Socialization through the life cycle. In O. G. Brim and S. Wheeler (Eds.), *Socialization after childhood: Two essays.* NY: John Wiley and Sons, 1966.

Brophy, J. Motivation in the classroom. In S. G. Paris, G. M. Olson & H. W. Stevenson (Eds.), *Learning and motivation in the classroom.* Hillsdale, NJ: Erlbaum, 1983.

Brophy, J. W., & Evertson, C. M. *Learning from teaching: A developmental perspective.* Boston, MA: Allyn and Bacon, 1976.

Brophy, J. E., & Evertson, C. M. Context variables in teaching. *Educational Psychologist,* 1978, *12,* 310–316.

Brush, L. *Encouraging girls in mathematics: The problem and the solution.* Cambridge, MA. Abt Books, 1980.

Buhrmester, D. *Assessing elementary-school aged children's school anxieties: The rationale, development, and correlates of the school concerns scale.* Unpublished masters thesis. University of Denver, 1980.

Byers, L. Ability-grouping: Help or hindrance to social and emotional growth? *The School Review,* 1961, *69,* 449–456.

Campbell, E. Q. Adolescent socialization. In D. A. Goslin (Ed.), *Handbook of socialization theory and research.* Chicago: Rand McNally, 1969.

Clausen, J. A. Perspectives on childhood socialization. In J. A. Clausen (Ed.), *Socialization and society.* Boston: Little Brown, 1968.

Connell, J. P. *A multidimensional measure of children's perceptions of control.* Unpublished masters thesis, University of Denver, 1980.

Covington, M. V., & Omelich, C. L. Effort: The double-edged sword in school achievement. *Journal of Educational Psychology,* 1979, *79,* 169–182.

Cox, F. N. Educational streaming and general test anxiety. *Child Development*, 1962, *33*, 381–390.

Crandall, V. C. Sex differences in expectancy of intellectual and academic reinforcement. In C. P. Smith (Ed.), *Achievement-related behaviors in children*. NY: Russell Sage Foundation, 1969.

Crandall, V. C., Katkovsky, W., & Crandall, V. J. Children's beliefs in their own control of reinforcement in intellectual-academic achievement situations. *Child Development*, 1965, *36*, 91–109.

deCharms, R. *Personal causation*. NY: Academic Press, 1968.

deCharms, R. Personal causation training in the schools. *Journal of Applied Social Psychology*, 1972, *2*, 95–113.

deCharms, R. *Enhancing motivation*. NY: Irvington Publishers, 1976.

deCharms, R. The origins of competence and achievement motivation in personal causation. In L. J. Fyans, Jr. (Ed.), *Achievement motivation: Recent trends in theory and research*. NY: Plenum Press, 1980.

Deci, E. *Intrinsic motivation*. NY: Plenum Press, 1975.

Deci, E. L., Schwartz, A. J., Sheinman, L., & Ryan, R. M. An instrument to assess adults' orientations toward control versus autonomy with children: Reflections on intrinsic motivation and perceived competence. *Journal of Educational Psychology*, 1981, *73*, 642–650.

DeVita, J. C., Pumerantz, P., & Wilklow, L. B. *The effective middle school*. West Nyack, NY: Parker, 1970.

DeVries, D., & Edwards, K. J. Learning games and student teams: Their effects on classroom process. *American Educational Research Journal*, 1973, *10*, 307–318.

Diener, C. J., & Dweck, C. S. An analysis of learned helplessness: Continuous change in performance strategy, and achievement cognitions following failure. *Journal of Personality and Social Psychology*, 1978, *36*, 451–462.

Doyle, W. Classroom tasks and students' abilities. In P. L. Peterson and H. J. Walberg (Eds.), *Research on teaching: Concepts, findings, and implications*. Berkeley, CA. McCutchan, 1979.

Dusek, J. B., & Flaherty, J. F. The development of the self-concept during the adolescent years. *Monographs of the Society for Research in Child Development*, 1981, *46* (4, Serial No. 191).

Dweck, C. S. The role of expectations and attributions in the alleviation of learned helplessness. *Journal of Personality and Social Psychology*, 1975, *31*, 674–685.

Eccles, J., Adler, T. F., Futterman, R., Goff, S. B., Kaczala, C. M., Meece, J. L., & Midgley, C. Expectancies, values, and academic behaviors. In J. T. Spence (Ed.), *Achievement and achievement motivation*. San Francisco, CA: W. H. Freeman, 1983.

Entwistle, D., & Hayduk, L. A. *Too great expectations: Young children's academic outlook*. Baltimore, MD: John Hopkins University Press, 1978.

Enzle, M. E., & Ross, J. M. Increasing and decreasing intrinsic interest with contingent rewards: A test of cognitive evaluation theory. *Journal of Experimental Social Psychology*, 1978, *14*, 588–597.

Epstein, J. L. *The quality of school life*. Lexington, MA: D. C. Health, 1981.

Epstein, J. L., & McPartland, J. M. The concept and measurement of the quality of school life. *American Educational Research Journal*, 1976, *13*, 15–30.

Epstein, J. L., & McPartland, J. M. Authority structures. In H. J. Walberg (Ed.), *Educational environments and effects*, Berkeley, CA: McCutchan, 1979.

Esposito, D. Homogeneous and heterogeneous ability grouping: Principal findings and implications for evaluating and designing more effective educational environments. *Review of Educational Research*, 1973, *43*, 163–179.

Flavell, J. The development of inferences about others. In T. Mischel (Ed.), *Understanding other persons*. Oxford: Blackwell, Basil, & Mott, 1974.

Frank, B. M. The effect of classroom activities on locus–of–control orientation. *Journal of Classroom Interaction*, 1980, *16*, 4–10.

Gardner, D. E. M. Personal and social relationships. In G. G. Harrap (Ed.), *First years in school: Aspects of children's development from ages 4 to 7*. London: Institute of Education, 1963.

Gatewood, T. What research says about the junior high versus the middle school. *The North Central Association Journal,* 1971, *46,* 264–276.

Gottfried, E. *Grade, sex, and race differences in academic intrinsic motivation.* Paper presented at the annual meeting of the American Educational Research Association, Los Angeles, CA: April 1981.

Gronlund, N. E. *Improving marking and reporting in classroom instruction: A title in the current topics in classroom instruction series.* NY: Macmillan, 1974.

Haladyna, T., Olsen, R., & Shaughnessy, J. *Determinants of class attitudes toward science.* Manuscript submitted for publication, 1980.

Haladyna, T., Shaughnessy, J., & Redsun, A. *Determinants of class attitudes toward social studies.* Paper presented at the annual meeting of the National Council for the Social Studies, New Orleans: November 1980.

Haladyna, T., & Thomas, G. The attitudes of elementary school children toward school and subject matters. *The Journal of Experimental Education,* 1979, *48,* 18–23.

Harter, S. A model of intrinsic mastery motivation in children: Individual differences and developmental change. *Minnesota Symposium on Child Psychology* (Vol. 14). Hillsdale, NJ: Lawrence Erlbaum, 1980.

Harter, S. A new self-report scale of intrinsic versus extrinsic orientation in the classroom: Motivational and informational components. *Developmental Psychology,* 1981, *17,* 300–312.

Harter, S. The perceived competence scale for children. *Child Development,* 1982, *53,* 87–97.

Higgins, E. T., & Parsons, J. E. Social cognition and the social life of the child: Stages as subcultures. In E. T. Higgins, D. W. Ruble & W. W. Hartup (Eds.), *Social cognition and social behavior: Developmental issues,* 1983.

Hill, K. T. The relation of evaluative practices to test anxiety and achievement motivation. *Educator,* 1977, *19,* 15–22.

Hill, K. T. Motivation, evaluation, and educational testing policy. In L. J. Fyans, Jr. (Ed.), *Achievement motivation: Recent trends in theory and research.* NY: Plenum Press, 1980.

Horowitz, R. A. Psychological effects of the "open classroom". In H. J. Walberg (Ed.), *Educational environments and effects.* Berkeley, CA: McCutchan, 1979.

Hoy, W. K. Pupil control ideology and organizational socialization: A further examination of the influence of experience on the beginning teacher. *American Journal of Education,* 1969, *77,* 257–265.

Johnson, D. W., & Ahlgren, A. Relationship between student attitudes about cooperation and competition and attitudes toward schooling. *Journal of Educational Psychology,* 1976, *68,* 92–102.

Johnson, D. W., & Johnson, R. Instructional goal structure. *Review of Educational Research,* 1974, *44,* 213–240.

Johnson, D. W., & Johnson, R. *Learning together and alone: Cooperation, competition, and individualization.* Englewood Cliffs, NJ: Prentice-Hall, 1975.

Johnson, D. W., & Johnson, R. T. Conflict in the classroom: Controversy and learning. *Review of Educational Research,* 1979, *49,* 51–70.

Kun, A., Parsons, J. E., & Ruble, D. The development of integration processes using ability and effort information to predict outcome. *Developmental Psychology,* 1974, *10,* 721–732.

Lawler, E. E. III, & Hackman, J. R. Impact of employer participation in the development of pay incentive plans: A field experiment. *Journal of Applied Psychology,* 1969, *53,* 467–471.

Lee, P. *A developmental study of children's prerogatives and constraints in several domains of school experience.* Report to the National Institute of Education, 1979.

Lepper, M., & Greene, D. Turning play into work: Effects of adult surveillance and extrinsic rewards on children's intrinsic motivation. *Journal of Personality and Social Psychology,* 1975, *31,* 479–486.

Lepper, M., Greene, D., & Nisbett, R. Undermining children's intrinsic interest with extrinsic reward: A test of the "overjustification" hypothesis. *Journal of Personality and Social Psychology,* 1973, *28,* 129–137.

Levy, P., Gooch, S., & Kellmer-Pringle, M. L. A longitudinal study of the relationship between anxiety and streaming in a progressive and a traditional junior school. *British Journal of Educational Psychology,* 1969, *39,* 166–173.

Lewin, K., Lippitt, R., & White, R. H. Patterns of aggressive behavior in experimentally created social climates. *Journal of Social Psychology,* 1939, *10,* 271–299.

Maehr, M. L. *Student expectations, rights, and privileges.* Unpublished manuscript, University of Illinois-Urbana–Champaign, 1979.

Maehr, M. L., & Nicholls, J. G. Culture and achievement motivation: A second look. In N. Warren (Ed.), *Studies in cross-cultural psychology* (Vol. 2). NY: Academic Press, 1980.

Maehr, M. L., & Stallings, W. M. Freedom from external evaluation. *Child Development,* 1972, *43,* 177–185.

Mann, M. What does ability grouping do to the self-concept? *Childhood Education,* 1960, *36,* 356–360.

Marshall, H. H. Open classrooms: Has the term outlived its usefulness? *Review of Educational Research,* 1981, *51,* 181–192.

McPartland, J. M., & Karweit, N. Research on educational effects. In H. J. Walberg (Ed.), *Educational environments and effects.* Berkeley, CA: McCutchan, 1979.

Meece, J. L., Eccles (Parsons), J., Kaczala, C. M., Goff, S. B., & Futterman, R. Sex differences in math achievement: Toward a model of academic choice. *Psychological Bulletin,* 1982, *91,* 324–348.

Metz, M. H. *Classrooms and corridors.* Berkeley, CA: University of California Press, 1978.

Miller, D. Adolescents and the high school system. *Community Mental Health Journal,* 1970, *6,* 483–491.

Miller, D. *Adolescence: Psychology, psychopathology & psychotherapy.* New York: Jason Aronson, 1974.

Minuchin, P. P., & Shapiro, E. K. The school as a context for social development. In P. H. Mussen (Ed.), *Handbook of child psychology,* 4th edition, (Vol. 3). NY: John Wiley and Sons, 1983.

Montemayor, R., & Eisen, M. The development of self-concepts from childhood to adolescence. *Developmental Psychology,* 1977, *13,* 314–319.

Moos, R. H. Educational climates. In H. H. Walberg (Ed.), *Educational environments and effects.* Berkeley, CA: McCutchan, 1979. (a)

Moos, R. H. *Evaluating educational environments.* San Francisco: Jossey-Bass, 1979. (b)

Moos, R. H. Evaluating classroom learning environments. *Studies in Educational Evaluation,* 1980, *6,* 239–252.

Neale, D. C., & Proshek, J. M. School-related attitudes of culturally disadvantaged elementary school children. *Journal of Educational Psychology,* 1967, *58,* 238–244.

Nicholls, J. G. The development of the concepts of effort and ability, perception of own attainment, and the understanding that difficult tasks require more ability. *Child Development,* 1978, *49,* 800–814.

Nicholls, J. G. Quality and equality in intellectual development: The role of motivation in education. *American Psychologist,* 1979, *34,* 1071–1084.

Nicholls, J. G. The development of the concept of difficulty. *Merrill-Palmer Quarterly,* 1980, *26,* 271–281. (a)

Nicholls, J. G. *Striving to develop and demonstrate ability: An intentional theory of achievement motivation.* In W. U. Meyer & B. Weiner (Chair), Conference on Attributional Approaches to Human Motivation. Center for Interdisciplinary Studies, University of Bielefeld, West Germany, June 1980. (b)

Nielsen, A., & Gerber, D. Psychosocial aspects of truancy in early adolescence. *Adolescence,* 1979, *14,* 313–326.

Oakes, J. O. *A question of access: Tracking and curriculum differentiation in a national sample of English and mathematics classes* (Tech. Rep. No. 24) Los Angeles, CA: University of California, Graduate School of Education, 1981.

O'Connor, J. L. Perceptions of self, ideal self, and teacher feelings in preadolescent children. *Elementary School Guidance and Counseling*, 1978, *13*, 88–92.

Parsons, J. E. *The development of children's evaluative judgements.* Unpublished dissertation, UCLA, 1974.

Parsons, J. E. *The development of expectancies, attributions, and persistence*, Unpublished manuscript, University of Michigan, 1982.

Parsons, J. E., Adler, T. F., Futterman, R., Goff, S. B., Kaczala, C. M., Meece, J. L., & Midgley, C. Expectancies, values, and academic behaviors. In J. T. Spence (Ed.), *Perspectives on achievement and achievement motivation.* San Francisco, CA: W. H. Freeman, in press.

Parsons, J. E., Adler, T. F., & Meece, J. L. *Sex differences in learned helplessness: Fact or fiction?.* Unpublished manuscript, University of Michigan, 1982.

Parsons, J. E., Kaczala, C. M., & Meece, J. L. Socialization of achievement attitudes and beliefs: Classroom influences. *Child Development*, 1982, *53*, 322–339.

Parsons, J. E., Meece, J. L., Adler, T. F., & Kaczala, C. M. Sex differences in attributions and learned helplessness? *Sex Roles*, 1982, *8*, 421–432.

Parsons, J. E., & Ruble, D. N. Attributional processes related to the development of achievement-related affect and expectancy. *Proceedings, 80th Annual Convention of the American Psychological Association*, 1972, 105–106.

Parsons, J. E., & Ruble, D. N. The development of achievement-related expectancies. *Child Development*, 1977, *48*, 1975–1979.

Pascarella, E. T., Walberg, H. H., Junker, L. K., & Haertel, G. D. Continuing motivation in science for early and late adolescents. *American Educational Research Journal*, 1981, *18*, 439–452.

Piers, E. V., & Harris, D. B. Age and other correlates of self-concept in children. *Journal of Educational Psychology*, 1964, *55*, 91–95.

Pittman, T. S., Emery, J., & Boggiano, A. K. Intrinsic and extrinsic motivational orientation: Reward-induced changes in preference for complexity. *Journal of Personality and Social Psychology*, 1982, *42*, 789–797.

Prawat, R. S., Grissom, S., & Parish, T. Affective development in children, grades 3 through 12. *The Journal of Genetic Psychology*, 1979, *135*, 37–49.

Prawat, R. S., Lanier, P. E., & Byers, J. L. *Attitudinal differences between students in general mathematics and algebra classes.* Unpublished manuscript, Michigan State University, undated.

Randhawa, B. S., & Michayluk, J. O. Learning environment in rural and urban classrooms. *American Educational Research Journal*, 1975, *12*, 265–285.

Rholes, W. S., Blackwell, J., Jordan, C., & Walters, C. A developmental study of learned helplessness. *Developmental Psychology*, 1980, *16*, 616–624.

Richter, F. D., & Tjosvold, D. Effects of student participation in classroom decision making on attitudes, peer interaction, motivation, and learning. *Journal of Applied Psychology*, 1980, *65*, 74–80.

Rosenbaum, J. E. *Making inequality: The hidden curriculum of high school tracking.* NY: John Wiley and Sons, 1976.

Rosenberg, M. *Conceiving the self.* NY: Basic Books, 1979.

Rosenholtz, S. J., & Rosenholtz, S. H. Classroom organization and the perception of ability. *Sociology of Education*, 1981, *54*, 132–140.

Rounds, T. S., & Osaki, S. Y. *The social organization of classrooms: An analysis of sixth-and seventh-grade activity structures* (Report EPSSP-82-5). San Francisco: Far West Laboratory, 1982.

Ruble, D. N., & Frey, K. S. Self-evaluation and social comparison in the classroom: A naturalistic study of peer interaction. In *Social comparison: Implications for education.* Symposium presented at the meeting of the American Educational Research Association, NY: March 1982.

Ruble, D. N., Parsons, J. E., & Ross, J. Self-evaluative responses of children in an achievement setting. *Child Development,* 1976, *47,* 990–997.

Rutter, M., Maughan, B., Mortimore, P., & Ouston, J. *Fifteen thousand hours: Secondary schools and their effects on children.* Cambridge, MA: Harvard University Press, 1979.

Salili, F., Maehr, M. L., Sorensen, R. L., & Fyans, L. J., Jr. A further consideration of the effects of evaluation on motivation. *American Educational Research Journal,* 1976, *13,* 85–102.

Schwarzer, R., Jerusalem, M., & Lange, B. *The development of academic self-concept with respect to reference groups in school.* Unpublished manuscript, undated.

Serow, R. C., & Solomon, D. Classroom climates and students' intergroup behavior. *Journal of Educational Psychology,* 1979, *71,* 669–676.

Shaklee, H., & Tucker, D. Cognitive bases of development in inferences of ability. *Child Development,* 1979, *50,* 904–907.

Shaughnessy, J., Haladyna, T., & Shaughnessy, J. M. *Relations of student, teacher, and learning environment variables to attitudes toward math.* Paper presented at the annual meeting of the American Educational Research Association, Los Angeles, CA: 1981.

Simmons, R. G., Blyth, O. A., & Carleton-Ford, M. A. *The adjustment of early adolescents to school transitions.* Paper presented at the American Research Association Annual Meeting, New York, 1982.

Simmons, R. G., Blyth, D. A., Van Cleave, E. F., & Bush, D. M. Entry into early adolescence: The impact of school structure, puberty, and early dating on self-esteem. *American Sociological Review,* 1979, *44,* 948–967.

Simmons, R. G., & Rosenberg, F. Sex, sex-roles and self-image. *Journal of Youth and Adolescence,* 1975, *4,* 229–258.

Simmons, R. G., Rosenberg, F., & Rosenberg, M. Disturbance in the self-image at adolescence. *American Sociological Review,* 1973, *38,* 553–568.

Slavin, R. E. Classroom reward structure: An analytic and practical review. *Review of Educational Research,* 1977, *47,* 633–650.

Slavin, R. E. Student teams and comparison among equals: Effects on academic performance and student attitudes. *Journal of Educational Psychology,* 1978, *70,* 532–538.

Slavin, R. E. Cooperative learning. *Review of Educational Research,* 1980, *50,* 315–342.

Stallings, J., & Robertson, A. *Factors influencing women's decisions to enroll in advanced mathematics courses.* Final report for the National Institute of Education, Washington, D.C.: Department of Health, Education, and Welfare, 1979.

Stipek, D. J., & Hoffman, J. Children's achievement-related expectancies as a function of academic performance histories and sex. *Journal of Educational Psychology,* 1980, *72,* 861–865.

Stipek, D. J., & Weisz, J. R. Perceived personal control and academic achievement. *Review of Educational Research,* 1981, *51,* 101–137.

Thomas, J. W. Agency and achievement: Self-management and self-reward. *Review of Educational Research,* 1980, *50,* 213–240.

Thompson, A. *A social climate perspective on early secondary school effects on student behaviors.* Presented at a symposium on Social Factors Affecting Student Learning at the meeting of the American Educational Research Association, New York, March 1982.

Trickett, E. J., & Moos, R. H. The social environment of junior high and high school classrooms. *Journal of Educational Psychology,* 1973, *65,* 93–102.

Tuckman, B. W., & Bierman, M. L. *Beyond Pygmalion: Galatea in the schools.* Paper presented at the meeting of the American Educational Research Association, New York, 1971.

Walberg, H. J., House, E. R., & Steele, J. M. Grade level, cognition, and affect: A cross-section of classroom perceptions. *Journal of Educational Psychology,* 1973, *64,* 142–146.

Wang, M. C., & Stiles, B. An investigation of children's concept of self-responsibility for their school learning. *American Educational Research Journal,* 1976, *13,* 159–179.

Weiner, B., & Peter, N. V. A cognitive-developmental analysis of achievement and moral judgments. *Developmental Psychology,* 1973, *9,* 290–309.

Weinstein, R. S. Reading group membership in first grade: Teacher behaviors and pupil experience over time. *Journal of Educational Psychology,* 1976, *68,* 103–116.

Welch, W. W. Curricular and longitudinal effects on learning environments. In H. J. Walberg (Ed.), *Educational environments and effects.* Berkeley, CA: McCutchan, 1979.

Willower, D. J. Some comments on inquiries on schools and pupil control. *Teachers College Record,* 1975, *77,* 219–230.

Yamamoto, K., Thomas, E. C., & Karns, E. A. School-related attitudes in middle-school age students. *American Educational Research Journal,* 1969, *6,* 191–206.

Yarborough, B. H., & Johnson, R. A. The relationship between intelligence levels and benefits from innovative, nongraded elementary schooling and traditional, graded schooling. *Educational Research Quarterly,* 1978, *3,* 28–38.

INDEX